HISTORY OF
United States Naval Operations

IN WORLD WAR II

*

VOLUME FOURTEEN

Victory in the Pacific

1945

HISTORY OF UNITED STATES NAVAL OPERATIONS IN WORLD WAR II

By Samuel Eliot Morison

Also
Strategy and Compromise

The Marine Corps men grasping the pole are Sgt. H. O. Hansen,
Pl. Sgt. E. I. Thomas and 1st Lt. H. G. Schrier. Pfc. J. R. Michaels holds
the carbine, Cpl. C. W. Lindberg stands behind

The First Flag-raising on Mount Suribachi, Iwo Jima

HISTORY OF UNITED STATES NAVAL
OPERATIONS IN WORLD WAR II
VOLUME XIV

Victory in the Pacific

1945

BY SAMUEL ELIOT MORISON

CASTLE BOOKS

HISTORY OF UNITED STATES NAVAL OPERATIONS IN WORLD WAR II

VICTORY IN THE PACIFIC
1945
VOL. XIV

ISBN: 0-7858-1315-2

To
The Memory of
WILLIAM FREDERICK HALSEY
1882–1959
Fleet Admiral, United States Navy

This was the greatest of all the achievements of the war and I think also of all the events known to us in history, the most decisive for the victor, the most ruinous for the conquered. They were utterly defeated at all points and endured no small sufferings, to no end.

— THUCYDIDES: *Peloponnesian War*, Book VII

Preface

I NOW DISCHARGE MY PROMISE, and complete my design, of writing the *History of United States Naval Operations in World War II*. Eighteen years have elapsed since I was commissioned in the Navy by President Franklin D. Roosevelt to do this task; thirteen years since the first volume came off the press. Fortunately good health, excellent assistance and the constant support and encouragement of my beloved wife, Priscilla Barton Morison, have enabled me to keep up a rate of production better than one volume a year.

A complete list of my assistants, with the exception of those who were given short temporary assignments, follows: —

Captain Bern Anderson USN, May 1952 to June 1960 [1]
Specialist 1st class Elinor M. Ball, April 1946 to April 1947
Dr. K. Jack Bauer, May 1957 to present
Commander Alexander C. Brown USNR, March 1945 to June 1946
Yeoman 1st class Antha E. Card W-USNR, March 1944 to September 1956 [2]
Yeoman 1st class Herbert M. Donaldson USNR, February 1946 to August 1948
Specialist 1st class Jane M. Donnelly, W-USNR, May 1946 to April 1947
Seaman 1st class Lawrence O. Donovan USNR, August 1945 to April 1946
Lieutenant Richard E. Downs USNR, May 1946 to April 1947
Commander George M. Elsey USNR, March to July 1944, and February to August 1949

---

[1] Retired as Rear Admiral 30 June 1960.
[2] Miss Card was separated from the Navy in Jan. 1946 but shortly after resumed work for the History as my personal secretary and continued to Sept. 1956.

Lieutenant Albert Harkness Jr. USNR, January 1946 to April 1947

Yeoman 3rd class Alexander D. Henderson USNR, August 1945 to May 1946

Yeoman 2nd class Edward Ledford USN, November 1956 to July 1958

Lieutenant Philip K. Lundeberg USNR, June 1948 and January to June 1950 [3]

Chief Yeoman Donald R. Martin USNR, February 1943 to present [4]

Ensign Richard S. Pattee USNR, June 1948 to June 1952

Lieutenant Commander Roger Pineau USNR, July 1947 to August 1957 [5]

Lieutenant Commander Henry D. Reck USNR, February 1944 to September 1948

Lieutenant Commander Henry Salomon Jr. USNR, February 1943 to December 1947 [6]

Yeoman 1st class Roger F. Schofield USN, September 1953 to November 1956

Commander James C. Shaw USN, November 1947 to June 1950 [7]

I also owe a debt of gratitude to Rear Admiral John B. Heffernan and Rear Admiral Ernest M. Eller, Directors of Naval History, under whom this History has been written. Fortunate indeed for an historian to have, as Directors, naval officers who are scholars themselves, and with whom he enjoyed the intimate relations of shipmate and friend during the period of hostilities.

The Naval War College at Newport, Rhode Island, under its successive presidents from Admiral Raymond A. Spruance (1945) to Vice Admiral Stuart H. Ingersoll (1960), has allotted office space for Captain Anderson and myself. The facilities of the drafting

---

[3] Lt. Lundeberg also did research on Volume X between and subsequent to his actual tours of duty, so that his total length of service to this History exceeded three years.

[4] Mr. Martin was separated from the Navy in Mar. 1947 but is still working for this History as a civilian.

[5] Lt. Cdr. Pineau was separated from the Navy in 1950 but continued working for this History as a civilian to Aug. 1957.

[6] Lt. Cdr. Salomon died 1 Feb. 1958.

[7] Now Rear Admiral USN retired.

room and cartographers, including Mr. Richard A. Gould, who did the maps for this volume, have also been available and extensively used. This association with the War College and its excellent library and staff has been a very pleasant and valuable experience.

Mr. Vernon E. Davis of the J. C. S. Historical Division helped me to unravel the tangle of events leading to the surrender of Japan.

Captain E. John Long USNR procured many of the illustrations.

Mr. Dean C. Allard, head of the Historical Records Branch of the Division of Naval History, has been most patient and helpful under my repeated requests.

Almost as important as those who actually worked on the research has been Miss Elizabeth Humphreys of Little, Brown and Company. She has copy-read the manuscript of each volume, and greatly improved it through her unerring scent for solecisms, contradictions and lack of uniformity in typographical style.

Writing the present volume began off Okinawa, an operation in which I participated on board Admiral Deyo's flagship *Tennessee*, as a member of the staff of her C.O., Captain John B. Heffernan. Before that operation was over I visited Iwo Jima, and spent some time at Fleet Admiral Nimitz's headquarters at Guam, reading action reports and talking with participants. After the end of the war I concentrated on the earlier years, and only returned to the subject matter of this volume in 1959. In it I have been particularly helped by Captain Bern Anderson, Dr. K. Jack Bauer and Mr. Donald R. Martin. Captain (now Rear Admiral) Anderson did much of the research for the text. Mr. Martin prepared Appendix I, and Dr. Bauer, Appendix II.

It must be repeated that this is not in the usual sense of the word an "official history," nor am I an "official historian." I was commissioned in the Naval Reserve in 1942 with the special mission to write it and have continued so to do as a civilian since my retirement from active duty in 1946. The Navy has given me every facility, but has not attempted to prejudice my conclusions or set the pattern of my writing. Little, Brown and Company of Boston, publishers of the classic works of Alfred Thayer Mahan, accepted this series as a regular publishing venture. The royalties are paid to the Navy, which has set them aside in a special capital fund which will be used to promote research and writing in United States Naval History.

This is the final narrative volume of the series. It will be followed by Volume XV, *General Index and Supplement*, which will contain (1) a general index of the entire series, including the task organizations which were not indexed in the separate volumes, (2) a description of different types of combatant ships, auxiliaries and naval airplanes used in World War II, (3) a summary of post-surrender operations in the Pacific, and (4) a cumulative list of errata, which will enable possessors of first editions to bring them up to date. So I make a special request to readers to send in promptly any additional errata that they may discover.

All times in this volume are of zone "Item" (Greenwich minus 9) and dates are east longitude dates, except where I am describing events in the United States itself.

Sources generally used without specific citation are the Action Reports and War Diaries of individual ships and commands, and the Cincpac Monthly Intelligence Summary, which was prepared by a staff under Captain Ralph C. Parker.

*   *   *

Every sailor must have a shore base whence he shoves off and whither, from time to time, he returns. From my base in Boston, where "every street leads down to the sea," I set sail in U.S.S. *Buck* in 1942 on the first leg of a long voyage. She went down in 1944; many of my old shipmates have departed; but I have been allowed to complete my voyage and my mission. So, thankful for past favors and hopeful for the future, I pick up my old mooring buoy and row ashore, happy to have reached home safely.

SAMUEL E. MORISON

44 BRIMMER STREET
BOSTON, MASSACHUSETTS
February, 1960

Contents

PART III

MISCELLANEOUS OPERATIONS

List of Illustrations

(All photographs not otherwise described are Official United States Navy)

List of Maps and Charts

Abbreviations

Officers' ranks and bluejackets' ratings are those contemporaneous with the event. Officers and men named will be presumed to be of the United States Navy unless it is otherwise stated; officers of the Naval Reserve are designated USNR. Other service abbreviations are USA, United States Army; USCG, United States Coast Guard; USCGR, Reserve of same; USMC, United States Marine Corps; USMCR, Reserve of same; RAN, Royal Australian Navy; RN, Royal Navy; RCN, Royal Canadian Navy; IJN, Imperial Japanese Navy.

A.A.F. — United States Army Air Forces
AK — Navy Cargo ship; AKA — Attack cargo
AP — Transport; APA — Attack transport; APD — destroyer transport
A/S — Antisubmarine
Batdiv — Battleship division
BB — Battleship
BLT — Battalion Landing Team
Bu — Bureau; Buord — Bureau of Ordnance; Bupers — Bureau of Naval Personnel; Buships — Bureau of Ships, etc.
CA — Heavy cruiser
C.A.P. — Combat Air Patrol
Cardiv — Carrier division
C.I.C. — Combat Information Center
Cincpac — Commander in Chief, Pacific Fleet (Admiral Nimitz)
CL — Light Cruiser
C.O. — Commanding Officer
C.N.O. — Chief of Naval Operations
Com — before cardiv, desdiv, etc., means Commander Carrier Division, Commander Destroyer Division, etc.
Cominch — Commander in Chief, United States Fleet (Admiral King)
CTF — Commander Task Force; CTG — Commander Task Group
CV — Aircraft Carrier; CVE — Escort Carrier; CVL — Light Carrier
DD — Destroyer; DE — Destroyer Escort
H.M.A.S. — His Majesty's Australian Ship; H.M.S. — His Majesty's Ship; H.M.N.Z.S. — His Majesty's New Zealand Ship; H.M.C.S. — His Majesty's Canadian Ship

H.Q. – Headquarters

IFF – Identification, Friend or Foe

JASCO – Joint Assault Signal Company

J.C.S. – Joint Chiefs of Staff

LC – Landing craft; LCI – Landing craft, infantry; LCM – Landing craft, mechanized; LCS – Landing craft, support; LCT – Landing craft, tank; LCVP – Landing craft, vehicles and personnel; LSD – Landing ship, dock; LSI – Landing ship, infantry; LSM – Landing ship, medium; LST – Landing ship, tank; LSV – Landing ship, vehicle; LVT – Landing vehicle tracked (or Amphtrac). (A), (G), (L), (M) and (R) added to above types mean armored, gunboat, large, mortar and rocket.

Op – Operation; Opnav – Chief of Naval Operations; op plan – Operation Plan

O.N.I. – Office of Naval Intelligence

O.S.S. – Office of Strategic Services

O.T.C. – Officer in Tactical Command

PC – Patrol craft; PCE – Patrol craft, escort

P.O.W. – Prisoner of war

RCT – Regimental Combat Team

s.f.c.p – Shore fire control party

S.O.P.A. – Senior Officer Present Afloat

SS – Submarine

TF – Task Force; TG – Task Group; TU – Task Unit

UDT – Underwater Demolition Team

U.S.C.G.C. – United States Coast Guard Cutter

USSBS – United States Strategic Bombing Survey

VB; VC; VF; VT; VOS – Bomber; Composite; Fighter; Torpedo Observation-Scout plane or squadron

YMS – Motor minesweeper; YP – Patrol vessel

Aircraft Designations
(Numerals in parentheses indicate number of engines)

United States

B–24 – Liberator, Army (4) heavy bomber; B–26 – Marauder, Army (2) medium bomber; B–29 – Superfortress, Army (4) heavy bomber

F4F – Wildcat; F6F – Hellcat; F4U – Corsair; Navy (1) fighters

OS2U – Kingfisher, Navy (1) scout-observation float plane
P–38 – Lightning, Army (2); P–47 – Thunderbolt, Army (1); P–51 –
     Mustang, Army (1) fighters
PBJ – Navy Mitchell (2) medium bomber
PBM–3 – Mariner, Navy (2) patrol bomber (flying boat)
PBY – Catalina, Navy (2) patrol bomber; PBY–5A, amphibian Cata-
     lina; PB4Y–1 – Navy Liberator bomber (4); PB4Y–2 – Navy
     Privateer bomber (4)
PV–1 – Ventura, Navy (2) medium bomber
SB2C, SBW – Helldivers; SBD – Dauntless, Navy (1) dive-bombers
TBF, TBM – Avenger, Navy (1) torpedo-bombers

Japanese

Betty – Mitsubishi Zero–1, Navy (2) high-level or torpedo-bomber
Fran – Nakajima, Navy (2) all-purpose bomber
Frances – Nakajima, Navy (2) bomber
Frank – Nakajima, Army (1) fighter
Jake – Aichi or Watanabe, Navy (1) reconnaissance bomber
Jill – Nakajima, Navy (1) torpedo-bomber
Judy – Aichi, Navy (1) dive-bomber
Kate – Nakajima, Navy (1) torpedo-bomber
Nate & Oscar – Nakajima, Army (1) fighters
Nick – Kawasaki or Nakajima Zero–2, Army (2) fighter
Sally – Mitsubishi, Army (2) medium bomber
Tojo – Nakajima Zero–2, Army (1) fighter
Tony – Zero–3, Army or Navy (1) fighter
Val – Aichi 99, Navy (1) dive-bomber
Zeke – Mitsubishi Zero–3, Navy (1) fighter

PART 1

Iwo Jima

CHAPTER I

Decisions, Plans and Preparations[1]

October 1944–February 1945

1. The Bonins and Ryukyus in Pacific Strategy

IT WAS a long, hard pull for the Navy across the Pacific to within striking distance of Japan; but, by the time Saipan in the Marianas had been conquered (August 1944) and the major part of Luzon liberated (February 1945), two practicable routes were open to the ultimate objective – the Nanpo Shoto and the Nansei Shoto island chains. The first, better known to Americans and Europeans as the Bonins,[2] begins not far off Tokyo Bay and continues southerly for some 700 miles to Minami Shima, which is 290 miles northwest of the northernmost Marianas, and 615 miles north of Saipan. Most of these islands are tiny volcanic cones, too small for an airfield. But Chichi Jima and Iwo Jima had distinct possibilities.

The other island chain, the Nansei Shoto (better known to Americans and Europeans as the Ryukyus), forms a great arc some 600 miles long, from Honshu, southernmost of the Japanese home is-

---

[1] This subject is also covered to some extent in Vols. XII Chap. I and XIII Chap. I. To the sources mentioned there add J. A. Isely and P. A. Crowl *The U.S. Marines and Amphibious War* (1951) chap. x, Lt. Col. Whitman S. Bartley USMC *Iwo Jima: Amphibious Epic*, published by Marine Corps Historical Branch 1954. In addition the writer discussed the strategic questions affecting the operations in this volume with Rear Admiral Forrest Sherman in May 1945, and profited by a perusal of his personal compilation, "Future Operations Recommendations to Cominch."

[2] The Bonin Islands (Ogasawara Gunto to the Japanese) properly are the central group of Nanpo Shoto comprising Muko, Chichi, and Haha. The southern group, which includes Iwo Jima, is called the Volcano Islands, but Bonins is often used for the entire chain. *Jima* or *Shima* means an island, *Shoto* an archipelago, *Gunto* an island group.

lands, to Formosa, making the eastern border of the East China Sea. This chain contains five or six islands suitable for air bases, the best and largest being Okinawa.

The spokesmen for taking Luzon (led by General MacArthur) and for taking Formosa (led by Admiral King) had held long discussions at Cincpac headquarters, at San Francisco, and with the Joint Chiefs of Staff at Washington. The Luzonites won because the Army estimated that securing Formosa would require nine combat divisions and more service troops than were likely to be available before the surrender of Germany. This was practically decided at the San Francisco Conference of 29 September – 1 October 1944, between Admirals King, Nimitz and Spruance and Generals Harmon and Buckner. Admiral Nimitz there submitted a carefully written memorandum, which not only urged that Luzon be the target but gave his opinion as to what should follow. He recommended a staggered, two-pronged advance, as follows. The first – target date 20 January 1945 – should thrust "up the ladder of the Bonins" to Chichi Jima or Iwo Jima; the second – target date 1 March – along the arc of the Ryukyus to one or more positions such as Okinawa or Amami O Shima. The purpose of the one would be to obtain emergency landing facilities for Saipan-based B–29s and a base for their fighter escorts in bombing Japan proper; and of the other, to secure and develop a sound air and naval base for the invasion of the Japanese home islands.

Admiral Spruance, who seems to have been the first high-ranking naval officer to appreciate the possibilities of Okinawa, observed with pleasure at San Francisco that Admiral King, who hitherto had been insistent on taking Formosa, had been reluctantly won over by Admiral Nimitz's logic. At this point in the discussion King turned to Spruance and remarked, "Haven't you something to say? I understand that Okinawa is your baby." To which Spruance, a man of deep thought but few words, replied that Nimitz had put the case so well that he had nothing to add.

From San Francisco Admiral King brought the word to the Joint Chiefs of Staff, who on 3 October issued the directive to General MacArthur and Admiral Nimitz, in pursuance of which the operations described in this volume were carried out: —

1. General MacArthur will seize and occupy Luzon, target date 20 December, and provide support for subsequent occupation of the Ryukyus by Admiral Nimitz's forces.
2. Admiral Nimitz, after providing covering and support forces for the liberation of Luzon, will occupy one or more positions in the Bonins-Volcano Group, target date 20 January 1945, and one or more positions in the Ryukyus, target date 1 March 1945.
3. Both C. in C.'s will arrange for coördination of forces and resources between themselves and with the Commanding Generals of XX Army Air Force,[3] and of the China-Burma-India area.

So there it was, on the line. The eastern (Iwo Jima) operation was placed first after Luzon because it was expected to be easier than the western (Okinawa) one. It was never anticipated that the same troops would be used for both operations, but the same Pacific Fleet would have to cover and support both, while the Seventh Fleet and Amphibious Force were engaged in covering and liberating the Southern Philippines, as described in our previous volume. It was necessary that Fast Carrier Forces (TF 38 or 58) be detached from supporting these Philippines operations in time to cover both the Bonins and the Ryukyus invasions.

2. Planning for Iwo Jima

Postponing consideration of the Okinawa plans to Part II, we shall explain why Iwo Jima of glorious though gory memory was chosen as the Bonins objective. The only alternative was the more northerly and larger Chichi Jima, which had a good protected harbor, Port Lloyd. But that island is too rugged for quick airfield

[3] XX A.A.F. included XX Bomber Command in China and XXI Bomber Command in Marianas.

construction, and air reconnaissance showed that it was more heavily fortified than Iwo.

The Bonin Islands might have been an American possession if
President Franklin Pierce's administration had backed up Commodore Matthew Calbraith Perry. Chichi Jima was first settled
from Honolulu in 1830 by two New Englanders — Aldin B. Chapin
and Nathaniel Savory — a Genoese, and 25 Hawaiians, who made
a living raising provisions for sale to passing whalers. Commodore
Perry called at Port Lloyd on 14 June 1853, next day purchased for
fifty dollars a plot of land on the harbor, stocked it with cattle
brought over in U.S.S. *Susquehanna*, set up a local government
under Savory, promulgated a code of laws, and took possession for
the United States. He intended to make Chichi Jima a provisioning
station for the United States Navy and American mail steamers.
But this action was repudiated by the Pierce administration in
Washington. Thus, in 1861 Japan was able to annex the Bonin Islands without opposition. The government did not disturb the
American colony, and serious colonization of the group by Japanese did not start until 1887.[4]

Iwo Jima, central island of the Volcano group, had great value
as a strategic outpost, but for nothing else. Situated in lat. 24° 45′ N,
long. 141° 20′ E, shaped like a bloated pear or a lopsided pork chop,
Iwo is only 4½ miles long and 2½ miles wide. The volcanic crater
of Mount Suribachi, 550 feet above sea level, at the stem of the
pear, remained inactive during World War II, but numerous jets
of steam and sulphur all over the island suggested that an erup-
tion might take place at any moment. The northern part of the
island is a plateau with rocky and inaccessible shores, but beaches
extended from the base of Mount Suribachi for more than two
miles north and east. These beaches, the land between them, and
a good part of the terrain are deeply covered with brown volcanic
ash and black cinders which look like sand, but are so much lighter
than sand that walking is difficult and running impossible. Marston
mat had to be laid to accommodate wheeled and even tracked ve-

[4] Lionel B. Cholmondeley *History of the Bonin Islands* (London 1915).

hicles. Up to 1944 the island was inhabited by about 1100 Japanese civilians who raised sugar and pineapples, extracted sulphur and ran a crude sugar mill; but all were evacuated before this operation began.

The unique importance of Iwo Jima for warlike purposes was derived from its location and topography. It lies almost midway between Honshu and the Marianas, 625 miles north of Saipan and 660 miles south of Tokyo. The Japanese constructed two airfields on the island, and a third had been started. On 14 July 1944 General "Hap" Arnold, head of the Army Air Forces, recommended to the Joint Planners that Iwo be seized to provide for emergency landings of the B–29 Superforts, and to base P–51 fighter planes to escort them in raids on Tokyo. The Joint Planners agreed, provided that the seizure of Iwo would not interfere with other and more important operations.[5]

As soon as the 3 October 1944 directive arrived at Cincpac headquarters, Admiral Nimitz's staff planners, presided over by Rear Admiral Forrest Sherman, moved fast. On 7 October they produced a staff study which became the basis for the plan and outlined the Iwo operation very much as it was carried out.[6]

Admiral Raymond A. Spruance, Commander Fifth Fleet, had the over-all command at Iwo Jima. Under him Vice Admiral Richmond K. Turner commanded the Joint Expeditionary Force (TF 51). As this was to be a Marine Corps landing, Lieutenant General Holland M. Smith USMC was made Commander Expeditionary Troops (TF 56), which consisted of the V Amphibious Corps, Major General Harry Schmidt USMC. Also under Turner were Rear Admiral Harry W. Hill, Commander Attack Force (TF 53), and Rear Admiral W. H. P. Blandy, Commander Amphibious Support Force (TF 52). Also in support of the operation were Vice Admiral Marc A. Mitscher's Fast Carrier Force (TF 58), an expanded Logistic Support Group commanded by Rear Admiral Donald B.

[5] Craven & Cate V 586–587.
[6] Cincpac-Cincpoa "Joint Staff Study DETACHMENT" 7 Oct. 1944. Operation DETACHMENT was the code name for the capture of Iwo, but it was little used.

Victory in the Pacific

Beary, and a Search and Reconnaissance Group (TG 50.5) under Commodore Dixwell Ketcham.

The landing force, the V 'Phib Corps, comprised the 3rd Marine Division (Major General Graves B. Erskine USMC), which had recently liberated Guam; the 4th Marine Division (Major General Clifton B. Cates USMC), then at Maui; and the new 5th Marine Division (Major General Keller E. Rockey USMC), then on the island of Hawaii. General Schmidt's headquarters were on Guam, but to plan for Iwo he moved to Pearl Harbor on 13 October. When General MacArthur was persuaded to postpone the Lingayen landings to 9 January, the two operations coming up were postponed for a full month — Iwo Jima to 19 February, and Okinawa to 1 April 1945.

There also had to be keen planning on the logistics end.[7] In operations for the liberation of the Philippines, a seagoing logistics group was set up in order to bring oil, replacement planes, spare parts and fleet tugs to the fast carrier forces at sea. This procedure proved so successful that the group was now enlarged and extended by adding ammunition ships and other auxiliaries, redesignating the group Service Squadron 6, and placing it under the command of Rear Admiral Beary, who had been head of Training Command Atlantic Fleet at Norfolk.[8] *Detroit*, one of the old light cruisers, was allotted to him as flagship. The Iwo operation, comparatively short, gave the new method of issue and transfer a good tryout. Twenty-seven fleet oilers were employed. Between 8 February and 5 March 1945 they delivered at sea 2,787,000 barrels of fuel oil (1,702,000 of them to Fast Carrier Force), 7,126,000 gallons of aviation gas (3,378,000 to the fast carriers), and 105,000 barrels of diesel oil. Ulithi, the headquarters of Commodore Carter's Servron 10, was the terminus of merchant tankers that supplied fleet oilers or floating storage.

Shasta and *Wrangell* on 19 February made the first successful

---

[7] Worrall R. Carter *Beans, Bullets, and Black Oil* (1953) chap. xxii; Comservron 6 (Rear Adm. Beary) "Logistic Analysis Iwo Operation" 8 Mar. 1956. For Leyte logistics see Vol. XII Chap. V.
[8] For brief biography see Vol. X 47*n.*

experiment in alongside transfer of ammunition at sea.[9] Three escort carriers, recently modified to carry replacement planes, and two of the older CVEs operated with oiler groups. By 1 March they had delivered 254 new planes and 65 pilots and crewmen to fleet, light and escort carriers. *Virgo,* fitted as a mobile general stores ship, made the first successful experiment in transferring by line packages of dry stores, small stores and clothing.

A valuable innovation was the conversion of two LSTs to be mother ships to landing craft.[10] Each had bunks, cooking and mess facilities for 40 officers and 300 men, 20 reefer boxes carrying 160,000 rations of fresh and frozen provisions, space for the same number of dry rations, and large evaporators. Now, at last, boat crews, left on the beach when transports retired for the night, had a chance for a shower bath, a hot meal and a "sack." During the first two weeks of the Iwo operation these mother ships also refueled and watered 54 small vessels such as PCEs and LCTs, and reprovisioned an additional 76.

3. Air Bombing and Naval Bombardment [11]

The Army Air Force setup in the Pacific was modified in August 1944 when Lieutenant General Millard F. Harmon assumed command of the newly formed Army Air Forces, Pacific Ocean Areas. General Harmon was also deputy commander to "Hap" Arnold of XX Air Force, which included the B–29s operating from Chinese bases, and of XXI Bomber Command of B–29s in the Marianas. In December 1944, Admiral Nimitz named him Commander Strategic Air Force, Pacific Ocean Areas, with control over all land-based aviation in the Pacific.

[9] *Serpens,* a Coast-Guard-manned cargo ship of Servron 8 refitted as ammunition carrier, blew up in Lunga Roads, Guadalcanal, on 29 Jan. 1945 with the loss of all hands but three.
[10] Commo. Carter (p. 290) credits this type to "Admiral Turner's ingenuity and initiative."
[11] Comcrudiv 5 (Rear Adm. Allan E. Smith) Action Reports of 17 Dec. 1944 and 21 Jan. 1945; Craven & Cate V chap. xix.

As air bases became available in the Marianas the VII Army Air Force (Major General Willis H. Hale) began to subject Iwo Jima to one of the longest sustained air bombardments of the war. This air force, widely scattered over the Pacific, was mainly engaged in keeping bypassed islands neutralized. Truk was the main target, but others — such as Ponape, Wotje, Marcus and Wake — were given attention from time to time. As new bases in the Marianas were developed, General Hale's fighters and bombers moved forward to attack the Bonins chain. On 10 August the first B–24s based on Saipan bombed Iwo Jima. Thereafter that island and others nearby were hit whenever the weather permitted. There were 10 such raids on the island in August, 22 in September, and 16 in October. Most of them were aimed at cratering the airfields, but some were anti-shipping strikes on harbors in Chichi Jima and Haha Jima. These were laid on to oblige the Navy, which was concerned over the extensive reinforcement of Iwo Jima that was being staged through Port Lloyd and other island harbors. General Hale protested that his B–24 pilots were not trained for anti-shipping attacks, but not until the B–29s began operating from Saipan were these strikes called off.

The first B–29 from the United States landed on Saipan on 12 October, and by the end of November there were enough to launch the first strike against Japan.[12] Before that happened the Japanese, realizing what they were in for, counterattacked the Saipan fields twice, and ineffectively; but after the first B–29 raid against the Japanese homeland, on 24 November, they hit back hard. Early on the 27th, as the Superforts were loading bombs for a second strike, two twin-engined Japanese bombers came in low, destroyed one B–29 and damaged eleven others. Around noon the same day 10 to 15 single-engined fighters evaded the radar screen, destroyed three more B–29s and severely damaged two. These raids, which continued intermittently until 2 January, succeeded in damaging six and destroying eleven B–29s.

Since the loss of a B–29 was serious, strenuous efforts were made

[12] For description of the Superfortress, see Vol. XIII 162.

to intercept or stop these raids. Vice Admiral John H. Hoover, Commander Forward Area, stationed two destroyers 100 miles northwest of Saipan as early warning pickets. They detected some raids, but not all. Since it was rightly suspected that the Japanese bombers staged through Iwo Jima, Admiral Nimitz gave that island top priority on 24 November. He ordered the curtailment of VII A.A.F. strikes on bypassed islands and shipping in order to concentrate a joint aërial bombing and naval bombardment on Iwo, 8 December.

A fighter sweep by 28 P-38s opened the attack at 0945; 62 B-29s bombed at 1100 and 102 B-24s at noon; Crudiv 5 (Rear Admiral Allan E. Smith), comprising heavy cruisers *Chester*, *Pensacola* and *Salt Lake City* with six destroyers, arrived off Iwo at 1330 and opened bombardment at 1347. "Hoke" Smith approached the island from the west, rounded Mount Suribachi and then reversed track in a half-circle. Unfortunately the sky was so heavily overcast as to force the planes to bomb by radar and to hamper ships' spotting. Surface visibility was good enough to enable the island to be well covered by a naval bombardment, which lasted for 70 minutes and expended 1500 rounds of 8-inch and 5334 rounds of 5-inch shell. The bombers dropped 814 tons of bombs. Photographs, taken three days later, showed that both airfields on Iwo were wholly or in part operational, but no more enemy air raids hit the Marianas until Christmas Day.

The job of keeping Iwo airfields neutralized was now turned over to B-24s of VII A.A.F. Between 8 December 1944 and 15 February 1945 they flew at least one strike daily over the island. The day before Christmas, Rear Admiral Smith's heavy cruisers, together with five destroyers, delivered a second bombardment, coördinated with a B-24 strike. This strike was slightly more eventful than the initial one in December, but even less effective. The bombardment, which expended 1500 rounds of 8-inch, provoked return fire from a 6-inch coast defense battery (designated "Kitty" on the target maps) in the northeast part of the island, but "Kitty's" claws managed to strike no closer than 200 yards. As proof of the slight damage inflicted by this bombardment, the Japanese were able to pay a vicious return visit to Saipan on Christmas Eve, a raid of 25 planes which destroyed one B–29 and damaged three more beyond repair.

Crudiv 5 returned 27 December for a repeat performance, lighter than the others; and a fourth bombardment was set up for 5 January 1945. While fighter planes and B–24s hit Iwo Jima the same cruisers and six destroyers bombarded Chichi Jima, 145 miles northward, and the slightly nearer Haha Jima. Their hope was to catch a convoy bringing Japanese supplies to these islands, whence they were forwarded to Iwo by small craft at night. Destroyer *Fanning*, steaming ahead of the group as radar picket, encountered at 0206 a surface target, later identified as *LSV–102*, which she sank. At 0700 Admiral Smith's group opened a one hour and 49 minutes' bombardment of Chichi Jima. During it, destroyer *David W. Taylor* suffered an underwater explosion, probably from a mine, which flooded her forward magazine. The Haha Jima bombardment by *Salt Lake City* and two destroyers lasted for an hour. Crudiv 5 then pounded Iwo Jima for another hour and three quarters. The reply was negligible, and a few aircraft which made passes at the cruisers were easily driven off.

The next bombardment came on 25 January, following a three-hour forenoon bombing by VII A.A.F. B–24s, escorted by P–38s. Rear Admiral Oscar C. Badger was now O.T.C., wearing his flag in battleship *Indiana*, and he brought along two more destroyers as well as Crudiv 5. The bombardment opened at 1400 and lasted for two hours. *Indiana* planted 203 rounds of 16-inch on the island and Crudiv 5 added 1354 rounds of 8-inch.

Beginning the last day of January, and for two weeks, VII A.A.F. bombed the island night and day. The Superforts also got in a few licks on 24 and 29 January and 12 February, adding 367 tons of bombs to the impressive total that hit, or at least were aimed at, the island.[13]

Probably no island in World War II received as much pre-

[13] "Analysis of Air Operations Pacific Ocean Areas and B–29 Operations," Nov.–Dec. 1944.

liminary pounding as did Iwo Jima. For ten weeks, until 16 February when the intensive pre-landing bombardment began, the island
was hit by land-based aircraft almost every day, and the total tonnage of bombs dropped was not far from 6800.[14] In addition, 203
rounds of 16-inch, 6472 rounds of 8-inch and 15,251 rounds of
5-inch shell were fired in the five naval bombardments. Under
ordinary circumstances, so heavy and prolonged a bombardment
would have been more than sufficient to pulverize everything on an
island of that size. Yet the Japanese restored the airfields on Iwo
Jima to operation a few hours after each attack, and continued to
fortify the island.

Staff planners and Admiral Nimitz himself anticipated no unusual
difficulty in taking Iwo Jima. Pacific Fleet technique for wresting
islands from the enemy had been worked out as the result of
abundant experience at Tarawa, Kwajalein, Eniwetok, Saipan,
Guam and Peleliu. Yet when the Marines landed on the island
19 February, after three more days of intensive bombardment, expecting to secure it in a few days, they were forced to fight for it
bitterly almost yard by yard over a period of one month and to
lose 6137 of their number. How that could happen becomes apparent when we examine the Japanese defense system on Iwo Jima.

4. *Japanese Preparations* [15]

Until after the American seizure of the Marshall Islands in February 1944, Iwo Jima was simply a whistle stop on the air line from
Japan to the Marianas and Carolines. Chichi Jima had been a small
naval base since 1914, and most of the Japanese armed forces in the
Nanpo Shoto were there; Iwo Jima had only a single airstrip capable
of accommodating about 20 planes and a garrison of about 1500
men. After losing the Marshalls, Imperial General Headquarters

---

[14] Comairpac "Analysis of Air Operations – Iwo Jima" 21 June 1945.
[15] Cincpac-Cincpoa Bulletin No. 136–145 *Defense Installations on Iwo Jima*
10 June 1945, Bartley *Iwo Jima*, MacArthur *Historical Report* II.

realized that the Marianas and Carolines were threatened and began to strengthen their next line of defense. In March 1944 the build-up of Iwo began in earnest. By the end of May there were over 5000 Army troops with artillery and machine guns, and a Navy guard force with a dozen coast defense guns of 120-mm caliber and upward, 12 heavy antiaircraft guns and thirty 25-mm twin-mount antiaircraft guns, manned by about 2000 men. The naval commander on the island was an airman, Rear Admiral Toshinosuke Ichimaru. By D-day the total strength of the island garrison was about 21,000 officers and men.

When the Americans invaded Saipan in June, Imperial General Headquarters placed the defense of the Volcano group directly under Tokyo, organized the 109th Infantry Division, and sent it to Iwo under the command of Lieutenant General Tadamichi Kuribayashi. Tokyo strategists correctly estimated that Iwo Jima would be the choice for an Allied landing and they set about to make it impregnable. Thanks to the energy and skill of General Kuribayashi, they almost did.

Troops originally intended to reinforce the Marianas were now diverted to Iwo Jima. Because the island had no harbor, and attack by United States submarines was feared, reinforcements were unloaded at Chichi Jima, whence they were sent on to Iwo by small craft. This procedure did not save them from loss. On 18 July 1944, for example, U. S. submarine *Cobia* sank *Nisshu Maru*, transporting a tank regiment from Japan to Iwo, about 180 miles northwest of Chichi. Most of the troops were rescued but 28 tanks were lost. In six months, the Japanese lost about 1500 men en route to Iwo by surface and submarine attacks on their vessels.

Occasional sinkings of transports did little to check the build-up. Now relieved of arming Marianas and Marshalls, Japan had plenty of steel, concrete and other material to spare. Keen-eyed aërial photo interpreters working for Admiral Turner watched prepared positions on Iwo grow in strength and intensity from day to day. Owing to cliffs on the bulgy northeastern part of the pear-shaped island, the only places possible to land on were the beaches north and east of Mount Suribachi, between which lay No. 1 Motoyama air-field with No. 2 not far north. General Kuribayashi figured out that the beaches and No. 1 airfield would be untenable in face of the naval and air strength which probably would be applied against them, and so decided to concentrate his defenses in and about Mount Suribachi in the south, and on the plateau around Motoyama village on the bulge. His naval advisers, on the other hand, insisted that the attack must be stopped at the water's edge. A compromise was made whereby the Navy constructed a series of pillboxes and strongpoints covering the beaches, and Kuribayashi assigned the troops to man them. Thus, Iwo had the benefit of the older tech-nique for repelling an amphibious attack ("annihilate it at the water's edge") plus the new technique, tried at Peleliu, Leyte and Lingayen, of a desperate defense in depth.

The Japanese naval coast defense guns of 120-mm (4.7-inch) and 155-mm (6-inch) caliber were so sited as to enfilade the beaches and approaches to them in a narrow arc of fire. Casemated behind four to six feet of concrete, they were so located as to have maxi-mum protection from naval gunfire. Behind the beaches on both sides was a system of concrete pillboxes so placed as to be mutually supporting. Large concrete blockhouses were also built in this part of the island. Antiaircraft guns were placed in pits so that a direct hit was required to knock them out. A system of tunnels connected the various positions, in each of which a deep cave shelter was pro-vided for the troops.

On the slopes of Mount Suribachi was a labyrinth of dug-in gun positions for coast defense artillery, mortars and machine guns. These were accompanied by elaborate cave and tunnel systems providing living quarters and storage space for servicing the weap-ons. From the volcano's rim, everything that went on at both sets of beaches, or on most of the island, could be observed.

General Kuribayashi's one main line of defense crossed the island between Nos. 1 and 2 airfields, taking full advantage of the terrain features. Here was a network of dug-in positions for artillery, mor-tars, machine guns and infantry weapons. These were in a system of caves connected by underground tunnels. A second line of defense ran between No. 2 airfield and the central Motoyama sector. Accurate range and firing data were provided at each weapon position, so that high accuracy could be obtained with minimum exposure. But the main feature of the bulbous part of the island was an intricate network of caves and excavated rooms, all connected by deep tunnels. In some places there were five levels of these caves, and few were less than thirty feet underground. One cave might have several entrances, and most served the double purpose of protection to men and a position for weapons. A mortar could be set up at a cave or tunnel mouth, fired and then withdrawn. Even tanks were emplaced in pits or narrow ravines with only the turret exposed. Added to the natural strength of the underground system was the use of camouflage with materials blending into the surrounding terrain and vegetation. Many of these positions were so cleverly prepared that they were not spotted until they opened fire, or the protective camouflage was blown away by our gunfire. Later, when the Marines were fighting ashore, a camouflaged rifle pit or machine-gun position might be exposed only when the troops were taken under fire from the rear.

All this followed the battle plan drawn up by General Kuribayashi in September 1944. He was to "transform the central island into a fortress." When the landings took place, the garrison must aim at "gradual depletion of enemy attack forces, and, even if the situation gets out of hand, defend a corner of the island to the death." "All forces will prevent losses during enemy bombing and shelling by dispersing, concealing and camouflaging personnel, weapons and matériel." The password for this operation meant "desperation," or "desperate battle."

Following the successful Allied landings on Luzon in January 1945 the Japanese high command was forced to take a new look at the strategic situation. In an atmosphere of pessimism and mutual suspicion it was difficult to reach any but the most general agreements on policy. But the need was urgent, and on 20 January 1945 an "Outline of Army and Navy Operations" was promulgated.[16] This new policy predicted that the final battle of the war would be fought in Japan itself. The outline attempted to provide a strategic defense in depth by prescribing an inner defense line running from the Bonins through Formosa to the coast of China and southern Korea. Key strongpoints to be developed on this defense perimeter were Iwo Jima, Okinawa, Formosa, the Shanghai area and the South Korea coast. China and Southeast Asia were classed as secondary theaters. When United States forces, the principal enemy, penetrated this inner defense perimeter, an intense war of attrition was to be waged against them in order to reduce their preponderance, shatter their morale and delay the invasion of the home islands. Air forces were to exert themselves fully over the perimeter defense zone, but air strength in general was to be conserved until a landing was under way, then concentrate on the invasion fleet, with emphasis on the use of the Kamikaze Corps. The planes themselves were to be concentrated in Kyushu, the Ryukyus, Formosa and Eastern China. Ground forces were to hold out as long as possible without reinforcement.

General Kuribayashi did his best to implement this directive, and his best was very good indeed. During the long series of air attacks and bombardments the garrison holed up, then came out to repair damage. Reinforcements and new guns and matériel were brought in at night and improvement of all defenses continued. If, as the Japanese expected, the assault could have been made shortly after the Marianas were secured in the fall of 1944, the island would have been ill prepared to meet it, but the postponement to February 1945 gave Kuribayashi his opportunity to sell the island at the highest price. Subsequent complaints by General Holland Smith and others about the amount and quality of naval bombardment and air bombing were completely off the beam: Iwo's defenses were of a nature that neither could possibly neutralize them. The only way to knock out most of the positions was for ships to close to point-

16 MacArthur *Historical Report* II 542 ff.

blank range, 2000 yards or less, and blast them out. This could not be done until the attack force was ashore, and one knew the location of the strongpoints.

Intelligence of Japanese defenses through aërial photographs was helped by submarine *Spearfish*, which snooped Iwo in early December and took photographs of the beaches through her periscope. The nature of the soil was correctly estimated, and the number of defensive positions seen was not far short of the truth. But she could not spot the caves and tunnels, and nobody in Marine headquarters seems to have put together the experience at Biak and Peleliu to anticipate the new Japanese tactics of defense in depth, which were to cost the Marine Corps dear.

The Japanese Navy's only contribution to the defense of Iwo Jima was in the form of submarines bearing the human torpedoes that they called *kaiten*, but the initial success of this gimmick, sinking a fleet oiler in Ulithi lagoon on 20 November, was not repeated.[17] A *kaiten* unit composed of *I–370*, *I–368* and *I–44* sailed for Iwo Jima 22–23 February 1945. The first-named ran afoul of destroyer escort *Finnegan* (Lieutenant Commander H. Huffman USNR), escorting a convoy from Iwo Jima to Saipan, on 26 February. She made a surface radar contact distant seven miles at 0555, sound contact at 0630, delivered three depth-charge and hedgehog attacks and hung on until 1034 when a very deep underwater explosion was heard and debris with Japanese markings rose to the surface. That marked the end of *I–370*.

Before the Iwo operation began, escort carriers *Anzio* (Captain G. C. Montgomery) and *Tulagi* (Captain J. C. Cronin) were made nuclei of hunter-killer antisubmarine units. A fighter plane from *Anzio*, flying a ten-mile-square search in the early hours of 26 February, at the request of destroyer *Bennion*, which had made and lost contact, sighted *RO–43* (not a *kaiten* submarine) and destroyed it west of Chichi Jima by a depth-bomb drop from 150 feet. Next day *Tulagi* sent planes after two submarines reported to be southeast of Iwo Jima but apparently missed them; *Anzio* planes, however,

17 See Vol. XII 51.

flew a repeat performance on the 27th and sank *I-368*, a few miles west of Iwo Jima.[18]

I-44 reached Iwo waters, but was kept down by destroyers for over 48 hours, almost suffocating the crew, and then returned to base. Vice Admiral S. Miwa, commanding Sixth Fleet (the submarines), was furious, and relieved the skipper of his command. A second *kaiten* unit of *I-36* and *I-58* (the boat that later sank *Indianapolis*) was then formed, and departed Kure 1 March. The first had to turn back shortly after its sortie, and *I-58*, after a frustrating cruise around Iwo, constantly harassed by antisubmarine craft, was recalled on 9 March.[19]

[18] CTG 52.2 (Rear Adm. Durgin) Action Report of 21 April 1945, Enclosure A, p. 8.

[19] M. Hashimoto *Sunk* (1954) pp. 139–143.

CHAPTER II

Preliminary Poundings

10–18 February 1945

1. Carrier Wings over Japan [1]

D URING the last three days before Iwo D-day, every effort was intensified, the most intense being a series of carrier-borne air strikes over and around Tokyo. These were laid on not only as a diversion — a shield, as it were, for Iwo Jima — but to destroy enemy planes and reduce Japanese capability for launching air attacks.

Admiral Halsey had been eager to hit Japan since October, but the support of Task Force 38 was urgently needed in the Philippines; and by the time this opportunity came, in February 1945, Halsey was no longer in command. Third Fleet completed its Luzon missions in late January and made for Ulithi, where the new "backfield" was waiting to take over. At midnight 26 January, Admiral Raymond A. Spruance relieved Admiral William F. Halsey, and Third Fleet again became Fifth Fleet. At the same time, Vice Admiral Marc A. Mitscher relieved Vice Admiral John S. McCain as Commander Fast Carrier Force, and TF 38 became TF 58. As the carriers would not have to depart in support of Iwo until 10 February, their fagged-out sailors and airmen enjoyed a welcome two weeks of upkeep and rest, swimming, playing softball and

[1] Action Report of Com Fifth Fleet (Admiral Spruance) 14 June, CTF 58 (Vice Adm. Mitscher) for 10 Feb.–4 Mar. 1945, 13 Mar., and of his task group commanders for the same period: CTG 58.1 (Rear Adm. Clark) 15 Mar.; CTG 58.2 (Rear Adm. Davison) 12 Mar.; CTG 58.3 (Rear Adm. F. C. Sherman) 28 Mar.; CTG 58.4 (Rear Adm. Radford) 1 Mar.; CTG 58.5 (the night carrier group, Rear Adm. Gardner) 12 Mar.

drinking beer on Mogmog. At the same time changes in the composition of Task Force 58 were made, partly owing to battle and storm damage to *Franklin* and *Monterey*, partly because new *Essex*-class carriers (*Bennington, Randolph* and *Bunker Hill*) joined the Fleet. And a new night-flying carrier group, TG 58.5, was formed around veterans *Enterprise* and *Saratoga*.

For the first carrier strike against the heart of Japan, Task Force 58 was organized as follows: — [2]

Fifth Fleet, Admiral Spruance in INDIANAPOLIS

TF 58, Vice Admiral Mitscher in BUNKER HILL

	TG 58.1 Clark	TG 58.2 Davison	TG 58.3 F. C. Sherman	TG 58.4 Radford	TG 58.5 Gardner
CV	HORNET WASP BENNINGTON	LEXINGTON HANCOCK	ESSEX BUNKER HILL	YORKTOWN RANDOLPH	ENTERPRISE SARATOGA
CVL	BELL. WOOD	SAN JACINTO	COWPENS	LANGLEY CABOT	
BB	MASS'TS INDIANA	WISCONSIN MISSOURI	S. DAKOTA NEW JERSEY	WASHINGTON N. CAROLINA	
CB			ALASKA		
CA	VINCENNES	S. FRANCISCO BOSTON	INDIANAPOLIS		BALTIMORE
CL	MIAMI SAN JUAN		PASADENA WILKES BARRE ASTORIA	SANTA FE BILOXI SAN DIEGO	FLINT
	15 DD	19 DD	14 DD	17 DD	12 DD

This first carrier strike against Japan proper since the Halsey-Doolittle raid of 1942 was regarded with some apprehension by Task Force 58, as almost half the air groups would be on their first combat mission. To meet expected counterattacks, especially those from the Kamikaze Corps, each air group on a big carrier now comprised at least 73 fighter planes (Corsairs and Hellcats), leaving only 30 units to be divided between dive- and torpedo-bombers.

Task Force 58 sortied from Ulithi 10 February and shaped a course eastward of the Marianas and Bonins. On the 12th, the air

[2] See Appendix I for complete task organization and C.O.'s.

groups rehearsed with the 3rd Marine Division on Tinian. Two days later the task force fueled at sea from one of Admiral Beary's replenishment groups. Everything possible was done to guard against detection. Measures included radio deception, scouting by Pacific Fleet submarines to dispose of any picket vessels there might be en route, scouting by B–29s and Navy Liberators from the Marianas to clear the air. On the 15th a scouting line of five destroyers ranged ahead of the carriers, and antisubmarine air patrol was set up. At 1900 a high-speed run-in began towards launching positions, where the carriers arrived at dawn 16 February. Thanks to these precautions, and to thick weather most of the way, they arrived undetected.

The launching position lay about 125 miles SE of Tokyo but only 60 miles off the coast of Honshu. Flying conditions were very bad — ceiling of 4000 feet, broken clouds at 1000 feet, rain and snow squalls, NE wind force 6 to 7. But, having come so far for what Admiral Mitscher predicted would be "the greatest air victory of the war for carrier aviation," [3] foul weather could not stop him. Heavy fighter sweeps were launched promptly on 16 February, to cover the airfields around Tokyo Bay.

Low overcast also hampered the Japanese, and the only offensive sweep to meet sizable opposition was the first from TG 58.2 over the Chiba Peninsula on the east side of Tokyo Bay. About 100 Japanese fighters attacked Admiral Davison's planes as they crossed the coast and about 40 of them were shot down. American pilots found the Japanese on the whole reluctant to engage; Admiral Mitscher had correctly told his pilots, "He is probably more afraid of you than you are of him." The fifth sweep, by TG 58.3 whose targets were to the westward, managed to find clear weather and had the honor to be the first Navy fighter planes to arrive over Tokyo. These initial sweeps, intended to clear the air of enemy fighters for bombing runs, found little opposition. Before return-

---

[3] CTF 58 Action Report, Encl. C, the Admiral's "Air Combat Notes for Pilots" posted in every ready room. For anyone wishing to know fighter-plane tactics at this stage of the war, this is an excellent source; so large a proportion of the VF pilots had had no combat experience that Mitscher took nothing for granted.

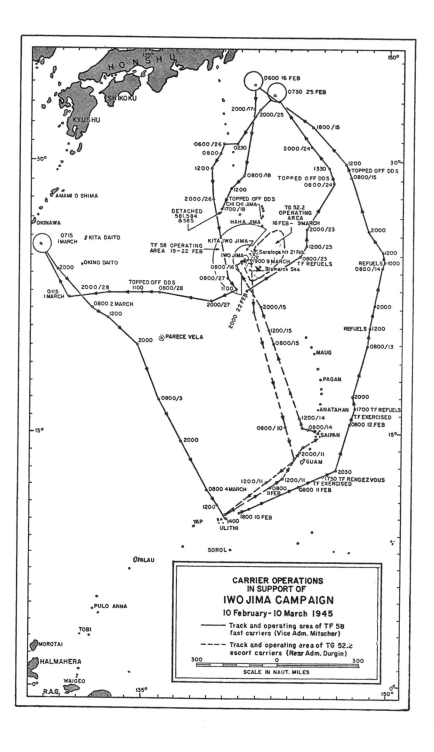

CARRIER OPERATIONS
IN SUPPORT OF
IWO JIMA CAMPAIGN
10 February-10 March 1945

——— Track and operating area of TF 58
fast carriers (Vice Adm. Mitscher)

- - - - Track and operating area of TG 52.2
escort carriers (Rear Adm. Durgin)

300   0   300

SCALE IN NAUT. MILES

ing to their ships the planes swept across the designated airfields, strafing planes that they caught grounded. Succeeding sweeps by Hellcats and Corsairs kept these fields covered throughout the day.

Admiral Mitscher, fearing that more targets would be weathered in during the afternoon, ordered bombing attacks against aircraft frame and engine plants in the Tokyo area at 1130, earlier than he intended. The first was directed against the Ota and Koizumi plants northwest of Tokyo. The Ota plant, previously damaged by B–29s, was almost completely destroyed in this and the next attack on 25 February, when Koizumi was first hit, as the aviators were unable to find it on the 16th.[4] Many planes that could not get through to their assigned target expended their bombs on airfields.

During the afternoon three Japanese picket boats that had evaded detection in the thick weather were spotted by destroyer *Haynsworth* and promptly sunk.[5] At sunset, after the daytime fighters had been recovered, TG 58.5 launched a sweep of night fighters to cover the enemy airfields at dusk. The task force was not disturbed during the night.

Before dawn 17 February, TG 58.5 sent off planes in search of shipping, and at dawn the other groups launched fighter sweeps. These were followed by bombing strikes on the Musashimo, Tama and Tachikawa plants near Tokyo. At about 1115, with weather growing steadily worse, Admiral Mitscher canceled further strikes. After recovering planes the task force retired towards Iwo Jima.

The results of these first carrier strikes at the heart of Japan were substantial but not spectacular. In addition to damaging aircraft frame and engine plants, a number of ships and small craft were attacked and sunk in Tokyo Bay, the biggest prize being *Yamashiro*

---

[4] USSBS "Report on Nakajima Aircraft Ltd." (June 1946) which does not distinguish between damage inflicted by the different attacks.

[5] *Haynsworth* recovered several survivors, who were transferred to *Essex* and placed in the brig under Marine guard. The prisoners became objects of considerable interest to the carrier's crew, who clustered around the cell doors, plied the prisoners with candy bars and cigarettes, and gave them their first lessons in Navy English. Thus, when Admiral Sherman came below to take a look at them, he was startled by the Japanese politely folding arms across stomach, bowing from the waist, and remarking what they had been told was the proper greeting to a flag officer, "F—— you, Joe!"

Maru of 10,600 tons. Best results were obtained against enemy aircraft, although the temperature was so low that a considerable number of our aircraft guns froze. TF 58 claimed 341 enemy planes shot down in the air and 190 destroyed on the ground, but this cannot be checked from enemy sources. Our losses were 60 planes in combat and 28 operationally out of 738 sorties which engaged the enemy, and a grand total of 2761 sorties, which included those for C.A.P.[6]

During the night of 17–18 February, en route to Iwo Jima, destroyers *Barton, Ingraham* and *Moale* destroyed three small Japanese picket boats. *Dortch* encountered a fourth, a PC type which fought back with 3-inch guns and killed three of the destroyer's sailors. This target was finally rammed and sunk by *Waldron.*

In passing Chichi and Haha Jima, Admiral Radford's TG 58.4 launched fighter sweeps and strikes which destroyed several small craft and cratered the airfield on Chichi Jima. During the afternoon of 18 February TGs 58.2 and 58.3 took stations west of Iwo Jima for direct support of the landings next day and the other three task groups made rendezvous with oilers south of that island.

2. *Two Days' Pounding, 16–17 February* [7]

Sunrise 16 February   0644
Sunset 17 February   1720

For the first time in a Central Pacific amphibious operation all pre-landing activities at the objective were under an amphibious group commander, Rear Admiral William H. P. Blandy.[8] "Spike"

[6] Vice Adm. Mitscher Action Report; cf. Comairpac "Analysis of Air Operations, Tokyo Carrier Strikes, Feb. 1945," 28 Apr.

[7] CTF 51 (Vice Adm. Turner) "Report on the Capture of Iwo Jima" 19 May 1945; CTF 52 (Rear Adm. Blandy) Action Report 22 Feb.; CTF 54 (Rear Adm. Rodgers) Action Report 10 Mar.; CTG 52.2 (Rear Adm. Durgin) Action Report 21 Apr.; CTG 52.3 (Com Minecraft, Rear Adm. Alexander Sharp) Report on Minesweeping Operations 6 Mar. 1945.

[8] Born N.Y.C. 1890, honor man of Class of 1913 Naval Academy, service in *Florida* during Vera Cruz landing and World War I; specialized in ordnance

Blandy was the sanguine Celtic type, with a humorous Irish mouth overhung by a large red nose. His quick mind, grasp of essentials and driving energy had served the Navy well during the first two years of the war, as Chief of the Bureau of Ordnance, especially in developing, adapting and manufacturing the Swedish Bofors and the Swiss Oerlikon as the indispensable 40-mm and 20-mm antiaircraft weapons. That signal service, though deeply appreciated throughout the Fleet, exposed him to good-natured gibes whenever a gun jammed or a shell failed to explode, which he accepted with good humor. He had taken part in the Kwajalein operation, commanded an amphibious group at Saipan, and now had the assignment to command and coördinate all pre-landing activities.

Directly under Admiral Blandy were an air support control unit commanded by Captain Elton C. Parker, a support carrier group of a dozen CVEs under Rear Admiral Calvin T. Durgin, minecraft under Rear Admiral Alexander Sharp, underwater demolition teams under Captain Byron H. Hanlon, and three groups of LCI(L) gunboats, mortar boats and rocket support boats under Commander Michael J. Malanaphy. The Gunfire and Covering Force (TF 54), consisting of six battleships, four heavy cruisers, a light cruiser and 16 destroyers under Rear Admiral Bertram J. Rodgers,[9] also came under Admiral Blandy until D-day.

Task Force 54, as finally constituted, included *Idaho* and *Tennessee*, freshly returned from overhaul at West Coast navy yards; *Nevada*, *Texas* and *Arkansas*, veterans of Operations OVERLORD and DRAGOON, which reached the Pacific in November; and 30-year-old *New York*, taking part in an amphibious operation for the first

---

engineering and developed formulas used for gun manufacture by autofrettage, asst. fire control officer *New Mexico* 1921, exec. *Vega* 1922, duty ashore at Cavite; squadron gunnery and torpedo officer for destroyers Asiatic Fleet in *Stewart* 1923; duty in Buord 1924; gunnery officer *New Mexico* 1927, and staff gunnery officer *West Virginia* 1929; U.S. Naval Mission to Brazil 1931; C.O. *Simpson* 1933; Comdesdiv 10, 1935; C.O. *Utah* 1938; Chief of Buord 1941–1943; Com 'Phib Group 1 at Kwajalein, Marianas and Peleliu; after Iwo Jima commanded the assault on Kerama Retto. Com Cruisers and Destroyers Pacific Fleet July 1945 and Com Joint Army-Navy TF 1 in the Bikini atomic tests. Cinclant Feb. 1947, retired 1950, died 12 Jan. 1954.

[9] For brief biographies of Admirals Rodgers and Durgin see Vol. XI 237 and 279.

time since TORCH in 1942. Heavy cruisers *Chester, Pensacola, Salt Lake City* and *Tuscaloosa* (also a European veteran) and the new light cruiser *Vicksburg*, with assigned destroyers, completed the gunfire support force. Admiral Spruance's flagship *Indianapolis*, together with battleships *North Carolina* and *Washington*, would join on February 19, D-day.

The combined task forces under Admiral Blandy arrived off Iwo Jima at 0600 February 16. The destroyers and APDs formed a screen seaward of the bombardment ships, and the escort carriers, operating about 50 miles south of the island, provided combat air and antisubmarine patrols. Embarked in *Wake Island* was VOC–1, a group of pilots trained as gunfire spotters, flying fighter planes designated VOFs. This unit, now making its début in the Pacific, had performed the same function successfully in Operation DRAGOON in 1944.[10] The weather at the target was poor. A low ceiling and intermittent rain squalls hampered the spotters. A sweep against airfield and shipping at Chichi Jima launched at 0643 was unable to get through.[11] Minesweeping off Iwo began at 0645 and the bombardment at 0707, but ten minutes later Admiral Blandy ordered the ships to fire only when efficient air spot was available so as not to waste ammunition.

Iwo Jima was subjected to bombardment throughout the day whenever spotting planes could observe the fall of shot. The highlight occurred at 1413 when an OS2U from *Pensacola*, piloted by Lieutenant (jg) D. W. Gandy USNR, first reported a Zeke on his tail; then that he was going after him; and, a split second later, "I got him, I got him!" It was amazing for a slow, flimsy Kingfisher to get a Zeke, but apparently this one did; the victim was sighted falling in flames. Shortly after, the UDT "frogmen," when setting up a navigational light on Higashi Rock a mile and a half east of the island, were fired on from Iwo Jima by small-caliber weapons. *Pensacola* noticed this and opened up on the weapons with her 5-inch guns, and within five minutes had silenced the enemy fire.

[10] See Vol. XI 280.
[11] CTG 52.2 (Rear Adm. Durgin) Action Report.

By 1800 the day's work was finished, and the results were disappointing. As Admiral Rodgers reported, "Little damage was apparent."

D-day minus 2, 17 February, gave a different story. The weather improved, with good visibility. On the day's program were fighter sweeps against Chichi Jima, minesweeping, and beach reconnaissance by UDTs, closely supported by the heavy ships, destroyers and LCI gunboats. Sandwiched between these activities was a bombing by B–24s at 1330.

Bombardment ships were in position off Iwo by 0700. Minesweeping began promptly and at 0803 the heavy vessels were ordered to close the beaches for destructive bombardment. *Pensacola* observed the sweepers being fired on, laid her secondary battery on the firing positions and silenced them within five minutes. But coastal batteries in the northeastern part of Iwo had their revenge. *Pensacola* around 0935 received six hits from 4.7- or 6-inch shells that wrecked her C.I.C., set fire to a plane on her starboard catapult, punctured her hull on the starboard side forward, killed 17 men and wounded 98. She withdrew temporarily to fight fires and treat casualties, but later returned to station and concluded her mission.

By 0911 *Idaho, Nevada* and *Tennessee* were 3000 yards off the beaches sending heavy direct fire at assigned targets. At 1025 Admiral Blandy ordered them to retire in order to clear the UDT operations, set for 1100. By that time the minesweepers were clear, having swept up to 750 yards of the shore in precise formation, banging away with their own weapons and occasionally coming under fire from the island.

So far, everything had gone almost "according to plan," but the attempt of the LCI(G) flotilla to cover UDT reconnaissance provoked an unexpected reply from the enemy. The four UDTs were embarked in destroyer transports *Bull, Bates, Barr* and *Blessman.* Seven destroyers provided cover at the 3000-yard line where the APDs launched their LCP(R)s carrying the swimmers. As the landing craft headed for the 500-yard line, where the swimmers would make the plunge, they were followed by seven LCI gun-boats under Lieutenant Commander Williard V. Nash USNR, firing 20-mm and 40-mm guns at the beaches and preparing to launch 4.5-inch rockets. Soon after these gunboats passed the 1500-yard line, mortar shells began falling among them; and a little later, as they were beginning to launch rockets, they came under intense fire from the flanks of the beaches. A heavy battery casemated at the foot of Mount Suribachi joined in with mortars, automatic weapons and small arms, all aimed at the swimmers and LCI(G)s, but the heaviest fire came from a hitherto unrevealed battery in the high ground just north of the beaches. As Admiral Rodgers reported, "These batteries had remained concealed through over two months of softening preparation. . . . Because of their pecul-iar nature they could be neutralized only by point-blank fire." Around 1100 the seven LCI(G)s, advancing in line abreast, began to take hits, but pressed on to support the swimmers until forced out by damage and casualties. Others dashed in to replace them, to be hit in turn, time after time. "*LCI(G)–471, –438, –441* and several others, although hit several times, gallantly returned to the fray after retiring just long enough to extinguish their fires and plug holes in the hull."[12] *LCI(G)–474,* after closing destroyer *Capps,* had to be abandoned and went down. *LCI(G)–409,* after going in twice and sustaining 60 per cent casualties, closed *Terror,* removed wounded, and took on board officers and men to help damage con-trol. In all, 12 LCI(G)s took part and all were hit, but they stuck to it until the swimmers were recovered and clear. Everyone who watched these vessels was inspired by their courage and persistence.

John P. Marquand, the novelist, who was gathering material in *Tennessee,* thus describes *LCI(G)–466* coming alongside: "There was blood on the main deck, making widening pools as she rolled in the sluggish sea. A dead man on a gun platform was covered by a blanket. The decks were littered with wounded. They were being strapped on wire stretchers and passed up to us over the side. . . .

[12] CTU 52.5.1 (Com LCI(G) Flot. 3, Cdr. M. J. Malanaphy) Action Report 24 Feb. 1945.

The commanding officer was tall, bare-headed and blond, and he looked very young. . . . There was a call from our bridge, 'Can you proceed under your own power?' . . . 'We can't proceed anywhere for three days,' the C.O. said. They had passed up the wounded — seventeen of them — and then they passed up five stretchers with the dead. . . ." [13]

Forty-four men in all were killed or missing and 152 wounded. Heavy support for the gunboats quickly developed. *Nevada*, being close inshore (Captain H. L. Grosskopf having turned a Nelsonian blind eye to Admiral Blandy's order to withdraw), was in the right position to silence the battery to the north, and concentrated on it for two hours. Captain Hanlon, in general charge of the reconnaissance, asked for an air strike at the base of Mount Suribachi and for the heavy ships to increase their rate of fire on known targets. At 1121, destroyer *Leutze* was hit, severely injuring the C.O., Commander B. A. Robbins, and 33 others, besides seven killed or missing.

By 1240 all swimmers but one had been recovered. The "frogmen" found no obstacles at the beaches and were able to produce accurate gradient maps of the approaches.

With every one of the eleven remaining LCI(G)s damaged, none were available for the afternoon reconnaissance of the western beaches. Hanlon asked for smoke planes, for the destroyers to fire white phosphorus shells, and for close gunfire support from heavy ships and destroyers. Blandy accordingly directed *Tennessee, Arkansas, Texas* and *Tuscaloosa* to cover the reconnaissance in that order, from south to north. Thus assisted, the UDTs made their reconnaissance and were back in their ships by 1755, with no casualties.

3. *D-day minus 1, 18 February*

Since the last two days of bombardment blasted away camouflage from batteries not previously known to exist, the island's defenses

[13] *Harper's* (May 1945) pp. 497–498.

were for the first time properly revealed; and formidable they were indeed. Fortunately for us, the support of UDTs with LCI(G)s had convinced General Kuribayashi that the main landing had started, and to repel it he unmasked batteries that would have caused very heavy casualties on D-day had they not been discovered two days before. This was the only serious mistake made by the Japanese general in his defensive tactics, which won the rueful admiration of his enemies.

These revelations on 17 February brought about a quick revision of the bombardment pattern for D-day minus 1, 18 February. Orders were issued to concentrate on the immediate vicinity and flanks of the eastern beaches, and for heavy ships to close to 2500 yards or less and deliver concentrated direct fire on all targets. At 0745 February 18 Admiral Rodgers ordered his gunfire ships to "close beach and get going." Each had her assigned target aiming to destroy as many as possible in the landing area and the nearby ground commanding the beaches. Bombardment ships delivered direct fire all day long. Both *Tennessee* and *Idaho* demolished their targets, literally blasting blockhouses and pillboxes out of the ground. The results of the bombardment, which ceased at 1821, were very gratifying. It was worth more than all the previous "softenings" by air bombing and naval gunfire, and was largely responsible for the assault teams' being able to touch down on D-day with few casualties. The sacrifice of brave sailors in the LCI gunboats was well rewarded.

A small enemy air raid developed about 2130 as the amphibious groups were retiring for the night. Destroyer minesweeper *Gamble* was hit by two 250-pound bombs amidships, one of which exploded in the after fireroom, causing extensive damage, and blowing two holes near the keel. Five men were killed or missing and nine wounded. *Hamilton* stood by to assist and remove casualties and *Dorsey* took *Gamble* in tow until she could be turned over to a salvage tug. *Blessman*, making 20 knots to close Admiral Rodgers's group, and carrying a UDT unit, was hit in the forward fireroom and troop spaces by a bomb dropped from a plane which approached from astern. She suffered extensive damage, lost 42 men killed or missing and 29 wounded.

Admiral Turner arrived off Iwo Jima at 0600 February 19 with the main body of the expeditionary force and assumed the duties of CTF 52, relieving Admiral Blandy, whose conduct during those three critical days had been characterized by keen intelligence in the face of unexpected situations.

February 18 (D-day minus 1) was Sunday. The chaplain on one of the transports had printed on cards, and distributed to each Marine, the words of Sir Jacob Astley's famous prayer before the Battle of Edgehill, in 1642: —

> O Lord! Thou knowest how busy I must be this day:
> If I forget Thee, do not Thou forget me.[14]

This well fitted the mood of United States Marines three centuries later.

[14] H. M. Smith *Coral and Brass* p. 254; but "Howlin' Mad" named the wrong author and garbled the prayer.

CHAPTER III

D-day at Iwo Jima [1]

19 February 1945

Sunrise	0641
Sunset	1725

1. Pre-landing Bombardment

D-DAY, observed Admiral Turner, opened with weather ideal for an amphibious landing — he had never seen it so good at Guadalcanal, the Gilberts, the Marshalls or Saipan. A light northerly wind floated fleecy clouds lazily over the island. A calm sea raised no surf on the beaches — a wonderful break for the assault, as beach gradients were so steep that even a low surf would embarrass landing craft. The island, wrote John P. Marquand, "never looked more aesthetically ugly than on D-day morning, or more completely Japanese. . . . It also had the minute, fussy compactness of those miniature Japanese gardens. Its stones and rocks were like those contorted, wind-scoured, water-worn boulders which the Japanese love to collect as landscape decorations. 'I hope to God,' a wounded Marine said later, 'that we don't have to go on any more of those screwy islands!' " [2] Only one more, Marine — the even screwier Okinawa — and the war would be almost over.

---

[1] CTF 51 (Vice Admiral Turner) Action Report; Action Reports mentioned in Chap. II, note 1 above; and those of Com Transgrp B (Commo. H. C. Flanagan); Com Transgrp A (Commo. J. B. McGovern), and C. G.'s V Phib Corps (Maj. Gen. Harry Schmidt USMC), 4th Marine Div. (Maj. Gen. Clifton B. B. Cates), 5th Marine Div. (Maj. Gen. Keller E. Rockey); Bartley *Iwo Jima;* Carl W. Proehl *Fourth Marine Division in World War II* (1946); Howard W. Conner *The Spearhead* (5th Marine Division) 1950; Robert Sherrod *On to Westward, War in the Central Pacific* (1945). The Navy has two excellent movies taken during the action, MN–5562 "Naval Guns at Iwo" and MN–5124 "To the Shore of Iwo Jima."

[2] "Iwo Jima before H-hour" *Harper's* (May 1945) p. 499.

Shortly after daylight 19 February there opened the heaviest pre-H-hour bombardment of World War II. Ships taking part were those of Task Force 54,[3] together with *North Carolina, Washington, Indianapolis, Santa Fe* and *Biloxi* lent by Task Force 58. This made a grand total of seven battleships, four heavy cruisers, three light cruisers and (during the last half hour) ten destroyers.

It began at 0640, two hours and twenty minutes before H-hour. Off the eastern shore were stationed *North Carolina* and *San Francisco*, whose assigned targets were in the bulbous part of the island. A line of four battleships and four cruisers, with eight destroyers between them, covered the southeastern coast from off the quarry overlooking the northernmost beach, to a point south of Mount Suribachi. Two battleships, five cruisers and one destroyer took care of the western beaches. Targets selected for this phase of bombardment were on and flanking the landing beaches, both airfields and the lower slopes of Suribachi. For the first 85 minutes fire was deliberate: 75 rounds each for the battleships, 100 rounds each for the heavy cruisers. At 0803 gunfire was lifted to permit air strikes to be made by planes from Task Groups 58.2 and 58.3.

These fast carrier groups were operating about 65 miles northwest of Iwo Jima, under the tactical command of Rear Admiral Frederick C. Sherman. At 0805 and 0815 their rockets, bombs, and napalm struck targets on the eastern slope of Suribachi, on high ground north of the landing beaches, and on the airfield in the center of the island. At 0825 the bombardment ships resumed with vastly increased tempo. For the next half hour shells literally rained on Iwo. Battleships fired 155 rounds each, the cruisers 150 rounds each, and the ten destroyers 500 rounds each.

Beginning at 0850 naval gunfire was adjusted, in a complicated and nicely timed pattern, so that the carrier planes could strafe the beaches during the last seven minutes before H-hour.

---

[3] Less *New York. Chester*, while approaching her firing station, was struck a glancing blow by *Estes*, but carried out her assigned bombardment.

It is impossible to assess the effect of this tremendous concentration of air bombing and gunfire, as distinct from what had been
done on the three previous days. Undoubtedly a number of gun
positions were damaged, but the Japanese garrison cozily sat it out
in their deep underground shelters.

At one minute short of H-hour naval gunfire shifted to targets
about 200 yards inland, at 0902 it moved another 200 yards inland
and thereafter formed a modified rolling barrage ahead of the
troops, constantly adjusted to conform to their actual rate of advance. This barrage was fired by the secondary batteries of the
heavy ships, to each of which was assigned a shore fire control party
with the troops. S.f.c.p. had the privilege of cutting in to request a
special shoot on some just-discovered target before the scheduled
fire of its ship was completed.[4]

2. H-hour, 0900

Admiral Turner ordered "Land the Landing Force" at 0645. It
was obvious that 0900 (H-hour) could easily be met. Iwo was
shrouded in the dust and smoke created by the bombardment, but
weather conditions were almost perfect. The operation looked like
a pushover. Optimists predicted that the island would be secured
in four days.

The assault troops were transported and landed by TF 53, the
Attack Force, commanded by Rear Admiral Harry W. Hill. The

---

[4] Comparative ammunition expenditure in D-day bombardments at Iwo Jima
19 Feb. and Okinawa 1 April 1945: —

No. Rounds	16-inch	14-inch	12-inch	8-inch	6-inch	5-inch
Okinawa	475	1325	175	2100	3000	36,260
Iwo Jima	1950	1500	400	1700	2000	31,000

Adm. Turner's Report for the two operations. See Col. Donald C. Weller usmc,
"Salvo-Splash!" U.S. Naval Institute *Proceedings* LXXX (1954) 1018–1021, for technical aspects of the naval bombardment.

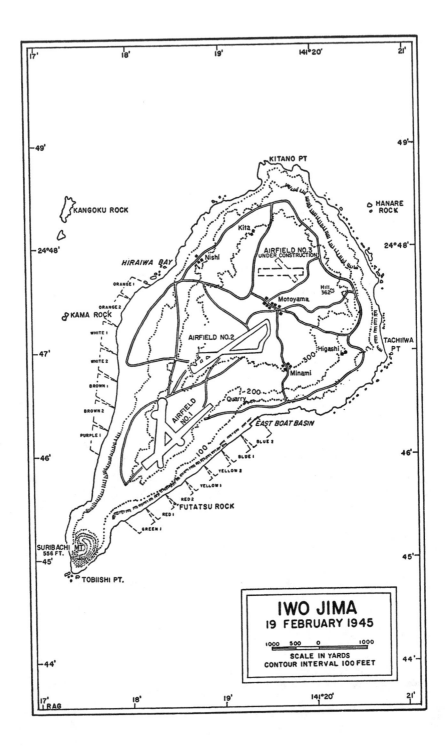

IWO JIMA
19 FEBRUARY 1945

SCALE IN YARDS
CONTOUR INTERVAL 100 FEET

5th Marine Division was embarked in the 22 transports of Commodore John B. McGovern's transport group; the 4th Marine Division in the 24 transports of Commodore Henry C. Flanagan's transport group. The first five assault waves were landed from LVTs,[5] which, with their troops, were embarked in LSTs of Captain Wilkie H. Brereton's Tractor Group.

The shore from the base of Mount Suribachi to the high broken ground 3500 yards northeastward had been divided on maps gridded for the assault into seven beaches, each 500 yards long, indicated by colors: one Green, two Red, two Yellow, and two Blue. The northeastern part of Blue 2 had been developed by the Japanese into a small boat harbor, which the Marines called the East Boat Basin. Their scheme of maneuver was relatively simple: — the 5th Division to land on the Green and Red beaches and drive across the island, a part to capture or isolate Mount Suribachi, the rest to deploy northward and advance up the island parallel to the 4th Division. The 4th would land on Beaches Yellow 1 and 2 and Blue 1 and drive inland to No. 1 airfield and to the north to protect their right flank.

In the midst of the thunder of bombardment the amphibious forces calmly took their positions. By 0730 the control parties had established line of departure 4000 yards off the beaches. LSTs of the tractor groups took station at the 5500-yard line, dropped ramps and began to discharge LVTs filled with troops, "like all the cats in the world having kittens," as John P. Marquand remarked. It was now time for the newest type of boat, the Landing Craft Support Craft, Large — designated LCS(L) — to do its stuff. Twelve of these 160-foot craft, each capable of firing a salvo of 120 4.5-inch rockets, and bristling with 40-mm and 20-mm and 50-caliber machine guns as well, were present. They headed for the beach at 0740, line abreast, launched their rockets aimed at positions 20 to 60 yards behind the beaches, turned 90 degrees to parallel the shore,

[5] The Marines' LVT amphibians again proved themselves at Iwo. Their low speed was no handicap since the equally slow LVT(A)s spearheaded the landings. But the LVTs could land their troops and supplies on dry land despite surf, steep beaches and soft sand.

firing everything they had, ceased fire at 0854, and withdrew to the line of departure just as the final air strike came in.[6]

At 0830 the first assault wave, consisting of 68 LVT(A), the amphtrac tanks, left the line of departure. It hit the beach almost precisely at H-hour, 0900. Within the next twenty-three minutes the remaining assault waves landed on schedule, and at 0944 twelve LSM, carrying medium tanks, beached.

Up to the point of actually touching land, this operation went off like a parade. Then trouble started. The LVT(A)s found their way blocked by the first terrace, which rose to as high as fifteen feet. The volcanic ash and cinders afforded poor traction, and as the men of the first wave left their vehicles on the run, they were slowed down to a walk. A few amphtracs reached the first terrace through breaches blasted by naval gunfire; some backed into the water and fired their turrets at inland targets; but many bogged down on the beach.

For a few minutes everywhere, and at some spots for as much as half an hour, only scattered small-arm, mortar and artillery fire fell along the beaches. Then both the volume and the accuracy of enemy resistance, mainly mortar fire, increased heavily. A situation developed somewhat similar to the one on Omaha Beach, Normandy, on 6 June 1944, with the important difference that here there was not even a sea wall for protection to the troops, who found it virtually impossible to advance in the face of withering fire. Enemy reaction developed earliest in the 4th Division sector. Colonel Walter Wensinger's 23rd Marine Regiment landed on Beaches Yellow; Colonel John R. Lanigan's 25th Marine Regiment on Blue 1. The Japanese had excellent observation posts on high ground north of these beaches. Four of the tank-carrying LSM which beached at 0944 were hit by mortar shells and suffered extensive damage.

General Kuribayashi's static defense now began to show itself.

---

[6] Lt.Cdr. H. D. Chickering usnr Action Report of *LCS(L)51* and letter of 4 Mar. 1945; Bartley p. 49. The LCI gunboats were to have gone in with the LCS(L) but were too badly shot up on D-day minus 2 to participate.

During the naval bombardment his troops retired deep into the ground and waited. As soon as gunfire lifted, they returned to their covered and protected positions and opened up on the advancing Marines. Their cleverly constructed pillboxes and larger gun and mortar positions could not be knocked out except by direct hit. Some of them, the "flush deckers," were built underground with only the firing slit uncovered, and the entire installation concealed from the view of ships or approaching troops by a sand bank. These were almost impossible to spot until they opened up. Gunports for the mortars were often only a couple of feet wide. Only a soldier on the spot could knock out positions such as these, with rifle fire, hand grenades, flame-throwers and demolitions. Aërial bombing, naval gunfire and artillery could contribute little to relieve this situation, which became hideously obvious within an hour of the landings.

As the Marines piled ashore they inched forward and took what shelter they could on the terraces, holding some momentum even though slowed to a crawl. On the left flank, the 5th Marine Division was going into action for the first time. On the extreme left, the 28th Marine Regiment (Colonel Harry B. Liversedge) landed two battalions in column on Beach Green while the 27th Regiment landed on Red 1 and 2. Opposition here was somewhat lighter than the 4th Division encountered, and heavy enemy fire developed more slowly, but within twenty minutes well-directed, accurate artillery, mortar and machine-gun fire began falling all along the 5th Division beaches. On the left, the 1st Battalion, 28th Marines, was to drive straight across the island at its narrowest point – 700 yards wide – while the 2nd Battalion, landing after the first, was to turn left towards Mount Suribachi. The 27th Marines had the job of driving straight inland and linking up with the 4th Division on their right. Having a little more breathing time than their comrades on the right flank, the 5th Division had a chance to get organized and start moving inland. Progress was slow owing to soft footing, heavy enemy fire, and occasional land mines, but never completely halted.

3. Build-up and Support

As the volume of enemy fire on the advancing Marines increased, the gunfire of supporting ships off shore stepped up. Prior to noon, most of the gunfire ships were busy delivering a rolling barrage with 5-inch shell. Fortunately, it had been arranged to repeat a scheduled shoot if progress ashore turned out to be slower than anticipated. This was done frequently. In addition, ships were instructed, whenever they observed fire coming from an enemy position, to lay on main batteries immediately and shoot it out. Other gun or mortar positions were spotted by planes, which called up ships' gunfire. The spotting was good and the shooting silenced many enemy positions, but they refused to stay silenced. A direct hit was the only certain way to silence a gun for good.

In no previous operation in the Pacific had naval gunfire support been so effective as at Iwo Jima. This was due in great measure to Lieutenant Colonel D. M. Weller USMC, V 'Phib Corps naval gunfire officer, who helped V 'Phib staff prepare the naval gunfire plan and had been beside Admiral Blandy during the preliminary bombardment. *Santa Fe* was the star of the fire support cruisers. She laid almost continuous 5-inch and 6-inch shell fire within 200 yards of the BLT on the left flank of 5th Division, with the result that hardly a shot was fired by the enemy from the base of Mount Suribachi, which commanded their line of advance. Battleship *Nevada* became the sweetheart of the Marine Corps. Her skipper, Captain H. L. ("Pop") Grosskopf, an old gunnery officer and a ruthless driver, had set out to make his battleship the best fire support ship in the Fleet, and did. *Nevada,* when firing her assigned rolling barrage about 0925, found that her secondary battery could not penetrate a concrete blockhouse and turned over the job to her main battery. This damaged a hitherto undisclosed blockhouse behind Beach Red 1, blasting away its sand cover and leaving it naked and exposed. At 1100 this blockhouse again became troublesome; the battleship then used armor-piercing shells, which took the position completely apart. At 1512 *Nevada* observed a gun firing from a cave in the high broken ground east of the beaches. Using direct fire, she shot two rounds of 14-inch, scoring a direct hit in the mouth of the cave, blowing out the side of the cliff and completely destroying the gun. One could see it drooping over the cliff edge "like a half-extracted tooth hanging on a man's jaw." [7]

An excellent illustration of the high state of training and versatility that existed in the Pacific Fleet at this stage of the war is shown by the experience of *West Virginia*, Captain Herbert V. Wiley. After outstanding performances at Leyte Gulf and Lingayen, she arrived at Ulithi 16 February to replenish from Service Squadron 10. At 0300 next morning Captain Wiley received orders from Admiral Nimitz to proceed immediately to Iwo Jima at best speed. Completing replenishment shortly after daylight, she began the 900-mile run to Iwo. At 1045 D-day, she arrived in the bombardment area, reported to Admiral Rodgers, received copies of all orders, charts, gridded maps, and an assigned firing position. Less than two hours after her arrival she was shooting at targets near Mount Suribachi.

A shore fire control party was assigned to each Marine battalion that landed. These parties suffered many casualties from enemy fire and lost much equipment but established communications with their assigned ships unusually early.

The Marines inched their way inland from the beaches preceded by heavy and continuous naval gunfire. At 1035 a small party of the 5th Division succeeded in making its way across the narrowest part of the island to the western beaches. But no continuous line of communications could be established as the troops which followed were forced to mop up Japanese positions that had inadvertently been bypassed; the defenders had held fire until they could shoot at the rear of the assault echelon.

Tanks began landing in the 5th Division sector at 0930. After considerable difficulty getting off the beaches they moved inland to support the troops. Some were disabled by land mines, but all be-

[7] Col. R. D. Heinl USMC, letter to writer 4 Dec. 1959.

came high priority targets for the enemy's antitank weapons and many were knocked out. In the final analysis it was the flame-thrower teams, riflemen with hand grenades, and engineers with demolition charges, blowing up pillboxes or sealing off cave entrances, that secured ground.

On the right of the 5th Division sector, resistance was heavy and progress was slow; yet, by 1130, RCT 28 was on and across the southern end of No. 1 airfield and, by 1500, RCT 27 had reached the cliffs overlooking the western beaches. Mount Suribachi was now cut off from the rest of the island's defenses.

The 4th Division on the right found the going very tough indeed. RCT 23, on the left flank, had gained only 500 yards by noon; it reached the edge of No. 1 airfield by 1405 but was unable to cross it or gain more ground. Tanks which landed in support at 1000 were slow in surmounting the beaches and some were knocked out by land mines. *LSM–216* beached four times under fire before she could find firm enough footing for her tanks to roll off.[8] RCT 25, on the right, attacked in two directions, inland towards the airfield and north against high broken ground. Here they were much distressed by fire coming from pillboxes located in the cliffs of the old quarry above East Boat Basin. To eliminate them, a new kind of spotting was tried. *LCS(L)–51* moved in to 650 yards off the boat basin and spotted for cruiser *Vicksburg*, gunfire support for that sector. Lieutenant J. J. Sweeney USMC, embarked in the LCS, directed her tracer fire to the hot spots, and the cruiser, following the tracers with her 6-inch guns, smashed them. This went on from 0910 to 1030. The LCS, followed by four more of the same class, fired both guns and rockets at spots indicated by troops ashore, and helped to break up a counterattack. During the afternoon these big support craft teamed up with destroyers to silence other positions. They thrust close inshore, drew enemy fire to themselves and replied with tracers which gave the destroyers their cue.

---

[8] The "high degree of coverage and tenacity shown by these ships in beaching . . . and landing this vital equipment in the face of the heaviest mortar and artillery fire yet seen" was praised in the 4th Division Report. Bartley *Iwo Jima* pp. 60n, 62n.

The 1st Battalion of RCT 25, assigned to the inland thrust, had made only 600 yards by 1130. The 3rd Battalion, with the northerly assignment, was pinned down almost from the start and casualties ran high, especially among officers. Enemy fire aimed at supporting tanks also fell among the troops, adding to their misery. Not until 1400 was Colonel Lanigan ready to launch a concerted attack to the north, and by late afternoon his battalion had reached only the first ridge behind East Boat Basin.

In the meantime a chaotic condition was developing on the beaches, under fire throughout the day. At about 1100 the northerly wind veered to SE, which made the beaches a lee shore; but "hot cargo" — such as ammunition, rations, water and high priority equipment — had to be landed. Most of the movement to the beaches had been by amphtracs, which brought in supplies that were manhandled by shore and beach parties and stacked up on the beaches. Some LVTs, however, carried supplies to forward troops and others returned to their parent LSTs for more high priority cargo. At about noon regimental commanders began calling for their reserve battalions to land, and during the afternoon the division commanders committed their reserve regiments. These reserves were sent ashore from their transports by conventional landing craft, LCVP and LCM. The beaches were so steep that when these craft touched down they found it very difficult to hold on. Rising surf broke over their sterns, and the backwash of rollers flowed over the downed ramp into the bow and flooded a boat so that it could not retract. A current which set parallel to the beach also caused many to broach, and others were hit and damaged by enemy mortar fire. As a result of this cumulative damage, the beach was so littered with wrecked boats by nightfall that it was difficult to find a spot to land. Available salvage equipment was inadequate, and with heaped-up supplies also clogging the beach a very serious situation developed. It is a tribute to the shore and beach parties, who worked throughout the day under enemy fire without flinching, and the UDTs who also turned to, that the increasing number of troops ashore did not run out of ammunition and supplies.

Approximately 30,000 troops were landed on 19 February. There were 2420 casualties, including 519 killed or missing in action; and 47 more died of their wounds. The beachhead established fell far behind the planned phase line. From East Boat Basin it extended inland, to and along the southeast edge of No. 1 airfield, across its southwestern end to the west beaches, returning to the east beaches along the northern base of Suribachi. The beachhead was only about 4000 yards long, 700 yards deep in the north and 1100 yards in the south, but it already contained six infantry regiments, as many artillery battalions and two tank battalions.

4. *Air Operations*

Admiral Durgin's escort carriers continued to supply observation and spotting planes, photographic flights, C.A.P. over the target, antisubmarine patrol, and strike missions for direct support of troops ashore. The VOF were especially useful in locating targets and spotting fall of shot for ships' gunners. Lieutenant Commander George Philip, skipper of destroyer *Twiggs*, recorded that this type had had a doubtful reception in the Pacific; but "his performance of a few minutes sold him. Work with the VOF was one of the highlights of the operation."

Of the fast carrier groups, TG 58.2 (Davison) and 58.3 (Sherman) operated about 65 miles northwest of Iwo Jima while TG 58.1 and TG 58.4 fueled and replenished off shore. After the prelanding strikes on the beaches, *Hancock* and *Lexington* sent fighter sweeps of twelve planes each against Chichi Jima and Haha Jima to destroy grounded planes and small craft. It proved to be an expensive mission. Five planes were lost operationally and a torpedo bomber was shot down by antiaircraft fire. During the afternoon Admiral Sherman sent some of his planes to report to Advance Commander Support Aircraft in *Estes*. This group made bombing, rocketing and strafing runs on designated targets on the hump of Iwo Jima that were not accessible to naval gunfire.

Since enemy planes could easily fly from Japan down the line of the Bonins to bomb ships at the beachhead, dawn and dusk air attacks were anticipated. The first of these came in at 1900 D-day; but, sighting two fast carrier groups en route, decided to make them the target. Over a period of two and a half hours an estimated 12 to 15 planes harassed TGs 58.2 and 58.3. Both task group commanders used radical maneuvers, cloud cover and smoke to conceal their ships' wakes and evade the attackers, and only two direct contacts were made. "Mighty Mo," the battleship *Missouri*, drew her first blood of the war by shooting down an enemy plane at a range of 9800 yards at 1953, and a second which approached nearer was splashed by the combined antiaircraft fire of several ships.

Task Group 58.5, the night carrier group, operated northwest of Iwo Jima and provided dusk C.A.P. over the island, night fighter cover, and night observers for naval gunfire.

The carrier planes inflicted very little direct damage. The performance of napalm or gasoline jelly bombs, which were expected to burn off camouflage and suck the oxygen out of dugouts, was disappointing, and a large percentage of them were duds.[9] Quarter-ton bombs were too small to smash Japanese installations. The principal contribution of carrier planes to the Iwo landings on D-day was to provide C.A.P. over the amphibious forces, which, in view of the fact that not one enemy air attack approached them, was hardly needed. But this was good practice for the Okinawa operation, where C.A.P. was desperately needed.

Darkness finally closed D-day, a day such as Iwo had never seen since it arose a hissing volcano from the ocean. The Marines dug themselves in where night overtook them. Gunfire support ships moved out to night withdrawal areas, leaving only *Santa Fe* and ten destroyers to supply star shell illumination and harassing fire on enemy positions. The Japanese tried a few infiltrations during the night, and on the west coast their feeble attempt at a counter-landing was wiped out by alert Marines. But the expected big counterattack never came off; banzai charges were no part of Gen-

9 CTF 51 (Vice Adm. Turner) Report p. (V) (E) 6.

eral Kuribayashi's plan. He intended to conserve his man power, knowing that American sea and air power had closed all hope of reinforcement, and that it was hopeless to try to drive the Marines into the sea. But he intended to fight for every yard of ground, and did.

Liberator over Iwo Jima, 15 December 1944

Planning for Invasion
Left to right: Rear Admiral W. H. P. Blandy, Rear Admiral Harry W. Hill, Lieutenant General H. M. Smith usmc, Vice Admiral Richmond K. Turner

The Invasion of Iwo Jima

Courtesy Admiral Deyo

LCIs Moving In, 17 February 1945

One of the Damaged LCIs

The Invasion of Iwo Jima

H-hour, D-day

Boat Waves Forming

The Invasion of Iwo Jima

Fifth Marine Division Advancing near Mount Suribachi, D-day

Fourth Marine Division Moving up the Beach

The Invasion of Iwo Jima

CHAPTER IV

The Conquest of Iwo Jima

19 February–16 March 1945

1. The Struggle Ashore, 20–21 February [1]

ROBERT SHERROD, the veteran correspondent who had
come ashore on the afternoon of D-day and spent the night
in a foxhole, picked his way forward early next morning among
corpses. "Whether the dead were Japs or Americans," he recorded,
"they had died with the greatest possible violence. Nowhere in the
Pacific war had I seen such badly mangled bodies. Many were cut
squarely in half. Legs and arms lay 50 feet away from any body. In
one spot on the sand, far from the nearest cluster of dead, I saw a
string of guts 15 feet long. Only legs were easy to identify; they
were Japanese if wrapped in khaki puttees, American if covered
by canvas leggings. The smell of burning flesh was heavy. . . ." [2]

The reduction and capture of Iwo Jima is a story of yard-by-
yard advance against a tough, resourceful enemy who allowed no
let-up, and who so used his terrain as to exact the maximum price
in blood. The Marines, advancing in the open with little natural
shelter, had to fight their way against an enemy burrowed underground and protected from everything but a direct hit. It was a
costly and exhausting grind, calling for higher qualities of courage,
initiative and persistence than a campaign full of charges, counter-
charges and spectacular incidents that raise men's morale. It was

---

[1] All sources mentioned in Chap. III, Note 1, especially Vice Adm. Turner's
Action Report; Sgt. Bill Miller USMC "Hot Rock, the Fight for Mt. Suribachi" and
Capt. F. A. Scott USMC "Ten Days on Iwo Jima" *Leatherneck* XXVIII, No. 5
(May 1945) 15–19.
[2] *On to Westward* p. 180.

like being under the lash of a relentless desert storm, from which there was no shelter, day or night; but this storm lasted six weeks and rained steel, not sand. General Holland Smith said that "Iwo Jima was the most savage and the most costly battle in the history of the Marine Corps." And Admiral Nimitz observed that on Iwo "uncommon valor was a common virtue." [3]

Supporting the Marines, and a factor that may have tipped the balance, was the impact of naval gunfire support and naval aircraft, whose shells, bombs and strafing wore the enemy down. No eight square miles in all World War II received such a sustained and heavy pounding by these means as did Iwo Jima. General Kuribayashi admitted the value of it. In a message to Tokyo at the height of the battle, he said: "I am not afraid of the fighting power of only three American Marine divisions if there is no bombardment from aircraft and warships. That is the only reason why we have to face such miserable situations." [4]

A pattern for the island campaign was promptly cut out. For daytime direct support, each Marine battalion had attached to it one or more destroyers with a liaison officer on board, and a Navy shore fire control party stayed with it ashore. At daybreak the heavy support ships closed the island to fire a preliminary bombardment on targets selected by divisional and regimental commanders the evening before. On the morning of 20 February (D-day plus 1), four battleships, three cruisers and an LCI mortar unit performed this service, each ship plastering her assigned targets for 50 minutes from 0740. After the Marines jumped off, the ships stood by for deep support on targets designated by the s.f.c.p.'s or by spotting planes. That afternoon *Washington* (Captain Roscoe F. Good) received a report from divisional headquarters of a strong point of enemy resistance near the southern end of airfield No. 2. And it was even stronger than we suspected. The Japanese had constructed more than 300 pillboxes, gun emplacements and traps in a space

[3] Isely & Crowl p. 501.
[4] Maj. Tokasuka Horie "Explanation of Japanese Defense Plan and Battle of Iwo Jima" 25 Jan. 1946. Horie, one of Kuribayashi's staff officers, was detached before the landings and sent to Chichi Jima, where he survived the war.

of 500 by 1000 yards. The air spotter, sent to investigate, reported many caves dug into a cliff and facing the Marines' front lines. He directed the battleship's main battery to one end of the cliff, then spotted three 16-inch salvos directly into its face at 50-yard intervals. These shells so ate into the cliff as to start landslides which sealed off most of the cave mouths. *Washington* was on the firing line with both main and secondary batteries for ten hours and twenty minutes on 20 February. Nobody could convince the Marines that battleships were obsolete!

Caves and excavated holes in the ground were the key to Iwo's defenses. On the extreme left, Colonel Liversedge's 28th RCT closed in on Mount Suribachi, supported by destroyer *Mannert L. Abele* and light minelayer *Thomas E. Fraser*. The latter, after illuminating the eastern slopes during the night, between 0715 and 1130 delivered preparatory and neutralization fire on the mountain's base from a point 1500 yards from the beach; then shifted fire to caves and other targets of opportunity on the slopes of the volcano. When relieved by her sister ship *Henry A. Wiley* at 1448 she had fired 775 rounds of 5-inch shell. Off the western slope of Suribachi, *Abele* supported the 3rd Battalion in a similar pattern, expending 971 rounds of 5-inch and 172 rounds of star shell. At 0830 RCT 28 jumped off to the assault. Only 50 to 70 yards were gained in the forenoon against well-placed, camouflaged pillboxes and caves, many of which were so close to the front lines that supporting weapons could not be used. When the tanks (delayed by lack of fuel) finally came forward at 1100, better progress was made; but RCT 28 gained only 200 yards that day towards the lower slopes of Suribachi.

The story was much the same on the right flank of the beachhead. Preceded by intense naval, air and artillery bombardment, the Marines jumped off at 0830 but found tough going from the start. On the extreme right the 4th Division was up against the first main line of Japanese defense and made slight progress. On the west coast the 5th Division did somewhat better; but the troops, mostly in the open, suffered heavy casualties from well-placed artillery and mortar barrages. By the end of D-day plus 1 the Marines occupied a line across the island that included No. 1 airfield. Now they were facing the main enemy line of defense in the higher, broken ground of the bulbous part of the island.

About noon 20 February occurred a change in the weather that hampered both air operations and unloading supplies. The wind veered from SSE to WSW and built up to 20 knots. At 1545 a sharp cold front passed over the island and the wind shifted to NNE, raising a heavy sea which added confusion to the already chaotic condition on the beaches. They became cluttered with wrecked boats and vehicles. The high surf, an insufficient supply of Marston mat to cover the soft ash, lost equipment, casualties, enemy artillery and mortar fire, all contributed to a horrible brew of congestion and confusion. As soon as the beach party pulled one wreck out of the way another landing craft came in and broached. Conditions would have been even worse but for the energy and skill of Admiral Hill's beach party commander, Captain Carl E. Anderson USNR. "Squeaky," as he was nicknamed from his high-pitched voice, commandeered men, bulldozers and weasels. Amphtracs and dukws justified themselves by rolling over the steep, soft beaches, carrying supplies to their destination without manhandling.[5]

In addition to morning and afternoon sweeps against Haha and Chichi Jima, aircraft from Task Force 58 and the escort carriers flew 545 sorties in 27 missions on 20 February, expending over 116 tons of bombs and 1331 rockets.

During the night of 20–21 February a destroyer was assigned to each battalion and a cruiser to each division ashore, for illumination and night harassing fire. The remaining ships withdrew to night operating areas and returned at dawn.

February 21 broke with showers and an 18- to 20-knot NE wind

---

[5] Bartley *Iwo Jima* p. 197. The Royal Navy liaison officer with the attack force remarked to this writer, about two months later, "On the beach was an extraordinary character, almost as wide as he was tall, wearing the insignia of a Navy captain, but delivering his commands in amazingly blasphemous language, with a strong Scandinavian accent. But he managed to get things done." That was "Squeaky" Anderson. Weasels were tracked vehicles, 15 ft. 9 in. long.

which continued to kick up choppy seas and heavy surf. At 0740 a heavy bombardment by naval gunfire and corps artillery opened in preparation for the Marines' jump-off at 0810. This was to be the daily pattern for the next three weeks. RCT 28 reached the base of Suribachi and some advance was made all along the line to the north of No. 1 airfield. Progress was painfully slow, as the Marines had to inch their way along, destroying pillboxes and sealing cave and tunnel entrances. Any position that was bypassed or missed was sure to come to life and start shooting again. Advance for the day was measured in yards and at the end of it No. 2 airfield was still in enemy hands.

Salvage work among the wrecked craft, vehicles and tanks on the beaches was hampered by the weather. Surf and sea conditions were such that unloading was limited to the big beaching craft and LSMs. During the day another RCT of the 3rd Marine Division, in floating reserve off the island, was landed and assigned to the hard-pressed 4th Division.

The Tokyo "Home and Empire" broadcast at the end of this day indicates that the enemy propaganda service was becoming really mad with Kelly Turner. The following is a partial translation: —

According to reports issued by the enemy, the man who commands the enemy American amphibious forces which effected landings on our Iwo Island is Vice Admiral Richmond Turner. He is the right-hand man to Commander in Chief Spruance of the enemy Fifth Fleet. He is the man who can be termed a devil man, being responsible for the killing of countless numbers of our own younger and elder brothers on the various islands throughout the central Pacific area. Turner's career in war against our own men began with the operations on the island of Guadalcanal.

This man Turner is called and known as the "Alligator" in the American Navy. He is associated with this name because his work is very similar to that of an alligator, which lives both on land and in the water. Also, the true nature of an alligator is that once he bites into something he will not let go. Turner's nature is also like this.

Spruance, with a powerful offensive spirit and Turner, with excellent determinative power, have led their men to a point where they are indeed close to the mainland, but they find themselves in a dilemma, as they are unable either to advance or retreat.

This man Turner, who has been responsible for the death of so many of our precious men, shall not return home alive — he must not, and will not. This is one of the many things we can do to rest at ease the many souls of those who have paid the supreme sacrifice.[6]

Nevertheless, "Alligator" Turner (the Japanese evidently got the name from the shoulder patch of the V 'Phib Corps) not only returned alive, but at the time we go to press (1960) is still very much alive.

2. Carrier Strikes and Air Support, 21 February–1 March [7]

On 21 February Task Groups 58.2 and 58.3 operated about 70 miles WNW of Iwo, providing C.A.P. and launching several bombing strikes. Admirals Sherman and Davison also sent a strafing sweep against Chichi Jima to interdict the airfield so it would not be used for staging. During the night of 20–21 February about 13 raids with a total of 18 to 20 planes came in on the task group. Several planes pressed in near enough to be fired upon; two were shot down. No damage was inflicted on the ships. The pattern of these attacks on Sherman's and Davison's groups reminded sailors of similar raids off the Gilbert Islands in November 1943, years and years ago as it seemed. But of very different design were the attacks on *Saratoga* that same evening by kamikazes from Hatori airbase near Yokosuka, which staged through Hachijo Jima in the Northern Bonins.

On the morning of 21 February *Saratoga* (Captain Lucian A. Moebus) and three destroyers were detached from TG 58.5 in order to provide C.A.P. the following night over the amphibious forces off Iwo Jima. Unfortunately the rest of the night carrier group, *Enterprise* with three cruisers and seven destroyers, was re-

---

[6] Foreign Broadcast Intelligence Service Bulletin 22 Feb. 1945.
[7] CTF 58 (Vice Adm. Mitscher) Action Report for 10 Feb.–4 Mar., 13 Mar. 1945, CTG 52.2 (Rear Adm. Durgin) Action Report for Iwo Jima, 21 Apr. 1945.

tained by Admiral Mitscher for night C.A.P. over TF 58; this gave
old "Sara" too little protection. At 1628 that day, when she had
just reached her operating area 35 miles NW of Iwo with most of
her planes on board, bogeys were reported 75 miles out. These were
evaluated by the air support commander as "friendly." Six fighters
of *Saratoga's* C.A.P. were nevertheless vectored out to inspect the
suspicious characters, and at 1650 came a "Tally-ho!" from a pilot,
followed by the word "Splashed two Zekes." The sky was overcast
and ceiling down to 3500 feet, favoring air attack. *Saratoga* went to
general quarters, commenced catapulting night fighters at maximum speed, and sent them out in all directions. At 1659 her antiaircraft guns opened fire on six planes bursting out of the clouds.
The first two, already blazing from hits, struck the water and
bounced into the carrier's starboard side at the waterline, hurling
their bombs inside the ship, where they exploded. "Sara" had just
completed launching 15 planes when she received these hits, and
had two standby fighters on the catapults when she received a bomb
from a third aircraft which exploded on the anchor windlass.
This knocked out a good section of the flight deck forward. The
fourth attacker splashed; the fifth made a flat turning dive, crashed
the port catapult and exploded. The sixth, also in flames, crashed
an airplane crane on the starboard side; parts of it landed on No. 1
gun gallery and the rest went overboard. All this happened within
three minutes, 1700–1703 February 21.

Saratoga's power plant was hardly touched, and she built up
speed to 25 knots while fighting fires. The blaze on the hangar deck
was brought under control by 1830; the fire in wing tank control
twelve minutes later. But the flight deck was in no condition to
recover airborne planes. Destroyer *McGowan*, which took over
fighter control, instructed them to land on one of the escort carriers near Iwo, until "Sara" had jettisoned her burning aircraft.

At 1846, just as things were beginning to look up, there came a
sinister glare of parachute flares, and five more kamikazes attacked.
Four were shot down clear of the carrier; the fifth came in unobserved, dropping a bomb which exploded on or just over the flight

deck, blowing a 25-foot hole in that deck as the plane bounced overboard. Even in this predicament there was something to laugh at. A confused pilot from a CVE landed his plane on *Saratoga's* deck, remarking as he alighted "Gee, I'm glad I'm not on that old Sara. All hell's broken out there!" A deckhand replied "Take a good look around, brother. This *is* hell!"

But old "Sara" was not yet dead. Although wounded in seven places, by 2015 she was able to recover planes on the after part of her flight deck. On Admiral Spruance's orders she steamed under her own power to Eniwetok, en route to a West Coast yard for repairs. She lost 36 planes by burning and jettisoning, and six by water landings, and sustained heavy casualties — 123 killed and missing, 192 wounded.[8]

The loss of *Saratoga's* services for over three months, and the discouraging results of this battle, coupled with the distaste of carrier-plane pilots for night work,[9] put a stopper on further development of special dusk-to-dawn carriers and planes. Admiral Mitscher was not favorably impressed by their performance. In the next operation, the one covering the Ryukyus, there was but one night-flying carrier, *Enterprise*. But, as we shall see, her performance in that operation caused the Admiral to change his mind about night fighters and bombers.

"Sara" was not the only flattop to catch it during the night of 21–22 February. At 1845, during twilight, escort carrier *Bismarck Sea*, operating with Admiral Durgin's group (to which *Saratoga*

[8] *Saratoga* Action Report 7 Mar. 1945.
[9] Discussed in letter from Cdr. William I. Martin (C.O. Air Group 90 in *Enterprise*) to Cominch 14 Apr. 1945. The reasons for this distaste were not so much the hazards of night flying as failure to receive target information from daytime fliers, dissatisfaction over not seeing targets, and irregular meals and hours. CTG 58.5 (Rear Adm. M. B. Gardner), in his Action Report of 12 March, stated that the effectiveness of a night carrier group was not properly tested during this operation. The losses of TG 58.5, 10–22 February, exclusive of *Saratoga's* in the 21 February attack, were eight planes (one over Yokosuka, one by "friendly" fire off Iwo, rest operational), five pilots and four other men, plus ten more planes jettisoned as a result of deck crashes. Admiral Spruance, in his endorsement to this report, observed that a special night carrier group was not a good solution because its requirements for daytime C.A.P. put too much load on the other groups. Night fighters were frequently called upon for emergency day missions; 71 per cent of their sorties in this operation were by day.

Marines Moving In on a Cave

Fifth Division Command Post
Left to right in Foreground: Brigadier General Leo D. Hermle,
Major General K. E. Rockey, Colonel James F. Shaw

The Battle for Iwo Jima

The farthest LST is carrying a pontoon causeway, and the next one, an LCT. The nearest craft is an LSM; the wreck in the foreground is Japanese

Beaching Craft Unloading under Mount Suribachi, 24 February

and *Enterprise* were temporarily attached) about 45 miles east of Iwo Jima, became a total loss to kamikaze attack. One Japanese plane attacking on her port bow was taken under fire but a second, coming in very low on the starboard side, was not seen until 1000 yards away. It was shot at until the guns could depress no more; already blazing, it crashed the ship abreast the after elevator, which dropped onto the hangar deck. About two minutes later a heavy explosion occurred. This started gasoline fires in planes on the hangar deck, the after end of which was blown out by a second explosion. The after part of the ship was a shambles and at 1905 Captain J. L. Pratt ordered Abandon Ship. *Bismarck Sea* burned and exploded for three hours, then rolled over and sank. Three destroyers and three destroyer escorts spent all night and until 1000 on the 22nd picking up survivors. Of her crew of 943 officers and men, 218 were lost.

Simultaneously with this fatal attack several Japanese torpedo bombers came in on the starboard side of escort carrier *Lunga Point*. The first, taken under fire at 1500 yards, launched a torpedo, then was caught by a shellburst and splashed only 200 yards away. The torpedo passed ahead. A second plane, closely following the first, dropped a torpedo which also crossed the carrier's bow safely; the plane then disappeared without being brought under fire. A third, close behind the second, after launching a torpedo which missed astern, hit the after part of the island with its wing, skidded across the flight deck with propeller chewing up the planking, then plunged into the sea over the port side. And a fourth plane was shot down. The fires in *Lunga Point* were soon quenched, the damage was slight, and nobody was killed.

Net cargo ship *Keokuk* [10] was cruising in formation with a group of LSTs and net tenders about 50 miles SE of Iwo Jima at 1720 February 21 when a Jill dived out of the clouds dead ahead, hit her on the starboard side just abaft the bridge, and slithered aft, wiping out all but one 20-mm gun of the starboard battery. All fires

[10] Designated AKN, an old train ferry converted to carry harbor nets and supplies for the net tenders.

were out by 1850, but *Keokuk* had 17 killed or missing and 44 wounded. *LST–477* was also hit by a kamikaze which apparently bounced overboard without doing much damage to this beaching craft or her embarked tanks.

Admiral Mitscher now ordered *Enterprise* to take *Saratoga's* place in close night support. Early 22 February she launched eight planes to search for "Sara's" missing pilots. Unfortunately two of these planes broke through a low, 500-foot cloud ceiling right over some of the fire support ships during an air alert, were mistaken for enemy and shot down. One crew of three was lost; the other, piloted by Ensign Henry G. Hinrichs USNR, was picked up by a PC which also mistook the men for Japanese and had the rail lined with armed bluejackets, in view of the enemy's propensity to toss hand grenades at would-be rescuers. Fortunately the "loud, continuous and explosive use of strong American invectives convinced them otherwise"; so much so that the patrol craft's skipper jumped over the side to aid the rescue.[11]

Enterprise had two main tasks off Iwo: to fly dawn and dusk C.A.P. over the escort carriers whose planes supported the troops by day, and to interdict the enemy airfield on Chichi Jima. On the evening of 23 February, her night fighter squadron, with the aid of five planes transferred from *Saratoga*, began hanging up a new record. Night and day for 174 consecutive hours, until midnight 2 March, this squadron kept planes airborne. Its pilots flew night, dawn, dusk and day air patrols, sweeps, and intruder missions on Chichi Jima. But the "jeep" carriers almost equaled this record of "Big E." Admiral Durgin's task group, during the 22 days that it furnished air support for Iwo (with only one day out for fueling), at one time kept planes airborne for 172 consecutive hours.[12] *Enterprise* remained off Iwo, under operational control of Rear Admiral Durgin, until 10 March. From her association with the escort carriers she acquired two new nicknames, "Enterprise Bay" and

[11] "History of Night Torpedo Squadron 90" p. 35, included in History Night Carrier Air Group 90.
[12] CTG 52.2 Action Report 21 Apr. 1945.

"Queen of the Jeeps." She entered Ulithi lagoon on 12 March for two days' upkeep before departing with TF 58 on the next operation to cover Okinawa.

Admiral Clark's TG 58.1 and Admiral Radford's TG 58.4 had been busy on D-day fueling and replenishing from the logistics group and filling up what would otherwise have been restful hours with antiaircraft practice. On 20 February "Jocko" Clark, who hated to see an idle plane on board, sliced off six whole deckloads to support the troops on Iwo Jima, and a few more next day.

During 23 February Task Force 58 fueled from Rear Admiral Beary's Servron 6 east of Iwo Jima and at 1850 shaped a northerly course for a high-speed run toward Tokyo. Next day the destroyers were topped off from the heavy ships, although hampered by high seas and strong winds. At about noon, destroyers were sent ahead to deal with Japanese pickets and give early warning of air attack. Weather forced a reduction of speed to 16 knots but the sea was so rough that *Moale*, hastening from TG 58.4 to take her picket station, smashed her bow and forecastle and flooded several forward compartments.

The first sweeps were sent off at 0715 February 25 when the task force was about 190 miles SE of Tokyo. The weather was so bad that most of the strikes hit secondary targets or those of opportunity. As the weather worsened rapidly during the forenoon, Admiral Mitscher at 1215 ordered all further operations canceled. This second strike on Tokyo was even less effective than the first.

Early in the afternoon, with unfavorable reports of weather over Tokyo for the next day, Admiral Mitscher decided to strike Nagoya on the 26th and shaped a course accordingly. En route, destroyers *Hazelwood* and *Murray* sank three Japanese small craft that were too tiny to be mentioned in postwar assessments. But a 100-foot-long Japanese picket boat, which refused to be disposed of easily, put up a spunky fight. She was picked up at 0030 February 26 by *Porterfield*, which opened fire with 5-inch and automatic weapons. The picket boat returned small-caliber shell fire, scoring hits which did considerable damage to instruments and radio sets around the destroyer's bridge structure, killed one man and wounded twelve. *Porterfield*, reporting that she had left the picket in a sinking condition, passed on; but the Japanesse vessel drifted into the inner screen of TG 58.3, where she almost collided with *Pasadena* and had the nerve to open fire on her at point-blank range, making 13 hits and wounding two men. The cruiser replied with 40-mm fire and passed on. Destroyer *Stockham* at about 0130 was ordered to destroy the enemy picket. She closed and opened fire with 5-inch and 40-mm guns. The boat still had considerable bite left, returned fire and hit *Stockham* several times with small bullets. By 0300 *Stockham* had silenced and dismasted the boat, leaving it awash in a sinking condition.

During that night both wind and sea made up and speed had to be reduced to 12 knots to avoid damage to the destroyers. Admiral Mitscher, realizing by 0514 February 26 that he could not reach a launching position off Nagoya in time, canceled the strikes and turned toward his fueling area, around lat. 23°30' N, long. 141° E., where the task force fueled on the 27th. Admiral Radford's TG 58.4 was then detached to Ulithi, while the other three steamed westward to make their third call on Okinawa.

Early in the morning of 1 March they reached a position 60 to 70 miles SE of the "Great Loochoo." Even in that hornets' nest of enemy air activity tactical surprise was obtained and no airborne opposition developed. Naha, the flimsy capital of Okinawa, was well bombed. Carrier planes roamed at will over the future scene of battle, bombing and strafing every likely target. Very important for future operations were the photographic missions. It was a fair day for once, and the photo planes obtained almost perfect coverage of Okinawa, Kerama Retto, Minami Daito and Amami O Shima, obtaining data for charts which were made and distributed before the end of the month.

Retirement commenced as soon as planes were recovered that evening, except that Rear Admiral F. E. M. Whiting's cruisers (*Vincennes, Miami* and *San Diego*) with Desron 61 were detached to bombard Okino Daito (also known as Borodino Island), an islet

195 miles east of Okinawa where the enemy was reported to have a radar station. Three firing runs were made there in the early hours of 2 March. Task Force 58 continued southeasterly and entered Ulithi lagoon on 4 March 1945 to prepare for the next operation, the capture of Okinawa.

During this two weeks' cruise, 16 February to 1 March, TF 58 claimed to have shot down 393 enemy planes in the air, and believed that it destroyed over 250 on the ground. It is now impossible to check these claims from Japanese sources. Plane and pilot losses were heavy — 84 planes with 60 pilots and 21 crewmen in combat, 59 planes with eight pilots and six crewmen operationally.

Escort carrier planes were the winged workhorses of the Iwo Jima campaign. *Anzio's* planes destroyed two Japanese submarines; [13] and while Task Force 58 raided Tokyo and Okinawa, Admiral Durgin's "jeeps," almost within sight of Mount Suribachi, were feeding out call-bombing and rocketing missions, and providing C.A.P. and antisubmarine patrol, from D-day minus 3 to D-day plus 18. "The daily task of providing air support," observed Admiral Durgin, "is not broken even for replenishing and refueling. It is a continual grind from dawn to dark each day."

3. *The Land Battle, 22 February–16 March*

On 22 February, worst day yet for weather, with a cold, drizzling rain, General Schmidt decided to give his front lines a rest, and the weather was so foul that afternoon air strikes had to be canceled. On the 23rd, after preliminary bombardment, the Marines jumped off, with main effort directed towards No. 2 airfield. The 4th Division fought in misery in terrain honeycombed with mines, booby traps, buttressed pillboxes, caves and blockhouses, all mutually supporting. Gains of 200 to 300 yards were made on the right, but there was little change in the center or on the left.

[13] See end of Chap. I.

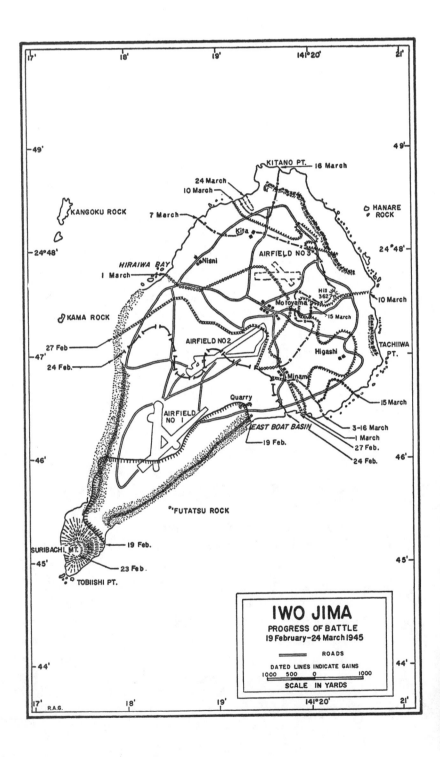

KITANO PT. 16 March

24 March
10 March

7 March

Kita

HANARE ROCK

KANGOKU ROCK

24°48'

24°48'

HIRAIWA BAY

Nisni

AIRFIELD NO 3

1 March

KAMA ROCK

Motoyama

Hill 362?

10 March

15 March

27 Feb.

AIRFIELD NO 2

Higashi

TACHIIWA PT.

24 Feb.

Minami

15 March

Quarry

EAST BOAT BASIN

3-16 March

AIRFIELD NO 1

1 March

19 Feb.

27 Feb.

24 Feb.

FUTATSU ROCK

19 Feb.

SURIBACHI MT.

23 Feb.

TOBIISHI PT.

IWO JIMA

PROGRESS OF BATTLE
19 February–24 March 1945

ROADS

DATED LINES INDICATE GAINS

1000 500 0 1000

SCALE IN YARDS

R.A.G.

The great event of 23 February was the successful scaling of HOTROCKS, the code name for Mount Suribachi. General Kuribayashi ordered his troops there to hold out to the last. But things got so hot on HOTROCKS — whose every slope could be reached by naval gunfire, air bombing and rocketing — that the local commander became desperate, and sent a message to headquarters requesting permission to make a banzai charge, rather than sit tight and be smothered. Whether or not the General deigned to reply is not known; but in any event, Colonel Harry ("the Horse") Liversedge USMC gave neither commander any time to make up his mind. Early on the 23rd a 40-man detachment from Liversedge's 28th Marines, commanded by 1st Lieutenant H. G. Schreier USMC, scaled the volcano. As they scrambled over the rim of the crater they were challenged by a small defense force on the opposite edge and a hot little fight developed. Before it ended, one of the Marines picked up a length of iron pipe, lashed to it a small American flag that he had brought up in his pocket, and raised it at 1020. This is the scene which we have used as a frontispiece to this volume. The flag was too small to be seen through the fog of battle, but fortunately a bigger one was coming up. A Marine had thoughtfully borrowed a big battle ensign eight feet long from *LST-779*, which had beached near the base. He carried it up the mountain, and Joe Rosenthal, Associated Press photographer, arrived in time to take the picture of the second flag-raising, at 1037, which became the most famous photograph of the Pacific War. It inspired the bronze monument to the Marine Corps by Felix de Welden that has been erected near Arlington National Cemetery, overlooking the Potomac.[14]

Secretary of the Navy James V. Forrestal was coming ashore with General Smith from *Eldorado* during the preliminaries. Symbolically, they touched Beach Green just as the second Stars and Stripes was flung to the strong north wind. "It was one of the proudest moments of my life," said General Smith; and the Secretary, turning to him, said gravely, "Holland, the raising of that flag

[14] Bartley pp. 73–78; *Coral and Brass* pp. 259–262.

on Suribachi means a Marine Corps for the next 500 years." [15] Old Glory, visible all over the island and far off shore, lifted the spirits of all hands.

But the end was not yet near. Even the 28th Regiment could not leave Suribachi and join the rest of the 5th Division on its way north, because the volcano slopes were a rabbit warren of caves and tunnels. Although some 600 Japanese had been killed in the assault, at least 1000 more were still there, holed up like mites in an over-ripe cheese.

Unloading conditions continued bad, even after a shift was made to the western beaches to avoid the cluttered wrecks of landing craft on the eastern side. Wind seemed to go around in circles at Iwo Jima, making first one side of the island and then the other a lee shore. Beach gradients everywhere were so steep that pontoon causeways broached, so the rest of the LSTs equipped with pontoons used them as lighters. Ordinary landing craft could not be used, as the backwash of each wave flooded them through the ramps, and all beaching craft had to keep motors running and use breastfasts in addition to two stern anchors. [16]

February 24 was a day of very heavy fighting in which significant gains were made. *Idaho* and *Pensacola* delivered an hour's naval bombardment of the heavily fortified area just north of No. 2 airfield; planes from the escort carriers then bombed it for a quarter of an hour and the Marines jumped off at 0915. During the day some of their tanks managed to reach the airfield by a rough road which first had to be cleared of mines. A foothold was secured near the middle of No. 2 airfield and gains of up to 800 yards were made on the left flank.

A feature of gunfire support rendered during the first week on Iwo Jima was the work of the LCI mortar unit under Lieutenant

<hr>

15 Walter Millis ed. *The Forrestal Diaries* (1951) pp. 29–30.
16 Notes from Commo. Robert C. Johnson USNR of the Seabees at Iwo Jima 21 Apr. 1945. From same source, 160 landing craft were damaged beyond repair the first two days.

Commander Stanley J. Kelley USNR. Thirty LCI(M)s were assigned, but owing to breakdowns not all were available at the same time. They provided direct support on call, and harassing fire to break up enemy counterattacks. With their shallow draft they could work close inshore on the flanks and often were in a position to shoot up gullies against enemy targets that were not visible to the Marines. Much of their fire was delivered at night. So impressed were the Marines with the performance of Kelley's craft that on 22 February the landing force commander sent them a special message: "Ships of mortar support group have been doing a splendid job. Believe your fire has had great effect in preventing large scale counterattacks." [17] Ammunition shortages curtailed their support at times, but when they retired to Saipan on 26 February they had expended over 32,000 mortar projectiles. Although frequently taken under fire by enemy batteries the only one damaged was *LCI(M)–760*, by a near miss.

Beginning 25 February the Marines ashore made slow but steady progress, gradually pushing Japanese defenders into the northern part of the island. The 3rd Division having completed landing on 24 February, the final drive was made by three divisions abreast, 4th on the right, 3rd in the center, and 5th, proud of having taken Suribachi, on the left flank.[18] By 1 March, No. 2 airfield and the village of Motoyama were in their hands. The naval gunfire support plan continued as on D-day, with destroyers assigned to battalions and heavier ships to divisions, or engaged in area bombardment. This continued until 9 March, when the enemy was contained in a narrow strip along the north and northeast coasts of the island. With fewer targets to take under fire, fewer ships were assigned.

Routine fire support duties were varied by many alarums and excursions. Few ships, however, had such a lively experience as destroyer *Terry* (Lieutenant Commander William B. Moore) on

[17] CTG 52.6 (Com. Mortar Support Group) Action Report 2 Mar. 1945.
[18] This advance is well described in Robert Sherrod *On to Westward* pp. 207–215.

1 March. In a screening station northwest of the island, she was ordered at 0215 to search for a submarine contact which had been lost
by another destroyer. At 0245 a low-flying Japanese plane coming
from the direction of Kita Jima closed and dropped a torpedo at
about 1000 yards' range. The plane had been picked up by radar
and tracked; the recognition officer saw it drop the torpedo and
sang out "Torpedo Away–" The skipper put rudder hard over and
rang up flank speed, which enabled *Terry* to escape, the torpedo
passing about 50 yards astern.

At 0720, en route to her next assignment, a screening station
north of Iwo Jima, *Terry* was passing Kitano Point at the north end
of the island and about 5200 yards off shore, when salvos from a
Japanese coastal battery began straddling her. Lieutenant Commander Moore rang up flank speed and began counterbattery fire
with his after guns. The destroyer received a 6-inch hit on the starboard side of her main deck over the forward engine room, losing
eleven men killed and 19 wounded and suffering extensive damage.
The Japanese battery fired continuously until about 0730, when
Nevada and *Pensacola* silenced it.

On the same day, *Colhoun*, anchored off the northeastern coast
of the island to repair damage received in a collision, absorbed a
three-gun salvo from an 80-mm dual-purpose battery. It wrecked
No. 2 torpedo tube, exploded the air flask of a torpedo, caused extensive damage, killed one man and wounded 16.

The same shore battery that bopped *Terry* almost got the number of ammunition ship *Columbia Victory*, anchored off the beach
close to V Amphibious Corps headquarters. A salvo fell near
enough to her fantail to wound a man. The skipper promptly
slipped his cable and got under way, pursued by enemy salvos. Generals Smith and Schmidt watched this performance with hearts in
their mouths, as one hit on the ammunition ship would have sent
them as well as her to kingdom come.[19]

[19] Rear Adm. Hill Action Report p. III 9; *Coral and Brass* pp. 217–218.

Beach and unloading conditions improved after 25 February. New beach exits were constructed, a lateral road leading inland was covered with Marston matting, good progress was made cleaning up wrecked landing craft and vehicles. But weather and surf conditions still prevented anything smaller than LST, LSM and LCT from unloading. Late on 2 March landing operations were shifted to the western group of beaches, and thereafter both sets of beaches were used whenever wind and surf permitted.

Escort carrier planes and B-24s from the Marianas continued to provide air support. Base development work on No. 1 airfield was pressed by Seabees. On the 27th (D-day plus 8) the first light Piper Cub observation plane, designated OY-1, was launched successfully from *LST-776*, which had been equipped with a special gear of booms and cables (the so-called "Brodie") for launching and recovering these small aircraft.

PBMs began to arrive that day to operate searches from their floating bases, tenders *Hamlin*, *Williamson* and *Chincoteague*, and the first searches went out on the 28th. But the sea off Iwo proved to be too rough and too full of flotsam to operate PBMs profitably, and they began to withdraw to Saipan 6 March when A.A.F. fighters arrived to take over covering duties. Thereafter searches were flown by PB4Ys, using the Iwo No. 1 airfield, which had received its first twin-engine plane, a C-47, on 3 March. Next day the island received its first call from a B-29, returning low on gas from Japan. The CVEs began to pull out on 9 March. Last of the heavy bombardment ships departed 12 March, leaving only destroyers and LCI(G)s for fire support.

Vice Admiral Kelly Turner, the "devil man" who the Japanese vowed would never return home alive, departed in *Eldorado* 4 March, after appointing Rear Admiral Harry Hill S.O.P.A., Iwo Jima. Transdiv 33 left the same day, taking to Guam one regiment of the 3rd Marine Division, which had suffered severely in the fighting. The other two regiments were ordered to remain until relieved by the 147th Infantry U. S. Army. Major General James E. Chaney

USA, commander of the future Army garrison, arrived with his headquarters on 27 February and the bulk of his troops began disembarking 21 March.[20] This overlapping of Marines and Army was a good thing, as it gave the GIs an opportunity to learn the peculiar methods that had been developed to meet the enemy tactics before becoming responsible for the final dig-out and mopping-up.

[20] Rear Adm. Hill Action Report pp. III 9, 14, XII 6. They arrived in cargo ships *Zaurak, Alkaid, Alderamin* and *Celeno,* escorted by DEs *John L. Williamson* and *French.*

CHAPTER V

Securing the Island[1]

17 March–1 June 1945

1. *The Mopping-up Process*

ALTHOUGH Iwo Jima was declared "secured" at 1800 March 16, and "operation completed" at 0800 on the 26th, there was a good deal of ground fighting between these two dates, and even later. The Marines suffered 3885 casualties between 11 and 26 March.

It took a week's work — 16 to 24 March — to overcome an exceptionally tough pocket of resistance, a rocky gorge that led down to the sea not far west of Kitano Point. By the 24th it was reduced to an area of about 2500 square yards. General Kuribayashi's radio informed Major Horie at Chichi Jima on the 21st: "We have not eaten or drunk for five days. But our fighting spirit is still high. We are going to fight bravely till the last." On the 24th Horie received the last word from his commanding general: "All officers and men of Chichi Jima, goodbye." [2]

These Japanese defenders did not simply hole up and die; they continued to do all the mischief they could. On 26 March, shortly before dawn, a body of about 350, including a large number of officers wearing swords, crawled out of the gorge. They were heavily armed with knee mortars, rifles and hand grenades (some of them

---

[1] Bartley *Iwo Jima* and Action reports cited earlier, especially those of Generals H. M. Smith and Harry Schmidt USMC.
[2] The Horie document (see Chap. IV Note 4).

American); a few were even wearing U. S. Marine uniforms. They took by surprise an insufficiently guarded VII A.A.F. and Seabee camp just south of Hirawa Bay. The Marine 5th Pioneer Battalion, which fortunately had bivouacked in this area, hastily formed battle line, and after a bitter struggle, lasting three hours, killed or drove off all attackers. The Japanese left some 250 of their number dead, but succeeded in killing 53 and wounding 119 American officers and men. General Kuribayashi may have been killed in this foray; but his body was not identified, and it seems more likely that this brave and resourceful officer committed hara-kiri in his subterranean command post.[3] The Japanese naval commander, Rear Admiral T. Ichimaru, also disappeared.

The smoke of this battle of 26 March had hardly cleared when General Harry Schmidt USMC announced that the Iwo Jima operation was completed. To all intents and purposes it was, with airfield No. 1 already doing business for the B–29s. Admiral Nimitz, upon his first visit to the island on the 24th, ascertained that so far 65 Superforts had been saved from destruction by being able to make emergency landings on Iwo, and between 24 March and 21 April about 230 more used the island facilities.

On 25 March, when the Japanese air forces attempted their last raid on Iwo, they were picked up by radar and intercepted by island-based P–61s which shot down several and drove off the rest.

General Schmidt closed his command post and departed on the afternoon of 26 March. The 3rd Marine Division began loading for Guam next day. The 147th Infantry Regiment U. S. Army, which had begun landing on 21 March, now took over responsibility for mopping-up and garrison duty. Major General James E. Chaney USA became island commander.

Down to 1800 March 27 the Marine Corps and Navy casualties incurred in capturing Iwo Jima were as follows: — [4]

---

[3] HQ Army Garrison Force G–2 Weekly Report No. 1, 2 Apr.; data obtained by the writer at Iwo 21 Apr. 1945. Different figures in Bartley p. 192.

[4] Bartley pp. 220–221.

	MARINE CORPS		NAVY [5]
	Officers	*Men*	*Officers and Men*
Killed in action	215	4,339	363
Died of wounds	60	1,271	70
Missing, presumed dead	3	43	448
Wounded in action	826	16,446	1,917
Combat fatigue casualties	46	2,602	?

Up to and including 26 March the count of Japanese killed and sealed up in caves was 20,703,[6] and only 216 had been taken prisoner. General Harry Schmidt then estimated that only 100 to 300 of the enemy were left alive on the island, which proved to be too optimistic.[7]

The Army now organized a systematic mop-up. An officer and ten men, Nisei who spoke Japanese, accompanied by prisoners who lent themselves to this work, broadcast invitations to surrender through loud-speakers, promising the Japanese good usage and plenty to eat and drink.[8] Caves on the northwest coast of the island and northeast of the East Boat Basin, whose occupants proved deaf to these appeals, were blasted by flame-throwers and explosives and sealed. These methods netted 867 more prisoners in April and May, during which time 1602 more Japanese were killed. Isolated pockets long held out in various parts of the island. During the week of 2 April about 200 Japanese attempted to rush an infantry command post just above East Boat Basin; this fight lasted all night and all Japanese participating were killed. They also managed to blow

---

[5] Including Navy Medical and Dental Corps officers and hospital corpsmen serving with Marines, Seabees, crews of gunfire support ships, aircraft carriers, transports and air units; but not including losses of TF 58 in strikes on Tokyo. There were also 37 casualties in Army units attached to V 'Phib Corps.

[6] Writer's notes from Col. John K. Gowen, Head of Intelligence Section A.A.F. Command at Iwo, 26 Apr. 1945.

[7] Writer's notes at Iwo Jima 21 Apr. 1945.

[8] A merry peasant-type Japanese soldier, nicknamed "Tojo," was particularly effective on these propaganda forays. He became a great pet of the soldiers, who, in answer to his request for a few English words of politeness, taught him the most horrible blasphemies. It became routine for any work party passing "Tojo's" group to call out "Hey, Tojo! How are you today, Tojo?" upon which the little fellow would come to attention, spread a broad grin, bow politely and call out an obscenity which he had been led to believe meant "Thank you very much!"

up a dump of 6000 cases of dynamite, which rocked the island and caused a number of casualties.[9]

2. *Air Base and Conclusion*

On 1 April a submarine gasoline pipeline, buoyed at its seaward end, was brought ashore to reduce dependence on drummed gas, and four 1000-gallon gas tanks were set up ashore. Aviation gas could now be delivered directly from tankers. A second pipeline was later established on the west side. Seabees began to construct No. 3 airfield in the north part of the island on 3 April. The 7th was a red-letter day, marking the first B–29 raid on Japan escorted by P–51 fighter planes based on Iwo. About 100 participated and they were aloft seven hours; 54 B–29s used Iwo fields during the day. Possession of Iwo more than doubled the efficiency of the Super-fortress bombing missions against Japan.

The writer, landing at Iwo 20 April 1945, counted 5330 crosses and stars in the Marine Corps cemetery. But there were about 31,000 soldiers, Air Force ground crews and Seabees on the island very much alive, healthy and in high spirits. Army officers said they wouldn't trade Iwo for any South Pacific island. The weather was cool and pleasant, and there was complete absence of mosquitoes and other wild life. The fact that everyone was active and helping the war effort kept morale high. The Seabees,[10] three of whose battalions landed on D-day, and who started to activate No. 1 airfield on D-day plus 5, did outstanding work; General Holland M. Smith on his departure sent a message: "Let us remember the skillful work of the Seabees who, laboring under fire, immediately began to transform this barren wasteland into a powerful advance base." Over 7600 of them were on the island 20 April; their sick list, an average of only 40 per day, was less than it had been in the United States.

[9] HQ Army Garrison Force G–2 Weekly Report No. 2, 8 Apr.

[10] These were the 8th Naval Construction Regiment, comprising the 8th, 90th, 95th, 106th and 23rd Naval Construction Battalions, and the 41st Naval Construction Regiment, composed of the 31st, 62nd and 133rd NCBs. (Notes from their War Diary, seen at Iwo 20–22 Apr. 1945.)

A Marine-Navy JASCO in Position

Effect of Naval Gunfire on a Japanese Pillbox

On Iwo Jima

Views from Mount Suribachi, 21 April 1945

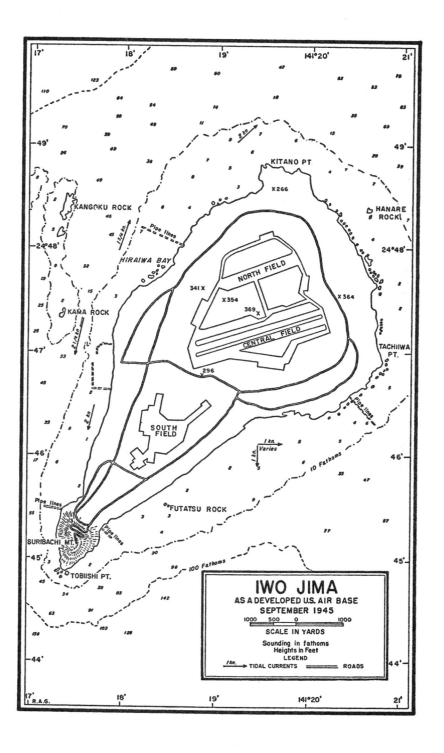

IWO JIMA
AS A DEVELOPED U.S. AIR BASE
SEPTEMBER 1945

SCALE IN YARDS

Sounding in fathoms
Heights in Feet
LEGEND
TIDAL CURRENTS   ROADS

Survey ship *Sumner* (Commander Irving M. Johnson USNR) was busy making soundings and erecting beacons off shore; she had already published a preliminary chart of the island and surrounding waters.[11]

Above all, let us not forget the United States Marines, who conducted this, one of the toughest battles in their entire history, with exemplary endurance, skill and valor. Never before had that great fighting arm of the United States Navy covered itself with so much glory; the more so because it was not a spectacular battle, but one of steady slugging against a relentless, dug-in enemy. Battle casualties amount to 30 per cent of the entire landing force, 60 per cent in the infantry regiments of the 3rd Division and 75 per cent in the infantry regiments of the 4th and 5th Divisions. During the five weeks of the campaign, 7500 battle replacements were provided, most of them coming under fire for the first time.[12]

The chief beneficiary of the seizure of Iwo Jima was the Army Air Force. Before the end of the war about 2400 B–29s landed on the island, carrying crews of some 27,000 men. One, nicknamed by her crew the "Oily Boid," crash-landed after being shot up over Tokyo so many times that the ground crew would bet every time a B–29 landed that it was she. Once a B–29 came down when the weather was so thick that the pilot had to land by guess, and when the plane stopped one wing was hanging over the cliff.[13] Air-sea rescue planes based on Iwo Jima also rescued many crews of planes that splashed. Not all would have been lost without the island's facilities; but the fact that these facilities were there gave a tremendous boost to aviators' morale. There is no doubt that the capture of Iwo Jima, expensive as it was, became a major contribution to victory over Japan.

Unfortunately, and, in my opinion, unjustifiably, there developed two controversies over this operation, one within the Marine Corps

[11] *Sumner* Monthly Report of Survey Activities for Mar. 1945; conversations with Cdr. Johnson at Iwo.
[12] Maj. Gen. Harry Schmidt Action Report 20 May 1945.
[13] Honolulu *Advertiser* 2 June 1945.

and the other in criticism of the Marine Corps. Marine historians have made much over the fact that General Schmidt originally asked for ten days' preliminary naval bombardment but Admirals Spruance and Turner would provide only three. Lieutenant General Holland M. Smith, in his pungent postwar narrative, denounced this decision, brushed off the reasons for it,[14] and implied that the adamant attitude of the Navy caused unnecessary casualties.

This serious charge deserves examination. All accounts agree that the nature of the defenses on Iwo was such that only direct hits on specific targets paid off. Aside from a lucky hit, about all that area bombardment could do was to blast off camouflage and reveal hidden targets. General Kuribayashi had purposely designed his defenses to minimize the effect of bombardment, so that rules about dropping so many rounds of shell per hundred square yards meant nothing. There is no reason to believe that ten or even thirty days of naval and air pounding would have had much more effect on the defenses than the bombardment that was delivered. The defenses were such, by and large, that the only way they could be taken out was the way they were taken out, by Marine Corps infantry and demolitions. Combat engineers of the 5th Marine Division destroyed 5000 cave entrances and pillboxes in their divisional zone of operations alone. As many as 1000 caves and underground entrances were blasted on Mount Suribachi.[15] Aërial bombardment and naval gunfire simply could not reach underground into the maze of caves and tunnels; yet these had to be cleared or sealed shut before the island could be secured as an air base on the Bonins' road to Tokyo. Robert Sherrod well said (in a dispatch that appeared in *Time* magazine on 12 March): "On Iwo the Japs dug themselves in so deeply that all the explosives in the world could hardly have reached them."

Commodore W. R. Carter has estimated that Iwo Jima, one-

[14] The reasons were (1) that the carrier strikes on Tokyo, necessary to keep the kamikazes away, could not be extended beyond three days; (2) difficulty in replenishing ships' ammunition so far from base; (3) by the law of diminishing returns, three days' bombardment should accomplish about 90 per cent of the maximum.

[15] 1st Lt. Walker Y. Brooks usmc "Engineers on Iwo" *Marine Corps Gazette* (Oct. 1945).

fifteenth the area of Saipan, had one-third more bombardment ammunition expended on it than was expended on the big Marianas
island. The total amounted to 10,650 tons.[16]

The other and more serious controversy began with an attack on
Navy strategy and Marine Corps tactics by the Hearst and McCormick press. This was largely a rehash of the arguments used against
taking Tarawa in 1943. Why sacrifice men for a useless piece of
real estate? Why do the Marines squander lives, in contrast to General MacArthur who saves them? To these criticisms Hanson W.
Baldwin patiently and convincingly replied in the *New York
Times*.[17] He pointed out that Iwo was necessary to protect and en-
hance the B–29 strikes on Japan and that there was no easy alternative. He defended Navy strategy and Marine Corps tactics as the
best suited to the situation. He replied to armchair critics who
demanded "Why wasn't poison gas used?" by pointing out that
poison gas is a defensive weapon, the use of which on Iwo would
have done the invaders more harm than good. He observed that
many false notions about what can be accomplished by air and
naval bombardment of islands stemmed from the fall of Pantelleria
in the Mediterranean in 1943, where the Italian defenders had no
heart to fight it out on the ground.[18] He reminded the public that
it cannot have an omelet without breaking eggs, and that the infan-
tryman, in the last resort, is the one who has to push a campaign
through to victory. All this is as true today as it was in 1945.

Peleliu, Iwo Jima and Okinawa were three operations conducted
in whole or in part by the Marines after the Japanese had adopted
their new tactics of defense in depth against an amphibious invasion;
and Iwo Jima was the hardest nut to crack because there the coastal
shell, too, was tough. But in all three the Japanese made a highly
intelligent use of natural features to exact the utmost in casualties.
A comparison of casualties in the three regimental combat teams

[16] *Beans, Bullets and Black Oil* pp. 289–290.
[17] Five installments, 5–9 March 1945.
[18] See Vol. II Chap. XII.

that suffered most in each of these three operations is instructive.[19]

On Peleliu the 1st Marine RCT had 1749 casualties, highest of the three involved. On Iwo Jima the 26th RCT of the 5th Marine Division suffered 2675 casualties. On Okinawa the 29th RCT of the 6th Marine Division had 2821. These comparisons indicate that losses at Iwo were not disproportionate to those in similar operations at that stage of the war.

Robert Sherrod wrote a succinct conclusion to this operation. "To the Marines, Iwo looked like the ugliest place on earth, but B–29 pilots who made emergency landings months later called it the most beautiful. One pilot flew eleven missions in the three months following the island's capture, and landed on it five times. Another said, 'Whenever I land on this island, I thank God and the men who fought for it.' " [20]

[19] This yardstick is best, as the total number of Marines in the three operations differed widely. The average combat strength of a Marine Corps RCT in World War II was 7500 officers and men.

[20] Sherrod *On to Westward* p. 153.

PART II

Okinawa

CHAPTER VI

Preparing for the Ryukyus

October 1944–March 1945

1. *Okinawa and the Okinawans* [1]

PLACE one leg of a pair of dividers on Shanghai, step off a radius of 450 miles, place the other leg on the tip end of Kyushu (the southernmost island of Japan proper), and swing it south and west, to the point where it hits Formosa. This outer leg will describe a 90-degree arc, about 700 miles long, through the Nansei Shoto. It will pass through Amami O Shima, and miss Okinawa and the Sakishima Gunto by a hair. And the quadrant that this arc subtends is the Tung Hai, the East China Sea. The Nansei Shoto (which means Southwestern Islands) are a series of drowned volcanic summits, about 140 in number, with a total land area of 1850 square miles, less than that of the State of Delaware. Over one quarter of this area, 485 square miles, is comprised in the central island of the chain that especially interests us: Okinawa.

The Nansei Shoto, commonly known as the Ryukyus,[2] are divided into three main groups (*Guntos*). Nearest Japan and longest under Japanese domination is the Amami Gunto. In the center is the Okinawa Gunto, which includes Okinawa, the Kerama Retto,

---

[1] Okinawa Studies, Nos. 1 and 2, issued by Office of Strategic Services in Honolulu (Alfred M. Tozzer, director) March 1944. Other useful documents are "Joint Staff Study – Okinawa Operation" 6 Dec. 1944; Cincpac-Cincpoa Info. Bull. No. 161-44 *Okinawa Gunto* 15 Nov. 1944; Second Supplement to same, 28 Feb. 1945; G. H. Kerr *Okinawa, the History of an Island People* (1958), an excellent scholarly history of the island.

[2] "Loochoo" or "Lew Chew" and "Ryukyu" are the Chinese and Japanese pronunciations of the same name, said to have been given by a Chinese poet in the seventh century, meaning "bubbles on the water" or something similar.

Ie Shima and several smaller islands. The south part of the arc, near-est Formosa, is the Sakishima Gunto. With Formosa, these islands form an eastern wall protecting the Japanese lifeline through the East China Sea. Whether the Allied Nations wished to invade Japan directly, or by way of China, airfields and an advanced naval base had to be set up somewhere in the archipelago. Formosa was the only alternative to the Ryukyus; and Formosa had been ruled out in September 1944. Once the Joint Chiefs of Staff had decided to seize and exploit "one or more positions in the Nansei Shoto" (as stated in their directive of 30 October), there could be no doubt that Okinawa would be position number one.

Okinawa or "The Great Loochoo" has plenty of room for air-fields, and two partially protected bays on the east coast suitable for a naval base. Its position is extraordinarily central. The nearest points in China, Formosa and Japan proper lie respectively 360 miles WNW, 340 miles WSW and 340 miles NNE. The 500-mile radius from Naha, the principal town of Okinawa, includes most of Kyushu, all Formosa and passes behind Shanghai and Foochow. The 600-mile arc includes Cape Engaño on Luzon and the Inland Sea of Japan. Iwo Jima is 760 miles distant. The 830-mile radius clips Hong Kong, Manila and the entrance to Tokyo Bay. But Oki-nawa was a long way from home for the United States Navy. Leyte, the nearest point where ground troops could be staged early in 1945, lies 900 miles to the southward. Ulithi and Guam are over 1200 miles away, and Pearl Harbor lies 4040 miles to the eastward on a great circle course – about the same as the air line from Ber-lin to Juneau, Alaska.

The Ryukyus are inhabited by a race apart. Their blood seems to be a mixture of Chinese, Malayan and Ainu. From early times there were one or more kings of the Ryukyus, and a single dynasty ruled from 1187 to 1879, when the islands were annexed by Japan. During the Middle Ages the king paid tribute to China, principal source of such culture as his people acquired; and, to be on the safe side, he gave a "cut" to the Japanese shogun or Prince of Satsuma, whose seat was in Kyushu. During the two centuries of Japanese isolation (1636–1853), when no foreign ships except a few Dutchmen were allowed to trade with Japan, and the Japanese were forbidden to go abroad, the Ryukyu kingdom acted as go-between in a smuggling trade between China and Japan; and as this trade brought rich profits to the Satsuma shoguns they permitted the Ryukyus to remain independent. The kings were real rulers, but paid tribute to the Emperor of China as their sovereign overlord; it was observed that their ancient castles at Shuri, Zachini and Nakagusuku faced the west, as a sign of fealty to China.

Except for an occasional Portuguese ship, the first European vessels to visit the Ryukyus arrived in the last decade of the eighteenth century. These visitors found the Okinawans polite but suspicious and evasive, anxious to protect themselves from prying foreigners, but with no armed forces to defend themselves.[3] In the 1840s France endeavored to establish a protectorate over the Ryukyus, but did not press the matter when the king politely declined. She did leave a Catholic mission at Naha, but neither Christianity nor Buddhism nor Islam made much inroad against the primitive animism and ancestor worship of the Okinawans. Commodore Matthew C. Perry USN in 1853 raised the American flag near Shuri on one of the hills that cost us dear to capture in 1945; he forced the regent (the king being a minor) to sign a treaty guaranteeing friendly treatment to American ships, and even established a temporary coaling station at Naha harbor.[4] Other nations then made treaties with the kingdom of the Ryukyus, but these were no protection when Emperor

---

[3] Captain Basil Hall, on his way home in 1816 after a visit to Okinawa, had an interview with Napoleon at St. Helena. In describing the Okinawans to the Emperor, "Nothing struck him so much as their having no arms. '*Point d'armes!*' he exclaimed. '*C'est à dire point de canons — ils ont des fusils?*' 'Not even muskets,' I replied. '*Eh bien donc — des lances, ou au moins, des arcs et des flèches?*' I told him they had neither one nor the other. '*Ni poignards?*' cried he, with increasing vehemence. No, none. '*Mais!*' said Buonaparte, clenching his fist and raising his voice to a loud pitch, '*Mais! sans armes, comment se bat-on?*' I could only reply that as far as we had been able to discover, they had never had any wars, but remained in a state of internal and external peace. 'No wars!' cried he, with a scornful and incredulous expression, as if the existence of any people under the sun without wars was a monstrous anomaly." Hall *Voyage to Loo-Choo* (Edinburgh 1826) p. 315.

[4] One of Commo. Perry's trophies, a great bronze gong dated 1458, hangs in the yard of the Naval Academy at Annapolis.

Meiji embarked on the policy of expansion which was doomed to be liquidated in 1945. The Emperor invaded the islands in 1875 and the Okinawans countered with passive resistance. Three years later, when General Ulysses S. Grant was about to visit China, a rumor reached Tokyo that the Okinawans intended to appeal to him for protection. Meiji then moved fast, reinforced his garrison in the islands, deposed the king, abolished the tribute to China and formally annexed the Ryukyus to Japan in 1879.

A semicolonial régime was maintained there until 1920. The Okinawans, despised by the Japanese for their poverty, lack of culture and failure to appreciate *bushido*, had the benefit of Japanese schools, but otherwise were treated as an inferior race. They seldom intermarried with the Japanese, continued to speak their own language and to observe their ancient rites and customs. Thousands of Okinawans emigrated to Hawaii, where they received news of every Japanese defeat with delight. This pacifist tradition and resentment against the "superior race" made it easy for United States forces to deal with the Okinawans as soon as they discovered that the stories of American brutality told them by the Japanese were untrue.

Compared with Japan or even with China, these islands were undeveloped and overpopulated. The southern part of Okinawa, in which we were chiefly interested, had a population density of 2700 per square mile as against 243 for Saipan, and 647 for Rhode Island. A population of over 800,000 [5] in 1940 owned only 331 motor cars, of which 88 were buses; two of the three narrow-gauge railroads were horse-drawn; there were only five movie houses in the entire archipelago. Most Okinawans lived in thatched huts or small frame houses, each surrounded by a stone wall and garden and clustered in villages of a few hundred or more inhabitants. They were predominantly farmers, each family owning several tiny fields in which were raised barley, sugar cane, beets, cabbages and sweet potatoes. There were only three towns of any size —

[5] For the entire Ryukyus 818,624; 463,000 for Okinawa.

Naha the capital, Shuri the ancient capital, and Toguchi on the Motobu peninsula.

Okinawa itself is shaped like a comic-strip dog, with an elongated neck and an overgrown jowl. The northern part is barren and mountainous, except for a portion of the Motobu Peninsula, the dog's uplifted ear. Three quarters of the population live in the southern portion, south of the Ishija Isthmus, the dog's neck. Naha, the one small harbor, is just forward of his stubby tail, on which the Naha airfield was situated. On the southeast coast there are two extensive bays protected by the Eastern Islands: the Nakagusuku Wan (Buckner Bay) between the dog's hind feet and forelegs, and the Kimmu Wan between forelegs and neck. Besides the Naha airfield three other important airdromes had been constructed by the Japanese by 1944: — the Yontan and Kadena fields close to the west coast, and the Yonabaru on the east coast. In addition there was a small airfield on the island of Ie Shima, which on the map looks like a bumblebee making for the dog's ear.

From the sea, the island had the appearance of a peaceful rural community, intensively cultivated. The countryside, with steep limestone hills, umbrella-topped pines, small cultivated fields and patches of woodland, recalled those Italian landscapes seen through the windows of Tuscan and Sienese paintings. But no church towers or domes break the skyline. Corresponding to the temples of other Oriental countries are the family tombs of the Okinawans. These large circular structures — built flush to a hillside and roofed with stone — dot the landscape, facing in the direction of Mother China. In front of each tomb is a porch, where the bodies of the dead are left exposed for a period of three years, after which their bones are cleaned and deposited in a handsome urn which is placed within the tomb. The suitability of these structures for machine gun installations was not overlooked by the Japanese Army, and American aviators occasionally bombed those suspected of interesting others than native morticians.

Such, in brief, is the nature of the island which was wanted as a

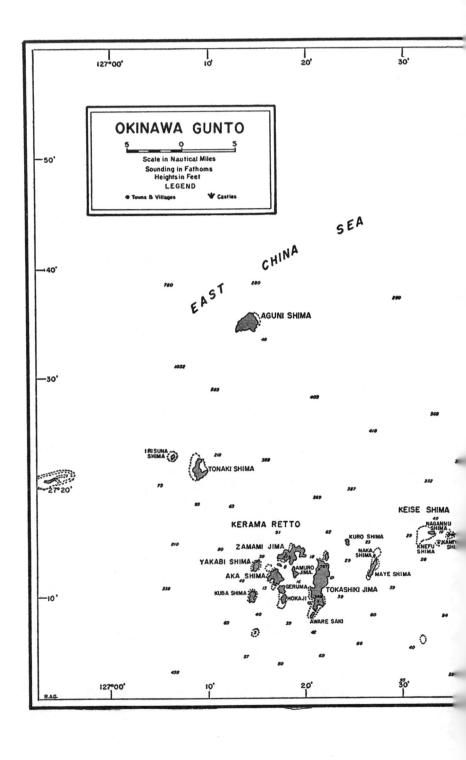

OKINAWA GUNTO

Scale in Nautical Miles
Sounding in Fathoms
Heights in Feet
LEGEND

● Towns & Villages   ♥ Castles

EAST CHINA SEA

AGUNI SHIMA

IRISUNA SHIMA

TONAKI SHIMA

KEISE SHIMA

KERAMA RETTO

NAGANNU SHIMA

KURO SHIMA

ZAMAMI JIMA

KNEFU SHIMA   KAMI SHI

YAKABI SHIMA

NAKA SHIMA

AKA SHIMA

AMURO JIMA

MAYE SHIMA

KUBA SHIMA

GERUMA

HOKAJI

TOKASHIKI JIMA

AWARE SAKI

R.A.G.

40'   50'   IHEYA 128°00'   10'   20'
              RETTO
                    171
              403
         35   IZENA SHIMA
       YANAHA SHIMA
   18   186   204
                    135   Hedo Saki   63
                          67
   150   171   145   148   43   50'
                                    X 1371   63
   206   46   52   X 1079
 56   210   IE SHIMA   17   X 1319   50
 Ie Shima   X   Bise   64 Akamaru Saki   35
 Airfield   567   Saki   23
        51   Nakijin KOURI SHIMA   1285   62 40'
 45   69   33   X 548   Shana Wan X   X 1650   117
      MENNA   754   YAGACHI Tako   X 902   69
         SESOKO   Toguchi SHIMA
 827   148   48   1999   Taira 1017   Kawata Wan   70
              1076   1211   X   Aruml Wan   88
              Nago   X   1020   Magari Saki   58
 240   59   28   892   329
         183   Besina   Abu Saki   58
              Misaki   Ora Wan   51
 199   221   606   Kushi   47   30'
 Zampa   X 953   Wan   53
 Misaki   Osunohana   OKINAWA
 (Point Bolo)   781   Kimmu   Ko   54
 150   Ishija   X 774   1   10   31
       Masuya   Castle   446
       Yontan   16   70
       Airfield   IKE SHIMA
      Kogosuku   52
       Castle   TAKA SHIMA   164
      Kadena   HEANZA SHIMA   22
 40   X 344   Airfield   358   HAMAHIKA SHIMA   169
        X 488   UKIBARU SHIMA
 39   141
 Kezu Saki   203   10   13   50
 achinato   21 TSUGEN JIMA
 Airfield   Yonabaru   Nakagusuku Wan   27°20'
      Airstrip   (later-Buckner Bay)
      Naha Shuri   UFU REEF
        Yonabaru   13   KUTAKA SHIMA   48   10'
 Naha Airfield   22
         X 283
       Kiyamu   29   134
 aki   Ara Saki   33   46
 40'   140   162   156   50'   128°00'   10'   20'

springboard for Japan, and whose securing would cost the United States more casualties than had been incurred in taking any other island in the Pacific.

2. *Planning Operation* ICEBERG

Planning for this massive operation, described by British observers as "the most audacious and complex enterprise yet undertaken by the American amphibious forces,"[6] started with a Cincpac-Cincpoa staff study, dated 25 October 1944, beginning "The Joint Chiefs of Staff have directed the Commander in Chief Pacific Ocean Areas to occupy one or more positions in the Nansei Shoto, with a target date of 1 March 1945." This staff study defined objectives, allotted forces and gave a rough outline of procedure. Rear Admiral Reifsnider,[7] designated to command the amphibious group to land on the northern half of the Okinawa beaches, arrived at Pearl Harbor 24 November 1944 for planning. He worked with the staffs of Commander Amphibious Forces Pacific (Admiral Turner), Commander Tenth Army (General Buckner), Commander III 'Phib Corps (General Geiger USMC). Rear Admiral John L. Hall,[8] to command the amphibious group that effected the southern landings, and Rear Admiral Blandy, in charge of amphibious support force and of all preliminary operations, were already there. They also

[6] British Combined Operations Observers Pacific Ocean Areas (Cdr. R. K. Silcock RN, Col. G. I. Malcolm, Grp. Capt. W. G. Tailyour RAF), Report to British Joint Staff Mission, Washington, 18 Apr. 1945.

[7] Lawrence F. Reifsnider, b. Maryland 1887, Naval Academy '10. Served in *Delaware, Maine, Rhode Island* and *Ozark*; qualified for submarine duty; C.O. of *C-1* in 1916 and fitted out several submarines to late 1917; C.O. of *E-2* and *O-5* during World War I. Shore duty 1919–1921; exec. *Chicago* to 1923; Comsubdiv 14 to 1925; duty at Naval Academy to 1928. C.O. *Corry, Broome* and *Evans* to 1930, duty in Bunav, 1st Lieut. *New Mexico* 1933–1935; senior course Naval War College, public relations officer Navy Dept. 1936–1937. C.O. *Memphis*, chief of U.S. Naval mission to Colombia, Comtransdivs 5 and 10, 1941–1943, and of Sopac Amphibious Group, July 1942 (see Vol. VI). Com 'Phib Group 4 in June 1944 (see Vol. VIII). After V-J Day commanded occupation Sasebo and Nagasaki; 4 Oct. 1945 Com V 'Phib Forces Western Japan; Com Administrative Command 'Phib Forces Pacific 1946; Com Eight and Gulf Sea Frontier 1947; retired 1949 as Vice Admiral.

[8] Brief biog. in Vol. IX, and see Vols. X and XII indexes.

took an active part in the planning of Operation ICEBERG, code
name for the invasion of the Ryukyus. The operation plan of Admiral Spruance, Commander Fifth Fleet, was issued on 3 January
1945. Next came the detailed operation plan of Vice Admiral Turner, dated 9 February.

Here let us consider the plan as a whole, keeping in mind that the
four principal commanders were Admiral Spruance, Vice Admiral
Mitscher (CTF 58), Vice Admiral Turner, who had charge until
the beachhead was established, and Lieutenant General Simon
Bolivar Buckner USA, commanding Tenth Army. Like the Gilberts
and Marshalls and Marianas and Iwo Jima, this was a Central Pacific
show. General MacArthur and Seventh Fleet were still engaged in
liberating the Philippines.[9]

D-day for Okinawa (L-day in the plan) was finally set for
1 April 1945. In order to obtain control of both air and ocean before invading an island so close to Japan, enemy air power, especially in view of the kamikaze technique, had to be pared down as
far as possible before the expeditionary force hit the Ryukyus. Not
much opposition was anticipated from the now decrepit Japanese
Navy.

The Okinawa plan contemplated a week of preliminary strikes
from the fast carriers and by B–29s based on the Marianas. Until the
Iwo Jima airfields were activated, the distance of Okinawa from
the nearest Army Air Force bases was too great (800 miles) for
anything smaller than a Superfort to splice out the work of carrier-
based bombers. Generals Arnold and LeMay of the Strategic Air
Force were reluctant to have their costly B–29s directed to what
they regarded as a mere tactical mission, but agreed to coöperate.
The question of how they should coöperate, and for how long, was
acrimoniously debated between General LeMay and Admiral
Nimitz in early March. According to the so-called "Strategic Air
Force Charter" (a directive of 1 April 1944 from the Joint Chiefs

---

[9] See Vol. XIII. About 24 Jan. 1945 Admiral Halsey, Vice Adm. McCain and
Vice Adm. Wilkinson (Com III 'Phib) left the Philippines for Pearl Harbor in
order to plan Operation OLYMPIC, the invasion of Kyushu that never took place.

of Staff), the B–29s constituted an independent kingdom under "Hap" Arnold within the Cincpac-Cincpoa empire; but Nimitz retained the right to direct the employment of the big bombers in a tactical or strategic emergency, which he considered this to be. Accordingly, on 27 March, when the advance expeditionary force for Okinawa put in at Kerama Retto, the B–29s flew the first of two missions against Japanese airfields and an aircraft factory on Kyushu.[10]

Two naval bombardment forces were brought up to the Ryukyus eight days before the landings, in order to give Okinawa and the vicinity a complete working-over. Admiral Blandy's amphibious support force of escort carriers, minecraft, light gunboats and the like, and Admiral Deyo's [11] bombardment group of battleships and cruisers, were given this job. Also under Admiral Blandy's command was placed a complete attack group, lifting an infantry division to take the Kerama Retto, a cluster of smalls islands off Okinawa. Here, six days before the main landings, he would set up an advanced fueling and repair base. No previous amphibious operation had included such important and vital preliminaries. Admiral Spruance, recognizing this, decided to be on the spot in *Indianapolis* from L-day minus 8.[12]

[10] Craven & Cate V 38, 629–631. In *The New Yorker* for 14 June 1958 is a souped-up account by Lt. Col. St. Clair McKelway, public relations officer on General LeMay's staff, of how he "blew his top" over this situation and tried to send a message to General Arnold demanding that Admiral Nimitz be court-martialed for obstructing the war effort!

[11] Morton L. Deyo, b. Poughkeepsie 1887, Naval Academy '11. Served in *Virginia, Duncan, Washington* and *Jenkins* to 1917; in *Allen* on the Queenstown station and in destroyer training at Boston in World War I. C.O. *Morris* 1919; aide to Com One 1920–1921; aide to Admiral S. S. Robinson, Com Battle Fleet and Cincus, 1921–1925. Instructor Naval Academy 1926–1929; C.O. *Sloat* and *Upshur* to 1932. Senior Course Naval War College and on staff thereof to Dec. 1934, when became exec. of *Milwaukee*. Operations officer staff of C in C Asiatic Fleet 1936–1939; aide to SecNav 1940 to Apr. 1941. Comdesron 11, 1941 (see Vol. I). C.O. *Monticello* Feb.–June 1942; C.O. *Indianapolis* July–Dec. 1942 (see Vol. VIII). Rear Adm. and Comdeslant in *Denebola* to 1943; commanded bombardment group in *Tuscaloosa* (flag) in operations OVERLORD and DRAGOON, 1944 (see Vol. XI). Comcrudiv 13 in *Santa Fe* with TF 38, Nov. 1944; and had this Okinawa command, relieving Vice Adm. Oldendorf after the latter's injury, to May 1945. Following V-J day, directed occupation landings in Kyushu and western Honshu and commanded Northern Japan Force. Com One 1946; retired as Vice Adm. 1949.

[12] He chose this 14-year-old heavy cruiser as his flagship because she was fast

Both planners and commanders were highly apprehensive of what enemy air might do to our forces before they had secured airfields on Okinawa. For the Japanese had several airfields in Okinawa and nearby islands, airdromes 150 miles away in the Amami Gunto, about 230 miles away in the Sakishima Gunto, and 65 airfields on Formosa, as well as 55 on Kyushu. Since no other operation would be going on at the time except the liberation of the Southern Philippines, there was no reason why the enemy should not concentrate his available aircraft, estimated at 2000 to 3000 planes, on the Allied expeditionary force and shipping off Okinawa – which is just about what he did. Nor was there any reason to suppose that he would not continue and even develop the effective kamikaze technique.

The Joint Expeditionary Force commanded by Vice Admiral Turner – gathered together from the West Coast, Oahu, New Caledonia, Espiritu Santo, the Solomons, the Philippines and the Marianas, and staged through Ulithi, Leyte and Saipan – would all be present off Okinawa on L-day, 1 April. Richmond Kelly Turner, having fairly earned the sobriquet that Napoleon bestowed on General Kléber (*l'enfant gâté de la victoire*), might have indulged in a little careless swagger. Having wrested one position after another from the enemy he was in fine fettle. He had been attacked in the American press for wasting lives, and compared unfavorably with General MacArthur, whose maxim "Hit 'em where they ain't" was hardly applicable to islands where enemy positions covered every beach and Japanese soldiers occupied every square rod of ground. Little he cared for that. He was still the same driving, swearing, sweating "Kelly" whose head could conceive more new ideas and retain more details than could any other flag officer in the Navy. He undertook the planning of the Ryukyus operation with more than ordinary meticulousness, and his voluminous plan was ready in time for subordinate commanders to study; it was so detailed that little was left for them to do.

The entire III Amphibious Corps (Major General Roy S. Geiger

---

enough to keep up with the carriers, yet old enough to be risked at the objective in an amphibious operation.

usmc), comprising three Marine divisions (the 1st, veterans of Guadalcanal and Peleliu; the 2nd, veterans of Tarawa and Saipan; the 6th, going into battle for the first time) and four infantry divisions of the XXIV Army Corps (the 7th, veterans of Attu, Kwajalein and Leyte; the 96th, veterans of Leyte; the 77th, veterans of Guam; and the 27th, veterans of Makin and Saipan), were to be employed in the invasion of Okinawa. A fifth infantry division, the 81st, was held in reserve at New Caledonia. The entire expeditionary force constituted the Tenth Army, under command of Lieutenant General Simon Bolivar Buckner, son of the like-named hero of the Southern Confederacy. If these plans worked out, some 172,000 combatant and 115,000 service troops would be landed on Okinawa before the operation was over.[13] About 77,000 Japanese troops were expected to be there to receive them.[14]

Troop-lift for this large force was a problem that vexed the planners, since war was still going on in Europe. Eight transport squadrons, each comprising about 15 assault transports, six assault cargo ships, 25 LST, 10 LSM and one LSD, were required. Four transrons could be culled from those used at Lingayen, but all eight would first have to do a job at Iwo. Two new transrons used at Iwo would be pulled out as soon as they had set the troops ashore, and proceed to Saipan or Espiritu Santo to load one assault and one reserve division for the Ryukyus. Two other new transrons were counted on to leave Pearl Harbor in early February for training, rehearsals, and loading of assault divisions at Guadalcanal and Nouméa.

The actual landings were planned for a four-division front, over five miles of beaches on the west coast of southern Okinawa. They were selected between two points known as Zampa-misaki and Kezu-saki. For want of a better name these were called "the Hagushi beaches," after a village at the mouth of the Bisha River that bisects the coastline and makes a convenient boundary between

---

[13] Joint Staff Study of 25 Oct. 1944.
[14] Estimate immediately before L-day. The 25 Oct. estimate was less than 50,000.

the Marines' sector on the north and the Army's on the south. Photographic reconnaissance showed that these beaches lay behind the usual shelflike coral reef, which meant that the first assault waves must be boated in amphtracs at or near high water, 0900. The mean range of tides there is 4.1 feet; but on L-day, which was Easter Sunday, there would be a spring tide of 5.2 feet.

The reason for choosing these particular beaches was the fact that they lay close to two important enemy airfields — Yontan behind the Marines' sector, and Kadena behind the Army's. In earlier operations it was deemed best if possible to land at some distance from airfields, which the Japanese usually defended fanatically. But at Okinawa it was the essence of victory that airfields be secured promptly, so that land-based planes could help the carrier planes to ward off enemy air attacks and eventually relieve them.[15]

From the landing beaches, the Marines would fan out to the east and north, and XXIV Corps to the east and south, capturing the two airfields within three days, the "waist" of the dog in fifteen, and the southern half of the island in thirty to sixty days. It was not expected that troops would advance beyond the Ishija Isthmus — the dog's neck. Mountainous northern Okinawa could be left to the enemy for the time being.

Phase II of the operation, the seizure of Motobu Peninsula (the dog's ear) and of Ie Shima, the little island with a big airfield, was planned to start about one month after the landings; and during that phase the conquest of Okinawa was expected to be completed.

A careful plan was worked out for the support of this operation by submarines of the Pacific Fleet. Besides wolf-packs hunting Japanese shipping in the unmined areas of the East China Sea, off Indochina and the coast of Honshu, "lifeguard" service was provided in the waters where TF 58 planned to strike.

Admiral Mitscher's fast carrier groups, TF 58, were depended upon to make preliminary neutralization strikes on Tokyo, the

---

[15] There was an alternate plan for landing on the eastern coast of Okinawa, between the dog's fore and hind legs, in case the wind backed to the westward and raised a dangerous surf on the Hagushi side.

Ryukyus, Formosa and airfields on the Japanese home islands, then to support the actual operation. In the latter mission they were to have the help of 18 escort carriers. Luzon-based planes of the Allied Air Forces Southwest Pacific were expected to keep Luzon Strait clear, and on 21 March Admiral Nimitz asked them to support the Ryukyus operation by strikes on Formosa. The Superfortresses based on the Marianas, now augmented to several hundred, were prepared to hammer at Tokyo, and industrial targets in Japan, right through the campaign.

3. *Japanese Preparations* [16]

The Japanese high command expected the Okinawa operation at about the correct date, and did everything in its power to put up a stiff ground defense supported by air and surface attack. This was in accordance with the "Outline of Army and Navy Operations" approved by the Emperor and promulgated 20 January 1945. Okinawa was designated one of the key strongpoints to be developed, the others being Iwo Jima, Formosa, Shanghai and the south coast of Korea. The defense of any or all these places was frankly stated to be a delaying action: —

> When the enemy penetrates the defense zone, a campaign of attrition will be initiated to reduce his preponderance in ships, aircraft and men, to obstruct the establishment of advance bases, to undermine enemy morale, and thereby to seriously delay the final assault on Japan. . . . Preparations for the decisive battle will be completed in Japan proper in the early fall of 1945.
>
> In general, Japanese air strength will be conserved until an enemy landing is actually under way on or within the defense sphere.

On 6 February the Japanese Army and Navy agreed to concentrate all air forces in the homeland around the perimeter of the East China Sea, and to emphasize training in kamikaze tactics. It was

---

[16] Rear Adm. Toshiyuki Yokoi "Kamikazes and the Okinawa Campaign" U. S. Naval Institute *Proceedings* LXXX (1954) 505–513; General of the Army Douglas MacArthur *Historical Report* II 543–555.

hoped that around 2000 aircraft could be assembled by 1 April, which happened to be Okinawa L-day, and that airplane production, which had declined to 1900 in January (and, as it turned out, to 1260 in February), owing to plant dispersal in anticipation of air raids, could soon be increased.

Less than two weeks after this agreement, on 19 February, American forces invaded Iwo Jima. As we have seen, the Japanese were unable to exert any great air effort on behalf of that hot little island, and the Japanese high command wrote it off on 22 March.

In the meantime the B–29s had begun their series of air raids, using incendiary bombs, on large urban areas of Japan. These, in the words of the Japanese collaborators to General MacArthur's *Historical Report*, "rocked the nation to its very foundations." The attack the night of 9–10 March, in particular, was "indescribably horrifying. Well over 250,000 houses were destroyed, rendering more than a million persons homeless, and 83,793 were burned to death." [17]

Air force training, with special emphasis on the kamikaze technique, was now accelerated in expectation of an attack on the Ryukyus. In a new Imperial General Headquarters directive of 20 March, these islands were designated "the focal point of the decisive battle for the defense of the Homeland." A massed air attack on our amphibious forces, both by kamikazes and conventional bombers, was planned and designated Operation TEN-GO. Already the high command had learned through Intelligence channels that the invasion force was beginning to leave Ulithi. C. in C. Combined Fleet (Admiral Toyoda) ordered Commander Fifth Air Fleet (Vice Admiral Matome Ugaki) in Kyushu to concentrate on enemy transports. Ugaki protested that if he did not send his aircraft out at once to attack anything encountered, they might all be destroyed on the ground.[18] The prohibition was then removed, but too late; Fast Carrier Force Pacific Fleet were about to swing into action again.

---

[17] MacArthur *Historical Report* II 551. Note that this was more destructive than the explosion of the first atomic bomb over Hiroshima.
[18] That is just what Admiral Nimitz wanted done, by the B–29s.

94 *Victory in the Pacific*

4. *The Fast Carriers' Contribution, 18–31 March* [19]

Vice Admiral Marc Mitscher's Task Force 58 sortied from Ulithi 14 March for an initial attack on Kyushu airfields. After replenishing on the 16th, the force began its run-in and reached launching position, about 90 miles southeast of the island, at dawn 18 March. Air opposition over Kyushu was light during the morning strikes, and the pilots were puzzled to find few planes grounded — for the good reason that, well alerted, they had taken off to attack the carriers. Consequently the TF 58 pilots expended their bombs on hangars and barracks. Afternoon strikes were directed against fields farther inland. Search planes located a concentration of warships, including battleship *Yamato*, around Kobe and Kure.

In the enemy counterattacks — for which Admiral Ugaki expended 50 of his carefully hoarded planes — Rear Admiral Radford's TG 58.4, operating about 75 miles south of Shikoku, received all the damage on 18 March. *Enterprise* was hit by a dud bomb at 0725, and a Betty trying to crash *Intrepid* was shot down so close aboard that two men were killed and 43 wounded; burning fragments started a fire in the hangar deck. Three Judys went for *Yorktown* shortly after 1300. Two missed; a third dropped a bomb which hit the signal bridge, passed through one deck, and exploded near the ship's side — blowing two big holes, killing or mortally wounding five men, and wounding another 26.

On 19 March Task Force 58's strikes were directed against Japanese ships in the Inland Sea and at Kure and Kobe. Seventeen ships, including such monsters as *Yamato* and carrier *Amagi*, were hit and damaged, but none seriously.

Shortly after sunrise Admiral Davison's TG 58.2 caught it. *Wasp* (Captain O. A. Weller) had just secured from general quarters and

[19] Com Fifth Fleet (Admiral Spruance) Action Report 21 June 1945; CTF 58 (Vice Adm. Mitscher) Action Report 17 July, and those of CTG 58.1 (Rear Adm. Clark), 58.2 (Rear Adm. Davison), 58.3 (Rear Adm. F. C. Sherman), and TG 58.4 (Rear Adm. Radford).

two thirds of her planes were away on strikes. An enemy plane arrived directly over the ship undetected, dived, and at 0710 dropped a bomb which penetrated to the hangar deck, exploded a plane, passed through crew quarters on No. 2 deck and burst in the galley on No. 3 deck, causing great slaughter among cooks and mess attendants who were about to serve breakfast. Fires broke out on five decks simultaneously, six water mains were ruptured, and avgas poured down onto the lower decks, adding to the blaze. Yet, so efficient was damage control that the fires were out in fifteen minutes and *Wasp* was recovering planes by 0800. A few minutes later a second kamikaze missed the carrier by a few feet, nicking the exterior plane elevator, and exploding alongside. Casualties resulting from the bomb explosion were very heavy — 101 killed or died of wounds, 269 wounded; but *Wasp* continued to operate for several days before retiring for repairs.[20]

Admiral Davison's flag carrier *Franklin*, "Big Ben" as her crew called her, was launching her second strike of the morning at 0708 when hit by two bombs from a plane which approached undetected. The first bomb exploded on the hangar deck at about frame 82, wrecking the forward elevator, spreading destruction throughout the hangar and No. 3 deck and lighting huge fires among parked and armed planes. Everyone on that part of the hangar deck was killed, and the fire spread quickly. The second bomb struck the flight deck at about frame 133, exploded above the hangar deck and spread fires through planes which were tuning up to launch. This explosion blew the after elevator up and to one side. Almost immediately the entire ship was enveloped in flames and a pall of heavy black smoke.

Captain Leslie H. Gehres, on the bridge, was knocked down by the first explosion. On picking himself up he noted the fires on the starboard side forward and ordered full right rudder in order to bring the wind on the port side, with the thought of keeping the flames away from planes on the after flight deck. When he managed to make his way inboard he saw that the after part of his ship

[20] *Wasp* Action Report; Carlyle Holt in Boston *Globe* 23 and 24 Oct. 1945.

was also on fire; he swung her to port to bring the wind on her starboard beam, and slowed to two-thirds speed. The bombs in the planes began a long series of explosions, some very violent. Admiral Mitscher, who was on board *Bunker Hill*, heard six enormous explosions in *Franklin* when she was still below the horizon.

One of the more spectacular displays was put on by twelve 11¾-inch "Tiny Tim" rockets with which a dozen fighter-bombers on the flight deck were armed. As described by Commander Joe Taylor, the executive officer, "Some screamed by to starboard, some to port, and some straight up the flight deck. The weird aspect of this weapon whooshing by so close is one of the most awful spectacles a human has ever been privileged to see. Some went straight up and some tumbled end over end. Each time one went off the fire-fighting crews forward would instinctively hit the deck." [21] Before the fires were brought under control all ready ammunition in lockers and gun mounts abaft the island structure had exploded.

Admiral Davison ordered *Santa Fe* to stand by and assist *Franklin*, and with members of his staff and Admiral Bogan (on board as observer) transferred to a destroyer in order to shift his flag to *Hancock*. As he was leaving, the Admiral advised Captain Gehres to issue the order "Prepare to Abandon Ship," but the skipper replied that he thought he could save her. While waiting to go alongside, *Santa Fe* began picking up survivors who had been forced overboard by the heat and flames. As soon as some measure of communication was regained within the ship, Captain Gehres passed the word to direct all but key officers and men to abandon ship. These men took to the water as best they could. Many were rescued by destroyers which were following the carrier for that purpose.

Shortly after 0930 *Santa Fe* closed, Captain Hal C. Fitz slamming her alongside the exploding carrier and holding her with his engines. By that time the fire on the forward part of *Franklin's* flight deck was under control, and wounded men were transferred to her deck. Fire and engine rooms now reported to Captain Gehres that, owing to intense smoke and heat, they had to be evacuated.

[21] Exec's Report enclosed with *Franklin* Action Report 11 Apr. 1945.

By about 1000 all way was lost and the ship lay dead in the water. By noon *Franklin* reported that her skeleton crew had brought the fires practically under control and stabilized the ship's list at 13 degrees, and all wounded had been evacuated. *Santa Fe* took on board 826 men in 30 minutes, and stayed alongside for three hours.

Pittsburgh (Captain John E. Gingrich) now reported that she was ready to pass the towline to *Franklin*, as Captain Gehres had requested. *Santa Fe* pulled clear and *Pittsburgh* brought the heavily listing carrier around to a southerly course — a difficult task in the easterly wind that was blowing. The cruiser gradually worked up to six knots as she and her tow, screened by *Santa Fe* and destroyers, made headway southward. Rear Admiral M. B. Gardner of TG 58.5 took over command of TG 58.2.

By 0300 March 20 *Franklin* had begun to regain power and reported that she could make two knots. By 0932, she had regained steering control in the pilothouse, although still without a compass; and at 1100 she was ready to make 15 knots. The appearance of her flight deck was graphically compared to that of a half-eaten Shredded Wheat biscuit. The tow gradually built up speed and at 1235 *Franklin* was clear of *Pittsburgh* and under her own power. "Down by the tail but reins up!" reported Captain Gehres. Admiral Spruance signaled on the 24th that the ability, fortitude and sheer guts of skipper and crew in saving their ship were in the highest degree praiseworthy.[22] She was by far the most heavily damaged carrier in the war — in much worse shape than *Lexington* at Coral Sea or *Yorktown* at Midway — to be saved. Under her own power and with only one stop, at Pearl Harbor, she made the 12,000-mile voyage to New York. Vice Admiral A. W. Fitch, the former carrier commander at the Battle of the Coral Sea, declared without exaggeration, "Only by the outstanding skill, stamina and heroism of the officers and crew" could this have been done; that there was no precedent in the annals of sea warfare for a capital ship returning to port after such severe damage.[23]

[22] Com Fifth Fleet to C.O. *Franklin* 0100 Mar. 25.
[23] *New York Times* 22 May 1945, with list of those decorated.

Actual casualties in *Franklin* were 724 killed or missing and 265 wounded; and there would have been 300 more killed but for the heroic work of Lieutenant Commander Joseph T. O'Callahan USNR, Catholic chaplain, who not only administered last rites but organized and directed fire-fighting parties, and led two sailors below to wet down a 5-inch magazine that threatened to explode. Lieutenant (jg) Donald A. Gary, who discovered 300 men trapped in a pitch-black mess compartment, found an exit, and returned thrice through smothering smoke to lead them to safety.[24] No fewer than 1700 men were rescued from the water by cruisers and destroyers.[25] Among those killed was Captain Arnold J. Isbell, the distinguished commander of Atlantic hunter-killer groups.[26] He was on board *Franklin* waiting for transfer to *Yorktown*, to which he had been ordered as commanding officer.

Something more than courage — know-how — was required to conquer fires such as those that raged in *Franklin*. Neither she nor many of the other ships crashed by kamikazes off Okinawa could have been saved but for the fire-fighting schools and improved technique instituted by the Navy in 1942–1943. The initial impulse came from Lieutenant Harold J. Burke USNR, deputy chief of the New York City fire department. He interested Rear Admiral Edward L. Cochrane, Chief of the Bureau of Ships, in the new fog nozzle, which atomized water to a fine spray and quenched a blaze much more quickly than a solid stream. Burke and Lieutenant Thomas A. Kilduff USNR, formerly of the Boston Fire Department, trained over 260 officer instructors and established schools with mock-up ships at every continental naval base, and on several Pacific islands. At one of these, the damage control party of every new warship was trained before going to sea. The major object of this instruction was to "get the fear of fire out of the sailor"; to teach

[24] Story by Richard W. Johnston, who was on board, in Honolulu *Advertiser* 18 May 1945.
[25] Bupers breakdown and *Santa Fe* Action Report. The casualties are a record for any United States ship which survived an enemy attack, and are exceeded only by those of *Indianapolis* for a ship sunk.
[26] See Vol. X 109.

him that, if properly equipped with fire mask and helmet, handling an all-purpose nozzle and applicator, he could boldly advance to the source of a blaze and not get hurt.

The big carriers, which already had fourteen fire mains dependent on ship's power, were now given two more, operated by individual gasoline engines. One of these in *Franklin* threw fog for eight hours continuously when all other mains were knocked out by power failure. All ships were equipped with 160-pound handy billies, and the destroyers and larger types with 500-pound mobile pumps, each operated by its own gas engine. Hoses and couplings were made standard throughout the Navy. Portable oxyacetylene steel-cutting outfits and rescue breathing-apparatus were provided. A foamite system was placed at every hundred feet of a carrier's deck. The foam generators in destroyers, originally located in the engine spaces, were moved topside. Salvage vessels (ARS) were especially fitted out to help fight fires in other ships; and occasionally — though seldom in the Pacific — fire-fighting teams were flown out from a shore base to burning ships at sea.[27]

Following the Inland Sea strikes on 19 March, TF 58 retired slowly, sending fighter sweeps over southern Kyushu to keep enemy aircraft grounded. A quiet morning on the 20th was followed by a very lively afternoon. Admiral Davison's TG 58.2, still covering *Franklin*, came under attack by enemy aircraft. At 1454 *Hancock* opened fire on a Zeke coming in on her port beam at about 500 feet. *Halsey Powell*, which had just topped off fuel alongside, cast off and was in the process of getting clear when the burning Zeke, having missed the flight deck of *Hancock*, crashed the destroyer's main deck near the after 5-inch mount. Her steering gear was jammed, a collision with *Hancock* narrowly averted, speed was reduced to about ten knots, and 12 men were killed and 29 wounded.[28] The

---

[27] See Vol. I 329 for an early instance of this, to salvage *Wakefield*. Navy Dept. Press Release 8 Sept. 1945; information from Lt. Cdr. T. A. Kilduff USNR, 1946 and 1960.
[28] *Halsey Powell* Action Report 4 Apr. 1945.

kamikaze's bomb went right through *Halsey Powell's* hull without exploding. Between 1600 and 2000 some 15 to 20 aircraft attacked TG 58.2 and at 1626 one plane bombed and strafed *Enterprise*. The bomb missed but fires were started on "Big E's" flight deck as a result of "friendly" antiaircraft fire, impairing her ability to operate night fighters.

Task Force 58 was shadowed during the night, but no serious attack developed until about 1400 March 21 when a large bogey was picked up by radar to the northwest of the task force. Extra fighters were launched, to a total of 150, of which 24 from Task Group 58.1 intercepted the enemy about sixty miles out. The raid numbered 48 aircraft, 18 of them Bettys carrying the new one-man piloted bomb slung under their bellies. This gimmick, called *oka* (cherry-blossom) by the Japanese and *baka* (screwball) by us, was a 4700-pound bomb provided with rocket propulsion and a human pilot. Fortunately for us the Japanesse did not have many of them, as they were so small and fast (up to 600 m.p.h.) as to be almost impossible to shoot down once cast off from the parent plane. In this instance the weight of the *baka* deprived the Bettys of all power to maneuver, and so made them and their fighter escort an easy prey to the carrier-based Hellcats.

On 22 March TF 58 replenished from Admiral Beary's Logistic Support Group. The same day Admiral Mitscher reorganized his force into three task groups, leaving TG 58.2 to support the crippled carriers *Franklin, Enterprise* and *Yorktown.*

The carrier airmen claimed to have destroyed 528 aircraft in the air and on the ground in this two-day strike, operating within range of Japanese air bases. Japanese authorities admit that "losses were staggering": 161 lost out of 193 aircraft committed, in addition to an indeterminate number destroyed on the ground. These losses prevented heavy participation by Japanese air forces in the defense of Okinawa until 6 April. Admiral Ugaki, however, claimed that his "eagles" had sunk five carriers, two battleships and three cruisers, and that the Americans would have to postpone their attack on the Ryukyus. Imperial General Headquarters doubted the accuracy of his figures but hoped for the best.

Once again, as in the Formosa air battle of October 1944,[29] the Japanese were victims of their own propaganda. On 23 March, when TF 58 began its last pre-landing bombings of Okinawa and Admiral Blandy's Advance Expeditionary Force appeared in the Kerama Retto, the Japanese high command assumed that the one was a Parthian shot of fast carriers returning crippled to Ulithi, and that the other was a diversion.[30] Within two days they learned better, and on 25 March issued an alert for the concentrated air attack on the amphibious forces, Operation TEN-GO.

By that time it was too late for the kamikazes to interfere with the landings; TEN-GO was no go until 6 April, when, as we shall see, it became really serious.

Admiral Spruance gave Admiral Mitscher and his fast carriers a fresh accolade for their work in these pre-invasion strikes. They had, he said, surpassed their already high standards, and inflicted heavy damage on the enemy. The efficiency of C.A.P. was unsurpassed. Extraordinary energy and courage had been shown in repairing and saving badly damaged ships. And Admiral Nimitz, from his advance headquarters at Guam, also praised the endurance, teamwork and skill that Fifth Fleet had shown in the 18–21 March strikes.[31]

One week later, on 27 and 31 March, came the B-29 attacks on the Kyushu air bases which Admiral Nimitz had asked for. These closed down each field several days for repairs, and their mine-dropping operation in Shimonoseki Strait closed that vital supply artery for an entire week.

Thus, the burden of repelling the invasion fell upon the Japanese ground troops on Okinawa, numbering over 77,000. These constituted the Thirty-second Army, commanded by Lieutenant Gen-

---

[29] See Vol. XII Chap. VI.
[30] MacArthur *Historical Report* II 554.
[31] Com Fifth Fleet to CTF 58 2347 Mar. 23; Cincpac to Com Fifth Fleet 1340 Mar. 24.

eral Mitsuru Ushijima. This formidable garrison had not been reinforced in 1945; it had in fact been reduced in December 1944 by
sending replacements to Luzon. In addition, there were about
20,000 Okinawan militia and labor troops.

Task Force 58 planes had taken numerous photographs of Okinawa, on the basis of which Admiral Mitscher notified Admiral
Turner 26 March that the entire island was a honeycomb of caves,
tunnels and gun positions; that tanks and armored cars had been
observed popping into caves; that as tough a fight as on Iwo Jima
should be anticipated. He assured Turner, however, that he would
give all possible air protection to the amphibious forces, day and
night, and informed him that TF 58 planes were searching the
Nansei Shoto daily as far north as the Osumi Gunto.[32]

5. *The Royal Navy's Participation* [33]

During the year 1944, the British government formed a plan to
send the major part of the Royal Navy to the Pacific by June of
1945. Prime Minister Churchill had often and eloquently voiced
this intention, and by the summer of 1944 it had become his firm
policy. By that time the situation in Europe had so improved that
the Admiralty believed it no longer needed to keep the Fleet in
home waters. Having decided to create a British Pacific Fleet, the
Admiralty sent for Commander Harry Hopkins RN, who had been
serving as British observer with Admiral Nimitz. He arrived at
London in August 1944, gave the Admiralty the fruit of his experience for planning purposes; and charts of the Pacific Ocean, a
part of the world half forgotten in England, began to appear on
bulkheads in the rambling Admiralty building in Whitehall.

[32] CTF 58 to CTF 51, 2155 Mar. 25.
[33] John Ehrman *Grand Strategy* VI 222–235 (*History of Second World War*,
U.K. Military Series, 1956); Capt. S. W. Roskill RN kindly allowed me to use the
appropriate chapter in his *The War at Sea* III, a volume of this series, in advance
of publication; story by correspondent Robert Trumbull, who was on board, in
New York Times 16 Apr. 1945; Action Reports of Vice Adms. Rawlings, Vian
and Brind RN, and other restricted Admiralty sources.

Kure, 19 March

Midget Submarine Pen, Okinawa, 27 March

Spring Bombing by U.S.S. Essex *Planes*

The Ordeal of U.S.S. Franklin, *19 March*

At the OCTAGON Conference in Quebec in September 1944, where the Combined Chiefs of Staff met with President Roosevelt and Prime Minister Churchill, a leading issue was the participation of the Royal Navy in the Pacific War. Admiral King did not want it. He feared that a British Fleet's breaking into the Pacific at a time when the United States Navy was having a difficult time to supply itself would put an undue strain on logistics. But the British naval representatives and Mr. Churchill were so determined to have the Royal Navy fighting in the Pacific that they met this objection by promising to create a fleet train of their own, and on that basis the question was settled. The "approved report" of the C.C.S. to the President and Prime Minister, of 16 September, states: —

We have agreed that the British Fleet should participate in the main operations against Japan in the Pacific, with the understanding that this Fleet will be balanced and self-supporting. The method of employment of the British Fleet in these main operations in the Pacific will be decided from time to time in accordance with the prevailing circumstances.[34]

On 22 November Admiral Sir Bruce Fraser RN, commanding the British Eastern Fleet in the Indian Ocean, was appointed Commander in Chief of the new British Pacific Fleet, and on 10 December he established his headquarters at Sydney. Six days later he and members of his staff arrived at Pearl Harbor to confer with Admirals Nimitz and Spruance and the Cincpac-Cincpoa staff. As a result of these meetings a "Memorandum of Understandings" between the two Navies was drawn up.[35] It was agreed that the Royal Navy's first contribution to the Pacific War should be a fast carrier task force, to operate in the Philippine Sea and approaches to Japan during Operation ICEBERG, separately from Admiral Mitscher's TF 58 but performing a similar mission on other targets. The British Pacific Fleet, with its carrier commander Rear Ad-

---

[34] C.C.S. Report to President and P.M., 16 Sept. 1944, C.C.S. 680/2.
[35] "Memorandum Record of Understandings Reached in Conference 17–19 Dec. 1944 concerning employment of the British Pacific Fleet." Approved by Admiral King 2 Jan. 1945.

miral Sir Philip Vian as O.T.C., got under way from Ceylon 16 January 1945 for Australia. En route it managed to work in two successful strikes on Japanese-operated oil refineries at Palembang, Sumatra, and on 4 February reached Fremantle. Before returning to Sydney, Admiral Fraser sailed to Lingayen in U.S.S. *New Mexico* and narrowly escaped death in the kamikaze attack of 6 January 1945.[36]

It was not yet settled what the main employment of this important reinforcement would be during Operation ICEBERG. The J.C.S. were in favor of assigning Indonesia as the Royal Navy target area, with a base at Brunei Bay, Borneo. That was also what General MacArthur and Admiral King wanted. But Admirals Nimitz and Spruance wished to use the British carriers in their theater, to keep the southern part of the Ryukyus pounded down. This exactly coincided with the views of all British strategists from the Prime Minister down; no sideshow for them! After much discussion the Cincpac-Churchill view prevailed in the J.C.S., and on 14 March Admiral Fraser was directed to report to Admiral Nimitz with the proviso that his Fleet could be withdrawn on seven days' notice. The reason for this condition was the desire of Admiral King to use the British Fleet as a flexible strategic reserve in case a new operation, such as the liberation of Indonesia, were decided upon later.[37]

By mid-March Task Force 113, the combatant elements of the British Pacific Fleet, was conducting training exercises near Manus in the Admiralties. TF 112, the Royal Navy service squadron, had also come up to Seeadler Harbor, which had been agreed upon between Admirals Fraser and Nimitz as an intermediate British base between Australia and the combat theater. TF 113 was under the tactical command of Vice Admiral Sir H. Bernard Rawlings RN, who also commanded the 1st Battle Squadron. It was organized as follows: — [38]

[36] See Vol. XIII 105.
[37] Vol. XIII 257–258 and Ehrman VI 224.
[38] See end of Appendix I below for details and replacements. TF 113 was designated TF 57 when it came under U. S. Fifth Fleet.

1st Battle Squadron, Vice Admiral Rawlings RN
H.M.S. KING GEORGE V and HOWE

1st Carrier Squadron, Rear Admiral Sir Philip Vian RN
H.M.S. INDOMITABLE, VICTORIOUS, ILLUSTRIOUS and INDEFATIGABLE

4th Cruiser Squadron, Rear Admiral E. J. P. Brind RN
H.M.S. SWIFTSURE, BLACK PRINCE, ARGONAUT, EURYALUS, H.M.N.Z.S. GAMBIA

Fifteen destroyers, Rear Admiral J. H. Edelston RN

This was a well-balanced force. Three of the five cruisers were of the *Dido* antiaircraft class; the destroyers were new and fast. Two of these carriers were no strangers to the Pacific. H.M.S. *Indomitable*, at the approach of war with Japan, was sent to support Vice Admiral Sir Tom Phillips's ill-fated battle squadron, but owing to a mishap arrived too late. H.M.S. *Victorious* had been lent by the Admiralty in 1943 to the United States Pacific Fleet, which at that time, owing to the loss of *Wasp* and *Hornet*, had only two fleet carriers.[39] Sir Philip Vian's air groups, numbering over 200 units, used both United States Navy types such as the Corsair, Hellcat and Avenger, and British types, such as the Seafire (Navy version of the famous Spitfire fighter), and the Firefly, a heavy fighter. The service squadron (TF 112), commanded by Rear Admiral Douglas B. Fisher RN, comprised ten oil tankers, five replenishment-plane escort carriers and a large number of salvage and repair ships.

At sea, during the forenoon watch of 15 March 1945, Admiral Rawlings received the signal to report to Cincpac. He canceled all exercises, and after considering his logistic problem sent off this signal to Admiral Nimitz: —

I hereby report TF 113 and TF 112 for duty in accordance with orders received from C. in C. British Pacific Fleet. . . . Anticipate TF 113 with units of TF 112 be ready 1200 17th March to sail from Manus as you may direct. . . . It is with a feeling of great pride and pleasure that the British Pacific Force joins the U. S. Naval Forces under your command.

To which Admiral Nimitz replied: —

The United States Pacific Fleet welcomes the British Carrier Task Force and attached units which will greatly add to our power to strike

[39] Capt. Stephen Roskill RN *The War at Sea* II 229–231.

the enemy and will also show our unity of purpose in the war against Japan.[40]

The Royal Navy task force sailed from Manus 18 March and arrived Ulithi on the 20th, where it fueled from United States Navy facilities. During the next two days plans were completed for supporting Operation ICEBERG as TF 57, a part of Admiral Spruance's Fifth Fleet, but independent of TF 58. The mission assigned to Admiral Rawlings was to cover the Sakishima Gunto, a group of islands between Formosa and Okinawa.

Sailing from Ulithi 23 March, TF 57 rendezvoused with its fleet train at a point east of Cape Engaño. The logistic group then proceeded to Leyte Gulf and set up a forward anchorage and supply base in San Pedro Bay.

Upon joining Fifth Fleet the British Pacific Force accepted United States Navy tactical publications and communications procedures. Communication teams were provided for each combatant ship, and Captain E. C. Ewen USN, an experienced carrier skipper, acted as liaison officer to Admiral Rawlings. The British found the transition easy. The Admiral reported that only one signal had to be added to the British general signal book in order to accommodate his Fleet to American tactical formations, and the appearance of American terms such as C.A.P., A/S and Dumbo in his ships' action reports indicates that Senior Service sailors fell easily into new habits. Their fleet train proved to be adequate, since the U. S. Navy undertook to bring all black oil and avgas up to Ulithi; Admiral Fraser informed the Admiralty that Service Force Pacific Fleet had interpreted the "self-supporting" provision of the 16 September memorandum very liberally.

After fueling at sea, TF 57 headed for its launching area 100 miles south of Miyako Retto, easternmost of the Sakishima Gunto. Beginning at sunrise 26 March, fighter sweeps and bomber attacks were launched against airfields on Miyako in order to render them inoperative. After the last strike of the day the task force withdrew southeasterly for the night. At sunrise it returned to the launching

[40] Vice Adm. Rawlings Action Report 9 May 1945.

area, where the first day's sweeps and strikes were repeated on airfields not before covered, and on coastal shipping. In the forenoon H.M. destroyer *Undine*, with fighter cover, was sent out to search for the crew of an Avenger which had ditched fifty-six miles from the launching point. She not only rescued this crew but picked up an American Corsair pilot who had been adrift for forty-eight hours. At 1805 lifeguard submarine U.S.S. *Kingfish* reported the rescue of a British Avenger pilot. Reports of a typhoon to the southward caused Admiral Rawlings to call off strikes planned for 28 March in order to fuel and replenish and be sure the task force would be in position to cover the Sakishima Gunto from 31 March through 2 April, the critical period at Okinawa. During its two days' absence, planes from the support carrier group of Rear Admiral Durgin USN took over its job.

Replenishment completed in the afternoon of 30 March, sweeps and strikes against Sakishima targets were resumed next day. Admiral Rawlings now borrowed another tactic from the American fast carrier book. Antiaircraft cruiser H.M.S. *Argonaut*, which mounted the latest radar, and H.M. destroyer *Wager*, were stationed 30 miles in advance of the task force to act as pickets and to prevent Japanese aircraft from returning with friendly strikes.

Having reached L-day minus 1 for Okinawa, we may break off the story of TF 57 until Operation ICEBERG really began. In that operation, the British carrier group became a flying buffer between the United States amphibious forces and the enemy airfields on Sakishima Gunto.

CHAPTER VII

Moving In on the Ryukyus[1]

18 March–1 April

1. Sorties from Ulithi and Carrier Support

HERE is a brief reminder of the principal elements of Vice Admiral Kelly Turner's Joint Expeditionary Force (TF 51) for Operation ICEBERG, the conquest of Okinawa: — [2]

TG 51.1 WESTERN ISLANDS ATTACK GROUP, Rear Admiral Kiland: One transport squadron and tractor flotilla, to land 77th Division on the Kerama Retto on L-day minus 6. Closely allied to this was TG 51.2, the Demonstration Group, Rear Admiral Jerauld Wright.

TF 52 AMPHIBIOUS SUPPORT FORCE, Rear Admiral Blandy: Escort carriers, minecraft, UDTs, LCI(G)s, etc.

TF 53 NORTHERN ATTACK FORCE, Rear Admiral Reifsnider: Two transport squadrons to land III 'Phib Corps, Major General Geiger USMC, on the northern group of Hagushi beaches, on L-day, 1 April.

TF 54 GUNFIRE AND COVERING FORCE, Rear Admiral Deyo.

TF 55 SOUTHERN ATTACK FORCE, Rear Admiral Hall: Two transport squadrons to land XXIV Army Corps on the southern group of Hagushi beaches on L-day.

The ships and craft employed in the amphibious phases of this operation numbered 1213, of 45 different classes and types, from 179 attack transports and cargo ships down, including 187 of the

---

[1] CTF 51 (Vice Adm. Turner) Action Report Capture of Okinawa Gunto Phases I and II 25 July; CTG 51.1 (Rear Adm. Kiland) Action Report 26 May 1945.

[2] For detailed breakdown see Appendix I.

handy, ubiquitous and greatly wanted LST. The over-all figure of 1213 does not include the 88 ships of Task Force 58, the 22 ships of the Royal Navy's TF 57, the 95 ships in Admiral Beary's logistic group or the service forces and fleet trains of both Navies, which together would add over 100 more. Assault troops numbered 2380 of the Navy, 81,165 of the Marine Corps and 98,567 of the Army.[3]

Routing so large a number of ships and groups to a single destination from widely spaced staging points, an old game for V 'Phib staff, now required more than usual dexterity. Leyte Gulf was ample for the Northern Attack Force, but even the big lagoon of Ulithi was insufficient to hold the Southern, in addition to the approximately 200 vessels of Service Squadron 6 and 10, which used it as a logistics base. Arrivals and departures had to be nicely calculated in order not to overtax berthing and shore facilities.

Ulithi was also the scene of intensive detailed planning. Rear Admiral Blandy arrived there 11 March from Leyte to find Vice Admiral Oldendorf, appointed to command the Gunfire and Covering Force, on the binnacle list.[4] Fortunately, Rear Admiral Morton L. Deyo, veteran gunfire support commander in Operation OVERLORD and DRAGOON, was available to relieve Admiral Oldendorf. The gunfire support plans promulgated by Admiral Turner, which had just arrived, had to be correlated with those of lower echelons. "Spike" Blandy's plan, appropriately ready on St. Patrick's Day, was promptly distributed to some 600 ships in Ulithi lagoon.

Task Force 58, Mitscher's fast carriers with the first echelon of their attendant service force, departed Ulithi 14 March.[5] On the 19th the minesweepers left. The Royal Navy contingent, with most of its fleet train, arrived that day from Manus and anchored in the southern part of the lagoon. Fire support ships straggled in by twos and threes, some from Pearl Harbor, some from Iwo Jima and others from the Solomons. Ships which had been engaged in

---

[3] Turner Action Report Part I.
[4] Admiral Oldendorf and his chief of staff, Capt. R. W. Bates, had been injured when the "skimmer" taking them from shore to flagship *Tennessee* rammed a mooring buoy.
[5] See Chap. VI for their strikes on Kyushu, 18–19 March.

the nervous business of fire support off Iwo for the past month were badly in need of rest, upkeep and refresher training – for which there was no time. On 18 March Admiral Blandy held a briefing conference of all group, unit and capital ship commanders on board his flagship *Estes*. Three days later he and they sortied, and next day transports which had lifted Marines from Guadalcanal, Tulagi and the Russell Islands, occupied their berths. It was "hot bunk" in Ulithi lagoon.[6]

Lagoon and atoll presented an astonishing appearance on 20 March. In addition to the 40 or 50 ships that flew British ensigns, several hundred vessels of the United States Navy and Merchant Marine were present. Mogmog, the former seat of the king of Ulithi, transformed into a fleet recreation center, was so full of bluejackets in shoregoing whites that from a distance it looked like one of those Maine islands where seagulls breed; one could hardly walk a step ashore without kicking an empty beer can. On the headquarters island, Commodore O. O. ("Scrappy") Kessing, atoll commander, was dispensing characteristic hospitality at the crowded officers' club, to officers of the fleet and nurses from the three hospital ships present, *Solace, Relief* and *Comfort*. Some of these courageous ladies had their last dance on this occasion, except their dance of death with the kamikaze boys. A "boogie-woogie" band of colored Seabees gave out "hot" dance music, and in the brief intervals when they cooled their lips, another Seabee performed marvels on the harmonica. Press correspondents, profiting by free drinks, staggered about in imitation of the traditional sailor on liberty. A few Royal Navy officers, who had flown to Ulithi to join TF 57, relieved the drab American khaki by their white tropical uniform of shorts and sleeveless shirts with shoulder bars. Some of the United States Navy's most noted officers were present: Rear Admirals "Mort" Deyo, "Spike" Fahrion, "Turner" Joy and John H. ("Babe") Brown; destroyer squadron commanders such as Captains Roland Smoot, H. J. Martin and A. E. Jarrell; and a sprinkling of young reservists commanding destroyer escorts, such as "Charlie"

[6] For occupation and development of Ulithi, with chart, see Vol. XII 47–54.

Adams, son of a former Secretary of the Navy, and "Frank" Roosevelt, the President's son. Gene Tunney, former heavyweight boxing champion, had just arrived to take charge of fleet recreation. This party was a modern version of the famous Brussels ball before the battle of Waterloo; but no cry was raised of "They come! They come!" since the enemy was conserving planes for ship targets nearer home. Everyone was happy over a somewhat blown-up press release on the fast carriers' strikes on Japan, and eager to start for the top-secret destination.

From Ulithi it was a run of only four days to the Ryukyus for the fire support ships. They arrived 25 March. Next day the Northern Tractor Flotilla, which had come from Guadalcanal, preceded Transport Groups "Able" and "Baker" out of Ulithi lagoon. These, as well as the Southern Tractor Flotilla from Leyte, and the Demonstration Group from Saipan, ran into a spell of foul weather.

From 25 through 30 March, heavy seas and wind of gale force from the ENE reduced the normal 8-knot speed of advance of the LSTs, forced them occasionally to change course, and resulted in some cargo shifting and damage.[7] Weather forecasts indicated a typhoon, but Admiral Turner stoutly held on. The tractor flotilla just managed to meet target date and hour by displaying excellent seamanship and increasing speed at every opportunity.

The LCI gunboats which accompanied these tractor flotillas also had a rough passage. Yet Mortar and Rocket Division 2 managed en route to assemble and fuze all its rockets in the magazines.

The Southern Tractor Flotilla en route from Leyte took a similar buffeting, and Rear Admiral Jerauld Wright's Demonstration Group, which brought up the 2nd Marine Division from Saipan, made schedule by a very narrow margin.

[7] CTG 53.3 (Capt. J. S. Laidlaw) Action Report 14 Apr. 1945 indicates for eve of 26 March a fresh ENE wind force 6 and a heavy beam sea, forcing change of course from 335° to 315°; same all day 27 March; man killed by tank that broke loose. Wind abated 28th to force 5-6, squally, heavy seas; *LST-268* lost pontoon barge; wind made up to force 8 early hours 30 March, heavy going, two men overboard, both rescued; 20 miles behind schedule at noon. Capt. Laidlaw in *LCI-1080* was operated on that day for an infected hip by Lt.(jg) Wilbur C. Sumner USNR, who had been transferred by breeches buoy from *LST-950* the day before.

On the last day of the approach, the Northern Tractor Flotilla was attacked from the air. It had just rounded Kerama Retto and steadied on a northeasterly course at 0200 April 1 when a number of torpedo-bombers began attacking destroyer *Hugh W. Hadley*, which was steaming ahead of the LSTs. She splashed one plane on the twelfth successive try, and drove off the rest. One went for the tractor flotilla and launched a torpedo which passed harmlessly under the shoal-draft LSTs.

Task Force 58 was still out there, about 100 miles east of Okinawa. Between 23 March and 1 April Vice Admiral Mitscher launched strikes on adjacent islands, including Kerama Retto, and fighter sweeps over Okinawa, as part of his preparation for the impending landing. At least one task group was on station daily, and those that needed replenishment were absent for one day only. In the early hours of 23 March destroyer *Haggard* (Lieutenant Commander V. J. Soballe), in Admiral Radford's TG 58.4, depth-charged submarine *RO-41* on a sonar contact, forced it to the surface and rammed it, smashing her own bow so that she had to pull out for repairs, but causing the submarine to roll over and sink with explosions of gratifying violence.

At 1300 March 24 Task Group 58.1 launched a strike of 112 planes to attack a Japanese convoy reported about 150 miles northwest of Okinawa. Postwar studies confirm the returning flyers' claim to have sunk an entire eight-ship convoy. The same day, battleships *New Jersey*, *Wisconsin* and *Missouri* and five destroyers, under Rear Admiral L. E. Denfeld's command, were detached from the screen to bombard the southeast coast of Okinawa, while *Massachusetts*, *Indiana* and six destroyers threw 16-inch and 5-inch hardware at another section of the coast. The only attack on TF 58 during this period came from a single Jill torpedo bomber on 27 March, against destroyer *Murray*. The plane was splashed and the torpedo passed through *Murray* from starboard to port, exploding close aboard and doing relatively little damage.

On 29 March, from a point about 120 miles south of Kyushu, three task groups launched fighter sweeps over airfields in southern

Kyushu. During the next two days, while TG 58.1 replenished, 58.3 and 58.4 launched sweeps and strikes against Okinawa and furnished C.A.P. for ships in the vicinity.

2. The Minesweepers [8]

"First to arrive and last to leave" might well have been the motto of Minecraft Pacific Fleet. The Okinawa campaign opened at 1720 March 22 when *Hambleton* encountered a floating mine on the approach, and sank it by gunfire. Next morning at 0630 *Adams* led in sweeping the outer approach areas, and from that time on the mine flotilla was doing business day and night, as well as beating off kamikazes. *Adams* sighted the peak of Kuba Shima in the Kerama Retto at 0749 March 24.

Except in certain waters of the Philippines, the Japanese had done little mining in the path of the United States Navy. But they were known to have purchased from us and the British thousands of mines at the end of World War I, and it had to be assumed that they would have acquired from Germany the formula for making those influence mines which were so fatally effective off the coast of Normandy. Fortunately they had not done so. Although their mining of Ryukyus waters was neither abundant nor technically good, there was enough of it to make a lot of trouble.

Rear Admiral Alexander Sharp's mine force (*Terror*, flag) was organized as a task group of Rear Admiral Blandy's Amphibious Support Force. It comprised 122 minecraft and patrol craft in addition to net and buoy tenders. Smallest and most numerous were the YMS (yard or motor minesweepers), diesel-powered vessels 138 feet long, fitted primarily for sweeping acoustic, magnetic or other influence mines in shoal waters. Backbone of the minecraft fleet were the 185-foot, 800-ton AMs of *Admirable* class, and the 221-

[8] CTG 52.2 (Rear Adm. Sharp) Action Report 23 July 1945; conversations in 1945 with him, and with Capt. R. D. Edwards of Administrative Command Minecraft Pacific at Pearl Harbor, and their publications *Mines Away* and *Mine Warfare Notes;* A. S. Lott *Most Dangerous Sea* (1959).

footers of the *Heed* class, which began coming out in 1942.[9] Next were the destroyer minesweepers (DMS), converted from destroyers either of the old four-piper World War I vintage (*Gamble*, for instance), or of the 1630-ton *Bristol* class. The four-pipers had borne the burden of minesweeping in previous invasions as well as minelaying up the Solomons' Slot in 1943; the *Bristol* class, converted in 1944, reached the Pacific in time for Okinawa. These 1630-ton high speed minesweepers had fire control radar, which none of the smaller classes at that time possessed, and they had sacrificed only one of their five 5-inch guns. They could sweep a 150-yard width of ocean when steaming 15 knots. Biggest of all were the DMs, destroyer minelayers. These were 2200-ton destroyers of the *Allen M. Sumner* class, converted to fast minelayers in the course of construction.[10] But fast minelayers are only wanted when enemy shipping lanes are so near our own that they can dash in, "lay eggs," and retire. So these big DMs were used off Okinawa as antiaircraft, mine disposal, buoy laying and fire support vessels for the sweeper groups, functions which they performed admirably. Each carried six dual-purpose 5-inch 38-caliber guns mounted in twin turrets, two 40-mm quads and two twins, and eight 20-mm machine guns; but no torpedo tubes. They were also employed as radar pickets after the kamikazes had whittled down our destroyer strength.

The destroyer minesweepers, organized as a group under Captain R. A. Larkin, were employed in units of four or five, with a supporting DM, to make fast exploratory sweeps outside the 10-fathom line. But the typical sweep unit for the Okinawa operation consisted of five AMs equipped with "O" gear [11] to sweep for

<hr>

[9] Four of those at Okinawa — *Sheldrake, Skylark, Starling* and *Swallow* — and others which began coming out in June 1945 were named after birds, but they do not belong to the World War I "Bird" class, all the survivors of which had been converted to ATOs and other auxiliaries by 1945.

[10] The Navy in February 1944 decided that, in view of the falling-off in German U-boat activity, it was building too many destroyers. It asked various branches of the Fleet if they could use any of the 2200-tonners. The minecraft office in Washington at first declined, but finally and fortunately accepted.

[11] So named after H.M.S. *Oropesa*, which first used it.

moored contact mines at a depth of 10 to 20 fathoms, together with one 2200-ton DM as support and one PC or PGM to destroy floaters by machine-gun fire. Admiral Sharp had seven of these units, organized in two groups under Commanders T. F. Donohue and L. F. Freiburghouse. One of the commonest (and most welcome) sights off Okinawa in April was an AM unit with the ships in echelon, sweep gear streamed, steaming methodically at 5 to 8 knots, patrol craft peeling off to explode a floating mine. These ships were equipped for sweeping ground or influence mines, which the Japanese did not have, but they were equally efficient for cutting moored contact mines in depths of less than 100 fathoms.[12] The AMs took care of most areas off the western and southern coast of Okinawa, while four of the six YMS units entered Nakagusuku Wan and Kimmu Wan on the east coast to clear them for future military operations. The sweeping plan was largely drafted at Admiral Sharp's headquarters by Captains Ralph Moore and Robley D. Clark; the latter was killed by the kamikaze which crashed *Terror* on 1 May.

The importance of the minesweepers may be gauged from their slogan "No Sweep, No Invasion." The Okinawa operation could not begin without extensive preliminary sweeps, nor continue without constant re-sweeping. Up to L-day, 2500 square miles of ocean were swept, six enemy minefields were discovered, and 184 mines, including floaters, were destroyed.[13]

No influence mines were encountered, but the sweepers had to cope with mines moored in shoal waters off the landing beaches. On 26 March, near sunset, destroyer *Halligan* (Lieutenant Commander E. T. Grace) hit a mine when she ventured into unswept waters less than 50 fathoms deep, about three miles southeast of Maye Shima. The mine exploded her two forward magazines, sending smoke and debris 200 feet aloft, and the entire forward part

---

[12] The 100-fathom curve was at that time considered the limit of mineable waters, but Admiral Turner directed clearance sweeps up to the 200-fathom curve and exploratory sweeps up to the 500-fathom curve. Rear Adm. Sharp's Action Report shows that this was done.

[13] For the loss of *Skylark* on 28 March see Chap. VIII below.

of the ship down to No. 1 stack was blown off. Most of the survivors gathered on the fantail. *PC–1128* searched the area by moonlight, picked up six swimmers, and after the senior surviving officer,
an ensign, had ordered Abandon Ship, the PC with the aid of
PC–584 and *LSM–194* took off the other survivors. During the
night *Halligan* drifted ashore. She lost 153 killed and 39 wounded
out of a total complement of about 325, a dreadful warning of what
to expect from enemy mines.[14]

A day in the life of a destroyer minelayer may be gathered
from the log of *Henry A. Wiley*, Commander P. H. Bjarnason. On
29 March, in the neighborhood of Kerama Retto, she splashed a
Japanese plane half an hour after midnight. At 0355 the bridge received 40-mm fire from a nearby LSM that was under attack. Six
minutes later a Jake from right overhead dropped a bomb that
missed. At 0402, *Wiley* fired on another plane, which escaped. At
0519 she fired on another. Around six o'clock, when it was getting
light, she joined two destroyers for mutual protection; within a few
minutes they were under attack by three planes, one of which was
splashed by the antiaircraft fire of a destroyer. At 0613 a sixth plane
came in on a steep glide; *Wiley's* 5-inch fire caused it to veer, and a
40-mm hit exploded it. Another kamikaze, then starting to dive, was
taken under fire. The forward 20-mm battery snipped one wing
clean off and the plane exploded 75 yards on the starboard bow.
This fight was hardly over when a plane from one of our escort
carriers splashed astern of *Wiley*, which recovered the pilot. Now
the real day's work began. "0700 commenced sweeping operations."
These were interrupted only by a "submarine contact" (later evaluated as non-submarine) on which a depth-charge pattern was
dropped at 1400. "1700, completed sweep." [15]

Wiley, *Tolman* and *Shea* shot down 15 enemy planes before
1 April while protecting minesweepers, and *Adams* was knocked
out the same day by a kamikaze which crashed her well aft, whose

[14] Com 'Phib Group 7 (Rear Adm. Kiland) Report of Loss of *Halligan* 1 Apr.
1945, with endorsements.
[15] *Henry A. Wiley* Action Report 1 Apr. 1945,

two bombs exploded under her fantail. One of the subordinate duties of these DMs, which helped the transports and combatant ships to thread their way through swept channels in the open ocean, was to plant a series of buoy markers that radar could pick up at night. As the operation progressed, and numerous screen and radar picket destroyers were sunk or damaged by suicide planes, Admiral Turner detailed more and more of the larger minecraft for these duties. Their exploits will be recounted in the course of the narrative. As a result, practically all the sweeping after L-day had to be done by the YMS, and only four out of eleven new, and five out of twelve old destroyer minesweepers were operational on 21 June, the day when Okinawa was declared secured. Minecraft suffered more than 15 per cent of all naval casualties during Operation ICE-BERG.[16]

3. *Kerama Retto Occupied* [17]

Moonset	1432	March 25
Sunrise	0627	March 26
Sunset	1842	March 26

Fifteen miles west of Naha in Southern Okinawa lies a group of mountainous, irregularly shaped islands known as the Kerama Retto. The capture of this small group, unsuitable for airfields, was decided upon as the geography of the Ryukyus was studied, and the need of some better place than open ocean for fueling and ammunition replenishment became clear. Admiral Turner was struck by the possibilities of the Kerama Retto for this purpose. The roadstead or Kerama Kaikyo, between the largest island of the group and five smaller ones to the westward, was capable of accommodating 75 large ships in 20- to 35-fathom anchorages, with good holding ground, and both entrances could be closed by nets; the smaller

[16] Rear Adm. Sharp Action Report pp. F–2, G–1.
[17] Rear Adm. Blandy "Report of Operations Against Okinawa Gunto including the Capture of Kerama Retto, March–April 1945," 1 May 1945; Rear Adm. Kiland Action Report; personal observations and conversations with Adm. Kiland and staff in *Mount McKinley* 31 March, and with Cdr. Draper Kauffman 13 Apr. 1945.

Aka roadstead offered sheltered anchorage for seaplanes and their tenders, with a two-mile runway for the takeoff. Thus an advanced naval base might be set up in these islands before the main airdromes on Okinawa were captured.

Admiral Turner's proposal that the Navy seize this group about a week ahead of the main attack on Okinawa is said to have been opposed at first by almost every officer whom he consulted. That is surprising, in view of the success of the Union Navy in the Civil War in holding Ship Island off Biloxi, and the islands off Port Royal, S.C. Probably the inability of the Royal Navy to hold islands off the coast of Norway in World War II was in everyone's mind. The bogy of land-based air was brought up, since the enemy would have five airfields within fifty miles of Kerama while we were engaged in occupying it. It was even predicted that the Fleet, after taking heavy losses in Kerama, would be forced to seek the open sea. But the Iwo operation, as it unrolled its bloody scroll, accented the need of a sheltered anchorage for replenishment. Admiral Turner figured that he could get away with it, and he did. Naval fire power, delivered by ships and planes, diverted the enemy's main forces while the pirate team of Blandy and Kiland "cut out" Kerama right under his nose.

Admiral Turner was willing to go into Kerama Retto with nothing more than a reconnaissance battalion, and could easily have taken it with that. But Rear Admiral Ingolf N. Kiland,[18] who, as CTG 51.1, was directly responsible for the Kerama phase, wished to take no chances. Instead of fighting fanatical rear-guard actions from island to island with a small force, he planned simultaneous landings on five of the six larger Keramas, and on 26 March (L-day minus 6), instead of two days later as originally planned. The Army provided the 77th (Statue of Liberty) Infantry Division commanded by Major General A. D. Bruce USA.

Admiral Kiland's Western Island Attack Group (TG 51.1) consisted of command ship *Mount McKinley* and 19 large transport types with a screen of destroyers and destroyer escorts, two de-

[18] For brief biography of Adm. Kiland see Vol. XIII 93–94.

General View of the Roadstead

Landing on Aka Shima, 26 March

Kerama Retto

Baka Bomb

Suicide Boat, Zamami Jima

Deadly Japanese Midgets

stroyer transports carrying underwater demolition teams, a tractor flotilla of 18 LST and 11 LSM, a flock of LCI gunboats and patrol craft for control and close fire support, survey ship *Bowditch*, a service and salvage group of two tugs and two repair ships, a couple of tankers and seaplane tenders; two Victory ships as ammunition carriers, several units of the minecraft flotilla with their net and buoy group, a transport converted to a hospital ship and miscellaneous auxiliaries. This Western Islands Attack Group was covered from enemy air or surface interference by one of Admiral Durgin's escort carrier units and by Rear Admiral C. Turner Joy's fire support unit, both to arrive in Okinawan waters within twenty-four hours of the Kerama landings.

The Kerama Retto covers a space about 7 by 13 miles, most of it water. The ten principal islands are precipitous, broken, rocky, covered with scrubby vegetation, and with deeply scalloped shores. The highest point on the biggest island, Tokashiki Jima, is 787 feet above sea level. There are white sand beaches in many of the coves, closed in by bothersome coral reefs. The general aspect of the group might well have reminded Admiral Kiland of the land of his Viking ancestors. They were thinly populated by the poorer sort of Okinawans, who lived on fishing and from tiny gardens terraced into the rocky hillsides. The only industrial plant was a copper mine, no longer being worked, on Yakabi Shima. Intelligence estimated 1000 to 1500 Japanese troops to be present, in this instance an exaggeration. Air reconnaissance (originally by Luzon-based Army planes, latterly by TF 58) showed six beaches, one on each of the six westernmost islands, that looked good for landing.

The Western Islands Attack Force was mounted at Leyte where the 77th Division had recently played an important part in the fighting. Rear Admirals Blandy and Kiland, General Bruce of the 77th Division, and Captain Hanlon of the Underwater Demolition Teams worked out the detailed plan, dated 17 March.

In Commodore T. B. Brittain's Transport Squadron 17, newly formed in 1945, half of the ships had never seen action. Their landing craft crews were inexperienced and the task of finding the right beach on the right island in early morning was certain to be difficult. By good fortune, Hinunangan Bay on Leyte and the Cabugan Islands made possible a remarkably lifelike rehearsal of the Kerama landings, which was held on 13–15 March. Admiral Kiland, moreover, had an efficient intelligence officer, Lieutenant Commander Ellery Sedgwick USNR, whose section got out an illustrated "Coxswain's Guide to the Beaches." [19] This the lads studied so carefully during the five-day passage from Leyte that they made no false move. The tractor flotilla, with support craft and net tenders, sailed from Leyte 19 March; Admiral Kiland, with the transports and the rest of the attack force, two days later. In company steamed escort carriers *Marcus Island, Savo Island* and *Anzio*. The minecraft, as we have seen, were first to arrive and first to be hit.

At 0530 March 25, Palm Sunday, Admiral Joy with two cruisers and three destroyers peeled off from Admiral Deyo's main body some 22 miles southeast of Okinawa to deliver preliminary fires on the Kerama Retto. Five destroyer transports carrying the UDTs had earlier broken off arriving off Kerama about 0600. Commander Freiburghouse's minesweepers were already there. Before daylight, radar picket destroyers were stationed at points around the Retto to give warning of approaching planes. Joy bombarded the beaches and such strong points of the central island as had previously been noted by photo interpreters, and the minecraft joined their fellows from Leyte in scheduled sweeps.

The UDTs, which next went into action, had a strenuous program. Team 19 from *Knudson* (Lieutenant G. T. Marion USNR) reconnoitered Kuba, Aka, Geruma and Hokaji; Team 12 from *Bates* (Lieutenant Commander E. S. Hochuli USNR) took care of the Yakabi, Zamami and Amuro beaches; while Team 13 from *Barr* (Lieutenant Commander V. J. Moranz USNR) concentrated on Tokashiki. Following standard doctrine, each team proceeded to a point about 500 yards off its assigned beach in an LCVP. The landing craft then turned parallel to the reef, casting off a swimmer about

---

[19] Almost this entire section had been with the late Rear Admiral Moon in the invasion of France.

every 50 yards. Each man, clad only in trunks, goggles and rubber feet, was festooned with the gear of his trade. He carried a reel of marked line knotted every 25 yards, the bitter end of which he secured to the edge of the reef. He then turned toward the beach, uncoiling the line as he swam, halting every time he felt a knot to take soundings with a small lead line; or, if the depth were one fathom or less, with his own body which was conveniently painted with black rings at 12-inch intervals. The swimmer recorded his soundings with a stylus on a sheet of sandpapered plexiglass wrapped around his left forearm. After an hour or more of reconnaissance, depending on the width of the reef, each swimmer was picked up by his LCVP, which in the meantime had been planting little colored buoys on dangerous coral heads. The method of recovering swimmers was simple and effective. A sailor held out a stiff rope to the swimmer, who grasped the "monkey's fist" at the rope's end, while the boat was making three or four knots, and was hauled on board. Landing craft then returned to their APDs where the swimmers' data were correlated and entered on a chart. All this went on under gunfire support from destroyers and gunboats, and "really beautiful air support," as Commander Draper L. Kauffman USNR described it, from escort carrier planes. This kept the enemy so busy ashore that he never even fired on the underwater demolition teams.[20]

One could follow these "frogmen," as they were nicknamed, from the ships; and as they calmly waded about the beach they looked (as Admiral Deyo observed) more ursine than ranine — like shaggy Kodiak bears fishing for salmon in an Alaskan river.

The teams that took care of Kuba and Yakabi Shima ascertained that the beaches in these two outer islands were impracticable for landing craft, and could only be approached by amphtracs. After this had been reported to Admiral Kiland and General Bruce on board *Mount McKinley* at 1625 March 25, they decided, since there were not enough LVTs for all six beaches, to postpone these

---

[20] Conversation with Cdr. D. L. Kauffman USNR 12 Apr. 1945; UDT plan; Com UDTs Pacific (Capt. B. Hall Hanlon) Action Report 4 Apr. 1945.

two landings and take only Zamami Jima, Aka Shima, Geruma (also called Keruma) Shima and Hokaji (also called Fukashi) Jima on the 26th.

In the meantime the transports had made their last right turn and were approaching from the westward, with rising Altair as guide. It was a beautiful night under a moon only two days short of full, and few clouds in the sky. The sea was calm, ruffled only by light southerly airs; the temperature was 61° F. At 0430 March 26 the transports hove-to in their assigned area about six miles west of Kuba Shima, the southwestern island of the group. Soon after, Admiral Joy's fire support unit (cruisers *San Francisco* and *Minneapolis* augmented by battleship *Arkansas*) resumed bombardment of beaches and installations. The tractor flotilla divided into two groups, the smaller, of four LSTs, steaming into a designated area two miles north of Yakabi, and the larger, of 14 LST and LSM, to an area about two miles SSW of Kuba. When the sun rose at 0640 over a bank of mist that obscured Okinawa, thirty miles distant, troop-laden amphtracs from the southern group were already on their way in, and those of the northern group were boiling out of their LSTs.

Owing to the position of these islands each landing group had to make a "dog leg" approach. These are very apt to go wrong, but none did here. The northern group made a 45-degree turn to pass through the narrow channel between Zamami and two small, reef-ringed islets, then turned 90 degrees left for the half-mile run to Beach Violet in front of Zamami village. The southern group divided into three units. Two steamed in company for six and three-quarters miles on a straight course, then split and landed on Geruma (Beach Yellow) and Hokaji (Beach Blue). The third, steaming parallel to the others about a mile northward, had another half mile to go before hitting Beach Gold on Aka Shima. Excellent bomb, rocket and strafing support was rendered by planes from the escort carriers, directed by CASCU (Commander Air Support Control Unit) in *Mount McKinley*. All landings but one were effected on schedule, between 0800 and 0900, without the loss of a man or an

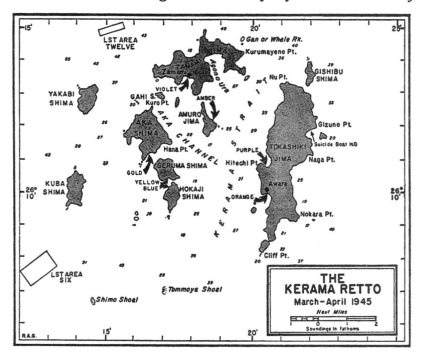

amphtrac; the Hokaji landing, delayed by congestion of landing craft, was made at 0921.

This neat though complicated landing took the Japanese completely by surprise; they had never imagined that the Kerama would interest us. The few hundred soldiers remaining there herded the natives into caves and tunnels and prepared to die fighting. On Zamami Jima the Japanese retired to the hills, leaving the invading troops to establish a beachhead almost unopposed. Two counterattacks were made during the following night, netting 106 Japanese dead. Resistance thereafter was individual and sporadic. The story at Aka Shima was similar. Five unoccupied pillboxes were found on the beach at Geruma, but there was no organized resistance. Twelve native women and a few children were found strangled in a cave by their own menfolk, who had been convinced by the Japanese that "fate worse than death" awaited them from the supposedly brutal and licentious Yanks. When the murderers, who were taken prisoner, found out what American troops were like, they begged their guards to allow them to "take it out" on the few Japanese prisoners. Civilians and Korean laborers generally surrendered easily, but most of the Japanese hid out in the hills.

All principal islands of the group except Kuba and Tokashiki were under American military control by the afternoon of 26 March. Net laying began at once and the first guide mooring buoys were set out before the close of that day.

Air opposition began at 1815 March 26, when nine kamikazes attempted unsuccessfully to crash ships of the Western Islands Attack Group and covering forces. At 0625 next morning two Vals attacked. *Gilmer's* galley deckhouse was hit by one that went over the side; she lost one man killed and three wounded. Destroyer *Kimberly*, on radar picket station about 20 miles southwest of Kuba Shima, was also attacked about the same time by two Vals of ancient vintage, one of which had a versatile pilot. He approached through the destroyer's full broadside, slipping, skidding, slow-rolling, zooming and weaving, until astern at 150 feet altitude. *Kimberly* maneuvered briskly, but Val stayed inside her wake and crashed a 40-mm mount, killing four men and wounding 57. The destroyer was not badly enough damaged to be taken off patrol until Kerama Retto was secured.

The only military use being made by the Japanese of Kerama Retto was to base Sea Raiding Units of "suicide boats," as we called them. Over 2300 troops had been brought in to set up and operate this base, but by 25 March their principal job had been completed and over half of them had pulled out. The rest were divided between Tokashiki, Zamami, Aka and Geruma. Immediately after our landings a careful search was made for the "suicide boats," and over 250 were discovered, mostly well hidden in camouflaged hangars and caves. They were only 18 feet long, each operated by one man, but carried two 250-pound depth-charges. On the night of 28 March net tender *Terebinth*, anchored 1000 yards off Hokaji, was surprised by one whose pilot seems to have had no stomach for

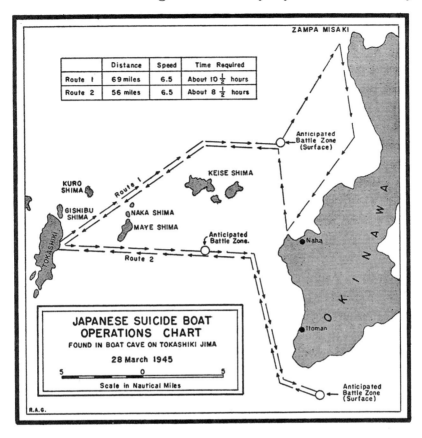

	Distance	Speed	Time Required
Route 1	69 miles	6.5	About $10\frac{1}{2}$ hours
Route 2	56 miles	6.5	About $8\frac{1}{2}$ hours

JAPANESE SUICIDE BOAT
OPERATIONS CHART
FOUND IN BOAT CAVE ON TOKASHIKI JIMA

28 March 1945

Scale in Nautical Miles

glory, as he dropped his depth charge 40 to 60 feet away and did no damage. That night three boats when attempting to retire from Tokashiki to Maye Shima were destroyed by patrolling LCIs; next morning *LSM(R)-189* destroyed three which attacked her. A talkative Japanese boat battalion commander who was taken prisoner told how they were to be employed in night attacks on the expeditionary force and produced the chart to guide them, which we have reproduced.

On 27 March the rest of Kerama Retto was secured. LCVPs from large transports, using channels through reefs blasted by UDTs, landed troops on Kuba Shima. No enemy being present, this island as well as Yakabi was soon evacuated. From Zamami as a base, a battalion landing team of the 77th Division, lifted across a bight of the roadstead to Beach Amber on Amuro Jima, secured that island. Two BLTs were staged via Geruma across Kerama Strait to Beaches Purple and Orange on the biggest island, Tokashiki Jima, which closed the roadstead on its eastern side. A shore battery there opened up on an LCI gunboat and killed one man — the only naval casualty in the Kerama landings. One company of Japanese put up a brief fight behind the beach, but resistance ended there. Since the Army made no attempt to control the whole of Tokashiki, about 300 Japanese troops remained in the hills until the end of the war. It was then discovered that they had at least one good coast defense gun on the western shore, literally looking down the throats of American ships anchored less than a mile away. Apparently awed by our show of overwhelming strength they lay doggo from 27 March to 23 August, when they surrendered. By late afternoon 28 March the entire group of eight islands was secured at the cost to 77th Division of 31 killed and 81 wounded; to the Navy, 124 killed or missing, 230 wounded. About 530 Japanese had been killed and 121 taken prisoner. Two battalions of the 77th were ashore on Zamami Jima and their supplies were 70 per cent unloaded; three battalions had been landed on Tokashiki, where two pontoon causeways were being set up on one of the beaches. The floating seaplane base had arrived.

Two 15-plane squadrons of Navy Mariners flew in next day, 29 March; they set up antisubmarine patrol near the island and began flying searches several hundred miles out.[21] Seven seaplane tenders under Captain G. A. McLean in *Hamlin* were anchored in Aka Channel, where they were soon joined by a fleet of auxiliaries. Fueling of combat ships had begun from two station oilers which refilled from a fleet tanker. Ammunition replenishment from specially equipped LSTs was about to begin; a boat pool was established and functioning. Japanese charts of the anchorage

[21] Michael G. Kammen *Operational History of the Flying Boat . . . World War II* (BuAer, 1959) p. 46.

were checked by survey ship *Bowditch*, and a new chart of the group, printed on board, was ready by 6 April.[22] Buoying of ship lanes was completed 28 March. Nets for the two entrances to Kerama Kaikyo, the principal roadstead, were then almost completed, and several of the little beaked net craft of the "tree" class (*Terebinth, Corkwood*, and the like) took up the boring but necessary task of net tending. All this, three days before Okinawa L-day. On 31 March when the writer entered Kerama Kaikyo on board *Tennessee*, the roadstead already had the appearance of a long-established base, and 35 vessels were anchored there.

Thus, the main objects of the Kerama operation were secured — the establishment of an advance logistics base and of a seaplane base for search and patrol. It also became home port for the mine-craft and their tender *Mona Island*. A landing craft base and boat pool was established in Agono Ura, the eastern harbor of Zamami Jima. Tractors dragged equipment up the steep mountain paths of Tokashiki Jima to place antiaircraft batteries and search radars on the summit, in order to intercept enemy planes attempting to sneak in over the mountains. As early as 27 March, Admiral Kiland was "serving customers" of the fire support groups with oil and ammunition. Replenishment from his LSTs and LCTs with Hanson crawler cranes on deck proved to be much more expeditious than from the regular ammunition ships.[23] So popular was his "store" that on 2 April he asked Admiral Turner for pontoon units and ten more LCMs, and got them.

Kerama Retto also served as base for the occupation of Keise Shima, one of two island groups that lay between it and Okinawa.[24] Keise Shima consisted of four low, sandy islets, the largest only 900 yards long, between six and eight miles off the southernmost coast of Okinawa. As they commanded the town of Naha and vicinity,

[22] H. O. Field Chart No. 2055, "Japan-Nansei Islands Okinawa Group-Kerama Retto and Passages."
[23] Rear Adm. Kiland Action Report Sec. VII.
[24] The other group, Maye and Naka Shima, when reconnoitered, was found to contain neither Japanese nor installations.

where the enemy had numerous strong points, they were wanted as emplacements for XXIV Corps 155-mm artillery to support the advance of ground troops on the big island.[25] The Japanese command made no attempt to defend them. A careful UDT reconnaissance, on 27–28 March, found good beaches but drew sniper fire. On the 30th, after all approaches and surrounding waters had been minswept, units of Captain Webb's tractor flotilla moved out from Kerama Strait to a position south of Keise and landed unopposed next morning on three of the four islets. The divisional artillery, promptly emplaced, was sited and ready for 1 April (L-day).

On 30 March the Western Islands Transport Group reëmbarked the 77th Division, excepting one battalion which was retained for the defense of Zamami Jima. The transports, under the command of Commodore Brittain, departed on the afternoon of 2 April and before nightfall were subjected to a heavy air attack.

Kerama roadstead became increasingly crowded with repair, service and ammunition ships, escort carriers fueling or bringing up replenishment planes, battleships, cruisers, destroyers and destroyer escorts taking on fuel, mail and ammunition; PBMs taking off and landing; mine and patrol craft enjoying a brief rest from their incessant labors; cripples from kamikaze attacks. The roadstead was not altogether free from air attack, but in general the kamikazes overlooked the plethora of profitable targets there. An occasional Japanese sniper troubled the troops ashore, and on the night of 1–2 April two bold fellows swam out to *LST-884*, anchored close to Zamami, climbed up the cargo net that she had carelessly left trailing, shot the deck sentry, and got away. Another climbed on board a damaged destroyer through the hole in her bow.

The natives soon lost their fear of Americans and went calmly about their simple occupations.

Between 28 March and 8 April, seven fleet tankers carrying 515,-000 barrels of fuel oil and 121,000 barrels of diesel oil arrived at Kerama and the three station tankers issued 425,000 barrels of the

---

[25] Compare taking Wakde Is. in the New Guinea campaign (Vol. VIII 91) and Ukiangong Pt., Makin (Vol. VII 123).

black and 82,000 barrels of the diesel, together with large quantities of lube oil and avgas, to 277 ships — an average of 23 per diem.[26]

Ships generally entered Kerama roadstead from the north, passing the isolated O Gan or Whale Rock, which shows a man's profile on one side and a woman's on the other. Inside the roadstead, despite frequent air alerts, one had a feeling of security, like having a roof over your head in an air raid. As Rear Admiral Allan Smith wrote, Kerama "gave a firmness to the Okinawa tactical situation that was felt by all. We were there to stay, with a place to tow damaged ships, look after survivors, replenish and refuel, drop an anchor." [27]

Aye, drop an anchor! For that boon alone, sailors blessed Kelly Turner, whose bright thought made it possible.

Although several days elapsed before the enemy made any serious effort to attack this concentration in the Kerama, he understood very well its significance. The aged Admiral Ito, in a Tokyo periodical of 1 April, said that America had stretched her supply line as far as she dared; and, with reference to an athletic event in which the Japanese have long held the record, the Admiral guessed that the United States was endeavoring to reach Japan by a hop to Kerama, skip to Okinawa, and jump to Kyushu. "In the Ryukyus we can best break the enemy's leg," the Admiral concluded. "He cannot continue his hop, skip and jump operations." [28]

[26] Memorandum from 'Phib Group 7 Logistics Officer to Rear Adm. Kiland, 8 Apr. 1945. See Chap. X for Okinawa logistics in general.

[27] Comcrudiv 5 (Rear Adm. A. E. Smith) Action Report on Okinawa 26 May 1945 p. viii–10.

[28] Broadcast by Radio Tokyo 2 April, translated by O.S.S. Honolulu. Admiral Ito also made the interesting remark that Kerama Retto was our substitute for Amami O Shima, which in the naval disarmament negotiations of 1921 we tried to persuade Japan not to fortify. In Article IX of the Treaty of Washington of 6 Feb. 1922, Japan agreed that the Kuriles, Bonins, Amami O Shima, "Loochoo," Formosa and the Pescadores should remain *in statu quo*, with no increase of naval facilities or coast defenses, and the United States made a similar agreement with respect to the Philippines, Guam and Wake.

CHAPTER VIII

More Preliminaries[1]

25–31 March

1. The Fire Support Group

REAR ADMIRAL Morton L. Deyo, gray-haired with bushy black eyebrows, a wiry, taut officer nearing his fifty-eighth birthday, commanded the largest gunfire and covering force (TF 54)[2] that had yet been assembled for a Pacific operation. It did not include any of the newer battleships, which as usual were attached to Task Force 58, and would have nothing bigger than a plane to shoot at for the next two months. Not that TF 54 was weak. It included that consistent slugger *Tennessee* (14-inch main battery) as flagship, three 16-inchers of the *Maryland* class, two of the 14-inch *New Mexico* class, 14-inch *Nevada*, the elderly 14-inch *New York* and *Texas*, and that thirty-three-year-old patriarch of the battle-wagons, 12-inch *Arkansas*. In addition, TF 54 had seven heavy cruisers, three light cruisers, 24 destroyers and eight destroyer escorts. The Advance Support Craft, a separate group under Blandy,

[1] CTF 52 (Rear Adm. Blandy) Action Report 1 May 1945; CTF 54 (Rear Adm. Deyo) Action Report 5 May; CTG 54.1 (Rear Adm. Rodgers) "Report of Gunfire Support Group 3, Fire Support Unit 3 and Crudiv 13 in Phases I and II of Okinawa Campaign, 21 Mar.–30 Apr. 1945" 30 Apr. 1945; Comcrudiv 5 (Rear Adm. Allan E. Smith) Action Report 26 May. Also the writer's personal observations and dispatches collected on board *Tennessee*, and Rear Adm. Deyo's series of personal accounts entitled "Kamikaze."

[2] Although CTF 54 was his designation and title, strictly speaking Deyo commanded TF 54 only on night retirement and in the event of a surface action. In daytime he "loaned" the fire support ships to Blandy, under whom Rear Adm. Rodgers became Com Fire Support Group. Deyo did not command gunfire on land objectives. This curious command arrangement was originally made by Admiral Turner because Oldendorf, the original CTF 54, was a Vice Admiral, and it was kept because Deyo was senior to Blandy.

included 53 LCI and LSM, mostly rocket and mortar ships. For fire support purposes this force was divided into six units.[3]

Plans for the pre-landing bombardment were largely prepared by the staff of Rear Admiral Blandy, the top commander in Okinawan waters until Admiral Turner arrived on L-day. One could not expect to destroy all possible targets on so big an island before the troops landed.

Photographic interpretation showed few defensive installations immediately behind the landing beaches. Consequently the ships were enjoined to seek out profitable targets through the eyes of their aircraft spotters, and to fire from the closest possible ranges.

During the midwatch on Monday, 26 March, the principal units of Admiral Deyo's Fire Support Force (as we shall call TF 54) began steaming at 10 knots in four close columns through the ten-mile-wide channel between Tonaki and the Kerama Retto, which Admiral Sharp's minecraft had already swept and marked with radar-reflecting buoys. The moon, two days short of full, was setting over the port quarter, casting a golden sheen on the calm waters and a bright glow on the edges of the few clouds. There was a coolness in the air that contrasted pleasantly with the steaming tropics left behind. The dark profiles of Kuba, Yakabi and Zamami were plainly visible, and a grass fire was burning on one of them. With the familiar triangle of Vega, Altair and Deneb to steer for, there was nothing to suggest that one was in the East China Sea save for a "distant and random gun that the foe was sullenly firing," somewhere in the Kerama Retto. Encouraging reports of progress in Kerama came over radio, but veterans of the Pacific War knew very well that the enemy never showed his hand at the start of an operation.

At dawn the ships deployed for their several bombardment missions. Helped by air spot, the battleships and cruisers attempted at long range (since they dared not close unswept waters) to knock out known targets furnished by photographic interpreters. There was no reply from the shore, except antiaircraft fire that damaged

[3] See Appendix I for details.

one of *Portland's* planes. Submarines, however, were lying in wait. *Wichita* reported a torpedo wake at 0940 passing her ahead, and a second passing ahead of *St. Louis.* Both cruisers and *Biloxi* sighted others within the next hour. Since these fire support ships were just loafing along, the enemy missed a very good chance to make a kill.

2. *Air Support, Naval Bombardment and UDTs*

The air aspects of this preliminary bombardment and other operations prior to L-day must be kept in mind. We have already mentioned the seaplane searches from Kerama Retto.

No land-based aircraft were available. Air support came mainly from the fast carrier groups (TF 58) which had already struck Okinawa on 23, 24 and 25 March, and from Rear Admiral Durgin's escort carrier group (TG 52.1), most of which arrived in the area on 25–26 March. These comprised five units of 18 CVEs under Rear Admirals C.A.F. Sprague, Felix Stump and W. D. Sample, all heroes of the Battle off Samar.[4] Planes from both fast and escort carriers performed the following services in this phase of the operation: daily strikes on Okinawan targets, C.A.P. over the amphibious forces, spotting for naval gunfire (in conjunction with the battleships' and cruisers' own float planes), photographic missions, and antisubmarine patrol.

All air operations during this phase were supposed to be controlled as well as coördinated by CASCU (Commander Air Support Control Unit) of the Amphibious Support Force, Captain Elton Parker in flagship *Estes.* The same amphibious command ship was the center for photographic interpretation and distribution by a special naval intelligence unit. On L-day – when Admiral Blandy relinquished the over-all naval command to Admiral Turner – Captain Whitehead, CASCU on board TF 51 flagship *Eldorado,* re-

---

[4] See Vol. XII for their brief biographies and exploits, and Appendix I, this volume, for details of TG 52.1.

lieved Captain Parker. A great deal of the success of this operation depended on the training, intelligence and quick wit of CASCU.

This system of directing escort carrier planes worked splendidly. C.A.P. was not so important in this preliminary phase as it became on and after 6 April, when kamikazes came out in startling numbers. The escort carrier planes began providing C.A.P. on 26 March. They also made an excellent set of photographs for the gunfire ships, and flew the great majority of air bombing missions on Okinawa prior to L-day. Their pilots were assiduous in spying out new targets and bombing concealed defenses. The fast carrier planes flew an average of five daily strikes against Okinawa during the same period and supported the landings on 1 April. But their great service in this campaign, one for which they were blessed by every man afloat, was to furnish C.A.P. for the amphibious forces until land-based air was ready to take over. They shot down many more enemy planes than did ships' antiaircraft fire. Without their aid, losses of the expeditionary force might well have been insupportable.

All bombardment missions of 26 March were concluded at 1630 and Admiral Deyo's fire support ships retired. All went well that night, except that a snooping Betty severed one of *Porterfield's* radar antennas. But dawn came up like thunder with bogeys on the radar screen, and no C.A.P. overhead. Seven kamikazes attacked; one ignored the screen and aimed at the circle of big battleships and cruisers. Repeatedly hit by antiaircraft fire, it burst into flames directly over *Nevada*. The burning carcass crashed her main deck abreast turret No. 3, knocking out both 14-inch guns, with three 20-mm mounts besides, killing eleven men and wounding 49. Another splashed on the port beam of *Tennessee*, a third near *Biloxi*, and a fourth hit that cruiser at the waterline, making two big holes in the plating. Its 1100-pound bomb, which fortunately failed to detonate, entered one of the cruiser's flooded compartments. She had no casualties, and was soon repaired at Kerama Retto. Destroyer *O'Brien*, detached from the retirement group to provide star shell that night over Kerama Retto, was severely damaged by a kamikaze in the dawn attack. She lost 28 men killed, 22 missing and 76 wounded, and had to return to the West Coast for repairs. Destroyer minesweeper *Dorsey* was crashed on her main deck but got off with minor damage and few casualties.

Naval bombardment on invisible targets is tedious enough, and even more tiresome to read about. For several hours, morning and afternoon, the fire support ships lay-to or steamed slowly as near shore as prior minesweeping permitted. They covered areas behind the Hagushi and the southern or demonstration beaches, firing deliberately with air spot. Between four and five in the afternoon, the different units assembled at a rendezvous 10 to 15 miles off Okinawa, formed a circular cruising disposition for antiaircraft protection, and retired seaward for the night, zigzagging in the light of the moon. A destroyer or two remained to help the patrolling LCI gunboats by delivering harassing fire and throwing up star shell. Before dawn the fire support ships returned to Okinawa, near which they usually sustained a routine early-morning kamikaze attack. The one on 28 March was ineffective, raising premature hopes that the self-sacrificing boys were going sour.

Since a minefield had been spotted off the Hagushi beaches, Lieutenant Commander Estep's Unit 7, *Skylark* leading, swept inside the fire support ships on the morning of 28 March. This observant "bird" had just signaled that she had seen 15 to 20 Japanese tanks scuttle out of a wood in order to avoid shellfire, when she ran smack into a mine. There was a great explosion, blowing out fuel oil which burned on the surface with bursts of flame and black smoke. Twenty minutes later she hit a second mine and took a heavy list. Within fifteen minutes her mast was under; her stern rose at a 90-degree angle and then plunged. Yet the rescue work by *Tolman* was so efficient that *Skylark* lost only five men, all killed by the explosions.

That night, enemy planes based on the Okinawa fields made a special go at small patrol craft. A dozen or so of these planes were destroyed, but one damaged *LSM(R)–188*, killing 15 men and wounding 32. From midnight to dawn 29 March, TF 54 was almost continuously snooped by enemy aircraft, ten of which were shot down. DMS *Ellyson*, when delivering short-range bombardment in the morning, saw what appeared to be a white man waving on the beach, and passed the word to *San Francisco*, which sent an SOC to the rescue. The man was Lieutenant F. M. Fox USNR of *Yorktown*, who after crashing had spent three days hiding near Kadena airfield. The SOC, piloted by Lieutenant (jg) R. W. Gabel USNR, damaged its float in the process but taxied out to *Ellyson* and delivered the rescued pilot.

On the same day the UDTs reconnoitered the Hagushi beaches, where the attack force proposed to land, and also those where they would pretend to land. The same technique was employed as at Kerama Retto. There was no enemy reaction except a little mortar and sniper fire. The swimmers reported that the reef was suitable for amphtracs, but only in a few places would there be enough water over it at high tide to float landing craft. The only artificial obstacles were about 2900 wooden posts driven into the coral.

From 29 March (L-day minus 3) battleships and cruisers delivered precision fire on the Okinawa airfields and other targets, the sweepers having enabled them to close the range. Special efforts were made by the escort carrier planes to interdict the Yontan and Kadena fields to the enemy by "intruder" missions. They caught a number of aircraft lining up to take off; and next morning there were no dawn attacks on the ships.

During the midwatch of 30 March, *Irwin, Hall, Tolman* and *LSM(R)-190*, on patrol off Okinawa, engaged two or three groups of Japanese motor torpedo boats which approached from the north. There was no damage to our ships, and at least one enemy boat was sunk.

Good Friday, 30 March, fifth day of bombardment, opened overcast and warm with a light southerly wind which later developed into a brisk breeze. This was the time for the UDTs to "blow the beaches," as they called the explosion of obstacles. From 1000 until noon the "frogmen" calmly worked along the wooden anti-boat stakes on the reef off Beaches Purple and Orange. Battleship sailors could see them placing their charges and being picked up on the run by LCVPs, while projectiles of the covering vessels screamed over their heads and exploded on the beach. The enemy did not reply with so much as a rifle shot.

So far as anyone could see, the entire island was depopulated. Not one human being was visible to ships, boats or even planes. The neatly tilled fields were completely deserted, even by cattle, and nobody moved abroad in the villages. If any military installations were there, they were deserted or effectively camouflaged. If the Japanese had been Christians, one might have assumed that they were all at church. As it was, everyone had the uncomfortable feeling that they were about to spring a very nasty surprise. Intelligence assured us that at least 60,000 troops were somewhere on the island, and actually there were many more. What were they up to, and where the hell were they?

Ie Shima, the little island with the big airfield off the dog's ear, was also reported by reconnaissance planes to be completely deserted, and a Japanese officer rescued from a sunk motor torpedo boat supported the delusion by insisting that it had been evacuated. Aircraft photos indicated that the airfield had been cratered, trenched and blasted to render it useless. No human being was visible, and no gun opened fire on our hedge-hopping planes. Two weeks later, the 77th Division had to kill about 3000 Japanese to secure Ie Shima.

When photo interpretation revealed a midget submarine nest in Unten Ko, a reef-fringed harbor on the east coast of the Motobu Peninsula (the Okinawa pup's upraised ear), escort carrier planes on 30 March bombed four of the pens and destroyed two loaded motor torpedo boats, expending two aircraft in the process. This attack wiped out the midgets; no more trouble from that source; but several Japanese fleet submarines were prowling about Okinawa. An hour before midnight 30 March, a night patrol plane sighted by moonlight a full-sized submarine on the surface about

30 miles southeast of Okinawa. Destroyer *Morrison* was ordered thither to conduct hunter-killer operations with the plane. *Stockton*, in the vicinity escorting an oiler to Kerama Retto, peeled off for this more congenial task. A coördinated depth-charge attack, at 0210 March 31, forced *I–8* to the surface, where the two destroyers opened fire and quickly sank it. They had the satisfaction of recovering one survivor.[5]

Despite the cumulative evidence of the enemy's having retired from the shoreline, reconnaissance pilots and officers who accompanied the UDTs ashore expected the landing to be resisted. The Hagushi beaches were bisected by the Bisha River, which was full of Japanese landing craft and motor torpedo boats, most of which (as they did not know) had been holed by our bombing planes. This river flowed into the sea between two outthrusting limestone bluffs, whose faces were honeycombed with caves and tunnels from which machine guns could enfilade the landing beaches. Like the installations at Iwo Jima and on Omaha Beach, they were inaccessible to naval gunfire or aërial bombardment. A similar limestone outcrop thrust down between and commanded the southernmost beaches, and a German-type concrete pillbox with stepped embrasures appeared ready to perform the same service for Beaches Yellow to the north of the river. Behind every beach was a thick six- to ten-foot-high sea wall of masonry and concrete, which had been very slightly breached by naval gunfire. Both airfields were dominated by tunneled and fortified hills. Only a few of these defenses, mainly new concrete emplacements, had been demolished by naval gunfire. It looked as if landing on the Hagushi beaches would be as bloody an affair as Tarawa, and that the three days allowed in the operation plan would be too little time for capturing Yontan and Kadena fields.

How wrong everyone was! What we thought to be difficult proved to be easy, and after the easy part was over the tough fighting began.

---

[5] Rear Adm. Blandy Action Report; the survivor's account is translated in M. Hashimoto *Sunk* (1954), p. 207.

3. L-day minus One, 31 March

At 0707 March 31 as Fire Support Unit 5 was proceeding to its station, four planes attacked. C.A.P. splashed two and *New Mexico* one; the third crashed Admiral Spruance's flagship, *Indianapolis*. The plane's wing struck an object on the port bulwark, twisting it so that it went overboard, but the bomb crashed through several decks and two messing and berthing compartments, killed nine men and wounded 20, and exploded in an oil bunker, damaging No. 4 shaft. *Indianapolis* could still steam at reduced speed and most of her guns could shoot; but the carelessness of a repair crew at Kerama Retto gave her damaged shaft the "deep six," and she had to go to Mare Island for major repairs. She was the first heavy ship in this operation to be knocked out by a kamikaze and, as we shall see, the last to be sunk in the war. Admiral Spruance transferred his flag to *New Mexico*.

All that day bombardment of the beaches continued at enhanced pace, with special attention to knocking breaches in the sea wall that ran behind them. Not many were made, and few in places whence vehicles could sortie. At 0830 the UDTs, covered by close gunfire from LCI and larger vessels, completed blowing the beaches.

XXIV Corps artillery now commenced landing on Keise Shima. By sundown half the artillery and rolling stock, and an antiaircraft battery, were ashore and ready to support troop landings.

During this Holy Week that preceded the landings, an enormous amount of ammunition was expended.[6] There was no want of bullets; only targets were wanting, and much ammunition was wasted on cratering the fields of the Okinawa peasantry. The bombardment was completely one-sided, since the Japanese shore and mobile batteries took care not to disclose their positions by firing. Planes and gunfire between them wrecked most of the enemy aircraft on the island, which was all to the good. Apart from this, the principal re-

[6] In rounds, 1033 16-inch, 3285 14-inch, 567 12-inch, 3750 8-inch, 4511 6-inch and 27,266 5-inch.

sults achieved by air bombing and naval bombardment were the destruction of villages and isolated farmhouses that had no strategic value.[7] The operation would probably have proceeded very much as it did from L-day on if there had been no preliminary naval bombardment whatsoever. Yet a bombardment there had to be, if only to cover the demolition teams, breach the sea wall and destroy beach obstacles.

General Ushijima had left only token forces behind the Hagushi beaches and on the two airfields. He concentrated east and south of Naha, and on the Motobu Peninsula. In view of the overwhelming strength that United States forces had displayed in earlier amphibious landings, this was his best bet for prolonging the defense and inflicting maximum casualties. But these tactics were unsuspected by Admiral Blandy's force on 31 March. It seemed inconceivable that the enemy would abandon two airfields without a fight. For aught we knew, the Japanese were holed up on and behind the beaches, ready to give the boys hell when they stepped ashore. Task Force 54 took no chances and prepared to afford Admiral Turner's amphibious force, when it landed next day, the most impressive gunfire support that any assault troops had ever had.

[7] The writer's personal observations behind the Hagushi beaches on 9 and 13 April.

CHAPTER IX

The Landings[1]
1 April 1945

Almanac for 1 April, Okinawa

Sunrise	0621
Sunset	1845

Moon rose (full 28 March) 2147

High water at 0900 (5.9 ft.) and 2140 (5.5 ft.)

Low water at 0246 (1.4 ft.) and 1508 (0.7 ft.)

1. *Organization of One Attack Group*

PRELIMINARIES ended and Phase I of Operation ICEBERG opened at 0600 Easter Sunday 1 April, when Vice Admiral Turner assumed command over all ships, groups and forces in Okinawan waters.[2] Rear Admiral Deyo retained command of the fire support ships to cover the main and demonstration landings and southern Okinawa.

It will be easier to comprehend the mechanics of this vast operation if we concentrate on a single transport group. Commodore Melton O. Carlson's Transport Group "Dog" formed half of Southern Attack Force commanded by Rear Admiral John L. Hall. This group, which had the duty of landing the 7th Infantry Division

---

[1] CTF 51 (Vice Adm. Turner), CTF 54 (Rear Adm. Deyo), CTF 53 (Rear Adm. Reifsnider), CTF 55 (Rear Adm. J. L. Hall), and CTG 55.1 (Commo. M. O. Carlson) Action Reports; the writer's personal observations in *Tennessee*.

[2] The Amphibious Support Force (TF 52) was now dissolved, and Rear Adm. Blandy as CTG 51.19 assumed command of Eastern Fire Support Group, with the job of coördinating fire and air support for the demonstration landing and other operations on the east coast of Okinawa, for which see Chap. XIV Sec. 2.

(Major General A. V. Arnold USA) on Beaches Purple and Orange, comprised four transport divisions and two tractor groups, with a total of 16 APA, 7 AKA, 1 LSD, 1 LSV, 30 LST and 22 LSM.[3] Multiply these numbers by four, and you will have a fair idea of the magnitude of the entire amphibious landing on the Hagushi beaches.

Group "Dog" began loading at Leyte 3 March, embarked troops on the 12th and 13th, rehearsed during the following week, topped off with fuel and provisions during the next few days, sailed in slow, intermediate and fast echelons between 25 and 27 March, and arrived off the Okinawa beaches during the early morning hours of 1 April. This was an unusually short troop lift for a Pacific amphibious operation. The 7th Division, old hands at amphibious work, had made a careful study of the initial landing. Besides the 23 combat-loaded transports and cargo ships and LSD *Epping Forest* and LSV *Ozark*,[4] Transport Group "Dog" included 30 LST. These handymen of the Navy were used in much greater numbers in Operation ICEBERG than in any previous Pacific operation. More had become available after the howls of the Atlantic Fleet and of our British allies for more and more LSTs had died in the Hitlerian twilight. Besides their primary employment for lifting tanks and amphtracs, LSTs had proved capable of discharging assault cargo much more rapidly than the big transports, and without transfer to landing craft. They could be used for general or specialized cargo, or specially equipped as hospital ships, and their young reserve officers were keen, intelligent and trained to cope with special demands and emergencies.

The landings followed the pattern which had been worked out during amphibious operations in the Central Pacific, from Guadalcanal through the Marianas. The landing diagram for Saipan, now standard amphibious doctrine for the Pacific Fleet, was adopted for Okinawa with only such changes as the different topography required.

[3] For names and other details see Appendix I below.
[4] A converted minelayer.

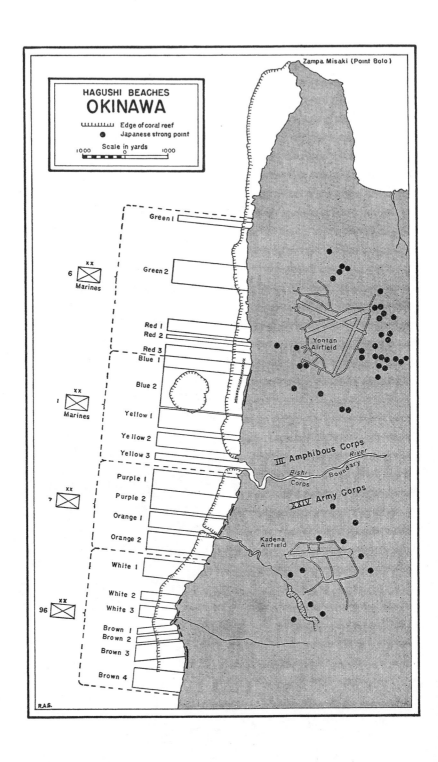

HAGUSHI BEACHES
OKINAWA

⊔⊔⊔⊔⊔⊔ Edge of coral reef
● Japanese strong point

Scale in yards
1000 0 1000

Zampa Misaki (Point Bolo)

Green 1

6 ⊠ Marines

Green 2

Red 1
Red 2
Red 3
Blue 1

Yontan Airfield

1 ⊠ Marines

Blue 2

Yellow 1

Yellow 2

Yellow 3

Ⅲ Amphibous Corps
River
Bishi Boundary
Corps

7 ⊠

Purple 1

Purple 2

Orange 1

XXIV Army Corps

Orange 2

Kadena Airfield

96 ⊠

White 1

White 2

White 3

Brown 1
Brown 2

Brown 3

Brown 4

R.A.S.

Experience had proved that a ship-to-shore movement involving several hundred landing craft of many different types required a well-trained control group as traffic policemen to oversee the forming, dispatch and movement of boat waves. Under Captain B. B. Adell, Commander Southern Attack Force Control Group in *PCE–877*, Lieutenant Commander J. M. Dundon USNR in *PCS–1452* acted as squadron control officer for our Group "Dog." He had two assistants, Control Purple in *PC–463* and Control Orange in *PC–469;* four division control officers in SC or PC; two LCC carrying the beachmaster of Transdiv 7 for the Orange, and of Transdiv 38 for the Purple beaches; four boat group commanders in landing craft, one for each beach; and four to eight wave guides in LCVPs for each boat wave.

The big transports caught up with the tractor and PC groups around midnight 31 March, and in the early hours of 1 April reached their respective unloading areas in the exact order of their stations. The APA and AKA hove-to in Transport Area Dog, with a front of 3000 yards and a depth of 7000 yards, about seven and a half miles from Beaches Purple and Orange. Twenty-three LST and 13 LSM proceeded to LST Area 2, which lay about three miles from the beach, while nine LSM, six specialist LST (supply, water, ammunition and gas, maintenance, hospital) and LSD *Epping Forest* with boated tanks, dropped off at the rear and occupied LST Area 5, a little further to seaward of the control vessels. *PCE–877* closed Admiral Hall's flagship *Teton* to pick up Captain Adell, who had concluded last-minute arrangements with the Admiral's staff, and then proceeded to a point midway between the 7th and 96th Division beaches. She flew the Zero ("five of clubs") flag.[5] Lieutenant Commander Dundon's *PCS–1452*, top control vessel for Group "Dog," flying a purple and orange banner to mark the boundary between the divisional beaches, took station broadside to

[5] *PCS–1402* closed Adm. Turner's flagship *Eldorado* to stand by for the use of Gen. Buckner and staff during the day; *PCS–1421* performed the same service for General Hodge, Commanding General XXIV Corps, alongside *Teton*, while *PCS–1402* and *PCS–1455* acted as tenders for the commanding generals of the 7th and 96th Divisions who were in transports *Harris* and *Mendocino* respectively.

Captain Adell's *PCE–877*, and slightly seaward of the Line of Departure. That line, about 4000 yards from the beaches, had been established by the five other control vessels, each displaying a banner corresponding to the colors of the beach she controlled. Thus, the Purple and Orange Beach Line of Departure was marked by five control craft, on station and anchored by 0700, an hour and a half before H-hour, as follows: —

SC–1060 Lieutenant (jg) J. B. Sneddon USNR: Purple banner with one stripe, marking northern edge of boat lane to Beach Purple 1.

PC–463 Lieutenant E. E. Boelhauf: Solid purple banner between the two beaches of that color.

SC–1049 Lieutenant W. B. Carter USNR: Orange banner with one black vertical stripe, marking northern edge of boat lane to Beach Orange 1.

PC–469 Lieutenant D. D. Baker: Solid orange banner, marking boundary between the boat lanes to Beaches Orange 1 and 2.

SC–1312 Lieutenant F. G. Carpenter USNR: Orange banner with two vertical black stripes, marking southern edge of lane to Beach Orange 2.

This color scheme was carried out consistently. Every wave's guide boat flew a pennant of similar color and design and every landing craft of the initial waves had the color of the beach for which she was destined painted on her topsides. First wave ashore set up corresponding beach markers about ten feet high, brightly painted on canvas. Each landing craft could recognize at a glance the place where she should cross the line of departure, and for what beach she should steer. The colors and flags also made it easy for beach parties and troops ashore to recognize their own boats. Captain Adell had under him two LCC (fast motor boats equipped with radio and radar) which, flying purple and orange pennants, preceded the boat waves to positions shoreward of Line of Departure, where they acted as floating fairway buoys.

At 0629 *Epping Forest*, a number of LSM, and 15 LST began discharging amphtracs and landing craft, flying the appropriate beach flag at the dip during the process and hoisting it two-blocks when completed. The LSTs carrying LCTs on deck then retired to an area slightly to the southwest and shed their burdens with a loud splash. LCTs thus activated hustled out to the big transports to be in readiness for lightering cargo in the afternoon. LSTs carrying pontoon barges and causeway units dropped them off in Area 2, where the pontoon sailors hastily clipped their units together and soon were chugging off, propelled by mammoth outboard motors, to await orders.

All assault-loaded LSTs had departed Leyte in the same order that they would be wanted off Okinawa. Thus, Nos. 11 through 24, carrying the LVT(A) armored tanks, found themselves in the two front ranks nearest shore; those carrying LVT-4 personnel amphtracs in the center; specialist LSTs in the rear. The LVTs did not waste time running around in circles (that picturesque feature of earlier amphibious operations, provoking unnecessary consumption of fuel and loss of breakfasts), but, led by guide boats flying the appropriate colored pennants, filed in column to positions a few hundred yards outside Line of Departure, ready to deploy from column into line when given the word to go.

In the meantime, the big ships in Transport Area "Dog" were lowering landing craft and boating troops for the ninth and subsequent waves that followed the initial assault. Those that carried dukws, the amphibious trucks that roll supplies over the reef, launched them promptly. Dukws had their own rendezvous area behind the first three ranks of transports, where they were met by guide boats which led them to *LST-734* in Area 2. There they loaded priority supplies for the shore. Other transports with landing craft which were not used to boat troops stood by to provide assault supplies on call. General unloading was to begin only when the beaches were clear enough to receive masses of supplies.

Certain designated landing craft and LCC boated the Navy's beach parties. These went in to stand by the reef and direct the negotiation of that hurdle after the tide fell and Line of Departure became obsolete. The assault waves were landed around high water, at 0900; hence, it was anticipated that by the time supplies began coming ashore, it would be necessary to transfer them from the landing craft to dukws and LVTs, which could climb over the reef. Floating barges with cranes were provided to help this transfer. Each control PC kept two circles of cargo-bearing landing craft orbiting about 1000 yards from the beach, ready to be sent in on signal from Army shore parties when there was room for them. Thus, beach congestion, the dam of matériel that had clogged earlier amphibious landings, was prevented.

In order to land the 16th and subsequent troop waves, a simple transfer plan was provided. Retracting LVTs formed circles on each flank of the "Dog" area. Each LCVP then went alongside an LVT and transferred her men. And as all amphtracs were of the latest type, LVT–4, they could accommodate as many men as an LCVP.

In order not to overwhelm the reader with more detail, yet do justice to the magnitude and complexity of this great amphibious operation, I shall now describe the landing of the 7th Division on the Purple and Orange beaches by boats and craft of Transport Squadron "Dog."

2. A Landing on the Southern Beaches

Easter Sunday and L-day, 1 April 1945, broke slightly overcast and cool, a pleasant change for GIs who were accustomed to fighting in the steaming heat of the Philippines. Many a member of the fighting 7th Division, as he wolfed a hearty breakfast, wondered whether he would be alive to enjoy another meal. His luck could not hold out much longer; Okinawa was "it." Recent casualty reports from Iwo did nothing to cheer him, especially as the shipboard briefing had stressed the fact that Okinawa was likely to prove a bigger and tougher Iwo. As soldiers and sailors peered over the rail, straining for a look at the top-secret objective, most of the lads were too intent watching the bombardment by fire support ships to indulge in conversation; but there was a considerable amount of assertion and denial respecting the immediate future. Imperial General Headquarters would have been interested in the exact and detailed knowledge of the "next operation," such as our gun-deck strategists pretended to possess, although they would have been astonished to learn how many GIs and Seamen 2nd class claimed to share the intimate thoughts of General Buckner and Admiral Turner.

At 0406 Kelly Turner signaled "Land the Landing Force." H-hour had been set for 0830, and at 0640 Admiral Hall confirmed it for Southern Attack Force. At about that time the sun rose over heavy, low-lying clouds and gave the amphibious forces their first real look at Okinawa through gaps in the smoke left by the bombing and naval bombardment. It was a beautiful morning, and a perfect day for an amphibious operation: calm sea, just enough offshore wind to blow the smoke away and to float the varicolored banners of the control craft. The morning sun cast a peach-like glow over the water and on the multitude of ships, some painted solid gray, some with striped Atlantic Ocean camouflage. This was the sort of weather one expected on Easter Sunday but seldom experienced. But the parade that was being prepared was a strange one for Easter, and left no time in its tight schedule for church. One could only pray that this tremendous effort might guarantee an infinite series of peaceful Easter morns in the future; that, as the Resurrection had promised eternal life to men of faith, the work this Easter might help to make faithful men free.

We may now shift to the viewpoint of the principal bombardment unit for Beaches Purple and Orange, battleship *Tennessee*, in which this writer was embarked. She packed a terrific fire power with her twelve 14-inch 50's, sixteen 5-inch 38's and forty 40-mm guns. Though scheduled to bombard the beach area from a range of 5000 to 6000 yards, which would have placed her astride the Line of Departure, her skipper, Captain John B. Heffernan, insisted on closing to 1900 yards from the beach, 3250 yards from her nearest target.[6] Since 0300 she and the other fire support ships had been cautiously threading their way through the tractor groups and control vessels, which required neat ship handling.

At 0620, when she was approaching with the rest of the fire support ships, a Val dive-bomber attacked the formation. After near-missing a destroyer-transport, it was shot down by one of the ships and splashed just astern cruiser *Birmingham*, which must have been surprised to have anything miss her. Ten minutes later the sun appeared, as if a signal for the bombardment to start. *Tennessee* lay-to about half a mile shoreward from the two control boats that marked the Orange sector of the Line of Departure. Destroyer *Paul Hamilton* lay close aboard, *Birmingham* took a fire support station to the southward, off the Brown beaches, and *Idaho* lay northward. It was clear overhead, but morning mist at water level obscured both the land and the big transports. Every visible expanse of water was covered with LSTs and landing and control craft, gently rocked by a slight ground swell.

As the bombardment progresses, more and more amphtracs issue from the LSTs and begin forming up in waves under the watchful eyes of their guide boats, taking station seaward of Line of Departure. *Tennessee* at 0722 concentrates on shattering the sea wall behind the beaches. At 0735 she checks fire while carrier-based planes fly parallel to the beach, bombing and launching rockets. The sound of naval cannon is stilled, but the air is filled with the drone of airplane motors, the rolling rumble of exploding bombs, and the sharp, unmistakable impact of rocket fire, which sounds like a giant lash being well laid on along the enemy coast by an almighty hand. One hears the swish almost at the same time as sharp flashes of the missiles exploding on the ground strike the eye; then a great backlash of smoke and dust whips into the sky accompanied by a loud c-r-r-rack from exploding rockets.

In a few moments the air strike is over and the ten battleships,

---

[6] She drifted out to about 3600 yards from the beach before the bombardment was over.

nine cruisers and 23 destroyers that are disposed along the ten-mile front resume close fire support. *Tennessee* fires her 5-inch 38 broadside at the rate of 54 rounds per minute, and throws in 40-mm fire for good measure. Then the hoarse roar of her main battery provides a bass to Amphibious Symphony No. 1 by maestro Kelly Turner. The yellow cordite smoke is blown back in our faces; Admiral Deyo sniffs it appreciatively from his catwalk outside flag plot and remarks, "That has a good, offensive smell!"

At 0800 the cry goes up, "Here they come!" In the van are the LCI gunboats, twelve for our four beaches alone, moving in perfect alignment at a deliberate 3 to 4 knots in order not to outdistance the LVTs. They pass around the battleships, and when about 1000 yards nearer the shore open fire with their 3-inch guns, crackling like old-time musketry. In the meantime the first wave of landing craft, the armored LVT(A), has swept around the battleship's bow and stern, reforming on her landward side directly under her guns, which are shooting 14-inch, 5-inch and 40-mm projectiles over the men's heads. The 40-mm bullets go out in clusters of white-hot balls which look as if they would fall among the boats, but their flat trajectory carries them clear to the beach.

In ten minutes' time three boat waves, one of LVT(A) and two of the ramped, troop-carrying LVT-4, each flanked by flag-flying guide boats, have passed the battleship. Each craft leaves a wake of white water which subsides into a smooth slick, and the slicks run parallel as railroad tracks. The alignment of the landing craft, while not exactly that of soldiers on parade, resembles that of a cavalry charge, each amphtrac having a personality like a horse. The men in green coveralls and camouflaged helmets gaze curiously at the battleships' flashing guns. They seem silent and grim as troops always do when about to land, for a soldier is never so helpless as in this situation. The LCI gunboats are now much nearer the shore; their gunfire sounds like a roll of drums. Just as the fourth wave passes the battleship, the planes come in for their last pre-landing strafing and rocket fire, making a noise like a gigantic cotton sheet being ripped apart. The fifth boat wave passes, troops standing on

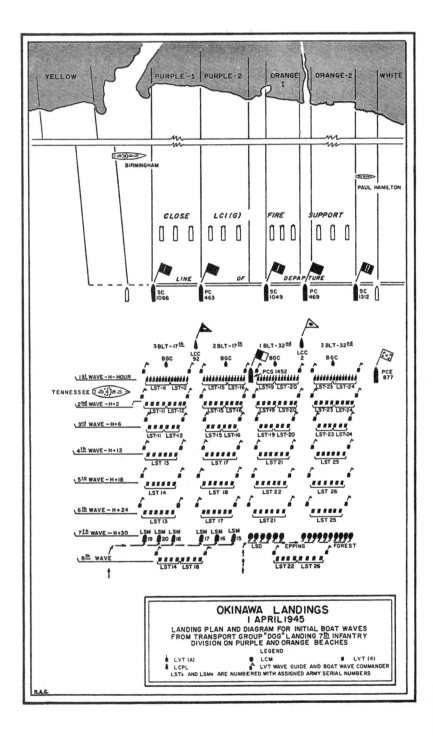

OKINAWA LANDINGS
1 APRIL 1945
LANDING PLAN AND DIAGRAM FOR INITIAL BOAT WAVES
FROM TRANSPORT GROUP "DOG" LANDING 7th INFANTRY
DIVISION ON PURPLE AND ORANGE BEACHES

the after deck to see "what goes on." And a marvelous sight it is, these waves of landing craft extending parallel to the coast as far as the eye can see, all moving with a majestic, precise deliberation that well represents the stout though anxious hearts that they embark. No finer military spectacle could be seen in the entire war.

Over the radio at 0828 word arrives that the first wave is only 75 yards from the beach. From the bridge of *Tennessee* comes the order "Cease Fire." The LCI gunboats have halted outside the reef; amphtracs of Wave 2 are already crawling over the reef to begin their last dash through the lagoon. At 0832 comes the long-expected word, "First wave has hit the beach!" Waves 2 and 3 are on the reef, 5 and 6 take off from Line of Departure; others are forming up as far as you can view to seaward.

As *Tennessee* winds ship, in order to give her starboard secondary battery a chance to shoot, the first signs of enemy opposition appear. A plume of white water rises up between her and the beach, and then another, fortunately in spots not covered by landing craft. A mortar battery on the bluffs of the Bisha River tries to get the range but never makes a hit. Boat waves are now composed of LCVP, whose troops will have to be transferred to retracting LVT in order to cross the reef. Then comes the 7th wave, one of a very different composition: 17 LCM landing craft for the Orange beaches, six of the 200-foot landing ships medium (LSM) for the Purple. These LSM, little brothers to the LST, are built more like a ship than their elders. They are camouflaged in great blobs of green, yellow and brown paint, which light up to a modernist fantasy of color when seen in echelon; yet there is something curiously medieval about them. Nearly amidships rises a tall, cylindrical pilothouse with round ports like the turret of a castle, and the numerous alidades, peloruses and other gadgets which crown the turret have the effect of battlements protecting the helmeted sailors. Could our designers have consulted the famous tapestry at Bayeux depicting another successful invasion? Can it be a coincidence that the control craft for Purple 1 is numbered 1066? As the LSM formation passes, bow gates are already open, ready to disgorge the newest variety of amphibious vehicle, known as the "Tare-6, Swimming Tank," a medium Sherman tank supported by pontoons. Nine centuries of warfare and military architecture seem to come to a focus off the beaches of Okinawa.

Calmly proceed the LSMs, as enemy mortars drop another sequence of shells. Some fall perilously near *LSM-87*, but she does not concede an inch and is not hit. About a dozen LVT(A) are firing at this mortar battery from the water with their 75-mm guns, and presently silence it forever.

Nine o'clock. The sun has burned away the mist, disclosing an almost solid mass of transports to seaward, beaches swarming with amphtracs and men, troops moving through cornfields toward the tableland, an inexhaustible supply of landing craft forming waves, boats of the earlier waves beginning to retract. Now the medieval-and-modern LSMs pass again as on parade, having shed their floating tanks, and a spotting plane radios that our troops are already several hundred yards inland. Tanks can be seen swarming up the slope, orange and purple beach markers are clearly visible, landing craft bearing bulldozers and cranes pass; one labeled PRESS in large white letters darts by, bearing delighted correspondents who are going to "see it all," complete with typewriters to tap out the story. Wind and sea have made up; no whitecaps yet but enough chop so that landing craft pitch and throw spray.

At 0956 word reaches *Tennessee* from the flagship that the Marines in the northern sector are now on the edge of Yontan airfield, and have suffered no casualties.

Never was there a more pleasant surprise. All hands are stunned by the lack of opposition. Where are those 60,000 Japanese? What is wrong with their elaborate installations? Are they sucking us into a pocket, only to open up with a fierce attack later? No one knows the answer. Officers look at each other, smile and shake their heads. The big joke that morning was the word passed by some Corps humorist: "The Marines are going so fast that they have already contacted the Russians coming up the other side!"

Ten o'clock. *Tennessee's* shore fire control party is already in touch with her, but the troops fan out so fast that they have to break off. The battleship follows the word of her spotting plane by firing on several objects which to the pilot seem to be military installations — more likely they are family tombs. She then checks fire and nothing is heard for several moments but the drone of landing craft motors. My own rough count of landing craft within sight yields the incredible figure of 700.

At 1011, after two LCVP waves (the 17th and 18th) laden with regimental reserves have passed, *Tennessee* reopens fire. Shore fire control party offers no target, so she delivers deep support fire as spotted by her own planes. By 1035 assault troops have reached the edge of Kadena airfield. One can see with the naked eye the UDTs wading along the outer line of reef, now lifting above the ebbing tide, looking for likely places to blast a channel. At 1200 a message comes through that Kadena and Yontan airfields are already in our hands. In the operation plan, we were not supposed to capture them until L-day plus 3!

Throughout the afternoon unloading goes on without impediment from the enemy. A simple but effective scheme is employed to prevent landing craft being stranded by the falling tide. A salvage LCM fitted with extra towing gear is stationed off each beach. Whenever a landing craft coxswain is unable to retract with his own power, he calls for the salvage LCM, which yanks the craft off before it becomes hopelessly stranded.

Around 1345 Admiral Hall's aërologist predicts heavy surf for the afternoon of L-day plus 1, 2 April, a forecast which happily was not fulfilled. But, in anticipation of foul weather next day, Commander Southern Attack Force puts the heat on transport skippers, warning them to land "hot" cargo at once, and to stand in closer to the beach.

Throughout the afternoon the absence of opposition continues to astound sailors and soldiers alike. No enemy aircraft are sighted until dusk. The enemy behind the southern beaches offers but a few bursts of mortar fire, with some light artillery fire laid down on the right flank. On the northern beaches, nothing. Our aircraft can locate no troop concentrations; advancing troops meet only scattered snipers, and find a few enemy tanks in a cave. In the northern sector the Marines encounter only 15 Japanese soldiers, but they round up 675 Okinawa civilians, mostly old people and children, to be removed to a place of safety.

At 1400 Admiral Turner gives the order for general unloading which continues all night. There is a suppressed note of triumph in the laconic summary that he sends to Admirals Spruance and Nimitz at 1600 April 1: "Landings on all beaches continued, with good progress inland against light opposition. Beachhead has been secured. . . . Approximately 50,000 troops have landed over beaches. . . . 420th Field Artillery Group with two battalions 155-mm guns on Keise Shima in support ground troops. . . . Unloading supplies over Hagushi beaches commenced, using LVTs, dukws, LSMs and LSTs."

Retirement of all fire support ships, and of all but six transports with screen, begins in late afternoon. At that moment a few kamikazes come in. *West Virginia* was crashed at 1913, killing four men, wounding 23 and wrecking the galley and laundry, but leaving the ship fully operational. Fortunate indeed for the crowded amphibious forces that the depredations of TF 58 planes in March prevented any massed kamikaze attack on L-day, or until 6 April.

Rear Admiral Jerauld Wright's force, which simulated a landing on the south coast, received more attention from enemy air forces on L-day than did the real landings.[7] At 0549, while this demonstration group maneuvered for final approach, a kamikaze crashed the port quarter of *LST–884*, with 300 Marines on board. The LST burst into flames, ammunition exploded, and she had to be abandoned temporarily; but a fire and rescue party from *Van Valkenburgh* boarded her, and with the aid of hoses from four LCSs had the fire out by 1100. Twenty-four sailors and Marines were killed and 21 wounded. Another kamikaze managed to hole

[7] CTG 51.2 (Rear Adm. Wright) Action Report of Demonstration Group, 15 Apr. 1945; LSM Flot 5 (Cdr. W. H. Carpenter) Action Report 3 Apr. 1945.

transport *Hinsdale* in three different places, resulting in complete loss of power, 16 killed, and 39 wounded. Fleet tugs from Kerama Retto, *Yuma* and *ATR–80*, towed the stricken ships to safety.

The demonstration landings, which were repeated next day, did not deceive the enemy, but gave him the opportunity to claim that "Jerry" Wright and his men were "forced to withdraw . . . after being mowed down one after the other."

CHAPTER X

"Iceberg" Logistics[1]

March–June 1945

1. The Logistic Support Group

TO MOUNT so distant an operation, at a moment when the
European war reached its final crisis, and supplies of every
sort were being rushed to General Eisenhower's immense army
groups, and when the Philippines were not yet completely liberated,
required fresh efforts in American war production and logistic
supply.

Even more troops had to be provided for an invasion of Okinawa
than for the capture of Leyte, and they were poured into the
Ryukyus much more quickly than they had been in the Philippines. Methods and procedures had been given a good test, and
the command structure was simpler. Logistic plans have to be
based on the organization and command relations of the forces to
be supported and the forces rendering support.[2] When Admiral
Nimitz moved to Guam in 1945 with part of his staff, he left the
large Service Force Pacific staff, including Service Squadron 8
(Commodore Augustine Gray's oiler outfit), at Pearl Harbor.

Logistics planning for a big operation in the western Pacific began
at Pearl Harbor well before the ice of Operation ICEBERG began

---

[1] Com Servron 6 (Rear Admiral D. B. Beary) War Diaries for 1945 and "Logistic
Analysis Okinawa Operation" 31 May 1945; W. R. Carter *Beans, Bullets and Black
Oil* chs. xxv–xxviii; Henry E. Eccles *Operational Naval Logistics* (published by
Bupers 1950), "Pacific Logistics" (lecture at Naval War College 30 March 1946)
and presentation of subject at Joint Army-Navy Staff College same month; also
many conversations with him since his retirement as Rear Admiral.
[2] Eccles *Operational Naval Logistics* p. 32.

to freeze. In the late summer of 1944 Admiral Nimitz issued a general planning directive which started the ball rolling toward Iwo Jima and Okinawa. Around October the staffs of the assault and type commanders made preliminary plans which later became reconciled at a series of conferences at Schofield Barracks, Oahu, with Brigadier General Bertram Hayford USA, head of the logistics division of planning staff Pacific Ocean areas. In these conferences, which lasted through Christmas week, the major gears of the vast machine were meshed, and the staffs concerned were able to do most of the time-consuming paper work before the ICEBERG directive was issued.

Admiral Royal E. Ingersoll,[3] relieved as Cinclant on 15 November 1944, was then appointed Commander Western Sea Frontier. Admiral King felt that an officer of high rank and experience was needed to control the flow of logistic support and personnel into West Coast ports and the Pacific Ocean. Admiral Ingersoll was given ample authority to do that through two additional commands: Deputy Cominch under Admiral King, and Deputy Cincpac under his Annapolis classmate Admiral Nimitz.

At a logistics conference between Admiral Ingersoll's representatives and Service Force Pacific Fleet at Pearl Harbor on 22 February 1945, the keynote for the Okinawa operation was struck: "Every available facility on the West Coast should be prepared to operate at the maximum capacity."

A special problem for the Navy was the logistic support of the growing number of B–29s of the Strategic Air Force based at Tinian and Guam. Each of these Superfortresses flew an average of eight missions per month; each mission consumed 6400 gallons of aviation gasoline, and required eight tons of bombs. All this, together with "housekeeping" supplies for the ground crew, the Navy had to bring out to the Marianas bases. Combat Readiness section of Cincpac–Cincpoa staff estimated in June 1945 that over 100 ships were employed supporting the Superforts.[4]

[3] Brief biog. in Vol. I 206n; portrait is frontispiece Vol. X.
[4] Figures then obtained from Capt. E. M. Eller.

As in the Iwo campaign, all oilers and other auxiliaries that fed the Fleet in the battle area were placed under the operational command of Rear Admiral Donald B. Beary, Commander Service Squadron 6.[5] This Logistic Support Group, designated TG 50.8, had the mission "To furnish direct logistic support at sea to the Fifth Fleet in and near the combat zone, in order to maintain mobility and striking power." [6]

Beetle-browed Commodore Gray, "the oil king of the Pacific," had to provide for an estimated monthly consumption of over six million barrels of fuel oil, which had to be met by commercial tankers bringing oil from the West Coast to Ulithi. There a floating storage of 100,000 barrels was maintained and a shuttle service of 40 fleet tankers operated between it and the Ryukyus. In addition, there would be 900,000 barrels of reserve fuel, divided among Saipan, Guam, and Kwajalein, and a 5,000,000-barrel reserve at Pearl Harbor. During the three weeks 4–24 April, the peak of this operation, a daily average of 167,000 barrels of fuel oil and 385,000 gallons of avgas were issued to Fifth Fleet. The cumulative issue through 27 May was 8,745,000 barrels fuel oil, 259,000 gallons diesel oil and 21,477,000 gallons avgas.[7]

Four escort carriers converted for plane transport [8] were employed to bring replacement planes from Ulithi and Guam for all three classes of carriers; 17 more shuttled carrier planes between

---

[5] Donald B. Beary, b. Montana 1888, Naval Academy '10. Served in *Tennessee, Washington* and *Maryland;* M.S. Columbia 1917; C.O. *Remlik* and *Lamson* in World War I. Service in Bunav; C.O. *Talbot, Parrott* and *Sumner* 1921–23. Service in fleet training div. C.N.O. to 1925, navigator *New Mexico* to 1928. Instructor in electrical engineering Naval Academy to 1931. Assistant chief of staff to C. in C. Asiatic Fleet to 1934; fleet maintenance div. C.N.O. to 1936; senior course Naval War College; exec. *Colorado* 1937; C.O. *Richmond* 1938; duty at Naval Academy 1939–41, when became C.O. *Mount Vernon* (see Vol. I, 110–112). Com N.O.B. Iceland 1942–43, Com Atlantic Fleet operational training 1943; Comservron 6 from Nov. 1944. After V-J Day, as head of U.S. shipping control for Japanese merchant marine, took charge of repatriating several million Japanese troops. Com Twelve and Westseafron 1946; President Naval War College 1948; retired 1950.

[6] Rear Adm. Beary Op Plan 2-45, 9 Mar. 1945.

[7] Beary "Logistic Analysis" pp. 3–6. An oil barrel holds 42 gallons.

[8] Sometimes designated CVET, but this was not official. On return passages the CVETs carried 212 "flyable duds" back to the West Coast. In addition, TF 57, the Royal Navy carrier force, had five replenishment escort carriers in its logistics group.

Avengers over the Beaches
Kadena Airfield under No. 57

LVTs Passing U.S.S. *Tennessee*

L-day at Okinawa

LVT(A)s of First Wave with Control Craft

Photos Courtesy of Cdr. R. A. Silcock RN

LSMs Going In

L-day at Okinawa

Unloading on Beach Yellow 3 — at Mouth of Bisha River
No. 1000 is an LST, No. 220 an LSM, and the four at the beach are
LCTs

Destroyer *Ault* Fueling in Heavy Weather

Okinawa and Off Shore

Commodore Augustine H. Gray USN

Rear Admiral Bertram J. Rodgers USN

West Coast and forward bases, just as the merchant tankers did with petroleum products; four CVEs brought up air units to be based on Okinawan airfields, and two constantly kept C.A.P. over the oilers. Altogether, 854 replacement planes and 207 pilots and crew members were issued to the Fleet at sea between 14 March and 27 May. The transport CVEs supplied aëronautical spare parts, including 3000 belly tanks, as best they could; but the enormous number of different items required, about 10,000 on a large carrier, made that service unusually difficult. Spare aircraft engines (weight 3500 pounds) and even jeeps to run on a carrier's deck, were transferred at sea by ammunition ship *Lassen*.

Fueling and provisioning at sea by now were an old story. Fueling was done by hose, but everything else had to be transferred on a line; and the principal limitation was a critical shortage of 3½- and 4-inch manila; for until the Philippines were liberated, manila line would not be back in production. Even so, the Logistic Support Group once managed to transfer 64,000 tons of cargo to Task Force 38 at sea in two days' time — which was more than the stevedores of a port like Boston then handled in a week.

Ammunition replenishment at sea had begun in the Iwo operation, and now two more floating services were added by Servron 6. Navy cargo vessel *Mercury* became a mobile general stores issue ship, a sort of floating variety store. In two days' time she delivered at sea to Rear Admiral Clark's carrier group 168 tons of dry and 84½ tons of fresh-frozen provisions, together with large quantities of general and miscellaneous stores. Among items delivered by *Mercury* at sea off Okinawa were uniform clothing and life jackets, blankets and steel helmets; signal flags, ship chandlery and electronics, rags, toilet paper, candy and cigarettes; copper tubing, valves, acetylene gas, chinaware, cooking utensils, gun sights and cartridges for line-throwing guns. *Mercury* also had refrigeration space for a limited amount of fresh and frozen foods, which were in such demand as to be all gone by the end of March, except for a few crates of apples and oranges. "Reefer" *Aldebaran*, a fresh-frozen provision ship, dispensed a chilled and frozen cargo at

Ulithi early in March and returned to San Francisco for more. *Virgo* helped by coming out with general stores, clothing and electronics. She also carried five civilian radar engineers, representing the major factories of that equipment, to service ships' radar. Thus, as Admiral Beary wrote, "This full logistic support of ships at sea wonderfully extended the endurance of the Fleet."

His Logistic Support Group (TG 50.8 or Servron 6) was organized at Ulithi in March into two replenishment units, comprising oilers, ammunition ships, provision ships and screen; a salvage unit of fleet tugs, and two carrier transport units of three CVETs each. Admiral Beary now had a suitable fast flagship, light cruiser *Detroit*, with sufficient space and communications for the complicated work that he and his staff had to perform. She led about 45 ships out of Ulithi on 13 March, ahead of the fast carriers, and proceeded to lat. 19°50′ N, long. 137°40′ E where all four carrier groups were replenished on 16 March. Two days later, when word came of the severe blow to carrier *Franklin*, four fleet tugs and two destroyers were dispatched to her aid, and assisted in saving her. All four carrier groups were again fueled on 23 March around lat. 22°23′ N, long. 131°38′ E. Floating mines were sighted almost daily, seven being destroyed on 22 March alone. No firm submarine contact was made until 14 May, when fleet tug *Sioux* destroyed a *kaiten* ("human torpedo") by 40-mm gunfire at lat. 23°43′ N, long. 132°07′ E.[9]

From 24 March, TG 50.8 remained within an ocean area comprised between lats. 22° and 24° N, longs. 128° and 132° E. This was about three days' steaming from Ulithi and less than two from Okinawa. Sometimes a fast carrier group closed for fueling, but usually a couple of oilers with screen were detached to seek out the thirsty ships. In either case the *ad hoc* fueling and service group was formed the previous evening and deployment completed at daybreak, so that the ships were ready to pass a line or a "tit" as soon as light permitted, and to finish early. Every few days empty oilers

9 This may have been launched by *I–47*, which according to Capt. Ohmae's notes on Japanese submarine action reports, was then patrolling in the vicinity.

were sent back to Ulithi and full ones arrived. The weather became dirty on the 31st and all ships water-ballasted and battened down. Between 26 March and 1 April three oilers with escorts were sent into Kerama Retto, and at short intervals other units were sent there or to the Hagushi beaches; for TG 50.8 was taking care of Admiral Turner's amphibious force as well as Admiral Mitscher's fast carriers. For a time two full oilers were required at Okinawa every three days.

On 1 April Admiral Durgin's escort carriers, having borne the burden of close support and patrol during the first week of the Okinawa operation, were in need of replacement planes. Ferry pilots were brought up from a rear area in destroyer *Helm* and transferred to CVE *Windham Bay* at about lat. 23° N, long. 132° E. They then manned 13 replacement planes and took off for Kerama Retto. Hospital ship *Bountiful*, on account of her illumination, operated about 75 to 100 miles from TG 50.8, but occasionally was ordered by airplane message drop to rendezvous and receive patients from a fast carrier.

Every other fleet auxiliary service was strained to the utmost. Servron 10 (Commodore Worrall R. Carter) sent a selection of all classes of salvage and repair vessels to Kerama Retto, leaving the majority at Ulithi or Guam until 20 May when he moved most of them to Leyte. These ships rendered essential services to ships damaged by enemy air attack, and saved many of them from being sent to mainland yards for repairs.

As wells on Okinawa were supposed to be contaminated (an assumption which proved to be correct), troops ashore had to be provided with fresh water until the Army could set up distilling units. The exceptionally large number of beaching craft, gunboats and other small craft with no distilling apparatus on board meant an unprecedented demand. Four fleet oilers converted to water tankers, *Severn, Ocklawaha, Soubarissen* and *Ponaganset*, with millions of gallons and several H_2O experts on board, were sent out. Two new water boats, *Pasig* and *Abatan*, with a distilling capacity of 120,000 gallons per diem, were completed in time. But even these were not enough, because Eniwetok, Ulithi and Saipan also had to be provided with fresh water.

The Pacific Fleet fitted out a number of LST, designated LST(H), to receive wounded from the beach and give them treatment before transfer to regular hospital ships. As Okinawa had the reputation of being infested with snakes and all manner of vermin, Service Force obtained from the anti-snakebite laboratory at Calcutta a supply of the right kind of serum to counteract the particular variety of poison packed by Okinawan vipers. And it provided planes to sprinkle the area with DDT mosquito and vermin repellent.

More than 2,700,000 packages of cigarettes and 1,200,000 candy bars were issued between 14 March and 27 May. The oilers were the principal mail carriers; they and other ships in five weeks delivered 24,117,599 letters to ships engaged in the Okinawan operation and units ashore.

A vital factor in the success of Operation ICEBERG was the Navy shipping control system, which after much trial and error nearly reached perfection in 1945. This intricate network, starting at Washington and extending through Admirals Ingersoll, Nimitz and Spruance to the port directors at Eniwetok, Guam, Saipan, Ulithi and Okinawa, finally brought a close relationship between call-up and flow of resupply shipping, and beach unloading capacity in the combat area. Commander John Huntington, a key man in planning and operating this system, did an outstanding job, working from a converted LCI(L) as Port Director Okinawa. He and his group received a handsome tribute from Admiral Hall for their efficient work in shipping control, as well as hearty thanks for taking that onerous duty off the hands of the attack force commanders' staffs.[10]

[10] Com 'Phib Grp 12 (Rear Adm. Hall) Action Report 31 July 1945 p. (V)(G) 2. Unfortunately the lessons here learned were largely forgotten by both Army and Navy tactical commanders in the Korean War, leading to as bad a foul-up of shipping in 1950 as had happened in 1942-44. Letter of Rear Adm. Eccles, 5 Jan. 1960.

2. The Provisions Problem

As in earlier operations, the Navy supplied fresh provisions for Army, Navy and Marine Corps, afloat or ashore, and dry provisions for these arms when afloat; the Army furnished dry provisions to all service personnel ashore.

Besides *Mercury* and *Aldebaran*, which belonged to TG 50.8, there were scores of provisions and general stores issue ships servicing the ships and men in this operation. First came the "reefers," carrying fresh and frozen provisions. On 1 March nine of these were issuing foodstuffs to combatant ships about to sail for Okinawa, at the Solomons, Ulithi, Leyte, the Marianas and Espiritu Santo. By 1 April they were loading or undergoing upkeep at Auckland or Pearl Harbor. On 1 May five of the new *Adria* class of reefers, loaded at Mobile, were beginning to discharge initial cargos in forward bases. *Bald Eagle* (a C–2) and *Antigua* (a converted banana boat), loaded respectively at San Francisco and Seattle, and three chartered Grace liners, were discharging provisions in the Marianas, and a fourth was doing the same at Ulithi. By 29 May all four vessels were on their way east, and six others, loaded in New Zealand, San Francisco and Norfolk, were also discharging at Guam and Saipan. Three of the *Adria* class with cargos from Mobile and Pearl Harbor were at Kerama Retto, and a merchant ship, San Francisco loaded, at Leyte.

There were good reasons for this tremendous movement of provisions to the Marianas. First, there were over 200,000 men of Army, Navy and Marine Corps ashore on Saipan, Tinian and Guam in January 1945 (and over 100,000 more by March),[11] and about 50,000 more men in ships in the harbors, who had to be fed. Second, although New Zealand furnished the Navy with large quantities of provisions, these were mostly fresh meat, so that ships which loaded "down under" were not prepared for fleet issue. They had to discharge into warehouses at Guam and reload with

[11] Cincpac Personnel Summary 14 Aug. 1945.

a balanced cargo for the ships. So as soon as a sufficient number of refrigerated warehouses had been constructed at Apra, Guam became the entrepot for fresh and frozen provisions for the Pacific Fleet. A shuttle service of reefers there took on balanced loads to be issued to TF 58, or at Kerama Retto, and in Japanese home waters after the surrender.

For issue of dry provisions, the Service Force had thirteen Navy cargo vessels and a number of War Shipping Administration ships, mostly of the C–1 type. By mid-March it was evident that too many WSA ships had been accepted. Certain loads already ordered were canceled, others were discharged into warehouses at Pearl Harbor, and five were offered to General MacArthur and Seventh Fleet. In spite of these diversions there was still an excess of dry provisions in forward areas all through the Okinawa operation. On 1 April, 15 dry provision ships were riding at anchor in Ulithi lagoon, doing very little business. *Azimech* and *Matar* were sent on to Kerama Retto, three others to Saipan and Guam, and ten went up to Leyte around 20 May, when Commodore Carter shifted base thither for his Service Squadron 10.[12] Yet *Ascella*, which arrived Ulithi 25 February, was still there 13 June. This long detention put Service Force "in the doghouse" with War Shipping Administration. It had indeed borrowed too many ships; but beyond its control were the main factors in this overestimate: —

(1) The Navy did much better in furnishing fresh provisions

[12] *Dry Provisions on Hand and Issued, in Units of 1000 rations, 1 Jan. to 1 June 1945*

On hand 1 Jan. in fleet issue ships, Central Pacific	3,130
Arrivals, 1 Jan. – 31 May, in 57 different ships	118,130
Total available	121,260
Issued, 1 Jan. – 31 May	55,760
On hand, 1 June	65,500

Fresh and Frozen Provisions Issued

Deliveries by 34 different reefers in forward area, in net tons, by month, 1945: —

January	18,150	April	28,500
February	17,050	May	35,200
March	23,550		

Data furnished by Provision and Supply Section of Servron 8 at Guam, June 1945.

than had been anticipated, and ships will seldom take dry when they can get fresh. (2) About one hundred ships which were sunk in the operation or returned to the West Coast for repairs, no longer had to be fed by Service Force Pacific Fleet.

3. *Ammunition — and Conclusion* [13]

Replenishment ammunition for a campaign over 4000 miles from Pearl Harbor and 6200 miles from San Francisco, respectively 17 and 26 days' steaming at 10 knots, was a problem that the Combat Readiness Section of Cincpac, the "Fun and Gun boys" headed by Captain Tom B. Hill, solved with their habitual cheerfulness. At least three times the amount used to reduce the Marianas had to be initially provided; and this estimate, based on consumption at Iwo Jima, was slightly exceeded before Okinawa was secured. Shortages developed of certain items for a few days, but none serious enough to affect gunfire support. The supply of reduced charges for 8-inch bombardment shells at one time became critical, but it did not run out.[14]

Replenishment at sea of the fast carrier forces by regular ammunition ships was much more extensively practiced than off Iwo, where this system was inaugurated. The carrier groups replenished while they refueled; one carrier while waiting to go alongside an oiler would close *Shasta*, *Wrangell* or one of the other AEs in TG 50.8, and take on ammunition by slings while she waited her turn to fuel.

The ships of TF 51 replenished in Kerama roadstead or off the Hagushi beaches by a new system. Victory ships converted to am-

[13] Data from Capt. Hill, Capt. E. M. Eller and Cdr. S. M. Archer, 1945.
[14] Beginning in the fall of 1944, conversion of the fire control system of heavy cruisers to accommodate charges of 2160 foot-seconds was started, as this reduced charge is better for close range bombardment and gives only one-sixth to one-seventh of wear on the gun as compared with the regular service powder charge of 2500 foot-seconds. Only one or two of the heavy cruisers were thus converted in time for Iwo, but all were ready for Okinawa. Reduced charges were not used for the light cruisers as their 6-inch guns wore so well as not to need them.

munition carriers brought powder, projectiles, bombs, demolition and pyrotechnics for the ground forces from the West Coast directly to Kerama Retto. There two of them, *Hobbs Victory* and *Logan Victory*, were sunk by kamikazes. This misfortune, together with unexpectedly heavy expenditure by the ground forces, caused a shortage of white phosphorus and 81-mm mortar shells. About 400 tons of the latter had to be flown up by plane from Guam. One or two converted Victory ships attended the fast carrier groups; but most of them discharged at Ulithi, Leyte or the Marianas into LSTs. Nine LST ammunition ships were used, and "type loaded"; i.e., they carried only ammunition used by one type of ship such as a cruiser or destroyer. With two hatches and a caterpillar crane working, these LSTs proved to be very quick and efficient at replenishment.

The following table of ammunition expenditures of 5-inch and upward during the Okinawa operation to 21 June, in round numbers, was furnished by Vice Admiral Hill when he took over the command of V Amphibious Force from Admiral Turner.[15]

OKINAWA OPERATION AMMUNITION EXPENDITURE IN ROUNDS

	Before 2 Apr.	2–30 Apr.	1–10 May	10–20 May	Total through 20 May	On hand Kerama or en route 20 May	Expended 17 May– 21 June [17]
16" HC	1,500 [16]	1,000 [16]	400	800	3,700	2,000	510
14" HC	4,600	5,500	1,800	650	12,550	5,200	4,300
12" HC	750	1,600	350	0	2,700	0	0
8" HC	5,800	11,000	4,300	4,700	25,800	12,900	7,050
6" HC	7,200	18,000	6,400	5,100	36,700	19,000	11,650
5" 51 HC	5,000	9,000	2,000	1,600	17,600	11,500	2,000
5" 38 AAC	50,000	115,000	40,000	42,000	247,000	100,000	99,525
5" 38 Star	1,500	18,000	6,000	6,000	31,500	12,800	13,150
5" 25 AAC	9,000	27,000	9,000	11,100	56,100	20,000	14,925
5" 25 Star	500	8,870	3,000	3,200	15,570	6,000	4,500
EQUIVALENT IN TONS	7,417	11,870	4,052	3,651	26,990		

In addition to the above, ammunition ships issued to TF 58 at sea, 77,582 5-inch 38 projectiles, 34,773 5-inch rockets, 19,297 500-pound General Purpose aircraft bombs, 18,579 100-lb G.P. bombs,

[15] Com V 'Phib Speedletter to Cincpac 23 May 1945.
[16] Not including 16" fired by TF 58.
[17] This column from CTF 51 (Vice Adm. Hill) Action Report 4 July p. (V)–40.

Vice Admiral John S. McCain USN

Vice Admiral Marc A. Mitscher USN in U.S.S. *Randolph*

CTF 38 and CTF 58

To: Sam Morison
Historian par excellence
and my good friend
With warm regards
and sincere best wishes
Turner Joy
5/28/52

Portrait by Hugh Cabot

Rear Admiral C. Turner Joy USN

3671 250-pound G.P. aircraft bombs, 798 G.P., A.P. and S.A.P. bombs from 500 to 2000 pounds, 83 torpedoes and 810 depth charges.[18]

The five ammunition ships regularly employed with TG 50.8 issued at sea 15,169 tons of ammunition between 22 March and 27 May, a daily average of 143 tons; *Wrangell* on her top day dispensed 460 tons.[19] Their average turnaround period was 20 days. Transfer at sea offered no difficulties aside from the shortage of manila; trouble came from a different source. When one of these ships, carrying 150 different items of powder and bullets, was about half discharged, her load became unbalanced from the issue point of view; she could no longer furnish all ammunition requirements of a capital ship. In port under similar circumstances a ship would "shop around" until she got what she wanted, but you couldn't shop around on the high seas. Nor was it safe to consolidate cargos in the open ocean.

As an experiment, *Shasta*, after her load had become too unbalanced to be useful to TF 58, was sent to Kerama roadstead to dispose of "remnants"; but this so reduced her availability to the fast carriers that it was not repeated.

A comparative table of annual ammunition expenditure by heavy cruiser *Salt Lake City*, which had been dishing it out in the Pacific since early in the war, illuminates the amount and kinds of shooting that took place around Okinawa. Yet her 1945 expenditures in this table are through 5 May only, and were exceeded by the end of the Okinawa campaign.

AMMUNITION EXPENDITURE IN ACTION BY U.S.S. *Salt Lake City, 1942–1945* [20]

	8″ AP	*8″ HC*	*5″ AAC*	*5″ VT*	*5″ Star*
1942	862	0	580	0	205
1943	1,031	711	483	118	100
1944	112	3,985	2,109	0	0
1945 1 Jan–5 May	32	10,613	8,478	79	1,756
TOTAL	2,037	15,309	11,650	197	2,061

[18] Beary "Logistic Analysis" p. 8.

[19] Same; the other AEs were *Shasta, Lassen, Mauna Loa* and *Vesuvius. Firedrake* issued rockets to the amount of 252 tons.

[20] Rear Admiral Allan E. Smith Action Report 26 May 1945.

The logistics aspect of the Okinawa operation was the most re-markable experiment ever tried of supplying a fleet at sea many thousands of miles from base. Admiral Beary, Commodore "Nick" Carter, Commodore "Gus" Gray and Vice Admiral W. W. ("Poco") Smith, who relieved Vice Admiral William L. ("Uncle Bill") Calhoun at the beginning of this operation as Commander Service Force Pacific Fleet, deserve the highest credit for so notably contributing to this capture of an important corner of the Japanese Empire. All regarded it only as a beginning, not a perfected system. As Admiral Beary modestly remarked in his Logistic Analysis of 31 May: —

"Many important requirements could not be completely supplied, but experience in the Okinawa operation has conclusively proved that full logistic support of a fleet at sea is entirely practicable, provided operations are being conducted in an area where reasonably satisfactory weather and sea conditions will be experienced."

Among the many tributes to Servron 10, that of Captain John B. Heffernan, C.O. of battleship *Tennessee*, stands out: — [21]

The *Tennessee* has been receiving supply services from Service Squadron 10 for more than fifteen months. The expansion and improvement in supply services during this period of time has been phenomenal, and has amazed experienced supply officers who understand the difficulties which had to be overcome. The actual achievement is indisputable evidence of the tireless energy, unceasing perseverance, and truly coöperative spirit of Commodore Worrall R. Carter, his hardworking staff, and the splendid personnel serving under him. Service Squadron 10 has labored under difficult climatic, living, and working conditions, without the compensation or personal satisfaction of combatant action, and in areas where typhoon danger was always present. Notwithstanding the difficulties inherent in their organization and situation, they have overcome the problems of communications; storage in large numbers of ships, barges, etc.; transportation between their wide-spread storage bottoms and the ships to be supplied; transportation from distant harbors and depots. Today their actual supply service compares very favorably with the service obtained from an efficient supply activity on shore in the continental United States. Their spirit of service and their help-

[21] Letter to Com Fifth Fleet 29 May 1945.

ful attitude is second to none. They made every conceivable effort to fill this ship to capacity, and they managed to "top-off" the ship in every instance when so requested.

The battle damage incurred on 12 April 1945, especially the damage to the after main battery director, was such that one competent and experienced maintenance officer who visited the ship expressed the opinion that she should go to a Navy yard. Commodore Carter, and Captain P. D. Gold, declared that Service Squadron 10 could do all the work, with some help from our ship's company, and the work was done in a most satisfactory manner, . . . thereby returning *Tennessee* to active combat duty with a minimum loss of time. Furthermore, these repairs were made while the ship was replenishing ammunition, supplies, fuel, etc., and carrying on routine upkeep.

Admiral Beary's group, while acting as mobile supply station in the open ocean about 200 miles south of Okinawa, was hardly ever attacked. Fleet ocean tug *Sioux*, as we have seen, destroyed a "human torpedo" that challenged her, and oiler *Taluga* "knocked down a Japanese plane with her bridge," as her action report humorously put it, but was promptly repaired and returned to duty. Admiral Clark, in his first action report for this operation, wrote, "the services received from CTG 50.8 were most excellent," and marked "a definite step forward in Fleet operations." They enabled the Fast Carrier Force to keep the sea for a period of over two months.

On 24 May Admiral Beary and staff held a conference with Admiral Halsey on board battleship *Missouri* at lat. 23°40′ N, long. 130°18′ E. Admiral Halsey took over command of the Fleet on the 27th when TF 58 became TF 38 and TG 50.8 became TG 30.8. The same organization was maintained and similar services were rendered.

CHAPTER XI

Feeling Each Other Out[1]

2–5 April 1945

1. Where Is the Enemy?

THE ASTOUNDING absence of enemy troops puzzled even Intelligence experts.[2] Some civilians who were interrogated said that the Japanese had withdrawn to the east, others said to the north, still others said to the south. In the amphibious forces it was generally believed that they had intrenched themselves in the rugged northern section of Okinawa.

Even without his hoped-for reinforcements, General Ushijima had about 100,000 troops, including the Okinawa home guard, which was greatly in excess of American Intelligence estimates. He used the tactics already laid down by Imperial General Headquarters for opposing a landing force of superior strength. There was no more wild talk of "annihilating" the enemy on the beach; on the contrary, he is to be allowed "to land in full" and "lured into a position where he cannot receive cover and support from the naval and aërial bombardment," and where the most effective fire power can be brought to bear. His force is then to be "wiped out."[3] These tactics were intelligent in that they gained time and inflicted maximum casualties; but the end product was the same,

[1] Action Reports already noted at head of Chap. IX; R. E. Appleman, James M. Burns and others *Okinawa: The Last Battle* (U.S. Army in W. W. II series, 1948) chaps. iv, v; Maj. Charles S. Nichols USMC & Henry I. Shaw *Okinawa: Victory in the Pacific* (a Marine Corps Monograph, 1955), chaps. v–viii.

[2] III 'Phib Corps G–2 Report 1200 Apr. 2.

[3] Battle Instructions of 32nd Japanese Army, Okinawa, 8 Mar. 1945, Cincpac-Cincpoa Translations, summarized in Cincpac *Weekly Intelligence* I No. 46 (28 May 1945) p. 5, and in Deyo "Kamikaze."

extermination of the Japanese garrison and total defeat of Japan. The General originally planned by thorough demolition to deny the Yontan and Kadena airfields to the invaders, but in the hurry of last-minute preparations he neglected this. Both airfields, as well as most of the hills that commanded them, were secured by Tenth Army on L-day. On the 2nd and 3rd, elements of the 7th Infantry Division and the 1st Marine Division reached the east coast. On 4 April the III 'Phib Corps (1st and 6th Marine Divisions) occupied the Katchin Peninsula and a good stretch of the east coast, putting a collar around the dog's neck several miles east of the Ishikawa Isthmus, which they had not expected to reach for twenty days. The Marines then rolled up into the northern half of Okinawa, meeting no serious resistance until they began fanning out into the dog's ear, the Motobu Peninsula.

Airfields were even more important than territorial gains. On 2 April the Kadena strip was operational for emergency landings, and next day two strips of the Yontan field could be used. One of the stories that went the rounds told of an enemy plane landing on the Yontan field the night of 1–2 April. The pilot taxied up to the filling station, hopped out and asked for gas in Japanese. A Marine sentry replied and the Emperor lost one pilot.

South of the Bisha River, in XXIV Corps territory, the 96th Division found stiffening resistance in rugged country on the afternoon of the second day. This resistance, by a rear guard covering the enemy withdrawal, was overcome on the 4th when the Japanese were reported to be falling back on Shuri, the ancient capital east of Naha. "Extensive reconnaissance and photographic flights see no sizable enemy concentrations, but report numerous targets for aircraft and ships," states Admiral Turner's summary at the close of 4 April. That night XXIV Corps was subjected to heavy artillery fire. On the 5th, cold and rainy, the soldiers advanced almost to the lines that they were destined to hold for the next two weeks.

The Allied assault on Okinawa could not have been better timed to hit the Japanese people where it hurt most; for 3 April, the day after they got the news, was Emperor Jimmu Day in Japan. Jimmu, some 2500 years earlier, had inaugurated Japanese expansion with the conquest of Yamato (whose namesake had but five days to live), and announced as his policy "I wish to make the universe our home." The Japanese government now admitted that a beachhead had been established and the situation was serious. Retired Admiral Takahashi pointed out in a broadcast on 2 April that the loss of Okinawa would cut Japan off from her southern conquests; he promised that the Japanese Navy would shortly take the offensive; and Premier Koiso blustered to the Diet that their heroes would drive the Americans off Okinawa, and then "retake Saipan and other points." But the sands were running out for Koiso. In a few days' time he resigned, and the aged Admiral Suzuki, chosen by the Emperor to find some honorable way for Japan to get out of the war, became Premier. Since any peace move would take time and require great circumspection and caution, to avoid a military *coup d'état*, there was no question but that Okinawa would be defended vigorously and to the last man. It is a sad reflection that this costly operation, and everything that followed until 16 August, was unnecessary from any point of view but that of keeping "face" for the military leaders who had started the war.

2. Unloading [4]

The Navy's main contribution to this rapid advance in Okinawa was unloading and fire support. The armored amphtracs (LVT–A), which were designed to get artillery ashore with the assault troops, had been used for the first time at Saipan, and had proved indispensable to fill the gap between the landing of assault waves and that of divisional artillery. Placed under the artillery

[4] The Action Reports already mentioned and personal observations. The Report of British Combined Operations liaison officer at Cincpac HQ (Col. G. I. Malcolm, British Army) to the chief of his mission at Washington, 18 Apr. 1945, has been particularly valuable, as Col. Malcolm and the other two observers (Cdr. R. K. Silcock RN and Grp. Capt. W. G. Tailyour RAF) are old Commando men who went ashore every day to see what went on.

regiment commander of each of the four assault divisions, they were used exactly like land tanks, and in the XXIV Corps area found plenty of targets.

Success in unloading an amphibious operation is dependent on everything both afloat and ashore working according to plan. Ships are combat-loaded with the expectation of so much ammunition, provisions, stores, and heavy equipment being needed at certain hours on definite days. If the enemy pins the attack force to the beach, as at Tarawa and Anzio, unloading gets fouled up; but an almost equal though less unhappy "snafu" occurs when the ground forces are unexpectedly successful and outrun their supplies. That is what happened at Okinawa. LVTs and dukws carrying "hot cargo" had to roll so far inland to reach the troops that their turn-around was delayed, and unloading consequently slowed down. This was particularly true of the northern beaches from which the Marines were distant twenty miles by 6 April. The Marines complained of Navy procedure on these beaches, but the Navy countered with the charge that the "leathernecks" used shore party as replacement troops, and withdrew almost all vehicles from the work of unloading. It made little difference in the end.

There were also difficulties on the southern beaches. LSTs of Captain J. S. Laidlaw's Northern Tractor Flotilla were overloaded with cargo, amphtracs, land tanks, dukws, wheeled vehicles, engineer equipment and naval ammunition. Twenty-nine LSTs carried pontoon barges or causeway sets secured alongside, 16 carried LCTs on their decks, and none of these could be unloaded promptly; vehicles stowed in an LCT, and naval ammunition stowed under them, had to be removed before the landing craft could be launched. LST stowage in this operation was something like those Chinese nests of boxes which must be unpacked in order, or not at all.[5]

Although each LST in the transport area discharged her men and amphtracs in time to land on schedule, the LSTs themselves were delayed coming into the northern beaches until L-day plus 1, when

[5] LST Flot 6 (Capt. Laidlaw) Action Report for Okinawa 1 Mar.–11 Apr.; LST Group 38 (Capt. J. R. Clark) Action Report 10 Apr. 1945.

eleven slots were ready for them on Beaches Blue 1 and Yellow 2. Unloading continued all night from 2 April on, with the aid of lights.

On Admiral Hall's southern group of beaches, below the Bisha River mouth, unloading ran very smoothly, probably because the shore parties there were composed of veterans of the Engineer Special Brigades. The Purple and Orange beaches lay behind made-to-order reefs of a uniform width (about 350 yards) and a smooth hard surface over which wheeled vehicles could run when the reef was bared at half tide. General unloading here began promptly at 1400 L-day. Bulldozers filled up holes in the reef with sand and thus made tracks by which trucks and jeeps could roll ashore from beaching craft. Any day after 3 April, the Orange and Purple beaches were lined solid with LST, LSM and LCT.

In an amphibious operation against a large island, where there must be a steady build-up by successive echelons, unloading never stops unless interrupted by weather or enemy action. On 4 April the north wind increased, a heavy surf built up on the beaches by midnight, all beaching craft that could retracted, and unloading was suspended by Admiral Turner's order. By 0400 April 5, the north wind had reached a velocity of 25 to 35 knots. Some 18 beaching craft were damaged that day, and the following night, by action of the surf. This suspension lasted until 6 April, when the wind changed to the regular NE monsoon and the sea moderated.[6] Admiral Turner sent every ship away as soon as she had discharged; the first departed 5 April. Very few casualties were suffered from enemy air attack in the transport areas and along the beaches. Landing craft crews were well trained, energetic and devoted. There were no complaints of their securing out of sight to "calk-off," or going souvenir hunting ashore. It was an inspiration to see these young boys and the winch crews swinging boats out smartly, and unhooking the lead-weighted welin davit blocks from the ringbolts of craft pitching and rolling alongside. Altogether, this was an operation for the amphibious forces to look back on with pride.

[6] CTF 51 Action Report p. (III)–16–22.

On 5 April, 29 empty attack transports and two LSV departed for Guam and Saipan with suitable escort. Admiral Wright's Demonstration Group had already gone. But several hundred transports, LSTs and smaller craft were left off Hagushi to receive the first serious enemy air attack, on 6 April.

After the 6th, XXIV Corps lines were stabilized for another two weeks. This gave Army engineers a good opportunity to enlarge beach exits, widen roads, and build a four-lane highway parallel to the shore front. The writer, who walked along the Purple and Orange beaches on 9 April when the 27th Division was coming ashore, and who also "thumbed" a series of rides inland, was impressed with the order and cleanliness of XXIV Corps sector.

3. *Retirement and Retaliation*

During the first two nights after L-day, Admiral Turner followed standard amphibious force practice in retiring his transports seaward for the night, in dispositions separate from the fire support ships. Twilight was the kamikazes' favorite hour for self-immolation; one at 1910 April 1 crashed transport *Alpine* about 15 minutes after she had got under way, blew two big holes in her side, killed 16 men and wounded 27. *Achernar*, in a different formation, was both crashed and bombed shortly after midnight, losing five killed and 41 wounded. Both transports discharged the undamaged part of their cargos before retiring for repairs. Transports of the Kerama Retto group were also attacked that night, but suffered no casualties.

Just as the Northern Force was getting under way, some trigger-happy gunner opened up on an imaginary enemy plane. Other ships in the formation commenced firing in the general direction of other ships' tracers or bursts, and the O.T.C. added to the confusion by giving the order "Make Smoke," so for the next half-hour the transports zigzagged under a cloud, in danger of collision as well as of their own gunfire.

Captain John W. McElroy USNR, C.O. of transport *Marathon,* thus described the confusion of that evening: —

For a radius of about fifty miles could be overheard on the voice radio every report made by every radar guard ship in the area of bogies here, there and everywhere. Regardless of whether the information originated five or fifty miles away, every word of this "hot" dope went over the J. A. sound-powered telephones into the ears of every gun crew and lookout. No one ever mentioned that fifty percent of the bogies turned out to be friendlies when interrogated; so the gun crews, like everyone else who was getting the dope, soon had the idea that the sky was full of enemy planes.

Ten minutes after the watch was relieved at midnight, this ship's C.I.C. passed the word "Bogey bearing 180° distant seven miles" — omitting to say that the report came from a radar picket ship about 17 miles away in the other direction. A gun captain, looking along that bearing, saw what he believed to be a low-flying enemy plane in the moonlight and promptly obtained permission to open fire. The skipper, clapping his binoculars on the reputed kamikaze, observed that it had a mast, two stacks and a set of torpedo tubes, dashed to the control station and managed to cancel the impending battle. In the meantime every ship in the column started blazing away. Fortunately nobody managed to hit the destroyer, one of their own screen.[7]

On 2 April the transports, which had reëmbarked part of the 77th Division from Kerama Retto, commenced retirement to a waiting position southward. At 1836, this group, when it had steamed only 16 miles, came under severe attack by ten or more kamikazes. One near-missed Commodore Brittain's flagship *Chilton.* A Nick crashed the bridge of destroyer transport *Dickerson,* killing her skipper, Lieutenant Commander Ralph E. Lounsbury USNR, the exec., Lieutenant A. G. McEwen, and 52 more officers and men, besides seriously wounding 15. She was towed back to Kerama

[7] Capt. McElroy informal "Reaction Report" 10 Apr. and letter to writer 16 Apr. 1945.

after the fires were out, but found unsalvageable, taken out to sea and scuttled.[8] *Goodhue* and *Telfair* of Transdiv 51 were attacked by three planes in rapid succession. One was exploded by gunfire in midair; a second, badly hit, bounced like a billiard ball from hell between the starboard and port kingposts of *Telfair*, hit her port bulwarks and toppled overboard, after killing one man and wounding 16. Next, a Nick headed for *Goodhue's* bridge. Her gunfire deflected its course sufficiently so that it clipped the mainmast at the yardarm and crashed an after 30-ton cargo boom, from which it slid into the after 20-mm gun tubs and finally into the sea. Five soldiers and 19 sailors were killed; 35 soldiers and 84 sailors wounded.

In this same dusk attack on 2 April, at 1838, a Fran came in unseen on *Henrico*, flagship of Transdiv 50, crashed the bridge and released two bombs which exploded. Captain Elmer Kiehl, the division commander; Captain W. C. France, the C.O.; Colonel Vincent Tanzola, commanding the 305th Infantry Regiment; and Colonel L. O. Williams, his exec., were killed, together with 21 other naval officers and men and eleven other Army officers and men. A dozen more sailors and one Marine were missing. The ship survived, but she was out of the war.

L-day plus 2, 3 April, broke beautifully clear for a dawn attack. When the Northern Group transports returned in formation to their anchorage off the Hagushi beaches, breakfast had to wait. In vain master-at-arms threatened that the cooks would "t'row it overboard"; every bluejacket on deck stayed there, hundreds of pairs of eyes scanning the heavens in hungry hope that "just one lousy Nip" would heave in sight. C.A.P. splashed every one that approached, but the ships at Kerama Retto were not so fortunate. There *LST–599*, carrying the gear for a Marine fighter squadron, took an attacking plane under fire at about 0715 and clipped off one wing, but the plane crashed and penetrated her main deck, where

[8] Lt.(jg) J. D. Ebert (gunnery officer and senior survivor) Interview 11 June 1945, Division of Naval History; *N.Y. Times* 12 July 1945.

it exploded and started fires. The Marine squadron lost most of its gear and 21 men were wounded, yet nobody but the kamikaze pilot was killed.[9]

As the big transports hauled in to their unloading stations off the Hagushi beaches they made smoke successfully. Admiral Turner, observing that the improvement of artificial smoking made the ships safer near shore than at sea, canceled night retirement thereafter.

Turner's screening plan for the protection of the expeditionary force in and around Okinawa was unusually comprehensive. He set up (1) a close antisubmarine screen of destroyers around the transport area; (2) a radar countermeasure screen of LCI inside it; (3) an outer antisubmarine screen, running from Motobu Peninsula around Kerama Retto to Abu Saki on the southeast coast; (4) an antimidget "flycatcher" screen, composed largely of LCI covered by a destroyer or light cruiser, patrolling in search of suicide boats, motor torpedo boats and enemy attempts to move troops and supplies by barge; (5) an anti-surface-craft patrol of five destroyer types, covering approaches by which the enemy might attempt a night raid; (6) and most important, the radar picket screen.

This last gave best protection against surprise air attack, and the radar picket stations were the posts of greatest danger. They were disposed around Okinawa at distances of between fifteen and one hundred miles from land, so as to pick up flights of approaching enemy planes and, with the aid of C.A.P., to intercept them. From 26 March on, each station was kept by a destroyer or DMS with a fighter-director team on board. This controlled the C.A.P. which was maintained overhead all day by Admiral Durgin's escort carrier planes. The picket vessel patrolled night and day within 5000 yards of her station, and when bogeys appeared on her radar screen, the fighter-director officer vectored out C.A.P. to intercept. By this means a large proportion of enemy planes approaching Okinawa were shot down before they reached the island, and our forces

[9] *LST-599* (Lt. R. P. Roney) Action Report 6 Apr. 1945.

engaged in landing, unloading or fire support were given timely warning of an air raid. Hundreds of sailors lost their lives and about a score of ships and craft were sunk rendering this service.

After L-day, as soon as the LCI gunboats, LCS support craft and LSM could be spared, Admiral Turner sent two or more of these to support the picket destroyers. They added punch to the anti-aircraft fire and proved a present and courageous help in time of trouble.

There was not much activity at radar picket stations before 3 April. Destroyer *Prichett* on station No. 1, directly north of Point Bolo, was under attack throughout the midwatch and until 0500 April 3. With the aid of a night fighter she splashed two. A bomb exploded under her counter, but the damage was quickly repaired at Kerama Retto. That afternoon *Mannert L. Abele*, a new 2200-ton destroyer, was patrolling radar picket station No. 4, on the northern approach, in company with *LCS–111* and *LCS–114*. The C.A.P. had just departed. The weak spot in air defense during the first ten days at Okinawa, before land-based night fighters were available, came at dusk. Planes could not land or take off from escort carrier decks in the dark, and TF 58 had no night fighters to spare for this service. Hence all picket stations and ships lost their air umbrella at dusk, children's hour for the kamikaze kids. At 1630 two Judys started diving on *Abele*, one after the other, while a third made figure-eights overhead. One was splashed by ship's gunfire; a second, already on fire, skimmed like a flying torch over her fantail and splashed; within a few seconds the third dropped a bomb which missed, and then flew away.[10] *Abele* was not damaged, but she had not much longer to live.

The escort carriers too were attacked on 3 April. *Wake Island* at 1744 picked up five planes on her starboard quarter. Two dived and missed, splashing close aboard, and the explosion of the second ripped a hole 18 by 45 feet in the carrier's side, all below the water-line. Casualties fortunately were not serious, but she had to go to Guam for repairs.

[10] *Mannert L. Abele* (Cdr. A. E. Parker) Action Report.

Wednesday, 4 April, when the weather made up, was relatively free from air attacks. "Be prepared for very heavy attacks by enemy aircraft from Kyushu throughout today," was the ominous opening message from Admiral Turner to his task force on the 5th.

The old formula, by which one could predict the first strong counterattack after an amphibious landing on D-day plus 4, still held good. As we have seen, the Japanese air forces were so depleted and their Kyushu fields so badly hit by the B–29 and TF 58 attacks before L-day that they needed four days before "throwing the book" at us. The kamikazes which had appeared so far were probably based on Okinawa itself or other airfields in the Nansei Shoto.

Rain and overcast on L-day plus 4, 5 April, gave Admiral Turner's ships another day's grace from air attack, but the battleships and cruisers supporting XXIV Corps drew return fire from a coastal battery near Naha. *Salt Lake City* was fired on, and then *Nevada*. At 1740 she took five hits of around 6- to 8-inch caliber, but this tough old battlewagon, which had survived the Pearl Harbor attack, remained operational and lost only two men killed and 16 wounded.[11] The 155-mm Army artillery on Keise Shima apparently silenced this battery, which was not heard from again.

[11] *Nevada* Action Report 19 Apr. 1945.

CHAPTER XII

"Ten-Go" Gets Going[1]

6–8 April

Almanac for 6 April at Okinawa

Last quarter moon rose	0030
Sunrise	0615
Sunset	1849

1. The Gallant Fight of Newcomb and Leutze

ADMIRAL TOYODA, commanding all Japanese air forces in the East China Sea sector, managed in the first week of April to effect a partial concentration on Kyushu and Formosa and to begin Operation TEN-GO in earnest. The numbers assembled fell short of his plan, which called for a total of 4500 aircraft, but the 699 (355 of them kamikazes) available for 6 and 7 April inflicted a distressing amount of damage. This was the first of ten massed kamikaze attacks to which the Japanese gave the name *kikusui,* "floating chrysanthemums."[2]

The wind on 6 April was NE, force 5 or 6, strong enough to raise whitecaps; the sky overcast, and the temperature unusually low — from 60° to 65°. Nothing happened until the afternoon. Admiral Deyo's fire support ships, as well as those supporting Admiral Blandy's operation off the east coast of Okinawa, were ordered to form up early, perform tactical exercises until dusk, and retire in

---

[1] CTF 51 (Vice Adm. Turner), CTF 53 (Rear Adm. Reifsnider) and CTF 55 (Rear Adm. Hall) Reports; writer's personal observations from *Tennessee;* MacArthur *Historical Report* II 555–56.

[2] A table of *kikusui* attacks will be found at head of Chap. XV.

company. Around 1635, as Deyo headed his formation toward the beach to pick up *Idaho* and Spruance's flagship *New Mexico*, the battleship sailors had the pleasure of seeing C.A.P. shoot down four planes which had been pursued from over Ie Shima. Up there a general air mêlée was going on, and minesweepers were catching it on the surface. By 1710 the transport area off the Hagushi beaches was ablaze with antiaircraft fire. About five enemy planes got through C.A.P. and four were shot down by ships. The transports' fire discipline was still poor, shooting on such bearings that the flak fell on their sister ships, and bringing friendly planes under fire.[3]

Admiral Deyo's night retirement disposition, still short of four heavy ships and six destroyers which had not got the word, consisted of nine battleships and cruisers steaming in circles respectively of 5000 and 12,000 yards' diameter, with a screen of seven destroyers 4000 yards outside. The disposition turned away towards Ie Shima. At 1753 destroyer *Leutze*, which had already been damaged off Iwo Jima, sighted a plane coming in eight miles distant and at 1800 opened fire. Within a few moments the clear evening air was spotted with black bursts from 5-inch gunfire, almost every ship was spouting red balls from her 40-mm quads, and the water was laced with spray from shorts. About twelve Kates and Oscars came in so low over the water that lookouts saw them before radar did. *Leutze* and *Newcomb* bore the brunt of this attack. In quick succession one kamikaze crashed *Newcomb's* after stack, a second was splashed, and at 1806 a third, carrying a large bomb or torpedo, crashed into her, amidships, gouging deep into the bowels of the ship with a tremendous explosion that cut off all remaining sources of power and blew "both engine rooms and the after fireroom into a mass of rubble." "With intentions of polishing us off," wrote Commander I. E. McMillian, "a fourth plane raced toward *Newcomb* from the port beam and although under fire by her forward batteries came through to crash into the forward stack, spraying the entire amidships section of *Newcomb*, which was a raging con-

[3] CTG 53.7 (Northern Defense Group, Capt. W. W. Weeden) Action Report.

Rear Admiral Donald B. Beary USN

From portrait by J. J. Capolino at U. S. Naval War College

Commander Leon Grabowsky USN

Commander I. E. McMillian USN

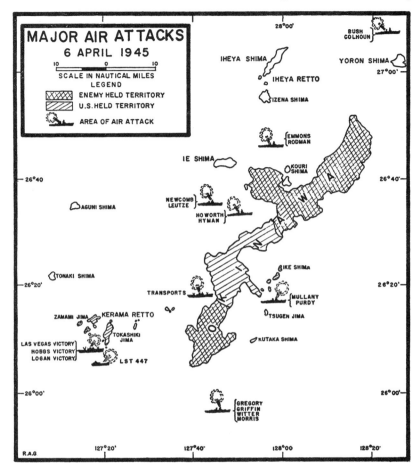

MAJOR AIR ATTACKS
6 APRIL 1945

SCALE IN NAUTICAL MILES
10   0   10

LEGEND

⬛ ENEMY HELD TERRITORY
▨ U.S. HELD TERRITORY
🔥 AREA OF AIR ATTACK

28°00'

BUSH
COLHOUN

IHEYA SHIMA

YORON SHIMA

27°00'

IHEYA RETTO

IZENA SHIMA

EMMONS
RODMAN

IE SHIMA

KOURI
SHIMA

26°40

26°40'

AGUNI SHIMA

NEWCOMB
LEUTZE

HOWORTH
HYMAN

OKINAWA

TONAKI SHIMA

26°20'

IKE SHIMA

26°20'

TRANSPORTS

MULLANY
PURDY

TSUGEN JIMA

ZAMAMI JIMA

KERAMA RETTO

KUTAKA SHIMA

TOKASHIKI
JIMA

LAS VEGAS VICTORY
HOBBS VICTORY
LOGAN VICTORY

LST 447

26°00'

26°00'

GREGORY
GRIFFIN
WITTER
MORRIS

R.A.G

127°20'   127°40'   128°00   128°20'

flagration, with a fresh supply of gasoline." [4] Flames shot up hundreds of feet, followed by a thick pall of smoke and spray which so completely covered the destroyer that sailors in nearby battleships (including the present writer) thought that she had gone down.

Destroyer *Leutze*, closing rapidly to render antiaircraft assistance to *Newcomb*, also assumed that she was sinking and swung out boats in preparation for rescue; but when close aboard she observed that McMillian's ship was still holding together. A solid mass of flame swept from bridge to No. 3 gun, but her valiant crew

[4] *Newcomb* Action Report 14 Apr. 1945; one of the best.

showed no intention of abandoning ship. Lieutenant Leon Grabow-sky (Naval Academy 1941), C. O. of *Leutze*,[5] gallantly risked his ship to help her sister, closed her weather side at 1811 (only ten minutes after the first crash), passed hose lines on board to help fight fires; and then, at 1815, a fifth plane approached, heading for *New-comb's* bridge. One of her 5-inch guns, fired in local control, made a hit which tilted the plane just enough so that it slid athwartship and on to *Leutze's* fantail, where it exploded.

Now *Leutze* too was in trouble. A fire sprang up in the after am-munition handling room. While one of her repair parties continued fighting fires on board *Newcomb*, the other two attempted to check flooding on their own ship and jettisoned topside weights. Steering control was lost with the rudder jammed hard right. Seven-teen compartments laid open to the sea by the Japanese bomb let in so much water that *Leutze* began to settle. Destroyer *Beale*, with all fire hoses streaming, now closed the disengaged side of *New-comb;* and not until then did *Leutze* signal "Am pulling away, in serious danger of sinking." At 1842 Lieutenant Grabowsky re-quested Admiral Deyo's permission to jettison torpedoes and depth charges. After permission had been granted *Leutze* signaled "Be-lieve flooding under control." Minesweeper *Defense* (Lieutenant Commander Gordon Abbott USNR), which had been slightly dam-aged by two kamikaze hits shortly after 1800, took *Leutze* in tow at 2005. While making her slow way to Kerama Retto *Defense* sent this cocky message: "Sorry to be late, have scratched a kamikaze and taken two on board. Now have destroyer in tow." [6] She arrived off Kerama Retto and cast off her tow at 0230.

Newcomb, one of the "fightingest" destroyers in the Navy (she had led a torpedo attack in Surigao Strait), lost nothing in compari-son with *Leutze;* Nelson's accolade to his sailors, "They fought as one man, and that man a hero," could well be applied to her crew.

<hr>

[5] Her former C.O., Cdr. B. A. Robbins, had been wounded off Iwo Jima.
[6] George L. Batchelder letter of 23 Jan. 1960; *Defense* Action Report 15 Apr. 1945.

The exec., Lieutenant A. G. Capps, after being pulled out from under the tail of a crashed kamikaze, directed the local-control fire of the forward gun and then handled the firefighting; the surgeon, Lieutenant J. J. McNeil USNR, carried several severely injured men to a place of safety, operated on surgical cases in the wardroom in the midst of the uproar, and so continued all the following night; Lieutenant (jg) D. W. Owens USNR "by his personal direction and fearless leadership" quenched a magazine fire. Two out of 78 enlisted men singled out for special commendation in the Action Report may also be mentioned here: fireman Francis J. Nemeth was securing steam lines when burned to death by the spreading fires, and machinist's mate Richard C. Tacey was killed trying to reach some of the black gang who were trapped by the flames. All crews of guns that could shoot fired until they were blown overboard or killed.

Newcomb had all fires under control before fleet tug *Tekesta* towed her, too, into the calm waters of Kerama Retto. One marveled at the sight of them there next morning: scorched, scarred and half wrecked, *Leutze* alongside repair ship *Egeria*, with part of a kamikaze plane still resting on her fantail; *Newcomb* with No. 2 stack gone, No. 1 leaning crazily to starboard, her entire deck abaft the superstructure buckled into the contour of a roller coaster, and her fantail about six inches above the water. *Leutze* had lost only 7 men killed or missing and 34 wounded, but *Newcomb's* casualties were 40 killed or missing and 24 wounded. Both ships had to be beached or dry-docked and there was some question whether they were worth repairing, but repaired they were.

Captain Roland N. Smoot, the squadron commander, paid this tribute to *Leutze* in his endorsement to her Action Report: —

"Without hesitation, and in the face of continuing attacks, raging fires, and the grave possibility of further damaging explosions, she committed herself exclusively to her stricken sister ship until her own serious condition made it necessary to haul clear. Thence she proceeded to save herself against what appeared at first to be hopeless odds. This she accomplished in the most expeditious and effective manner possible." [7]

2. Radar Pickets Blooded

Two destroyers fared even worse that afternoon. *Bush* (Commander R. E. Westholm), on radar picket station No. 1, and *Colhoun* (Commander G. R. Wilson), on station No. 2, were the first to be encountered by "floating chrysanthemums" flying southwest along the Nansei Shoto. The ships had been out there since April 1 and 3 respectively, with "seldom a dull moment." Advance elements of the massed air attack heckled them all through the midwatch and *Colhoun* received eleven bombing attacks, all of which missed, between 0230 and 0600 April 6. The forenoon watch was fairly quiet. Around 1500, 40 to 50 planes flew down from the north, stacked at various altitudes between 500 and 20,000 feet, and began orbiting and attacking *Bush*, while about 12 others went after *Cassin Young* (Commander J. W. Artes) at station No. 3, next to the eastward.

Bush shot down two Vals and drove off two more, a few minutes before 1500. Thirteen minutes later a Jill was sighted heading low for her. Commander Westholm promptly swung ship to bring it abeam and unmask his main battery. Fire was opened at a range of 7000 to 8000 yards. The plane jinked and weaved at an altitude of 10 to 35 feet above the water, and although every gun on the destroyer was firing, it kept coming and crashed between the two stacks. The bomb exploded in the forward engine room, killing every man there, and most of those in the two fire rooms. Flooding started immediately and *Bush* took a 10-degree list, but escaping steam smothered the fires and power was regained as the auxiliary diesel generator cut in. Handy-billys were used to control the

[7] Action Reports of both ships; story by S. R. Linscott in *Boston Globe* 6 July 1945.

flooding, the wounded were treated on the fantail or in the ward-room and although the ship had gone dead, everyone expected to save her, and all hands cheered when a C.A.P. of four planes appeared overhead.

Colhoun at 1530, learning by radio that *Bush* was in need of help, began to close at 35 knots, bringing along her C.A.P. for the short time it could remain. The chief fighter-director commander in *Eldorado*, Admiral Turner's flagship, sent out another C.A.P. which encountered so many Japanese planes en route that a general mêlée developed some 15 miles south of *Colhoun's* course. This C.A.P. splashed bandits right and left, but ran out of fuel and ammunition before it could help the destroyers. At 1635 *Colhoun* closed *Bush*, then dead in the water, smoking badly and apparently sinking. She signaled a support craft, *LCS-64*, to rescue the crew and tried to interpose herself between the sinking ship and a flight of about 15 Japanese planes. They approached, and one went for *Bush* at 1700. Commander Westholm ordered about 150 of his men fighting fires topside to jump overboard for self-protection, and trailed knotted lines for them to climb on board again. All his 5-inch guns that would bear were jammed in train, but his 40-mm guns opened fire and frightened one Val away.

Colhoun in the meantime was shooting everything she had at an approaching Zeke, which missed and splashed midway between the two ships. "This left one down, eleven to go," remarked Commander Wilson. Another was hit by a 5-inch shell at 4000 yards, and its port wing caught fire. *Colhoun's* guns Nos. 1, 2 and 3 were quickly trained on a third Zeke diving at her starboard bow, and the first salvo hit him square on the nose; he splashed 50 yards abeam. Just then Wilson received a report that a fourth Zeke was about to crash his port bow. Too late he ordered full left rudder. The plane, already aflame, hit *Colhoun's* main deck, killing the gun crews of two 40-mm mounts. Its bomb exploded in the after fire room, killing everyone there and rupturing the main steamline in the forward engine room. Lieutenant (jg) John A. Kasel, the engineer officer, opened the cross-connection valve before diving for the bilge, so the after engine room had steam and a speed of 15 knots was maintained.

Colhoun was already getting her fires under control (despite loss of all handy-billys) when, at 1717, commenced the fifth attack on her within 15 minutes, by two Vals and a Zeke. The gunnery officer had the presence of mind and found the time to assign target sectors to his five-inch guns. One Val was splashed 200 yards on the port quarter. One missed *Colhoun* and was shot down by fire from *Bush* and *LCS-84*. The third plane crashed the forward fire room, where the bomb exploded, piercing both boilers, blowing a 4-by-20-foot hole below the waterline, and breaking the keel. *Colhoun* went dead in the water; all power and communications were lost. The indefatigable damage control party then applied CO_2 and foamite fire extinguisher. The gunnery officer reëstablished communication with guns 1, 2 and 4 of the main battery. The wounded were treated, fires brought under control; and the men had just begun to get rid of depth charges and torpedoes when at 1725 the sixth attack on *Colhoun* (and fourth on *Bush*) started.

Three planes dove on each bow and one on her quarter. All *Colhoun's* guns were now manned in local control; and it takes such strength and determination to point and train a 5-inch 38 without power, that the strong young bluejackets had to be relieved after two minutes. One Zeke was splashed 150 yards away. The other two were hit by 40-mm fire but only slightly damaged. One, a Val, caught its wing in the after stack, caromed on No. 3 gun, knocking off its gas tank which burst into flames, and then bounced off main deck into the water. There the bomb exploded, knocking a 3-foot-square hole below the water line and so deluging the after part of the ship with water that all fires were extinguished and everyone on the fantail was washed overboard. The third plane missed *Colhoun*, pulled out and started to dive on *Bush* against her 40-mm fire, the best she could now deliver. It missed the bridge, and crashed main deck between the stacks. The impact almost bisected *Bush*; only the keel held her together. Her men already overboard climbed back, the repair party threw water on the fire and

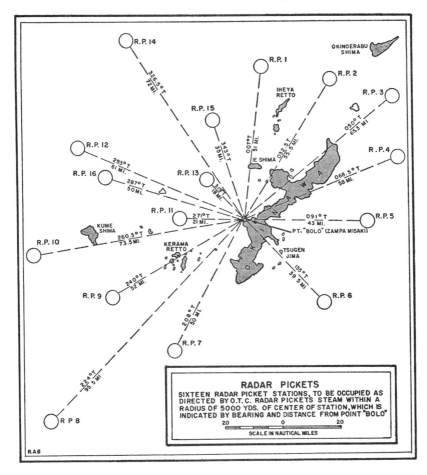

almost had it under control when, at 1740, a fourth plane, a Zeke, made a weaving dive. *Colhoun's* No. 4 fired at it but missed. For the last time the 20-mm and 40-mm guns of *Bush* spoke. The kamikaze cleared her by five feet, gained altitude, did a wingover, came in again, and crashed her port side at 1745, starting a terrible fire and killing or fatally burning all the wounded in the wardroom. A handy-billy, shifted to this fire, was no better than a garden hose on such a blaze; the entire forecastle was enveloped in flames, and ready ammunition began to explode.

Still neither crew would give up its ship. *Colhoun,* with only a bucket brigade operating, was taking water fast, but *Cassin Young* and a tug were coming in to assist. Commander Westholm counted on the fires in *Bush* above the main deck burning themselves out, as his ship was well buttoned up below; and although she could hardly fail to break in two in the heavy sea, he hoped that each half might be salvageable. Shortly before 1800 the bow began to settle. Suddenly a Hamp appeared "out of nowhere" and, evidently deciding that *Bush* was a goner, dived on *Colhoun*. Direct hits were scored on the plane at very close range. Already aflame, it hooked the pilothouse and crashed the port side. *Colhoun* was so badly damaged already that this additional hit did not make things much worse.

By that time daylight had begun to fade. Other Japanese planes were visible, but not another ship was within hailing distance. Damaged *LCS-64*, with many survivors on board, had cleared out. At 1830 a big swell rocked *Bush*. She caved in amidships, jackknifed until bow and stern sections were at a 135-degree angle, and quietly went down in a 350-fathom deep.

Commander Wilson of *Colhoun*, after consulting his exec. and heads of departments, decided to abandon ship. When *Cassin Young* closed at 1900, he begged her to search for *Bush* survivors. *LCS-84*, which also closed, commenced the arduous work of rescuing men in the rough sea. About 200 were transferred to *Cassin Young* between 2015 and 2100. *LCS-87* then came alongside and took over all who remained in *Colhoun* except a skeleton salvage crew of four officers and 17 men. Fires flared up again, and the men ran out of foamite and CO_2. When fleet tug *Pakana* arrived from Kerama Retto at 2320, *Colhoun* was listing 23 degrees and awash up to her No. 4 gun. The tug had no pumps to lend, so Commander Wilson ordered *LCS-87* to take off the skeleton crew, and, at his request, *Cassin Young* sank her by gunfire. She had lost 35 men killed or missing and 21 were wounded.

The plight of *Bush* survivors was desperate. To keep afloat they had one gig, a number of floater nets which were constantly breaking up and capsizing, and a few rubber life rafts inflated by CO_2, which were excellent — one supported 37 men. The seas were ten to twelve feet high and whitecapped. Both air and water were cold. The men had taken a beating in the successive attacks on their ship and were suffering agonies from their burns. Many could stand no more, slipped out of their life jackets and went down. The gig finally attracted the attention of *LCS–64*, which commenced rescue operations at 2130; a fleet tug from Kerama and a PC arrived shortly after. They had to work in complete darkness as Japanese planes were still about. As the rescue vessels approached survivors some became excited and tried to swim to them, and drowned from exhaustion; or when alongside were broken against the hull, or caught in the propellers. Other men died after being taken from the water. Seven officers out of 26, including Comdesdiv 98, Commander J. S. Willis, and 87 men out of 307, were lost.[8]

3. *Attacks on Antisubmarine Screen and Minecraft*

There was air-surface action all around Okinawa on that bloody afternoon and evening of 6 April. Destroyer *Gregory*, Lieutenant Commander Bruce McCandless, was part of the outer antisubmarine screen off southern Okinawa, with APD *Daniel T. Griffin* and destroyer escort *Witter* in an adjoining station. Two Vals attacked at 1612. *Gregory* shot down one; the other went for *Witter*, nine miles distant, crashed her and killed six men. *Gregory* and fleet tug *Arikara*, escorting *Witter* to Kerama Retto, saw *Morris* in another patrol station under attack at 1815. She was crashed between her two forward turrets. *Griffin* and *R. P. Leary* closed with fire hoses ready; and although the kamikaze's gas tank had soaked compartments below deck, making a very hot and dangerous fire, they got it under control by 2030. *Morris* lost 13 men killed and 45 wounded; and, as in all these actions, many suffered ghastly burns.

Destroyer *Howorth* (Commander E. S. Burns) was steaming north off Zampa Misaki at 1600, with cruiser *St. Louis* about 1800

[8] Action Reports and conversations with the surviving exec., Lt. Malcolm G. Evans USNR.

yards away, when the air raid on the transport area approached. The kamikazes decided to attack the cruiser and the destroyer. Antiaircraft fire of both ships splashed one 25 yards astern of *St. Louis*. A Val dove on *Howorth* at 1623, passing between her stacks and splashing. At 1700, when patrolling her station between Nago Wan and Ie Shima, not far from the spot where *Newcomb* and *Leutze* were attacked, *Howorth* got word that *Hyman* on a nearby station had been hit, and went to her assistance. She had barely changed course when two groups of four Zekes each went for her. The first to attack, a slow glider, was knocked down 200 yards short. Two missed and splashed. The fourth, a steep diver, passed over her fantail with wing scraping the deck, and splashed. Another was shot down 250 yards away. The sixth to attack charged directly at the main battery director and crashed. Nine men were killed or missing and 14 wounded, but the fires were quickly brought under control; and while the damage control party was working another plane was shot down by her 40-mm fire, dead astern. Nevertheless, *Howorth* was able to make Kerama Retto unassisted.

Hyman (Commander R. N. Norgaard) had been attacked by four planes at 1612, when proceeding to a "flycatcher" picket station northeast of Ie Shima. She shot down three, but at 1627 was crashed by a Hamp on the torpedo tubes between the stacks. A tremendous explosion, to which torpedo warheads probably contributed, followed, and the flooded forward engine room had to be abandoned. *Hyman* was so severely damaged that destroyer *Rooks* was told off to escort her, and en route to Kerama the pair was attacked but not hit. Lucky *Rooks* (Commander J. A. McGoldrick) had already taken part in the destruction of five kamikazes in the course of the day. She was in the thick of things around Okinawa until 25 June, but suffered neither damage nor casualties — surely a record for good fortune.

On the east coast, destroyer *Purdy* (Commander Frank L. Johnson) was patrolling antisubmarine station A-2 off Kimmu Wan at 1730 when the word was passed that destroyer *Mullany* on a nearby station had been crashed by a kamikaze. Half an hour later Captain

Moosbrugger, commanding this east coast screen, ordered *Purdy* to go to *Mullany's* assistance, and she bent on 30 knots. At 1845 she found *Mullany* on fire, dead in the water and abandoned, with minesweepers collecting survivors from the water. Commander Johnson ordered the smaller minecraft to leave and destroyer mine-sweeper *Gherardi* to stand by, and requested a tug and a C.A.P. from Admiral Turner, while he started salvage operations. Presently the C.O. of *Mullany* boarded *Purdy* from his whaleboat and gave a gloomy report of the condition of his ship; but Johnson decided to persist in his efforts. At 1930 he closed *Mullany* with fire hoses rigged and played streams of water on her. When the fires began to die down, the C.O. boarded with his own salvage party, and was able to take *Mullany* to Kerama Retto under her own power.

Nor does this conclude the story of 6 April. A unit of six mine-craft, *Ransom* flag, under Lieutenant Commander W. W. McMil-len, supported by destroyer-minesweepers *Rodman* (Commander W. H. Kirvan) and *Emmons* (Lieutenant Commander Eugene N. Foss USNR) was sweeping the channel between Iheya Retto and Oki-nawa, when it suddenly became the target for a large flight of kami-kazes. *Rodman* was surprised by the first of the gang. Diving out of the clouds it crashed her forward. Almost immediately thereafter its bomb exploded under her superstructure. Sixteen men were killed or missing and 20 wounded; but *Rodman's* engineering plant was still intact, and fires were under control by 1600, when she was crashed by two more kamikazes of the group that was after *Emmons*, and one that hit the skipper's cabin gutted the superstructure.

Emmons was about to go alongside *Rodman* to assist when her radar screen showed the air to be full of "bandits." She circled *Rodman* to provide antiaircraft support, and to such good purpose that six enemy planes were splashed by her gunfire. A large C.A.P. of Marine Corps Corsairs from one of the fast carriers went after these bandits like all-get-out; *Emmons* would put a 5-inch burst as near one as she could, and in a split second a Corsair would drop down from topside and splash the kamikaze. At least 20 victims of this C.A.P. were counted from the ship, which splashed six more before being hit herself. The Corsairs boldly pressed attacks right into the DMS's antiaircraft fire, but could not save her. In rapid succession *Emmons* was hit by five kamikazes as she was making 25 knots, and four others missed by yards. Two crashed her stern simultaneously, blowing off both fantail and rudder. A third crashed the forward gun and blew a large hole in the bow. A fourth hit under the bridge on the port side, slithering into the C.I.C. and killing the four officers and ten men who manned that brain center of the ship. Flames roared up through the pilot house, into which Lieutenant Commander Foss and most of the bridge personnel had ducked; they rushed out to take refuge on the bridge, but no bridge was there and overboard they went. The fifth kamikaze came in on a strafing run at 1833 which killed the machine-gun officer, then circled and crashed the wrecked superstructure.

With the wounded captain overboard, the executive killed and the first lieutenant wounded, the gunnery officer, Lieutenant J. J. Griffin USNR, took command.

Fires were raging in all spaces from the forward gun to frame 67, small fires were burning elsewhere, ready ammunition was exploding, the ship had a 10-degree list and appeared to be settling aft; but the sprinkling system in the handling rooms functioned, the engineering plant was little damaged, and the gun crews continued to fire in local control, No. 3 splashing a sixth kamikaze. Lieutenant Griffin had the less severely wounded removed to life rafts and ordered topside gear to be jettisoned. The fire in the superstructure was brought under control, but the fire forward could not be quenched owing to lack of water pressure, and the port engine conked out. At 1930, after a heavy explosion in the handling room, Lieutenant Griffin ordered Abandon Ship. *Emmons* might yet have been saved had she received assistance in fire-fighting and pumping; but *Rodman* had all she could do to reach Kerama Retto alive, the minesweepers under strafing fire fished from the water a number of survivors, including the skipper; and all fleet tugs were helping other cripples. *PGM-11*, a small mine-disposal vessel, bravely stood by. She boldly closed the burning and exploding ship and took off the 60-odd remaining men around 2000. Two hours later *Ellyson* closed the derelict, still burning but floating high; she was unable to put a rescue party on board, because of the rough sea, and, upon orders by Admiral Turner, sank her with gunfire lest she drift onto an enemy-held beach. Eight out of 19 officers and 53 out of 237 men were killed or missing, and three more officers died of their wounds.[9]

I doubt whether anyone could fully appreciate the results of this desperate fury of the Kamikaze Corps unless he were present, or in a hospital where wounded survivors were treated. Men wounded in these attacks were for the most part horribly burned. They suffered excruciating agony until given first aid; but if blown overboard, hours might elapse until a pharmacist's mate could relieve them. The medical officers did wonders if the wounded survived long enough to receive attention. And many men in rear hospitals, who looked like mummies under their bandages, breathing through a tube and being fed intravenously while their bodies healed, were cured by virtue of new methods of treating burns.

4. Raid on Kerama

Kerama roadstead, where many vulnerable ammunition and fuel ships were concentrated, had been largely neglected by enemy air until this great attack of 6 April, and not many planes got through to it then. At 1627 *LST–447* (Lieutenant Paul J. Schmitz), having discharged cargo at Okinawa, was proceeding to Kerama when at a point about a mile and a half below the southern entrance to the roadstead she sighted two planes 200 feet above the water, heading in. She opened fire on a Zeke and scored a hit at 3000 yards. The Japanese pilot, evidently figuring that he could not make the

[9] *Emmons* Action Report by Lt. Griffin; story in *New York Daily News* 19 June 1945; conversations at Aiea hospital with Lt. Cdr. Foss, who, badly burned, was picked up by *Recruit* after an hour in the water, went completely blind for two weeks, but eventually recovered both sight and health. My statement of casualties is that of Lt. Cdr. Foss.

crowded harbor, shifted target to the LST, and kept on coming, black smoke streaming out of his tail, despite more hits from her machine guns. He crashed the ship about two feet above the waterline and his bomb penetrated and exploded, completely gutting the LST and starting such fierce fires that within ten minutes Lieutenant Schmitz passed the word to abandon ship. Destroyer escort *Willmarth* and rescue tug *ATR–80* closed to fight fires, but, owing to the large amount of diesel oil on board, *LST–447* burned for about 24 hours, when she sank. Five men were missing and 17 wounded.

During this action, escort carrier *Tulagi* and three Victory ships converted to ammunition carriers – *Las Vegas Victory*, *Logan V.* and *Hobbs V.* – were moored just inside the southern entrance to Kerama roadstead. These received the full attention of other kamikazes which passed up the LST. One attempted to dive on *Tulagi* but swerved and crashed *Logan V.* as second choice. *Hobbs V.*, anchored nearby, weighed and stood out, but at 1845 another kamikaze crashed the after part of her bridge. Both ships were abandoned by their merchant marine crews. *Las Vegas V.*, Navy-manned, was discharging ammunition from both sides into an LCS, an LCT and two LCMs when this action began. She splashed a plane that picked on her, and most fortunately was not hit. The other two ammunition carriers, owing to their understandably prompt abandonment, sustained few losses – mostly to their Naval armed guard units; but the ships themselves were a total loss. They drifted, burning and exploding, for over a day, when they were sunk by gunfire.

A mile off Cape Zampa Misaki (Point Bolo) a number of LSTs of Lieutenant Commander J. R. Keeling's group 46, anchored and waiting their turn to beach, caught the eyes of kamikazes looking for meaty victims. At 1711 one dived on *LST–739*. Fired on by her and the other LSTs, it was splashed 200 yards from the group flagship; and between 1800 and 1815 five were shot down by the screen and by a group of minesweepers which were then returning to base.[10]

[10] Com LST Group 46 (Unit 4, Lt. Cdr. Keeling) Action Report.

Admiral Turner's staff estimated that 182 Japanese planes in 22 groups attacked the expeditionary force during the afternoon of 6 April; that 55 were destroyed by C.A.P., 35 by ships' antiaircraft fire, and 24 by crashing — a total of 108. On the same day, TF 38 claimed to have destroyed 249 attacking planes, *Essex* airmen alone splashing 65; and of the total, 136 were shot down over Okinawa. That these claims were not much exaggerated is proved by the fact that the Japanese themselves counted 355 kamikaze planes and 341 bombers committed to this, the first and greatest of their massed *kikusui* attacks; and kamikazes never returned home.

On the other hand, we had lost three destroyer types, one LST and two ammunition ships sunk; and ten ships, including eight destroyer types, a DE, and the minelayer *Defense*, suffered major damage and many casualties. This, however, fell far short of Japanese claims and expectations, which amounted to 60 vessels (including 2 battleships and 3 cruisers) sunk and 61 badly damaged. A comparison of our losses with the almost 700 enemy planes thrown into the battle indicated that the kamikazes planes were no longer so lethal, plane for plane, as they had been over Lingayen Gulf in January.

This particular blitz slipped over into Saturday 7 April, the day that *Yamato* was sunk. A kamikaze crashed *Maryland*, causing the loss of 16 men and wounding 37 more. Twenty planes approached the transport area, but did no damage; 12 were shot down, half by C.A.P. and half by ships. En route, one plane crashed radar picket destroyer *Bennett*, killing three men, wounding 18 and causing severe damage in the engineering spaces; she was escorted to Kerama by *Sterett*. Destroyer escort *Wesson*, in a screening station north of Ie Shima, was crashed by a plane which dove out of the clouds while she was engaged in firing on three others. Fires sprang up, engineering spaces flooded, and power was lost for a time; but she made Kerama on one shaft.

Radar picket stations Nos. 1, 2 and 3, where *Bush* and *Colhoun* were sunk, received more attention on 8 April, but no more damage was done to the ships. *Gregory* on station No. 3 was attacked by a

Sonia that evening. Although pieces were shot off it by machine-gun fire, it kept coming, and crashed amidships, abreast of the forward fire room. Then a second and a third came in, and were shot down close aboard. Commander McCandless got his fires out in short order, and *Gregory* steamed into Kerama roadstead under her own power.[11]

At the conclusion of these three days Admiral Spruance congratulated the escort carriers, and the search and reconnaissance planes operating from Kerama, for their outstanding performance and fine teamwork. At the same time he notified Admiral Nimitz that the situation respecting pilots and planes was not good, and might become critical if enemy air attacks continued. He requested that replacement pilots and planes be expedited by the transport CVEs of Service Squadron 6, even if our obligations in other Pacific areas had to be reduced. Everyone realized that the situation was serious for the destroyers and other screening ships, and might even get out of hand.

---

[11] *Gregory* Action Report. She proceeded to San Diego for repairs.

CHAPTER XIII

Fast Carrier Support[1]

1–12 April 1945

1. The End of Yamato, 7 April

ON 6 APRIL, the day when Operation TEN-GO was unleashed, two groups of Task Force 58, "Jocko" Clark's 58.1 and "Ted" Sherman's 58.3, were operating some 70 miles east of the Okinawa dog's forelegs, the Katchin Peninsula. C.A.P. and a radar picket unit of six destroyers were thrown out 30 miles northeastward. *Cabot* had a very close shave from a kamikaze that skimmed over her deck but missed; three carriers, two cruisers and two destroyers were also near-missed, and about 30 planes were shot down over or near the disposition. It seems that the pilots who attacked TF 58 that day were second-string kamikazes. One even bailed out when his plane was shot down by C.A.P. He was picked up, as Admiral Mitscher signaled, "from a fancy red life raft, wearing silk scarf with Nip inscription 'Kamikaze Special Attack Unit 3.' Says he flew from Kikai Jima. Graduated from Kisarazu late 1944 and is a flight instructor. Now matriculating in *Hornet*."

Throughout this day, and for many days preceding and following, TF 58 also maintained C.A.P. over the amphibious forces around Okinawa; the importance of their work, in concert with the

[1] CTF 58 (Vice Adm. Mitscher) Action Report 17 July 1945 pp. 8–11, and Action Reports of CTG 58.1, 58.2, 58.3 and 58.4; Mitsuru Yoshida "The End of *Yamato*" U.S. Naval Institute *Proceedings* LXVIII (Feb. 1952) 117–130, translated by M. Chikuami and edited by Roger Pineau (copyright 1952 by the Institute); Combined Fleet Notice No. 24, 30 July 1945, trans. by Robert S. Schwantes; *Yamato* War Diary, and Desron 2 Action Report, translation in *Campaigns of Pacific War* 334–338; Naval Technical Mission to Japan "*Yamato* and *Musashi*" O.N.I. *Review* I No. 8 (June 1946) 3–17.

ships, we have already seen. *Essex* claimed that her planes alone shot down 65 of the enemy's on 6 April, and total TF 58 claims added up to 249 — a mighty achievement, even if discounted 50 per cent. And only two planes were lost by the Task Force.[2]

At 1745 April 6, Pacific Fleet submarine *Threadfin*, patrolling off the Bungo Suido entrance to the Inland Sea, picked up a surface contact of two large and about six smaller ships, moving southwest at 25 knots. In accordance with her orders she passed up a chance to attack in order to get off her contact report, which was promptly received by Task Force 58. *Hackleback* also sighted this group and sent off four contact reports.

This last-gasp effort of the Japanese Combined Fleet comprised super-battleship *Yamato*, light cruiser *Yahagi* and eight destroyers. As an integral part of Operation TEN-GO, their objective was the Hagushi roadstead off Okinawa, to attack "survivors" of the day's air blitz, at daylight 9 April. The sacrificial nature of this sortie is indicated by the fact that *Yamato* was given only enough fuel for a one-way trip to Okinawa.[3]

Yamato and her sister ship *Musashi*, the world's biggest battle-wagons, were the pride of the Imperial Japanese Navy. The remains of *Musashi* were already on the bottom of the Sibuyan Sea, whither Avengers of the Fast Carrier Forces had consigned her on 24 October 1944.[4] But *Yamato* had come through the Battle off Samar and the subsequent air pursuit with relatively little damage, and was theoretically capable of outshooting any ship of the United States Navy.

Designed in 1937 and completed in December 1941, *Yamato* displaced 68,000 tons on trials and 72,809 tons fully laden. Her main battery consisted of nine 460-mm (18.1-inch) guns. These enormous cannon threw a projectile weighing 3200 pounds, as compared with the 2700-pound shell of our 16-inchers, and had a maxi-

---

[2] CTF 58 (Vice Adm. Mitscher) Action Report p. 8.
[3] Rear Adm. Yokoi in U.S. Naval Institute *Proceedings* LXXX 509.
[4] See Vol. XII 162, 186, and air photo of *Yamato* in that battle facing p. 190. For sinking of aircraft carrier *Shinano*, which was converted from a similar BB hull, see Vol. XII 410–411.

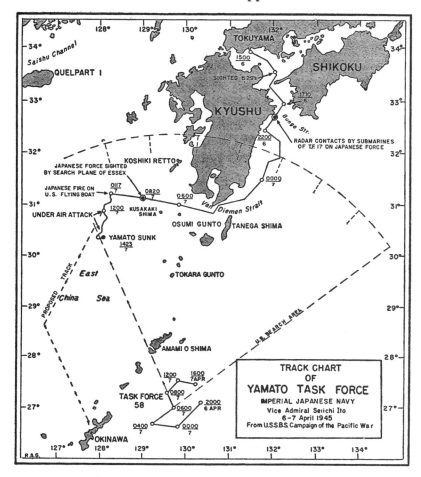

TRACK CHART
OF
YAMATO TASK FORCE
IMPERIAL JAPANESE NAVY
Vice Admiral Seiichi Ito
6-7 April 1945
From U.S.S.B.S. Campaign of the Pacific War

mum range of 42,000 meters (22½ miles), the flight time being a little over one minute and three quarters. Her planned complement of 2200 officers and men had been increased to 2767 on account of radar and additional antiaircraft guns, of which she possessed about 100. She measured 863 feet over all and drew 35 feet with full load. Her engine rooms were protected by 16.1-inch vertical and 7.9-inch horizontal armor plate. Her propulsion came from four turbine engines developing 150,000 horsepower; and in spite of her great weight she was capable of a maximum speed of 27.5 knots and a standard cruising speed of 25 knots. This ratio of speed to armor and weight was attained by electrical welding and a unique hull design, the principal feature being a gigantic bulbous bow to reduce hull resistance. *Yamato*, moreover, was a singularly beautiful ship, with a graceful sheer to her flush deck, unbroken from stem to stern, and a streamlined mast and stack. She was built at the Kure navy yard under conditions of extreme secrecy, and special dry docks to accommodate her and *Musashi* had been constructed at Sasebo and Yokosuka.[5]

The *Yamato* task force was set up by Admiral Ozawa, Commander Third Fleet, as "Surface Special Attack Force" (also called "First Diversion Attack Force"), with the objective to "destroy the enemy convoy and task force around Okinawa," in coöperation with the Japanese Air Forces and Army.[6] The task organization follows: —

> *Surface Special Attack Force,* *Vice Admiral Seiichi Ito
> Battleship   *YAMATO, *Rear Admiral Kosaku Ariga
> *Comdesron 2* Rear Admiral Keizo Komura in light cruiser *YAHAGI, Captain Tameichi Hara
> *Comdesdiv 41* Captain M. Yoshida in FUYUTSUKI, with SUZUTSUKI
> *Comdesdiv 17* *Captain K. Shintani in *ISOKAZE, with *HAMAKAZE and YUKIKAZE
> *Comdesdiv 21* *Captain H. Kotaki in *ASASHIMO, with *KASUMI and HATSUSHIMO
> * Sunk or killed in this action.

This forlorn hope of the Japanese Navy was rendered hopeless for want of air cover. According to one account, two fighter planes were over *Yamato* as late as 1000 April 7 but retired before the fighting began. In view of what had happened to another naked fleet, Admiral Kurita's in the Battle for Leyte Gulf, it seems inexplicable that the now unified Japanese air command should have hurled all its available fighters against TF 58 and the amphibious forces on 6 and 7 April, instead of covering these ships.

---

[5] Capt. K. Matsumoto and Capt. M. Chihaya (who took part in her construction) "Design and Construction of the *Yamato* and *Musashi*," U.S. Nav. Inst. *Proceedings* LXXIX (Oct. 1953) 1103–14; U.S. Naval Technical Mission, Japan Summary Report 1 Nov. 1946 p. 9; data from Capt. T. Ohmae, 1959.

[6] Combined Fleet Notice No. 24. The 32nd Army on Okinawa, according to this, "was to open a general attack and wipe out the enemy landing party."

Admiral Ito's force got under way from off Tokuyama at 1520 April 6 and sortied from the Inland Sea by Bungo Suido at 2000. The crew of *Yamato* were assembled at 1800, when the exec. delivered a message from Admiral Ozawa, "Render this operation the turning point of the war." The crew sang the national anthem and gave three banzais for the Emperor. At 2020 a U.S. submarine was sighted "and repulsed," according to a subsequent Combined Fleet release. *Hackleback* reported that a destroyer peeled off three times in pursuit, but never came near enough to force her to submerge.

Special Attack Force skirted the eastern shores of Kyushu, turned west through Osumi Kaikyo (Van Diemen Strait), passed Sata Misaki, the southernmost point of Kyushu, and steered about WNW, leaving the big lighthouse on Kusakaki Shima well on the port beam, with the idea of circling around as far from TF 58 as possible and pouncing on Okinawa during the evening of 7 April.

Admiral Mitscher was expecting this, and made every possible preparation to see that *Yamato* and her consorts did not get very far. After receiving the two submarine contacts he ordered all four of his task groups to a suitable launching position northeast of Okinawa. Rear Admiral Radford's TG 58.4, which had been fueling on 6 April, managed to rejoin TF 58 during the night; only Rear Admiral Davison's TG 58.2, fueling, failed to get into the fight. Searches were flown by TGs 58.1 and 58.3 at daybreak 7 April. All strike planes were held on carriers' flight decks until results of the search were known.

At 0823 April 7 an *Essex* plane flushed the *Yamato* group southwest of Koshiki Retto. Nine minutes later the pilot sent an amplifying report giving the enemy course at 300°, speed 12 knots. The big battlewagon was actually making 22 knots, at the center of a diamond-shaped formation screened by the destroyers, with light cruiser *Yahagi* in the rear.

Admiral Spruance promptly transmitted these contacts to Rear Admiral Deyo of the gunfire and bombardment force off Okinawa, indicating that the *Yamato* group was fair game for him. Deyo held a conference of flag and commanding officers on board Admiral Turner's flagship *Eldorado* at 1030 April 7, as a result of which a battle plan was drawn up for six battleships, seven cruisers and 21 destroyers. Deyo planned to keep his ships between the Japanese and Okinawa, to prevent their getting at the transports. TF 54 sortied from the roadstead at 1530 and performed exercises and battle maneuvers, during which *Maryland* was hit by a Japanese aërial bomb on turret No. 3, which was temporarily knocked out. An eagerly anxious evening followed for TF 54. Staff officers familiar with range tables took care to remind others that *Yamato's* 18.1-inch guns should have a maximum range of 45,000 yards, as against 42,000 for the 16-inch gunned battleships in Deyo's force and 37,000 for *Tennessee;* and that her speed should enable her to make an "end run" and thrust at the transports. They were cheered by a signal from Turner to Deyo, "Hope you will bring back a nice fish for breakfast"; and just as Deyo had begun to write his answer on a signal blank, "Many thanks, will try to . . ." an intercepted message, to the effect that Mitscher's scouts had already picked up the enemy, suggested the conclusion, ". . . if the pelicans haven't caught them all!" — which is what they did.[7]

Of great assistance in reaching this much desired consummation were two amphibious Mariners belonging to VPB 21 based at Kerama Retto, piloted by Lieutenant James R. Young USNR and Lieutenant (jg) R. L. Simms USNR. These made contact on the *Yamato* force and shadowed it for the next five hours. Ito fired at them in vain; they sent out regular reports and homed carrier strikes onto the target. They also made a notable air-sea rescue, as we shall see.

From lat. 31°22' N, long. 129°14' E, where the *Essex* plane picked up *Yamato* at 0823, she and her consorts made frequent radical changes of course and evasive maneuvering, but the general trend of the disposition was south.

Admiral Mitscher, as soon as he received definite reports of the

[7] CTF 54 (Rear Adm. Deyo) Action Report pp. 38–41, and his Ms. "Many Sparrows."

enemy force and its location at sea, launched a tracking and covering group of 16 fighter planes at 0915. At 1000 the main strikes from TGs 58.1 and 58.3 commenced launching. These consisted of 280 planes, 98 of them torpedo-bombers. *Hancock's* contingent (53 planes) was 15 minutes late in launching and failed to find the target. Admiral Radford's TG 58.4, which could contribute only 106 units, as it had C.A.P. duty over Okinawa, did not reach launching position until 0945 and its planes were late reaching the target.

The approach of the first strike was spotted by *Yamato* at 1232. Rear Admiral Ariga ordered Open Fire, and scores of guns in the flagship "burst forth simultaneously," according to Ensign Yoshida. At 1241 she received two bomb hits near the mainmast, and, four minutes later, her first torpedo hit. (Carrier *Bennington* claims both for her boys.) *San Jacinto* planes at the same time got a bomb and a torpedo into destroyer *Hamakaze*, which plunged to the bottom bow first. Light cruiser *Yahagi* was also hit by a bomb and a torpedo at this time and went dead in the water.

Between 1300 and 1417 the force was under almost continuous attack. Ensign Yoshida gives a graphic picture of the big battleship's predicament, and what it felt like to be on board a mighty ship, helpless under an expertly delivered air onslaught. Her antiaircraft gunners, for want of practice on live targets, were unable to hit anything. After five torpedo hits on her port side between 1337 and 1344 had created serious flooding, Rear Admiral Ariga ordered the starboard engine and boiler rooms, as the largest and lowest compartments in the ship, to be counter-flooded. Yoshida phoned the occupants to warn them, but it was too late. "Water, both from torpedo hits and the flood valves rushed into these compartments and snuffed out the lives of the men at their posts, several hundred in all. Caught between cold sea water and steam and boiling water from the damaged boilers, they simply melted away." This sacrifice failed to correct the list, and with only one screw working, *Yamato* lost speed rapidly.

Now came in the fourth major attack wave. Aërial torpedoes blew more holes in the port side and at least ten bombs exploded on the decks. The wireless room, supposedly watertight, flooded so completely that thenceforth *Yamato* had to rely entirely on flag and light signals. From 1345 she enjoyed a precious 15 minutes free from attack, but it availed her nothing. As Yoshida relates, bombs, bullets and torpedoes had reduced the mighty battleship "to a state of complete confusion. . . . The desolate decks were reduced to shambles, with nothing but cracked and twisted steel plates remaining. . . . Big guns were inoperable because of the increasing list, and only a few machine guns were intact. . . . One devastating blast in the emergency dispensary had killed all its occupants including the medical officers and corpsmen. . . ."

At 1400 began the final air attack. Hellcats and Avengers were able to make selective runs on the slowly moving, almost helpless ship. A terrific torpedo detonation aft reverberated throughout the ship and ended all communications from the bridge. The distress flag was hoisted, steering room flooded, rudder jammed hard left, and the list increased to 35 degrees. "As though awaiting this moment, the enemy came plunging through the clouds to deliver the *coup de grâce*. . . . It was impossible to evade. . . . I could hear the Captain vainly shouting, 'Hold on, men! Hold on, men!' . . . I heard the Executive Officer report to the Captain in a heartbroken voice, 'Correction of list hopeless!' . . . Men were jumbled together in disorder on the deck, but a group of staff officers squirmed out of the pile and crawled over to the Commander in Chief for a final conference." Admiral Ito "struggled to his feet. His chief of staff then arose and saluted. A prolonged silence followed during which they regarded each other solemnly." Ito "looked around, shook hands deliberately with his staff officers, and then went resolutely into his cabin." The Captain concerned himself with saving the Emperor's portrait.

It was now 1420. "The deck was nearly vertical and *Yamato's* battle flag was almost touching the billowing waves. . . . Shells of the big guns skidded and bumped across the deck of the ammunition

Twilight Air Attack on Transport Area

U.S.S. *Newcomb* after Kamikaze Crash

Operation TEN-GO *Gets Going*

U.S.S. *Zellars* after Kamikaze Crash

U.S.S. *Tennessee*, after Splashing One on Each Bow, About to Be
Crashed by a Third

U.S.S. *Tennessee* Fighting Fires

The Air Attack of 12 April

The Last of Battleship Yamato

The Black Spots Are Heads of Swimmers

Going, Going, Gone! (The Last of Light Cruiser Yahagi)

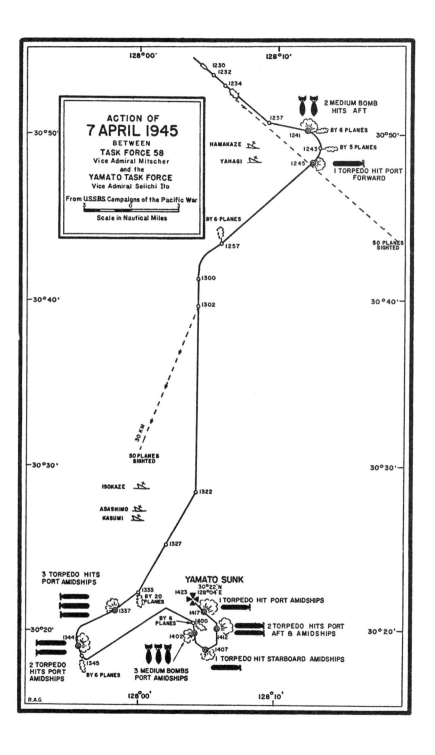

ACTION OF
7 APRIL 1945
BETWEEN
TASK FORCE 58
Vice Admiral Mitscher
and the
YAMATO TASK FORCE
Vice Admiral Seiichi Ito

From U.S.S.B.S. Campaigns of the Pacific War

Scale in Nautical Miles

128°00'   128°10'

1230
1232
1234

2 MEDIUM BOMB
HITS AFT

1237

30°50'   30°50'

1241
HAMAKAZE
YAHAGI
1243   BY 6 PLANES
1245   BY 5 PLANES
1 TORPEDO HIT PORT
FORWARD

BY 6 PLANES
1257   50 PLANES
SIGHTED

1300

30°40'   30°40'

1302

30 KM

50 PLANES
SIGHTED

30°30'   30°30'

ISOKAZE
1322

ASASHIMO
KASUMI

1327

3 TORPEDO HITS
PORT AMIDSHIPS

YAMATO SUNK
30°22'N
128°04'E

1333   1423
BY 20   1 TORPEDO HIT PORT AMIDSHIPS
PLANES

1337   1417
BY 6   1400
PLANES   2 TORPEDO HITS PORT
AFT & AMIDSHIPS

30°20'   1344   1402   1412   30°20'
1 TORPEDO HIT STARBOARD AMIDSHIPS
1407

1345
2 TORPEDO   BY 6 PLANES   3 MEDIUM BOMBS
HITS PORT   PORT AMIDSHIPS
AMIDSHIPS

R.A.G   128°00'   128°10'

room, crashing against the bulkhead and kindling the first of a series of explosions." At 1423 "the ship slid under completely," followed by "the blast, rumble, and shock of compartments bursting from air pressure and exploding magazines already submerged."

One American had a grandstand seat for seeing this queen of the battlewagons go down. He was Lieutenant (jg) W. E. Delaney USNR from carrier *Belleau Wood*. His Avenger had made bomb hits on *Yamato* from so low an altitude that the explosion set him afire and all had to bail out. The two crewmen had parachute trouble and were drowned, but Delaney managed to get into his rubber raft, from which he witnessed the death throes of *Yamato*. There he was spotted by Lieutenants Young and Simms who had been following the battle in their PBMs. While Simms acted as decoy to attract enemy gunfire, Young made a neat water landing, taxied toward the pilot, whose raft was in the midst of floating Japanese survivors, took him on board, made a jet-assisted takeoff, and subsequently landed him safe and sound at Yontan airfield.[8]

About two hours later another PBM, observing a mass of wreckage and many floating survivors, made a water landing and took prisoner some survivors, who admitted that *Yamato* was no more. At 1701 Admiral Mitscher sent a signal to Admiral Spruance, "We attacked *Yamato*, *Agano*, one light cruiser and seven or eight destroyers. Sank first three, two others burning badly, three got away. . . . We lost about seven planes."

Light cruiser *Yahagi*, which the pilots had wrongly identified as *Agano*, proved almost as tough as the battleship, taking 12 bomb and seven torpedo hits before going down. Besides *Hamakaze*, sunk early in the fight, three other destroyers were so heavily damaged that they had to be scuttled. The four destroyers remaining were damaged in varying degrees, but managed to get back to Sasebo. *Yamato* lost all but 23 officers and 246 men of her complement of 2767; *Yahagi* lost 446; *Asashimo* lost 330; the seven destroyers, 391

[8] *Belleau Wood* Action Report 14 Mar.–28 Apr., 4 May; VPB 21 War Diary for April; Delaney's story in *N.Y. Times* 11 Apr. 1945.

officers and men. Among the survivors were 209 wounded.[9] Losses on our side were 10 planes and 12 men.[10]

As we have seen in Chapter XII, the Kamikaze Corps was far from idle during this attack. It not only pulled off the first massed *kikusui* assault on the amphibious forces, but struck back at Task Force 58. At 1212 April 7 *Hancock* opened fire on an enemy plane at 3000 feet. It crossed her bows, then turned and headed for the ship, sharp on her starboard bow. After dropping a bomb that hit the flight deck forward it crashed the same deck aft, setting fire to parked planes. The bomb explosion holed and damaged the flight deck, set fire to nearby planes and to the forward part of the hangar deck. By 1230 damage control party reported the fires under control, and by 1300 only an occasional wisp of smoke could be seen from other ships as evidence of the attack. *Hancock* recovered her own strike group at 1630 and was able to handle aircraft on an emergency basis, but she lost 72 men killed and 82 wounded.

2. Task Force 58 Operations, 11 April

On 8 April Task Force 58 resumed routine support of Operation ICEBERG, and that day TG 58.2 rejoined.

Since the P.O.W. whom *Hornet* picked up on 6 April conveniently boasted that 11 April would bring another massed attack, Admiral Mitscher canceled all support missions over Okinawa for that day, and had all dive-bombers and torpedo planes debombed and degassed and parked on their hangar decks. C.A.P. was increased to 12 aircraft over the TF 58 picket destroyers and 24 over each of the two carrier task groups present. The other two were fueling.

---

[9] Information from Capt. Ohmae.

[10] Mitscher Report p. 9. Of the 386 carrier planes engaged, TG 58.1 contributed 113, TG 58.3, 167, TG 58.4, 106. By types they were 180 VF, 75 VB and 131 VT. CTF 58 Action Report p. 8. Each VF carried three 500-lb. bombs and each VB one 1000-lb. semi-armor piercing or GP bomb, and two 250-lb. bombs.

The expected attacks began to develop at 1330 April 11 and continued throughout the afternoon watch. At 1443 a kamikaze crashed battleship *Missouri* near her starboard quarter about three feet below main deck level. Parts of the plane and the mutilated body of the pilot were strewn over the after part of the ship, but the resulting fire was brought under control within three minutes and damage was confined to scorched paint. *Enterprise*, now back with TG 58.3, caught it again. At 1410, just as she was in a port evasive turn, a Judy sideswiped her port quarter and struck the shields of two 40-mm mounts. Parts of the plane were left in the gun tubs and the bomb continued into the water, exploding under the carrier and causing minor damage. At 1510 another Judy crashed close under her starboard bow, raising a shock wave and causing more damage. Parts of the Judy were hurled onto the flight deck where a plane on the starboard catapult caught fire; it was catapulted free, still burning, and the fire on the flight deck was quickly quenched. But "Big E" had to curtail her flight operations for 48 hours.

Destroyers on picket duty for TF 58 had a rough time on 11 April. At 1357 a plane was observed by *Kidd* to dive out of the sun onto *Bullard*, which took it under fire and splashed it about 50 yards astern. Eleven minutes later *Kidd* took a second aircraft under fire about 5000 yards on the port bow. This one passed ahead and out of range. Two enemy planes were next seen indulging in a mock dogfight (apparently to convey the idea that one was friendly) on the other side of the destroyer *Black*, which was about 1500 yards on *Kidd's* port beam. One dog-fighter peeled off and made a low-level run on *Black* in such a direction that *Kidd* could not bring her batteries to bear. As it reached *Black* the plane pulled over that ship and continued low over the water toward *Kidd*. Although already smoking from hits, it crashed the destroyer's forward fire room at the waterline. The skipper, Commander H. G. Moore, was seriously wounded by the bomb, which passed through the ship and exploded on the port side. In less than five minutes the forward fire room was isolated from the engineering system, while the ship was still making 22 knots. She had 38 killed or missing and 55 wounded. Most of the enemy plane was carried back to Ulithi in the fire room. It was found not to be a kamikaze but a fully equipped fighter with instrument panel and self-sealing tanks.

At 1507 April 11 *Essex* took a near-miss on the port side from a bomb which caused extensive damage to fuel tanks and in the engineering plant. She lost 28 wounded but remained in action. *Hale* was jolted by a near-miss bomb while maneuvering to put her surgeon on board *Kidd*. *Hank* had three killed or missing and one wounded when a kamikaze crashed close aboard, causing minor damage to the ship.

All this belongs to the second *kikusui* assault, involving 185 kamikazes.[11] Next day the "floating chrysanthemums" concentrated on radar pickets and ships off Okinawa. April 12 proved to be one of the most trying days for the Navy in this campaign.

3. *Royal Navy off Sakishima Gunto, 1–12 April* [12]

As we have already seen, Vice Admiral Rawlings RN in H.M.S. *King George V* brought all combatant elements of the British Pacific Fleet, including four fast carriers, up to the Sakishima Gunto, where their planes struck airfields and installations on 26, 27 and 31 March. Still designated Task Force 57, these ships contributed to the success of Operation ICEBERG by neutralizing airfields in the southern group of the Nansei Shoto and, to some extent, those on Formosa. Their efforts were neatly dovetailed with those of Rear Admiral Durgin's escort carrier support group (TG 51.2), so that Sakishima Gunto had no respite.

The Japanese air forces first counterattacked TF 57 on Okinawa L-day, 1 April. Rear Admiral Sir Philip Vian's carriers sent off first fighter sweep at 0640. Ten minutes later bogeys, 75 miles westward, registered on radar screens. The sweep was recalled to intercept and

---

[11] See table at head of Chap. XV.
[12] See footnote to Chap. VI Sec. 5 for authorities, and end of Appendix I for task organization.

additional fighters were launched. Interception took place about 40 miles from the task force and four aircraft were shot down. This failed to break up the Japanese formation. On it pressed, pursued by Hellcats, Corsairs and Seafires, and reached the carriers shortly after 0705. One plane made a low-level strafing run on H.M.S. *Indomitable*, killing one man and wounding six, then turned its attention to *King George V* but did no damage there. Next, a kamikaze crashed the base of the island of H.M.S. *Indefatigable*, killing 14 men and wounding 16. Her steel flight deck was out of action only briefly and she continued to launch and recover on a somewhat reduced scale. H. M. destroyer *Ulster* received a near-miss from a 500-pound bomb, which ruptured the bulkhead between the engine room and after fire room. She had to be towed to Leyte by H.M.N.Z.S. *Gambia*.

At 1215 the carriers launched a strike against Ishigaki airfield and runways in the Sakishima Gunto, and destroyed a few more grounded aircraft. At 1730 a low-flying bogey was picked up 15 miles to the northwest and Hellcats were sent to intercept. The bogey, which proved to be two planes, evaded them in the clouds, and one dived on H.M.S. *Illustrious*, which evaded by use of full rudder; one wing touched the edge of the flight deck and the plane splashed in the sea, where its bomb exploded harmlessly. The Japanese pilot's instructions, listing the priority of kamikaze targets, were blown on board by the explosion and made very interesting reading for Captain Lambe and staff, and for Fifth Fleet Intelligence.

Inferring from his experience on L-day that the enemy was launching planes from Sakishima airfields at first light, Sir Philip Vian sent off two aircraft at 0510 by moonlight to cover Ishigaki, and two more for Miyako, but they had to return owing to radio failure. No activity was noted and at daylight 2 April a fighter sweep was launched to cover all airfields in the Sakishima Gunto. The task force then retired for fueling and was relieved, during its absence, by planes from Admiral Durgin's escort carrier group.

Bad weather prevented the fueling scheduled for 3 April and it was not completed until the 5th. On 6 April pairs of aircraft were launched to be over the Miyako and Ishigaki airfields at daybreak, but no enemy planes were there to be found. At about 1700 bogeys were picked up by radar and the fighter intercept shot down one Judy. One kamikaze out of four dived on *Illustrious*. Again this carrier successfully took radical evasive action. The wing tip hit the island and the plane spun into the sea; there were no casualties and but slight damage.

During the day a message was received from Admiral Nimitz indicating that in his opinion all-out enemy reaction to Okinawa by kamikazes was under way; and he was only too right. Consequently, TF 57 canceled a bombardment of Ishigaki planned for 7 April. Fighter cover was maintained over Sakishima Gunto all that day, and when it appeared that craters previously blown in the airfields had been filled, three bomber strikes were sent to re-hole them. Admiral Rawlings's task force was enjoying a peaceful sail; sailors were reading, playing chequers and shooting darts, and a Royal Marine barber was cutting hair on the deck of *King George V*, when the Stand-to was sounded and everyone jumped to battle stations. The fleet chaplain, Canon J. T. Bezzant (survivor from the sinking of H.M.S. *Repulse* on 10 December 1941), explained over loudspeaker that enemy planes were flying about. One Judy was splashed by Seafires close aboard *Illustrious*; Seafires shot down a second at a safe distance, and the only air attack of the day was over.[18]

That evening TF 57 retired to fuel, while a veteran U.S. escort carrier division — *Sangamon, Suwannee, Chenango* and *Santee*, with Rear Admiral Sample as O.T.C. — took over the job of pounding targets in the Sakishima Gunto.

Fueling completed 9 April, Sir Philip Vian's carriers had already started back to their launching area when a message was intercepted from Commander Fifth Fleet to Cincpac, recommending that TF 57 strike the northernmost airfields of Formosa on 11 and 12 April, while Luzon-based aircraft of the Southwest Pacific command took care of those in southern Formosa, and Admiral Durgin's escort

[18] Trumbull in *N.Y. Times* 16 Apr. 1945.

carriers covered Sakishima Gunto. Admiral Nimitz approved this diversion and the Royal Navy carriers reached launching position 30 miles off Formosa at 0600 April 11. Weather conditions were so unfavorable that the strikes were postponed to the 12th. Warned by Admiral Spruance that heavy air attacks were to be expected, Sir Philip Vian put up an unusually heavy C.A.P. when reaching his launching position. But no planes molested the four carriers as they sliced off 48 bombers, accompanied by 41 fighters, in two waves to hit Formosan airfields. The first wave well performed its mission. The second, impeded by weather, shifted attention to Kiirun and attacked a chemical plant, docks and shipping. Strikes were repeated next day, after which TF 57 withdrew for another drink of oil. Very few enemy aircraft were seen in or over Formosa, but the British carriers' C.A.P. had to deal with strikes from the Sakishima Gunto. Consequently, on Admiral Rawlings's advice, Admiral Spruance decided to leave Formosa to the Southwest Pacific command and let TF 57 concentrate on the smaller islands which were giving trouble.

CHAPTER XIV

The Second Week at Okinawa

7–13 April 1945

1. The Situation Ashore, 8–11 April [1]

ON 8 APRIL, first Sunday after Easter, when the second week of the assault on Okinawa opened, the ground situation was about as follows. In the north the rapid advance of the 6th Marine Division across the neck of the Motobu Peninsula came to an end. On Monday morning it began to meet stiff opposition. In the south, XXIV Corps had already encountered stubborn resistance from strong defensive positions, implemented by massed artillery fire of a quality never hitherto received from the Japanese Army. By Sunday the Corps was stopped cold. Shore fire control parties and planes were having trouble locating targets in this southern area that could be reached by naval gunfire. But these difficulties did not then seem serious. Hope sprang up that all might be over by Whitsuntide, so rapidly had the troops advanced.

Kamikaze attacks, especially that of 6–7 April, were disquieting. But Admiral Turner expressed the general sentiment when he signaled at noon 7 April, "If this is the best the enemy can throw against us, we shall move forward." Next day, in view of the sinking of *Yamato* and the favorable situation on Okinawa, Turner sent this jocular message to Admiral Nimitz: "I may be crazy but it looks like the Japs have quit the war, at least in this section." To

[1] Books and Action Reports mentioned at heads of Chaps. IX and XI; Robert Sherrod *History of Marine Corps Aviation* (1952) chap. xxv; the writer's personal observations and field notes. The Japanese version of the *baka* bomb attacks is in Inoguchi & Nakajima *The Divine Wind* (1958) chap. xvi.

which Commander in Chief Pacific Fleet made the succinct reply: "Delete all after 'crazy'!"

Overconfidence prevailed in many quarters. "Old hands" of the Luzon campaign insisted that the present crop of kamikazes was inferior to the one encountered off Lingayen. That was correct, but there was a lot more of them. Intelligence, after many estimates and much figuring, reached the comfortable conclusion that the Imperial Air Forces were scraping the barrel, and that the 6 April performance could not be repeated more than once.

Pessimism there was, too. Some destroyer officers insisted that a pilot bent on crashing could not be stopped by anything smaller than 5-inch shell, and that with the existing system of gunfire control, it was impossible to knock down planes in one-two-three order. Radar picket duty could be as suicidal for the picketing sailors as for the attacking Japanese, unless two or more destroyers were placed at each station and C.A.P. provided at dawn and dusk. A summary of battle damage issued by Admiral Turner 10 April, adding up the Navy, Army and Marine Corps casualties through the 9th, indicated that the taking of Okinawa was going to be very costly: — [2]

	Killed	*Missing*	*Wounded*
Army & Marine Corps	650	129	3010
Task Force 51	246	330	737

The most encouraging factor was the early capture of airfields and prompt building-up of a land-based air force. Yontan and Kadena fields were no beds of roses for tired airmen. Japanese artillery shelled them daily; strafers and bombers paid frequent visits. Yet, by the evening of 8 April, 82 Marine Air Wing Corsairs and seven night fighters were based on Yontan field, and more were brought up within a day or two by escort carriers. Of this number, 41 were already available for C.A.P.; in another week if all went well these would be increased to 144. But the land-based night fight-

[2] CTF 51 Action Report and Admiral Turner's 20th summary for 1800 Apr. 10. These figures do not include the casualties in TF 58. For Navy casualties Lingayen, see Vol. XIII 325–326.

ers could not be used for C.A.P. before 14 April as their radar and calibration gear had not yet been unloaded. So the holes in the Fleet's air cover, at dawn and dusk, were not yet covered. If Admiral Spruance hoped soon to release TF 58 from close support duties, he was disappointed. Close support duties for Operation ICEBERG tied it down until well into June; it got away only to sink *Yamato* and strike Kyushu airfields.

The Japanese made Sunday night 8–9 April a rough one for the troops ashore. Turner assigned five battleships, five cruisers and 17 destroyers for night support of Tenth Army, whose "gratitude for our silencing rocket and mortar emplacement was almost heart-rending." [3] Every night thereafter, naval vessels stood by off southern Okinawa to deliver call fire and illumination, as requested by shore fire control parties. Star shell, the best way to uncover Japanese attempts at infiltration, was expended liberally, and its quality had greatly improved during the past year. "Up the Slot" in 1943 one expected half the star shell to be duds or fizz-outs; but off Okinawa a 100 per cent performance was not unusual.

Commodore McGovern's transports lifting the floating reserve arrived 9 April. Landing the 27th Division was completed next day; there were now some 160,000 American troops ashore on Okinawa.[4] In order to relieve shipping congestion, the 2nd Marine Division, still part of the floating reserve, was ordered by Admiral Turner to return to Guam, a move which turned out to be unwise. To shorten the supply line to the Marines on Motobu Peninsula, a secondary beachhead was established on the shores of Nago Wan.

In the early morning hours of 9 April the enemy delivered out of Naha Harbor his first successful suicide-boat attack. One 18-foot stinger hit destroyer *Charles J. Badger* off the Brown beaches and knocked out both engines temporarily, but hurt nobody. A second boat was detected by destroyer *Purdy*, and, when fired upon, dropped its depth charge and fled. In the transport area, assault

[3] Destroyer *Zellars* (Cdr. L. S. Kintberger) Action Report.
[4] Estimate by General Bruce at the time. Tenth Army G-1 Report says 175,000 landed by 21 April.

cargo ship *Starr*, target of a third, was conveniently protected by an LSM moored alongside which took the hit, not a lethal one except for the Japanese boat crew. At least three other boats and 15 swimmers carrying hand grenades were detected and destroyed in this attack. Thereafter "flycatcher" patrol was intensified, with one heavy ship and two destroyers assigned nightly to illuminate the mouth of Naha Harbor with star shell. But there were midgets also on the east coast, where *LCI(G)-82* had been sunk in the early hours of 4 April.

During the rest of this week the Marines were engaged in isolated actions against enemy strong points on the Motobu Peninsula; XXIV Corps was consolidating positions, getting ready for a big push in southern Okinawa. The soldiers were now up against the lines that the enemy intended to defend, the edge of a complicated and heavily fortified region across the three-mile-wide waist of the dog, from a point south of the Brown beaches to the Nakagusuku Wan. This area included pillboxes with steel doors impervious to flame-throwers. And Japanese artillery fire on our troops was increasing in volume and accuracy.

2. *East Side* [5]

One reason why Okinawa was chosen as the final springboard for Japan was the prospect of creating an advanced naval base on the shores of Nakagusuku Wan and Kimmu Wan. The one bay is located between the Okinawa dog's legs, and the other in the bend of his neck. Both lie directly across the island from the Hagushi landing beaches. Each is partly protected from the sea by a cluster of small islands and barrier reefs.

Before either bay could be used, the waters and their approaches had to be swept for mines, and the enemy removed from his vantage points on the offshore islands. This section of the Okinawa operation was called for short "East Side," and Rear Admiral Blandy,

[5] CTG 51.19 (Rear Adm. Blandy) Action Report 1 May 1945.

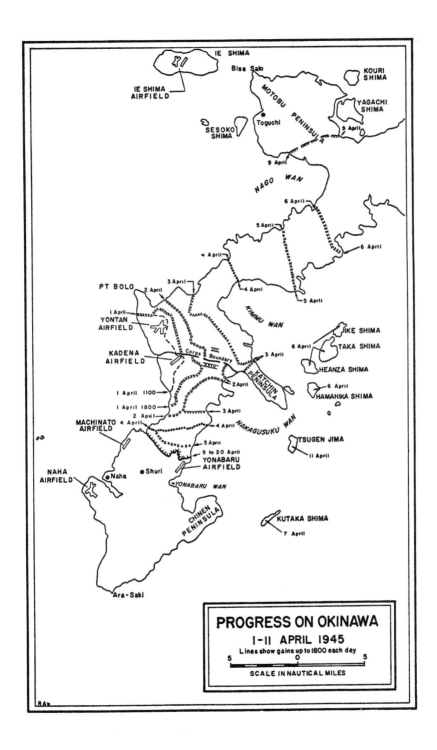

PROGRESS ON OKINAWA
1-11 APRIL 1945
Lines show gains up to 1800 each day
SCALE IN NAUTICAL MILES

who was given the job, earned a new nickname, "King of the Bowery."

Minesweeping the approaches to the two bays began 3 April and lasted six days. Commander E. D. McEathron had charge of these sweeps, and as depths in the bays were under 30 fathoms, his group was composed largely of small diesel-powered YMS. By the end of the second day's sweep, fire support ships were able to close the entrance to Nakagusuku Wan. On the 5th Admiral Deyo sent over three battleships, two cruisers and several destroyers to bombard East Side and islands, and that evening a Marine Corps reconnaissance battalion was landed on Tsugen Jima, which had to be secured before the bay could be developed. The Marine raiders were embarked in destroyer-transports *Scribner* and *Kinzer*, screened against possible attack of suicide boats by a "flycatcher" unit composed of an LCI gunboat and six LCS(L) support craft. After the landing, the Japanese garrison of Tsugen Jima came to life and the Marines, although not really run off the island (as they intended only to reconnoiter), had their departure expedited by a shower of machine-gun and mortar fire.

The casualties to Admiral Blandy's task group, during the eventful day of 6 April, we have already noted.[6] Minecraft worked all day clearing the East Side approaches and swept good sections of both bays. On the 7th *PGM-17* was sunk by a mine.

That night the Marine raiders reconnoitered three small islands of Kimmu Wan and found no military present. It was now clear that Tsugen Jima was the only East Side island that had to be taken, since it commanded the main channel to Nakagusuku Wan; and taken it was, on 10 April, by a battalion of the 105th Regiment, 27th Division, lifted from Kerama Retto in two transports and two LST, covered by *Pensacola* and two or three destroyers. The Japanese were entrenched in a village at the center of the island and let go as soon as the troops approached. With plenty of naval gunfire support the battalion had overrun the island on the afternoon of 11 April. Of the Japanese defenders, 234 were killed; about 50 more

[6] See Chap. XII: *Witter, Morris, Purdy* and *Mullany*.

fled, but were rooted out a few days later. All enemy installations, including three 6-inch guns, were captured or destroyed. Losses on our side to Army and Navy were 24 killed and about 100 wounded. The troops were reëmbarked to join the rest of the 27th Division in reinforcing XXIV Corps, and another unit had to mop up.

Every day through 11 April, assigned fire support battleships, cruisers and destroyers bombarded East Side targets designated by air spotters, and delivered call fire for the Marines and XXIV Corps.

3. *Air Battles of 9 and 12 April* [7]

Almanac for 12 April

Sunrise 0609   Sunset 1851
New moon rose 0354   Set   1838

Destroyer *Sterett* (Commander G. B. Williams), after success-fully driving off kamikazes on 6–7 April and rendering aid to others not so lucky, now caught one herself. In company with *LCS–36* and *LCS–24*, she was patrolling No. 4 radar picket station north-east of Okinawa, on the evening of the 9th. Five Vals approached in loose V formation. The first, when taken under fire, waggled wings and turned away. The second started a gliding attack. Main battery took it under fire so close that it exploded and splashed on *Sterett's* starboard beam. The third then began its run, and in spite of many hits, retained sufficient control to crash the destroyer at her water-line. When the smoke had cleared, the fourth Val was seen to be coming in on the starboard bow. It was immediately taken under fire by two 5-inch guns in local control and by the machine-gun battery. When 1000 yards distant, 40-mm fire sheared off one wing, which splashed 20 feet on the starboard bow, while the Val turned belly-up, then righted itself and continued over the destroyer. It splashed, after a landing wheel had near-missed the gunnery officer's head and the Japanese pilot's body had hurtled over No. 2 gun. As *Sterett* was making 32 knots when hit by the third Val, the in-

[7] CTF 54 (Rear Adm. Deyo) Action Report 5 May 1945.

rush of salt water put the fires out automatically, but the destroyer received enough structural damage to be sent to a rear area. By good fortune she suffered no loss of life.

The weather on 10 April was too foul for kamikazes, and there was only one air attack, on destroyer escort *Samuel S. Miles*. The plane nicked a gun shield, killing one man, and then splashed along- side, showering the ship with bomb fragments and debris. The fol- lowing night a Japanese attempt at a counter-amphibious landing against the northern sector was detected steaming northward in Yonabaru Harbor. Destroyers *Anthony* and *Morrison* were sum- moned, and took the barge completely apart with a direct hit.

On Thursday 12 April the weather was gorgeous, as clear and cool as a summer day in Maine when the wind blows off shore. But there was blood on the new moon. The Japanese chose this day for a second *kikusui* attack of 185 kamikazes, together with 150 fighters and 45 torpedo planes. Early that morning Admiral Turner warned all hands to expect strong air attacks and added, "Don't let any re- turn." Some did return; but ships of TF 51 with the aid of C.A.P. shot down about 147, and TF 58 claimed an additional bag of 151.

As usual radar picket ships were the first to catch it. At 0600 about 25 planes in ten groups approached from the north. A night C.A.P. from damaged *Enterprise* and a few shore-based planes were on duty, but shot down only four of the enemy. Three of the groups flew on to the Hagushi beaches, whence they were driven off, largely by ships' antiaircraft fire, without doing any damage; *LCI(R)–356* splashed one with her 40-mm. In the afternoon about 30 Vals concentrated on station No. 1, manned by destroyers *Purdy* and *Cassin Young* and four 158-foot support craft. At 1340 one kamikaze was splashed only 15 feet on *Cassin Young's* port quarter, a second was shot down at a safe distance, and at 1346 a third struck her port yardarm and disintegrated, knocking out the destroyer's forward fire room, killing one man and wounding 59. While this was going on, a second plane dived on *Purdy* out of the sun. She fired everything she had and splashed it 2500 yards away.

Damaged *Cassin Young* now retired to Kerama Retto and on her way saw something which made the men rub their eyes and wonder if the bombing had affected their wits. On passing Ie Shima, earlier reported to be completely deserted, they saw a Japanese plane making simulated bombing attacks on the island, and being met with antiaircraft fire so inaccurate as to suggest that this was a war game. The plane then landed on the supposedly ruined airfield, a group of Japanese suddenly appeared out of nowhere like a band of gnomes, folded the plane's wings and trundled it out of sight.

After *Cassin Young's* departure from station No. 1, another raid approached around 1445. C.A.P. began splashing "bandits" all around the horizon. One dived at *LCS (L)–33*, parted her radio antennas, and splashed. At 1500 two Vals dived on her from opposite bearings. One was shot down 500 yards away, the other hit her amidships, starting fires all over the vessel; and as the pumps were knocked out the wounded skipper, Lieutenant C. J. Boone USNR, wisely ordered Abandon Ship. Four men were killed and 29 wounded. *LCS(L)–57* (Lieutenant H. L. Smith USNR) also caught it. One plane crashed her forward 40-mm mount, a second exploded in the water close aboard, blowing a hole in her side, and a third hit her forward; three others were shot down. Her casualties were surprisingly low, two killed and six wounded, and she made Kerama roadstead under her own power.

At the same moment that *LCS(L)–33* was hit another Val, hotly pursued by three planes of the C.A.P., approached *Purdy*. The destroyer checked fire at 9000 yards for fear of hurting friends, then reopened at 6000 yards since the plane kept on coming. Hit by a 5-inch burst, it lost control and splashed 20 feet from the destroyer, ricocheting into her side. The bomb exploded, blowing ten men overboard. *Purdy* lost steering control from the bridge, most of her power, 13 men killed and 27 wounded. Under the division commander, Captain C. A. Buchanan, she crawled to Hagushi roadstead.

On another patrol station, destroyer *Mannert L. Abele* under her first skipper, Commander A. E. Parker, had the dubious honor of being sunk by the first *baka* bomb seen by our forces in action. This little horror was a one-way glider with three rockets as boosters, only 20 feet long with a wing span of 16½ feet and a warhead carrying 2645 pounds of tri-nitro-anisol. *Baka* arrived in the combat area slung under the belly of a two-engined bomber. Its pilot had an umbilical communication with the bomber's pilot, who released him near the target. The suicide pilot had to pull out of a vertical dive into a glide toward the victim, if necessary increasing speed by the rockets to over 500 knots. The small size and tremendous speed of *baka* made it the worst threat to our ships that had yet appeared, almost equivalent to the guided missiles that the Germans were shooting at London.

This initial *baka* attack was well timed. At about 1445 April 12, *Abele* was crashed by a Zeke which penetrated the after engine room. Its bomb exploded, breaking the keel and the shafts, and *Abele* went dead in the water and lost power. About one minute later, in came a *baka* at 500 knots. It hit the ship on her starboard side beneath the forward stack, penetrated No. 1 fire room, and exploded. The ship's midship section disintegrated, bow and stern parted, and *Abele* went down so quickly that five minutes later there was nothing on the surface where she had been except wreckage and survivors, who were being bombed and strafed by other Japanese planes. "A bomb exploded close enough to lift me out of the water," said Ensign David Adair USNR; "I heard several around me scream from pain caused by the blast."

Fortunately, that picket station was also manned by two LSM(R)s — "worth their weight in gold as support vessels," *Abele's* skipper said. As they closed to pick up survivors they shot down two planes which were strafing men in the water. A third plane crashed *LSM(R)-189* abaft her conning tower, smashing things up and wounding four men, but she continued her work of rescue, as did *LSM(R)-190*. *Abele* lost 6 killed, 73 missing and 35 wounded.[8]

[8] *Mannert L. Abele* Action Report 14 April; survivor's stories in *N.Y. Times* 22 June 1945. The C.O. especially commended Lt. George L. Way, who, blown overboard by *baka*, climbed back to help release life rafts for the men and opened hatches that permitted trapped sailors to escape.

As soon as Admiral Turner heard that *Cassin Young* was knocked out, he ordered destroyers *Stanly* (Commander R. S. Harlan) and *Lang* (Lieutenant Commander J. T. Bland III) from the adjacent station No. 2 to close No. 1, about 24 miles westward. En route they shot down a diving Val. Twenty minutes later *baka* suddenly dove out of a mêlée between C.A.P. and enemy planes, and, although frequently hit by automatic fire, crashed *Stanly's* starboard bow about five feet above the waterline, continuing right through to the port side, where its warhead exploded. This made *Stanly's* bow look like the face of a man who had lost his false teeth, but it did not stop her. Within ten minutes, as she was maneuvering radically under another aërial battle, a second *baka* zoomed in at a speed that appeared to be over 500 knots, passed over the ship, ripping her ensign off the gaff, attempted to bank, hit the water some 2000 yards away, bounced, and disintegrated. *Stanly* now received orders to close the transports off Hagushi. While steaming south she ran under a dogfight between five Zekes and the C.A.P., assisted by four Marine Corsairs. One Zeke peeled off and made for the destroyer, a Corsair began chasing him down, but retired when *Stanly* commenced firing. The Zeke, after being hit by 40-mm fire all the way down, straddled the destroyer's bows, fuselage on one side and bomb on the other, each splashing only about 15 yards from the ship. She had only three men wounded, and the damage to her bow was repaired in a few days at Kerama Retto. During these fantastic engagements *Stanly's* fighter-director controlled the C.A.P. and saw it shoot down seven kamikazes.

At 1453 a twin-engined plane, at which destroyer minesweeper *Jeffers* on radar picket station No. 12 was firing, cast off a *baka* at her. It missed and splashed about 50 yards away. *Jeffers* then steamed to the spot where *Abele* had gone down and helped to rescue survivors.

Destroyer minelayer *Lindsey* (Commander T. E. Chambers) was passing outside Kuba Shima at 1450 April 12 when she was crashed by two Vals. Her bow down to No. 1 gun was blown off. She lost 56 killed or missing and 51 wounded, and looked like a total loss

but the crews of repair ships at Kerama Retto fixed her up well
enough to be towed to Guam. Minesweeper *Gladiator* and destroyer escort *Rall* were also attacked by kamikazes on this day of
blood. The former, on a screening station, was at general quarters
when a Val splashed close aboard, spattering debris over the ship
but doing only superficial damage. *Rall*, on antisubmarine patrol,
was jumped at 1445 by a Nate which crashed on her starboard side
amidships. The bomb went straight through and exploded; 21 men
were killed and 38 wounded. Her internal damage was extensive
but the engineering plant largely escaped.

On this fateful morning of 12 April, Admiral Deyo did not as
usual disband his gunfire and covering force into its fire support
components. "Keep your group under way," Admiral Turner ordered him, "and disposed for best protection against air attack."
Deyo placed it in the best disposition for mutual antiaircraft support. Ten battleships, four heavy and three light cruisers steamed
in circular formation 9000 yards in diameter; twelve destroyers (all
too few) were widely spaced on a circle 6500 yards outside. Morning and forenoon watches were successively relieved, a sandwich
lunch was eaten at battle stations, but TF 54 still steamed at 16
knots around the great bight between Okinawa, Kerama Retto,
Aguni Shima and Ie Shima, as if admiring the scenery.

Would the enemy never come? Was this all a bluff? "Flash Red"
at 1326 signaled that they were coming at last. The radar pickets
had passed the word. But another hour elapsed before the kamikazes
that escaped picket ships, and C.A.P., appeared.

Literally out of a clear sky came the signal — two or three distant
planes, shot down by C.A.P., flaming and falling as one sometimes
sees a big meteor fall on a bright day. Deyo's disposition was then
headed east toward Okinawa, and Motobu Peninsula showed up
clearly on the port bow. *Porterfield* was the van destroyer; astern
of her came battleship *Texas* and cruiser *St. Louis*. Eleven different
groups of bogeys were on the radar screens. *Porterfield* at 1448 reported three planes in sight. Every ship within range opened fire,
filling the air with tight balls of black smoke from the bursts but
shooting down only one plane. Immediately after, at 1450, three

Jills were sighted on the port flank of the disposition boring in only 15 feet above the water. There destroyer *Zellars* (Commander L. S. Kintberger) steamed parallel to *Tennessee*, 2000 yards on her port beam. The first and the second attackers were splashed at 1800 and 3000 yards respectively. Gunfire then shifted to the third kamikaze, and 40-mm hits were observed; but before the main battery computer had caught up with it, this plane crashed the destroyer's port side at No. 2 handling room. A great sheet of flame roared up from *Zellars*. The crew fought fires, set up jury rigs, restored power to some pieces of equipment, administered first aid to the wounded, removed casualties to undamaged sections topside, "and did those thousand and one tasks attending major damage with a dogged determination and an air of unfrantic, concentrated effort." All fires were under control by 1500 when destroyer *Bennion* closed and sent over her surgeon; and at 1540 *Zellars* got underway at 15 knots, using "judicious profanity for communications." [9] Casualties were 29 killed or missing and 37 wounded. She had to return to the West Coast for repairs.

Tennessee (Captain John B. Heffernan) had just noted with dismay the crash on *Zellars* when her attention was absorbed by five planes of the same kamikaze formation. They were partly concealed by the smoke pall over the destroyer and difficult to detect among the bursts from 5-inch shells. The first was shot down 4000 yards on the port quarter. Three which came in low on the port beam forward, as if determined to hit Admiral Deyo in flag plot, were splashed by 5-inch fire between 100 and 500 yards away. Immediately after, another descended in a 45-degree dive from ahead, at about the same angle to the ship's course. It caught fire from a 5-inch burst about 1000 feet in the air, and without altering its course plunged into the sea and disappeared shortly after it had crossed the ship's bows, port to starboard. Possibly this kamikaze

---

[9] *Zellars* Action Report 1 May 1945. *Bennion,* the veteran destroyer which seemed to have a charmed life, had had seven men wounded in this action by a "friendly" shell bursting over her No. 3 40-mm gun mount. Two of her seamen jumped overboard to rescue an officer blown overboard from *Zellars* who was so badly burned on head and shoulders that he subsequently died. *The Story of the Bennion* (1947) p. 90.

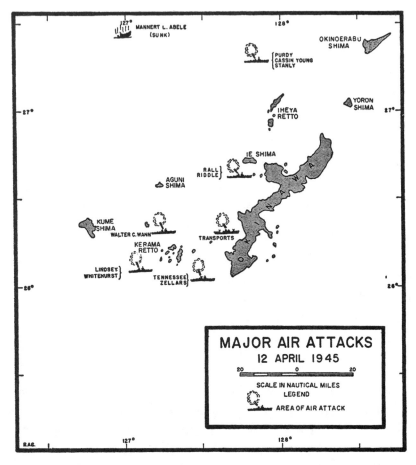

MAJOR AIR ATTACKS
12 APRIL 1945

SCALE IN NAUTICAL MILES
LEGEND

AREA OF AIR ATTACK

was intended as a decoy to attract the ship's attention from one that really meant business; for at the same time (1450) a Val about 45 degrees on the port bow straightened out and headed directly for the battleship's bridge. When about 2500 yards away it was detected and fired on by two 40-mm quads and eight 20-mm guns on the starboard side. One of the 40-mm bursts saved the lives of everyone on the bridge by shooting off the Val's left landing wheel; the right wheel then acted as rudder and deflected the plane's course slightly. Its right wing clipped the awning stanchions on the starboard wing of the bridge and parted the signal halyards. The plane then crashed one of the 40-mm quads, manned by Marines who had been firing on it, and slithered aft over fire-directors and 20-mm mounts, scattering flaming gasoline, burning to death many of the gunners, and coming to a shuddering stop abreast 14-inch turret No. 3. Its 250-pound bomb went through the deck, exploded in warrant officers' country, started fires there and blew some of the debris overboard. Chief Boatswain's Mate W. A. Dean, in charge of the damage and repair party on that side, was killed while pulling his men under cover. One sailor, blown into the air, landed on top of a 5-inch gun turret, where he very calmly stripped off his burning, gasoline-soaked clothes while awaiting a stream of water from the nearest fire hose. Corporal W. H. Putnam USMCR, pointer of a 40-mm mount, had one of the strangest adventures to befall anyone in a kamikaze attack. When trying to jump down into the gun tub, he tripped and fell overboard. When he came to the surface he found himself near burning pieces of the plane. He dived to avoid the flames, and came up close aboard a big life raft. Climbing on board, he found there the headless body of the Japanese pilot, tossed into it by the explosion. In this grisly company the Marine remained for several hours, until picked up by a destroyer, which returned him to his ship.[10]

New Mexico splashed a Val that dove for her at about 1458, and *Idaho* splashed a Jill close aboard; it exploded in the water so close that several dozen cases of beer in her blisters were ruined. In the meantime TF 54 had overrun, and engulfed as it were, a solitary minesweeper that was doing her best to keep out of trouble. Enemy planes seemed to use her for a rendezvous; and although she escaped a hostile hit, it is feared that shell fragments intended for them fell on the poor minecraft.

In ten minutes this air battle was over, but the radar screens were still full of bogeys and the formation maneuvered in the hope that C.A.P. would get them all. Shortly after 1545, *West Virginia* splashed two and *Hutchins*, one. At 2040, after dark, the disposition was brilliantly illuminated by Japanese pyrotechnics, the

[10] *Tennessee* Action Report 16 May; the writer's personal observations.

brightest flares that anyone on board had ever witnessed. Knowing by experience what this meant, Admiral Deyo ordered an emergency turn to avoid torpedoes, and immediately after, heavy explosions were heard in the wakes of *Tennessee* and *Idaho*, indicating a torpedo plane attack that missed; one of the "fish" was sighted passing astern of *Rooks*.

Tennessee's material damage was slight; she was able to continue fire support and, after temporary repairs, returned to duty. Owing, however, to the kamikaze having struck an exposed section of the deck, her casualties were many: — 23 officers and men killed, 106 wounded (33 of them horribly burned), and two of these died that night. Every member of the gun's crew of 12 which the kamikaze first crashed was either killed or wounded, costing the Marine Guard on board half its strength. Captain A. L. Adams USMC, the detachment's commander, was badly wounded by bomb fragments in the feet and thighs; but when the bodies of his men were committed to the deep that night, the Captain was there, supported by two unhurt Marines, to render them a final salute.

At least three destroyer escorts on screening duty were hit or near-missed on this fateful 12th. *Whitehurst* (Lieutenant Commander J. C. Horton USNR), on antisubmarine patrol southwest of Kerama, was attacked by three planes around 1500. She shot down two, but the third crashed her C.I.C. The bomb passed through the ship and exploded close aboard, knocking out the forward guns, and she had 37 killed or missing and an equal number wounded. *Riddle* splashed two close aboard; one of their bombs passed right through her, killing one man and wounding six. A kamikaze passed over *Walter C. Wann* just abaft the stack, cut several antennas, splashed and exploded 20 feet on the port bow, showering the ship with debris.

4. *The Death of President Roosevelt*

Friday, 13 April, broke bright and clear, but in every other respect it was a black Friday. Just as first light dawned over Okinawa, devastating news came over ships' loudspeakers: —

"Attention! Attention! All hands! President Roosevelt is dead. Repeat, our Supreme Commander, President Roosevelt, is dead."

Almost at the very moment, 0100 April 13, when the last rites were being performed for the kamikaze victims in *Tennessee*, Franklin D. Roosevelt was stricken with a cerebral hemorrhage. Half an hour after the morning watch came on duty, he breathed his last.[11] Many refused to believe it until confirmed by a signal from Admiral Turner.

"We were stunned," recorded one bluejacket in attack transport *Montrose*. "Few of us spoke, or even looked at each other. We drifted apart, seeming instinctively to seek solitude. Many prayed, and many shed tears." [12] No wonder, for in no section of the American people was the President so beloved as in the Navy. Bluejackets went about their duties sadly, officers looked anxious, mess attendants appeared as if they had lost their only friend. The question frequently asked of officers, "What will become of us now?" indicated that sailors looked to Franklin Delano Roosevelt as their champion in peace, their leader in battle, and their guarantee of a better world after victory.

By order of the Secretary of the Navy, James V. Forrestal, memorial services for the President were held at every shore station of the Navy and in every ship, on the second Sunday after Easter, 15 April. The form of the service was left to the chaplains, or to the commanding officer on ships that had no chaplain. As an example of what was taking place on board thousands of United States ships all over the world, here is the order of service on one of the relatively small and humble vessels of the Pacific Fleet, *LST-1122*, off Okinawa: — [13]

[11] The hour of his death, 1535 April 12 by Atlantic Coast time, was 0435 April 13 by the Item (Z–9) time we were using off Okinawa.

[12] Boatswain E. F. Stuckey, letter to writer, who received the same impression on board *Panamint* where he heard the news, and in *Tennessee* where he was serving. One felt a little better toward the Japanese because Radio Tokyo reported the President's death simply and decently, whilst the tone of Radio Berlin was low and insulting.

[13] Sent to the writer by the exec., Lt. (jg) Charles A. Smart USNR.

U.S.S. LST-1122

Commanding Officer
L. L. HUTCHINSON
Lieutenant USNR

Acting Chaplain
W. E. MITCHELL
Ensign USNR

MEMORIAL SERVICE FOR FRANKLIN DELANO ROOSEVELT
32nd President of the United States of America

Remarks on the President's death   The Captain
Invocation   The Chaplain
     Hymn — "Nearer My God To Thee," Sung by All Hands
Prayer from the Burial Service, Book of Common Prayer:
O God, whose mercies cannot be numbered; Accept our prayers on behalf of the soul of thy servant departed, and grant him an entrance into the land of light and joy, in the fellowship of thy saints; through Jesus Christ our Lord. *Amen.*

Almighty God, with whom do live the spirits of those who depart hence in the Lord, and with whom the souls of the faithful, after they are delivered from the burden of the flesh, are in joy and felicity; We give thee hearty thanks for the good examples of all those thy servants, who, having finished their course in faith, do now rest from their labours. And we beseech thee, that we, with all those who are departed in the true faith of thy holy Name, may have perfect consummation and bliss, both in body and soul, in thy eternal and everlasting glory; through Jesus Christ our Lord. *Amen.*

     The Lord's Prayer, Said by the Ship's Company
     Selections from Speeches of President Roosevelt, on "The Four Freedoms" and "A World Civilization," read by the Executive Officer.
     Ship's Company Comes to Attention. Five minutes' silence.
Three Volleys Fired.
Benediction   The Chaplain
     The National Anthem, sung by All Hands

CHAPTER XV

The Crucial Fortnight

14–30 April

1. The Radar Pickets' Ordeal [1]

IN ADDITION to small missions of one to twenty planes each on "off" days, the Japanese made ten major kamikaze attacks on our forces off Okinawa, including the first two in April, the story of which we have related in earlier chapters: — [2]

Attack No.	Date	NUMBER OF PLANES		
		Navy	Army	Total
1 (TEN-GO)	6–7 April	230	125	355
2	12–13 April	125	60	185
3	15–16 April	120	45	165
4	27–28 April	65	50	115
5	3–4 May	75	50	125
6	10–11 May	70	80	150
7	23–25 May	65	100	165
8	27–29 May	60	50	110
9	3–7 June	20	30	50
10	21–22 June	30	15	45
	TOTAL	860	605	1465

These mass attacks were designated by the Japanese *kikusui* ("floating chrysanthemum") operations. Together with individual kamikaze attacks not counted in this table, about 1900 suicide sorties were launched against American naval forces in the Oki-nawan campaign.[3] In addition there were hundreds of attacks by

[1] CTF 51 (Adm. Turner) Action Report, amplified by those of the ships concerned.
[2] USSBS *Campaigns of the Pacific War* p. 328, with dates extended by observed enemy air activity. This table does not include the VF which escorted the kamikazes, or VB and VT which sortied against U.S. forces the same day.
[3] Navy 1050, Army 850. Same reference.

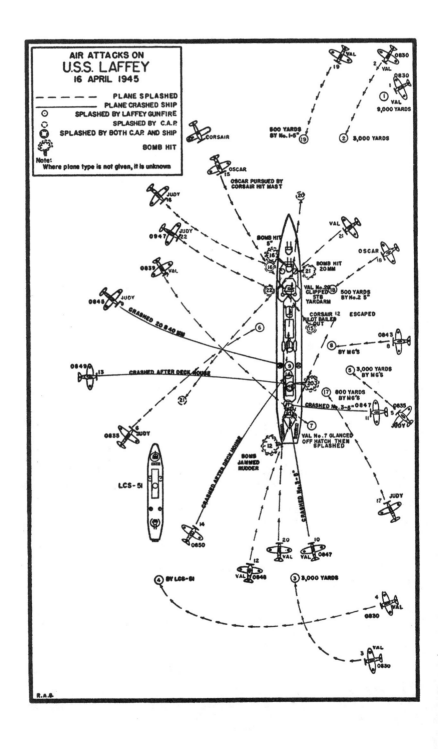

conventional dive-bombers and torpedo planes. The total number of Japanese aircraft involved is not known, but the Japanese Navy reports 3700 sorties by their own planes, including fighter escorts and conventional bombers; presumably the sorties of Army planes were at least half as much again.

Radar picket stations were the premier posts of danger in the Okinawa operation. Destroyers and other vessels assigned to this duty suffered tremendous losses, and protected other ships around Okinawa from sustaining even greater losses. By giving early warning of approaching kamikaze attacks, vectoring out C.A.P. to intercept, and most of all by bearing the brunt of these attacks, the pickets gave the finest kind of self-sacrificing service. Air alerts were daily and nightly occurrences except when the weather was too foul for Japanese planes to fly. By 10 April the more exposed stations were manned by two destroyers and four LCS. On 16 May, with radar stations on Ie Shima and Hedo Saki in operation, the number of picket stations was reduced to five.

Following the 12–13 April attacks, the story of which has been told in the previous chapter, pickets enjoyed a brief quiet period until the 16th, when hell broke loose in the third *kikusui* attack, 165 planes strong.

Laffey (Commander Frederick J. Becton), in radar picket station No. 1, was the first to catch it, at 0827. Probably no ship has ever survived an attack of the intensity that she experienced. From first light she had bogeys on her screen, and at one time her radar operator counted 50 planes closing from the northern quadrant. The kamikazes came in from every quarter of the compass. C.A.P., apprised of the situation by the fighter-direction officer on board, and warned to avoid the ship's antiaircraft fire, was just in the process of being relieved while the bogeys began to close. Nevertheless, C.A.P. accounted for a number of planes outside the ship's gun range, and boldly flew into the orbit of her gunfire to intercept. During a period of 80 minutes, in 22 separate attacks plotted by *Laffey's* officers (as indicated on our chart), she was hit by six kamikazes, by four bombs and by strafing, as well as being near-missed by a bomb and by a seventh kamikaze which splashed close aboard. Her guns, fired in local control after the director was knocked out, splashed eight more would-be crashers. Most of the damage was inflicted abaft No. 2 stack; there fires raged and several compartments were flooded. At 0947 when the action finished, *Laffey* had only four 20-mm guns still shooting and was down by the stern with her rudder jammed. While survivors of damage control parties, many of them wounded, worked to control the fires, the skipper tried various engine combinations to move her on a straight course, but none worked. At 1247 "the longest three hours ever experienced by all hands," as Commander Becton put it, ended when she was taken in tow by DMS *Macomb*. During the afternoon, when fleet tug *Pakana* relieved *Macomb* of the tow, her pumps just kept abreast of the flooding but were unable to gain. Then a second tug came alongside to help pump, and the two managed to tow *Laffey* into Hagushi anchorage. There she was patched up and proceeded to Guam under her own power on 22 April. She had 31 killed or missing and 72 wounded in this memorable action.

Commander Becton, who declared at the height of the action, "I'll never abandon ship as long as a gun will fire," was justly proud of his crew. "Performance of all hands was outstanding . . . the engineers played a vital part in saving the ship by the manner in which they furnished speed and more speed on split-second notice . . . gunnery personnel . . . demonstrated cool-headed resourcefulness and continued to deliver accurate fire throughout the action, often in local control. Damage control parties were undaunted, although succeeding hits undid much of their previous efforts and destroyed more of their fire-fighting equipment. They were utterly fearless in combating fires, although continually imperiled by exploding ammunition. . . . Especially deserving of mention were the 20-mm gunners of whom at least four were killed 'in the straps,' firing to the last." One of the many heroes was an eighteen-year-old coxswain, Calvin W. Cloer. Seriously burned when serving a gun, he went to the dressing station in the wardroom; but, deeming the wounded there to be in more need of attention, returned to serve his gun, where he was killed by a bomb. Not a single gun was abandoned, despite the flames and explosions.[4]

The squadron commander, Captain B. R. Harrison, observed that although *Laffey* was attacked by 22 planes of which six crashed and others were bombed, her gunners were able to shoot down nine of the enemy and she retained full engine and boiler power. He attributed this to superb ship handling by the C.O., which resulted in her taking most of the damage aft, and in many cases avoiding the full effect of the crashes. And Rear Admiral Joy added that *Laffey's* performance "stands out above the outstanding."

LCS-51 (Lieutenant H. D. Chickering USNR), then between one-quarter and one-half mile from *Laffey*, shot at four or five of the planes that were after the destroyer, splashed one, and at 1010 blew up another only 25 feet from her port side; its engine bounced into her, knocking a big hole at the waterline. *LCS-116* (Lieutenant A. J. Wierzbicki USNR), about six miles east of *Laffey*, was attacked by three Vals, one of which crashed her after 40-mm mount, badly damaging the vessel, killing 12 and wounding 12 men.

Bryant (Commander G. C. Seay), on radar picket station No. 2, received word that *Laffey* needed help. When steaming at top speed to assist her at 0934 she was attacked by six planes, one of which crashed the base of her bridge, demolishing C.I.C., radio and plotting rooms, and killing 34 men. The resulting fire was soon brought under control, and when Commander Seay learned that other vessels were standing by *Laffey*, he headed for Kerama Retto with 33 wounded on board.

Destroyer *Pringle* (Lieutenant Commander J. L. Kelley), minesweeper *Hobson* (Commander J. I. Manning) and *LSM-191* were on radar picket station No. 14 when attacked by three Vals at about 0910 April 16. Two came weaving in through the flak and one crashed *Pringle* just abaft the base of No. 1 stack. A violent explosion buckled her keel, the ship broke in two and sank within

---

[4] *Laffey* Action Report; story by the communications officer, Lt. Frank Manson USNR, in *N.Y. Times* 26 May 1945; *Washington Post* 14 Apr. 1958.

five minutes. Nearby vessels recovered 258 survivors, but 62 were missing and 43, of whom three died, badly wounded. *Hobson* fired at the plane which hit *Pringle* and shortly after spotted another coming in on her starboard quarter. She shot it down so close that the engine lodged in the midship deckhouse, a wing flew over the bridge, and the bomb exploded, kindling a fire in the forward engine room. After chasing off several other planes she recovered *Pringle* survivors and returned to the anchorage under her own power, having lost four killed and eight wounded.

Bowers, in the antisubmarine screen about six miles north of Ie Shima, shot down one plane at 0545 April 16 and four hours later was attacked by two more. One she splashed, but the second, after gliding over the ship, turned and crashed the flying bridge, spraying burning gasoline all over it. The fire was brought under control in about 45 minutes. *Bowers* made her own way into Hagushi anchorage, but her casualties were heavy – 48 killed or missing and 56 severely wounded, including her captain, Lieutenant Commander C. F. Highfield USNR and his exec, Lieutenant S. A. Haavik USNR.

Minesweeper *Harding* (Lieutenant Commander D. B. Ramage), on her way to radar picket station No. 14 at 0959 April 16, had a kamikaze crash so close aboard that the explosion blew a hole 10 by 20 feet in her topsides and twisted her keel 45 degrees for a distance of ten feet. She managed to back slowly into Kerama Retto, having lost 22 killed or missing and with ten wounded on board.

After this attack the radar pickets had a respite of twelve days while the Japanese were readying more "floating chrysanthemums." The fourth major *kikusui* attack was spread over 27 and 28 April. At about 2040 April 27 destroyer *Ralph Talbot,* in the outer screen, was hit by a kamikaze and narrowly missed by another. Her casualties were relatively light, five killed and nine wounded. *Rathburne,* in the transport screen, was also hit in the bow by a suicider. Both ships made Kerama under their own power. Converted merchant ship *Canada Victory* (Master William MacDonald), loaded with ammunition, having the bad luck to be caught in a rift in the smoke cover off Hagushi, was hit in the stern by a kamikaze and sank within ten minutes. She had 12 killed or missing and 27 wounded; unusually low casualties for an ammunition carrier.

On 28 April two destroyers and three smaller craft in picket station No. 1 sustained ten separate air assaults but suffered no damage. In station No. 2, *Daly* and *Twiggs* were kept busy all afternoon repelling attack. At 1639 a C.A.P. of six Corsairs was vectored out to a group estimated as 30 Zekes, approaching from the northeast. The Corsairs, though greatly outnumbered, shot down a good dozen of them and broke up the raid. Then, between 1730 and 1739, both ships came under attack by a large group of Vals. By high-speed maneuvering they avoided direct hits, but at least five kamikazes came very near crashing *Daly;* one hit the water within 25 yards of the ship and its bomb explosion punctured her badly, killed two men and wounded 15. The explosion of another Val that crashed close aboard *Twiggs* dished in her hull and buckled the main deck, but wounded only two men. Both ships retired to the transport area under their own power. Vessels on other picket stations had lively fights on the 28th but got off easily. *Brown*, in station No. 10, had her gig smashed. *LCI–580* too was hit but sustained only minor damage.

Few missiles or weapons have ever spread such flaming terror, such scorching burns, such searing death, as did the kamikaze in his self-destroying onslaughts on the radar picket ships. And naval history has few parallels to the sustained courage, resourcefulness and fighting spirit that the crews of these vessels displayed day after day after day in the battle for Okinawa.

2. *Progress Ashore; Ie Shima; Naval Gunfire Support* [5]

By 13–14 April, the northern sector of Okinawa, bailiwick of the III Amphibious Corps, was relatively quiet. Two battalions of Japa-

[5] *Okinawa: The Last Battle; Okinawa: Victory in the Pacific;* Action Reports of Admirals Turner, Deyo, Reifsnider, Hall and Joy.

nese troops on Motobu Peninsula had been cornered by the 6th Marine Division, which was about to have a very rough time rooting them out. Patrols from this division had reached Hedo Saki, the northern point of the island. The 1st Marine Division, which had been given the underside of the dog's muzzle, was mopping up the few pockets of Japanese there. In the southern sector, XXIV Corps lay across the island at the dog's neck and waist, still 5000 yards short of Shuri. Here the Japanese were concentrated and ready to put up stiff resistance which almost resulted in a stalemate.

By this time naval gunfire support had settled into a pattern that would be maintained steadily for more than two months while Tenth Army slowly overcame the enemy. For direct support two ships, one a destroyer for night illumination, were assigned to each regiment. Each division was assigned a cruiser or battleship with her own air spot, for deep support on targets in the divisional sector. Each corps had one or two heavy ships assigned for bombarding targets developed by corps artillery. For instance, when shortly after dusk 13 April, enemy flares blazed up from the neighborhood of Shuri, a signal that the Japanese meant mischief that night, shore fire control parties alerted *Colorado, Nevada, San Francisco, Biloxi* and two destroyers. Soon after, a heavy Japanese artillery bombardment began, followed by infantry assaults. With the help of naval gunfire the enemy was stopped cold and by dawn of 14 April this onslaught was over.

Things had gone so well in the Marine Corps sector that on 10 April Admiral Turner and General Buckner advanced the target date for the seizure of Ie Shima to 16 April. Rear Admiral Reifsnider commanded the attack group; the 77th Division, which had been standing by, furnished the landing force. After three days of naval and aërial bombardment and a UDT beach reconnaissance, the 77th Division landed on the southwestern beaches of Ie Shima at 0758 April 16. Initial opposition was light and the troops quickly overran the field, but ran into trouble as they approached the center of the island. Here the terrain was dominated by the Iegusugu pinnacle, a dead volcano rising to a height of 607 feet just north of Ie town. Built-in Japanese strong points, connected by a system of tunnels, made this pinnacle almost as formidable as Mount Suribachi on Iwo Jima; yet it was secured by 1730 April 21. Major General Bruce called the last three days of the fight for Ie Shima the bitterest of his experience. This small island, which plane reconnaissance had reported to be deserted by the enemy, had a strong enough garrison to kill 172 and wound 902 of our troops before it fell into their hands. The war correspondent Ernie Pyle was killed instantly by a machine-gun burst on 18 April when closely following the troops. I had visited Ernie only five days before. He was in the sickbay of Admiral Reifsnider's flagship *Panamint*, suffering from a severe cold. A frail little man, a gentle soul who hated war, he had come out to the Pacific owing to his sense of duty to tell the American people about the war with Japan, and how the ordinary soldier and sailor felt. He had spent many months on European fronts where the GIs were far from enthusiastic for their tasks, as he faithfully reported. In the Pacific he had recently spent a few days on board carrier *Cabot*, where he was impressed by the fighting spirit of the sailors and aviators. He had gone ashore with the Marines on L-day and written an amusing account of a night ashore, fighting fleas and mosquitos. It is a great pity that he was not spared to tell the public, in his simply eloquent prose, how it felt to be crashed by a kamikaze.[6]

On Okinawa the lines for XXIV Corps remained unchanged from 14 to 19 April. This delay was because our troops were up against a carefully planned defensive system. General Hodge had to make long and careful preparations for the first all-out attack. There were complaints in the Navy about XXIV Corps "dragging its feet" during these days when ships off Okinawa were under constant air attack. But General Geiger's Marines were similarly slowed

---

[6] Aside from Pyle's few and brief articles from the Pacific, which must be sought out in the daily press, the best correspondents' accounts of Okinawa are by John Lardner in the *New Yorker* 19 & 26 May 1945; Walter Davenport in *Collier's* 26 May; W. Eugene Smith in *Life* 18 June 1945; Warren Moscow's dispatches to *N.Y. Times;* and Robert Sherrod *On to Westward.*

down in the north; and now that the facts are known, there seems no ground for wardroom "beefs." Faced with such defensive works as General Ushijima devised, no army on earth could have done better than General Buckner's Tenth.

On 19 April three divisions of XXIV Corps attacked along a line running across Okinawa from a point about four miles north of Naha. The key point in the Japanese defense line was the ancient capital of Shuri, and the whole terrain was well adapted to Ushijima's defense tactics, based on underground caves connected by tunnels, to protect troops against artillery and naval bombardment. H-hour for the jump-off on 19 April was 0640, except that the 27th Division on the right started 50 minutes later to fit in with the artillery and bombardment plan. Naval gunfire support was provided at near maximum weight. After a night devoid of illumination, in order to screen troop deployment from the enemy, an intensive bombardment of enemy positions was laid on at 0540 by six battleships, six cruisers and eight destroyers. In addition, *Washington, North Carolina, South Dakota* and Desron 48, on loan from Task Force 58, arrived before dawn to bombard the south and southwest coasts. Ashore, 27 battalions of artillery rained 19,000 rounds of shell fire on enemy lines for 40 minutes before the jump-off. Some 650 Navy and Marine planes added bombs, rockets, napalm and strafing to the general din. The assault platoons then advanced, hopeful that the great mass of explosive metal had destroyed the enemy or had left him so stunned that he would be helpless. They were soon disillusioned. They were stopped cold when the relatively untouched Japanese came out of their deep caves and manned their well-designed defense positions. Only on the extreme right, where the 27th Division had bridged and crossed Machinato Inlet during the night, was any substantial progress made, and that over low and largely unprotected terrain.

For the next five days bitter fighting continued and progress was measured only in yards. The Japanese fought tenaciously. Although naval gunfire and air support were applied, it was essentially an infantry battle, as on Peleliu and Iwo Jima, with tanks playing an important rôle. By the evening of 23 April, General Ushijima's outer line had been penetrated at several points and he decided to withdraw to his next ring of defenses around Shuri. This retirement was effected secretly at night under cover of fog and artillery barrage. When the American troops jumped off next morning they encountered only a few stragglers.

Such was the pattern. Each line of defense was stubbornly held by the Japanese until the sheer weight of attack penetrated and forced abandonment. Then the process was repeated. The battle for Okinawa was the toughest and most prolonged of any in the Pacific war since Guadalcanal. It was similar to Iwo Jima but there were more Japanese to eliminate here and more terrain to capture. The details have already been well told in the Army and Marine Corps histories; here we shall mention only a few high spots and examine the contribution of the Navy to the final victory.

Ashore in mid-April the airfields at Yontan and Kadena were being improved and extended by Seabees to accommodate the Army planes and Marine Air Groups 31 and 33, which furnished C.A.P. and air support. Afloat, "flycatcher" operations destroyed large numbers of suicide boats, but occasionally one slipped out and damaged an anchored merchant ship. Destroyer *Hutchins* also was hit by a suicide boat in Nakagusuku Wan on 27 April. The explosion lifted her several feet, knocked down everyone on deck, and put the port engine and shaft out of business; but the ship was not sunk, and nobody was killed.

The Japanese Navy did not commit many submarines to the defense of Okinawa, and most of those that it did were destroyed. Four submarines were sent out from Saeki Bay, Kyushu, on 18 March to try to intercept Task Force 58 after its strike on Kyushu fields. All four were sunk: *RO-41* (as we have seen) by *Haggard* on 23 March, *I-8* by *Morrison* and *Stockton* on the 31st, *RO-49* by *Hudson* on 5 April and *RO-56* by *Monssen* and *Mertz* on the 9th. Two more were deployed in mid-April along a 200-mile circle off Okinawa;[7] one of these, *RO–109*, was sunk by *Horace A. Bass* on 25 April. A *kaiten* (human torpedo) carrier, *I–361*, was sunk by planes from hunter-killer CVE *Anzio* on 30 May.

Thanks to the efficient work of the radar pickets and C.A.P., most attempts of enemy aircraft to get at ships operating in Okinawa coastal waters were ineffective. Kamikazes did, however, break into the inner area on 22 April at 1751 and one crashed *Isherwood* on antisubmarine patrol. A fire from a ruptured depth charge spread to the other depth charges, which exploded, causing extensive damage and many casualties – 42 killed or missing and as many wounded. *Isherwood*, nevertheless, managed to make her way into Kerama Retto. At 1830 *LCS–15* was crashed so squarely and lethally as to go down within three minutes, carrying 15 men with her. Half an hour later, as the sun was setting, minesweeper *Swallow* on antisubmarine patrol was badly crashed by a kamikaze. She flooded immediately and within seven minutes capsized and sank, losing two men missing and nine wounded. Other vessels had close calls or received minor damage during this attack, which lasted until 2300.

This was not a *kikusui* attack, but it did more damage than the fourth one of that description, on 27–28 April. The "floating chrysanthemums" were successfully fought off by all combatant ships, but one pilot took a nasty revenge for his frustration. Hospital ship *Comfort* (Lieutenant Commander Adin Tooker USNR), fully lighted according to the Geneva Convention, and crowded with wounded, was steaming toward Saipan at lat. 25° 30′ N, long 127° 40′ E, about 50 miles southeast of Okinawa. She was crashed amidships by a kamikaze at 2041 April 28, under a full moon. The plane crossed the ship at masthead height, made a complete circle and dived into the superstructure, where it exploded. The surgery was demolished and every member of the medical corps, engaged in operating on the wounded, was killed instantly. Extensive damage was caused in the upper works but the power plant was unaffected. Two sailors and 21 soldiers, including six Army nurses, and seven

[7] Capt. Ohmae's notes and letter of 17 July 1959.

patients, were killed; seven sailors and 31 soldiers, including four nurses, and ten patients, were wounded.[8]

"Naval gunfire," state the Army historians, "was employed longer and in greater quantities in the battle of Okinawa than in any other in history. It supported the ground troops and complemented the artillery from the day of the landing until action moved to the extreme southern tip of the island, where the combat area was so restricted that there was a danger of shelling American troops." Assignments from Admiral Deyo's TF 54 were made daily and nightly to support troops ashore. A rotation schedule was devised which enabled these ships after a few days' shooting to retire to Kerama Retto for replenishment. Night illumination with star shell, usually delivered by destroyers, was also a great help to the troops, thwarting Japanese tactics of infiltration and night attack. "Time and again," write the Army historians, "naval night illumination caught Japanese troops forming or advancing for counterattacks and infiltration, and made it possible for the automatic weapons and mortars of the infantry to turn back such groups. . . . It was very difficult for the Japanese to stage a night counterattack of any size without being detected." [9]

The statistics of fire support at Okinawa through 17 May are impressive. During that period of 46 days, 17 of the 34 ships assigned to these duties were with TF 54 for the entire period, during which they spent between 28 and 36 days each in day fire support, in addition to 21 to 30 nights on the same duty.[10]

Mississippi, whose special assignment was the demolition of Shuri Castle, fired 2289 rounds of 14-inch and 6650 rounds of 5-inch in six weeks. *Colorado* through 21 May expended 2061 rounds of 16-inch and 6650 rounds of 5-inch. Among complimentary messages from the troops, on 18 May, General Del Valle, then engaged in the reduction of Shuri, signaled:—

[8] *Comfort* Report of Aërial Attack 1 May 1945; stories by Robert Trumbull in *N.Y. Times* 30 Apr. and *Honolulu Advertiser* c. 5 May 1945.
[9] *Okinawa: The Last Battle* p. 253.
[10] Each day or night here means a twelve-hour period; smaller periods were not counted.

"Your superb shooting has been a constant inspiration to our troops. . . . Every Jap captured reveals the awe and fear with which all Japs regard your gunfire." [11]

Wichita, prior to 18 May, rendered 36 days and 30 nights of fire support, and remained off Okinawa until the 28th, giving tongue almost daily. Her ammunition expenditure was 4800 rounds of 8-inch and 14,125 rounds of 5-inch of all types.

Light cruiser *St. Louis* also had a very long spell of duty, shooting off 13,175 rounds of 6-inch and 13,090 rounds of 5-inch ammunition. Eleven of the 16 destroyers assigned to TF 54 were with it for the full 46 days. Some concern was felt over the effect of this on their ordnance; that such heavy calls would dangerously wear down the rifling of their guns. To check the effects of this excessive use, *Hall* and *Richard P. Leary*, which had expended 4270 rounds per gun, fired an offset practice at 6000 and 12,000 yards on 27 May. *Leary* showed a range pattern of 260 yards at the shorter range and 470 yards at the longer, both normal. This proved that their 5-inch 38-caliber guns had remained accurate beyond all reasonable expectation.

The total ammunition expended by ships in Task Force 54, from the beginning of the operation to 21 June 1945, was 23,210 rounds of 12-inch and upward, 31,550 rounds of 8-inch HC, 45,450 rounds of 6-inch HC, and over 475,000 rounds of 5-inch, including star shell. [12] Two thirds of the 5-inch was expended in ships' defense against air attack, but over 184,000 rounds were in direct support of troops ashore.

Occasionally the enemy hit back. His coast defense batteries as usual were ordered to fire only on a landing force, so as not to disclose their positions; but once in a great while a Japanese artillery officer found such a juicy target in his sights that he could not resist taking a crack at it. As a Texas shipmate remarked, the Japanese gunner was like a mule that behaved himself until someone started fooling around his hind quarters. We have already told the case of

[11] *Colorado* Action Report 6 June 1945.
[12] Compiled from tables in Turner and Hill Action Reports.

Nevada, and on 18 May the same or a nearby coast defense battery let go on a sitting duck, destroyer *Longshaw*. During the previous week this ship had expended 1500 rounds of ammunition in fire support. On 17 May she put in for fuel, provisions and ammunition at Kerama Retto, where her crew were at general quarters until 2300, and spent the rest of that night firing star shell to support troops ashore on Okinawa. Immediately after she was dispatched on a day support mission. Pardonably, since her entire crew were in a state of exhaustion, she ran aground on a reef off Naha airstrip. *Picking* stood by and tried to pull her off but the light tow wire parted. Fleet tug *Arikara* then passed a line and was just taking up strain at 1100 when accurate enemy artillery fire started falling around the destroyer and hit her four times. One hit forward touched off a magazine explosion which blew off her bow back to the bridge. With many fires burning and the position of the ship hopeless, the C.O., Lieutenant Commander Becker, who had been severely wounded, ordered Abandon Ship, and never did make it himself. Besides him, 85 of her crew were killed, missing or died of wounds, and 97 others wounded.[13] *Longshaw*, so badly battered as to be unsalvageable, was destroyed by gunfire and torpedoes.

3. *Fast Carriers of the United States Navy and Royal Navy* [14]

In Chapter XIII we followed the operations of fast carrier forces, American and British, through 12 April. The kamikazes got in their next lick at Task Force 58 on 14 April when about 15 planes attacked the carriers' own radar picket line. One plane grazed *Hunt*, passing between her bridge structure and No. 1 stack and splashing alongside. The damage was slight and only five men were wounded. Five minutes later *Sigsbee* (Commander G. P. Chung-Hoon) took

---

[13] Vice Adm. Hill Action Report; Navy Department interview with Lt. R. L. Bly USNR and Lt. (jg) F. H. Sonntag USNR 10 July 1945.
[14] Same references as in Chap. XII note 1 and Chap. XIII note 1.

a crash on her main deck abaft No. 5 gun. Damage was extensive; the port shaft snapped off together with its propeller, the starboard shaft strut was sprung, and the ship flooded aft. After she had settled to main deck level she had to be towed to Guam. Surprisingly, only four men were killed, but 74 were wounded.

On 15 and 16 April, in addition to furnishing C.A.P. and air support for the troops at Okinawa, Task Force 58 launched fighter sweeps to cover airfields in southern Kyushu. The first day's attack was a complete surprise and the airmen claimed to have shot down 29 and destroyed 51 aircraft on the ground. But for this and the 16 April sweep, the third *kikusui* attack would doubtless have been even worse than it was.[15] Not only Okinawa radar pickets, but Task Force 58 received a share of attention from the 165 kamikazes that participated. At 1336 two of them dived on unlucky *Intrepid* (Captain G. E. Short). One narrowly missed her flight deck and splashed close aboard. The other crashed the flight deck near the after elevator, blew a hole in the deck 15 by 20 feet, and started intense fires. They were quenched within an hour but her structural damage was so extensive that *Intrepid* had to be sent to a navy yard, and she lost ten killed or missing, as well as 21 seriously and 66 slightly wounded.[16]

In the same action destroyer *McDermut* was hit by two "friendly" 5-inch shells with influence fuzes. One burst on impact and the other about four feet above the main deck, punching some 400 holes in the superstructure, damaging steam and water lines, killing five men and wounding 31.

On 17 April Rear Admiral Davison's Task Group 58.2, having lost *Enterprise* and *Franklin*, was dissolved, and its two remaining carriers, *Independence* and *Randolph*, were allotted to the other three groups. During the forenoon of 18 April, planes from carrier *Bataan*, aided by destroyers *Heermann*, *McCord*, *Collett*, *Mertz* and *Uhlmann*, sank submarine *I-56*, one of the *kaiten*-carriers on which the Japanese placed high hopes.

[15] See Sec. 1 of this Chapter.
[16] For her earlier damage see Vol. XIII.

During almost the rest of April, TF 58 was little molested by the enemy while it continued to furnish air support and C.A.P. over Okinawa and to make daily fighter sweeps over the northerly Nansei Shoto. "Jocko" Clark's TG 58.1 went to Ulithi 28 April for a ten-day upkeep. The relative quiet that had settled over the carrier groups was broken during the fourth *kikusui* attack on 29 April. At 1657 *Haggard* (Lieutenant Commander V. J. Soballe), of Rear Admiral Radford's TG 58.4, was crashed by a kamikaze at her water line amidships. She had just joined *Uhlmann* in a picket station 12 miles up-sun from the task group. Her forward engine room and both fire rooms were flooded to the waterline and all way was lost. After a second kamikaze had splashed close aboard her skipper decided to jettison torpedoes and depth charges. Fortunately the sea was calm as *Walker* towed *Haggard* into Kerama Retto, where she was patched up before going to a navy yard for major repairs. Eleven of her crew were missing in the action and 40 were wounded.

At 1728 on the same day destroyer *Hazelwood* (Commander V. P. Douw), ordered to *Haggard's* assistance, opened fire on a plane diving at her. It flew over No. 4 gun and splashed close aboard. Two minutes later a second kamikaze hit the port side of No. 1 stack and crashed the superstructure at main deck level. Oil and gasoline fires broke out and the forward fire room became inoperative. Within an hour the fires were under control and *Hazelwood* was taken in tow by *McGowan*. By 0415 next morning, 30 April, damage control parties had her engineering plant repaired to a point that she was able to cast off the tow line and proceed under her own power. *Hazelwood's* damage was great and her casualties heavy. Commander Douw and 45 other officers and men were killed and 26 wounded.

We return now to Admiral Rawlings's carrier task force off Sakishima Gunto. H.M.S. *Illustrious*, which had developed structural trouble, was detached and sent to Leyte with two destroyers. Her place in the carrier squadron was taken by H.M.S. *Formidable*.

Strikes were launched against Sakishima Gunto on 16 and 17 April. Upon their completion Admiral Rawlings reported to Admiral Spruance that TF 57 would be available for further strikes on 20 April, although his original schedule called for retirement to Leyte by the 16th. This offer was not only approved but brought an appreciative message from Admiral Nimitz. On 18 and 19 April, while the British carriers fueled, the *Sangamon* escort carrier unit again took over their duty of cratering airfields in the Sakishima Gunto. Task Force 57 returned for one more go at them on the 20th and then departed for Leyte. It had launched strikes on 12 days out of a possible 26, lost 19 aircraft and claimed 33 enemy aircraft shot down and 38 destroyed on the ground. And it had set a record for the Royal Navy in days of steam by keeping the sea for 32 days continuously.

While the British carriers were replenishing at Leyte Gulf, the *Sangamon* unit took over for a third time, and from 28 April on was augmented by escort carriers *Makin Island*, *Fanshaw Bay*, *Manila Bay*, *Lunga Point* and *Salamaua*.

This concludes the story of naval activities in the Okinawa campaign during the month of April. For the Navy it was one of the toughest months in the entire Pacific War; but it was some compensation that the *Yamato* task force and most of the submarines committed by the enemy had been sunk, and that at least one thousand aircraft with their pilots, including 820 of the first four *kikusui* attacks, had been expended.

CHAPTER XVI

May Days at Okinawa

1. *The Radar Picket Line*

ON 3 MAY when Japan delivered her fifth *kikusui* attack, station No. 10 was the hardest hit. Weather had been bad during the morning but cleared in the afternoon. At 1822, when visibility was excellent, *Aaron Ward* (Commander W. H. Sanders), veteran of many battles, went to general quarters in anticipation of air attack. An incoming Val was taken under fire at 7000 yards, but went into a glide smoking heavily and splashed abreast No. 3 mount, about 100 yards on the starboard quarter. Momentum carried the engine, the propeller and a portion of one wing into the destroyer's after deckhouse, but inflicted slight damage and no casualties. Immediately after, a second kamikaze was shot down 1200 yards to port. Before it splashed, a Zeke was seen coming in from astern. Although brought under gunfire and ablaze from hits, it bore in, dropped a bomb which exploded in the after engine room, crashed just below the port after 40-mm mount and sprayed burning gasoline all about. No. 3 five-inch mount lost all power and communication and thereafter fired in local control. During the next twenty minutes several planes were taken under fire, but as none of them pressed home their attacks, *Aaron Ward's* damage control parties had a chance to keep fires and flooding from spreading and to relieve the sufferings of the wounded. But steering control from the bridge had been lost, and the destroyer had to be steered at the rudderhead by hand.

At 1859 the entire group at station No. 10 became targets of a particularly vicious attack. Of six vessels, four were hit. *Aaron*

Ward disintegrated one Val in the air by a direct hit. At 1904 a
Betty was shot down. Immediately after, two Vals came in under
heavy fire. One apparently aimed at the destroyer's bridge but
missed, clipped her forestay, cutting the steam line to the whistle
and severing several antennas before splashing alongside. At 1913
another Val, although hit repeatedly, crashed *Aaron Ward* amidships, releasing its bomb just before the impact and blowing a hole
in the side which flooded the forward fire room and caused the
destroyer to lose propulsion. And this was not all. Within a few
seconds a fifth plane, unobserved because of smoke and flame,
crashed the midships deckhouse, and about one minute later a Zeke
crashed the superstructure near the after starboard 40-mm mount
and spread flames and destruction over the remainder of the deck.
Aaron Ward was now almost dead in the water with uncontrolled
fires raging and ammunition exploding; her only remaining source
of power was the forward diesel generator. And on top of all this,
at 1921 a seventh plane came at her through fire of the forward
40-mm guns; it hit the base of No. 2 stack, blowing the stack, a
searchlight, and two 20-mm guns into the air. Two LCS(L) came
alongside at 1935 to help. Through heroic efforts by the crew —
who worked amidst exploding ammunition — fires were under control by 2024. Casualties were 45 killed, missing or died of wounds;
49 others wounded.

At 2106 *Shannon* took *Aaron Ward* in tow and proceeded to
Kerama at about five knots. She arrived at 0723 next morning, to be
greeted by a message from Admiral Nimitz to Commander Sanders:
"We all admire a ship that can't be licked. Congratulations on your
magnificent performance." After six weeks' work she was able to
make her way to New York on one engine, to be decommissioned
as beyond economical repair.

Little (Commander Madison Hall) kept company with *Aaron
Ward* at station No. 10 during this memorable third day of May.
She estimated from her plots that 18 to 24 enemy planes were in-
volved in attacks which began at about the same time as those on
Ward. At 1843 a kamikaze crashed her port side and its engine

demolished her after low-pressure turbine and condenser. A second plane was shot down by automatic weapons, but in less than a minute a third crashed at about the same place as the first and added to the engine-room damage. A fourth now bored in, hit her port side amidships and displaced No. 3 boiler. Almost immediately a fifth, making a vertical dive, crashed her after torpedo mount. The torpedo air flasks exploded and the plane's engine or bomb burst No. 3 and No. 4 boilers, which probably broke the ship's keel. *Little* was now dead in the water with neither power nor internal communication. She settled rapidly; by 1850 her main deck was awash and Commander Hall ordered Abandon Ship. Five minutes later, only twelve minutes after her first hit, *Little* sank. Her survivors reported six dead, 24 missing and 79 wounded.

Rocket-equipped *LSM(R)–195* (Lieutenant W. E. Woodson USNR), on the same No. 10 station, was hit at about 1910 May 3 while rushing to assist *Aaron Ward* and *Little*. The crash started her rockets exploding, the fire main and auxiliary pumps were knocked out, and the landing ship had to be abandoned. After heavy explosions she sank, losing eight killed or missing and 16 wounded. Many of her survivors were picked up by *Bache*, which had had a narrow squeak herself in station No. 9 and had come over to No. 10 to assist. *LCS(L)–25*, also in station No. 10, was damaged by a near-miss while en route to assist the destroyers, and lost three killed or missing and 12 wounded; but she made Kerama Retto under her own power with many *Little* and *Aaron Ward* survivors on board.

Thus, two destroyers, two other ships and 86 men were lost in one day at a single radar picket station; and that was not the only station to be attacked. In No. 9 at 1830 May 3, *Macomb* was hit on No. 3 gun by a kamikaze which sprayed burning gasoline around the mount and on deck. In two minutes the fires were brought under control. Damage was not serious, but she lost seven killed or missing and 14 wounded.

Next day, May the 4th, into which the fifth *kikusui* assault continued, proved to be even worse for the radar pickets. *Luce* (Commander J. W. Waterhouse) was on station No. 12. By 0750 there were numerous bogeys on her screen. C.A.P. splashed several but at 0808 two broke through. *Luce* opened fire on them at about 8000 yards. One, badly hit, splashed only a few feet on her starboard hand; the bomb explosion caused a brief power failure and knocked out all radars. Another plane was then seen coming in on the port quarter. Guns were trained on it manually, but only a few had time to fire before it crashed the ship in the vicinity of No. 3 mount. She flooded rapidly on the starboard side. At 0814, when the stern was going under, Commander Waterhouse ordered Abandon Ship. One minute later this destroyer, named after a distinguished admiral, up-ended and sank, exploding heavily underwater. Her casualties were exceedingly heavy – 149 killed or missing, 57 wounded (including the skipper) who required hospitalization, and 37 others wounded; only 93 of her complement of 335 escaped uninjured. *LSM-190* was also sunk in the same attack, losing thirteen killed or missing and 18 wounded.

Picket station No. 1, manned by *Morrison* (Commander J. R. Hansen), *Ingraham* (Commander J. F. Harper, with Comdesdiv 120, Commander J. C. Zahm, embarked), three LCI(L) and *LSM(R)-194*, had an even worse experience than No. 12 on 4 May. Raids started coming in at 0715, C.A.P. was vectored out to intercept the first three, but a Val pursued by four Corsairs headed for *Morrison*. Although hit repeatedly it flew over her forecastle, grazing No. 2 gun and the bridge, then splashed in her wake not ten yards away. Within a few minutes another Val with Corsairs on its tail headed for the same destroyer, whose guns splashed it 2500 yards short. Then a Zeke, also chased by C.A.P. fighters, dropped a bomb 50 feet on *Morrison's* port beam and crashed the same distance to starboard. The forenoon watch opened with still another Val, also pursued, zooming past the bridge where it left parts of a wing and landing gear, splashing 25 yards away. A fifth performance of the same kind was put on at about 0825, the enemy plane skimming over the after stack and splashing. So far *Morrison* was almost untouched, but her luck ran out when two Zekes made a vertical dive on her. One grazed the after stack and hit the base of the forward stack, its bomb exploding No. 1 boiler. The second hit No. 3 five-inch gun a glancing blow and crashed the main deck, opening the starboard shell plating of the after engine room to the sea. Even after absorbing these hits the destroyer might have survived; but the Japanese now added insult to injury by dealing her a deathblow from two wood-and-canvas twin-float biplanes of ancient vintage. Seven of these were seen closing at low altitude and slow speed. One was hit repeatedly by 20-mm fire as it came in. Bits of the fabric of its wings fell on the crew of the after 20-mm mount as it passed over them, and it then crashed a 40-mm mount and No. 3 five-inch gun. Powder in the upper handling room exploded, blowing the gun off its foundation. Another antique came in from astern under attack by Corsairs and landed in the destroyer's wake, but that did not stop the pilot; he taxied up the wake, took off and crashed gun No. 4, igniting more powder. These two successive explosions caused such rapid flooding aft that Commander Hansen ordered Abandon Ship, and just in time; she upended and went down with her bow pointing heavenwards, within ten minutes of the last two hits. Casualties were exceedingly heavy — 153 killed or missing. Only 179 were rescued from her complement of 331 officers and men; and 108 of the survivors, of whom six subsequently died, were wounded.[1]

On this same fatal picket station No. 1, on 4 May, *Ingraham* received two near-misses and was crashed by a Zeke near No. 2 five-inch which flooded the forward fire room, killed 14 men and wounded 37.[2] And the rocket landing ship, *LSM(R)-194*, was hit by a kamikaze at 0850 and sank quickly, losing 13 men missing and 23 wounded.

In picket station No. 14 *Shea* (Commander C. C. Kirkpatrick) took a *baka* bomb on 4 May. Although this station lay 50 miles northwest of Hagushi beaches, it was bothered by haze from the morning smoke cover at the transport area drifting over it in the

[1] *Morrison* Action Report 11 May 1945.
[2] *Ingraham* Action Report 8 May 1945.

forenoon watch and cutting surface visibility to 2000 yards. At 0857 *Shea* sighted a Betty five to six miles at the upper edge of the haze. C.A.P. did for the Betty, but the *baka* that it carried suddenly appeared out of the haze only 1000 yards distant, gliding at terrific speed toward the ship. Automatic weapons opened fire but the tiny human-directed missile hit the starboard bridge structure, passed through the ship and exploded close aboard on the other side. This attack cost *Shea* 27 killed and 91 wounded, but she was able to make her own way to Hagushi roadstead.

Lowry and *Massey*, at picket station No. 2 on 4 May, escaped with superficial damage from kamikaze near-misses. In station No. 10, on the evening of this same grim day, *Gwin* had her after 40-mm director carried away and a 40-mm mount put out of business by a kamikaze that overshot and splashed. *Gwin* carried on, having suffered two killed and nine wounded. *Cowell* on the same station, twice near-missed by kamikazes, was showered with debris and gasoline which fortunately did not ignite.

Thus, total losses to radar pickets on 4 May amounted to two destroyers, two LSM and 370 officers and men. This fifth *kikusui* attack, indicating that the kamikazes were becoming even more deadly, created something approaching dismay at Cincpac headquarters. When the bad news arrived in the evening, Admiral Nimitz asked Admiral Forrest Sherman in my presence whether he didn't think the kamikazes would soon lay off the picket destroyers in search of bigger game. Sherman replied that he thought not, "You could get a man down quicker by hitting him on the same tooth than by punching him all over." Nimitz said, "Anyway we can produce new destroyers faster than they can build planes." But Sherman's gloomy prediction proved to be correct.

The next serious damage to the pickets occurred during the sixth *kikusui* attack on 11 May to which 150 planes were committed. Picket station No. 15 was occupied by *Evans* (Commander Robert J. Archer), *Hugh W. Hadley* (Commander Baron J. Mullaney), three LCS and one LSM(R). From 0750 to 0930 this station, northwest of Okinawa, was under heavy attack. By 0755

Hadley had more than 150 enemy planes on her radar plot. She vectored out C.A.P. in several directions; these interceptors were too busy to report, but it was estimated that they downed about 50 enemy planes and that 50 more, in *Evans's* estimate, attacked her and *Hadley*. Action was fast and furious. The two destroyers, maneuvering independently at high speed, became separated by as much as three miles. *Evans* claimed to have shot down 15 planes; but four more, and parts of four others, crashed her. The first crash, on the port bow, did not affect her fighting ability. It blew her exec. over the side, but a seaman dove in and supported him until both were picked up. The second kamikaze hit her below the water line at the after fire room, which flooded, together with the after engine room. Within two minutes she was hit by two more kamikazes almost simultaneously, near the galley. One of their bombs detonated in the forward fire room, exploding two boilers, and flooded all remaining engineering spaces. *Evans*, now powerless, went dead in the water. To cap it off a fifth suicider came in at 0925 with the C.A.P. on his tail. The pursuers' bullets and the ship's automatic fire deflected this plane so that it passed down her port side and splashed. In the meantime the flooding was being fought by bucket brigades, handy-billys and craft that came alongside, including *Harry E. Hubbard*. By 1350 *Evans* was under tow to Ie Shima where she was patched up and then towed to Kerama Retto. She had lost 30 killed or missing and 29 wounded.

While all this was going on, *Hugh W. Hadley* was under attack by groups of planes coming in on both bows; she claimed to have shot down twelve. At 0920 she was attacked by ten planes simultaneously, on both bows and from astern. All ten were destroyed by her or destroyed themselves, but they inflicted a variety of blows — one bomb hit aft, a crash by a *baka*, a crash by a kamikaze aft, and a side-swipe in the rigging by another. The ship was badly holed, both engine rooms and one fire room were flooded, a heavy fire raged abaft No. 2 stack and ammunition began exploding on all sides, and the ship threatened to capsize. Commander Mullaney ordered all but 50 members of the crew over the side in life rafts;

those on board worked like heroes and saved their ship, while the Corsair pilots of C.A.P. overhead, running out of ammunition, literally rode kamikazes into the water. *Hadley* was towed to Ie Shima, patched up and taken to Kerama. She had 28 killed and 67 wounded, including her skipper. He survived to write a report which reflects a great and proper pride in his ship's performance; and if other destroyer skippers were as proud, none was so eloquent as Commander Mullaney: —

No captain of a man of war had a crew who fought more valiantly against such overwhelming odds. Who can measure the degree of courage of men who stand up to their guns in the face of diving planes that destroy them? Who can measure the loyalty of a crew who risked death to save the ship from sinking when all seemed lost? I desire to record that the history of our Navy was enhanced on 11 May 1945. I am proud to record that I know of no record of a destroyer's crew fighting for one hour and thirty-five minutes against overwhelming aircraft attacks and destroying twenty-three planes. My crew accomplished their mission and displayed outstanding fighting abilities. I am recommending awards for the few men who displayed outstanding bravery above the deeds of their shipmates in separate correspondence. . . . Destroyer men are good men and my officers and crew were good destroyer men.[3]

Small groups of enemy planes, not part of a *kikusui* mass attack, were active on 13 May. *Bache* (Lieutenant Commander A. R. McFarland), attacked by several low-flying planes, managed to knock down two, but a wing of the third clipped No. 2 stack and the fuselage was swung onto the main deck; its bomb exploded, severing steam and power lines. This lone kamikaze managed to kill 41 and wound 32 of *Bache's* sailors. Fires were under control by 1912 and within two hours the ship was being towed to Kerama Retto.

On 16 May construction of a new search radar station began on an island of the Iheya Retto, about 20 miles northeast of Ie Shima. It was hoped that this could detect approaching enemy planes ear-

---

[3] *Evans* and *Hugh W. Hadley* Action Reports 15 and 22 May; *N.Y. Times* 15 July 1945. The crew later found the remains of two kamikaze pilots in the bilges.

lier than ships' radar, and eliminate some of the radar picket stations.[4] In the meantime they carried on.

On 17 May *Douglas H. Fox* (Commander R. M. Pitts) was in "hot" picket station No. 9 with *Van Valkenburgh* and four LCS. All ships here had been at general quarters for three previous nights, when bogeys were flying about, but were alert though weary at 1929 on the 17th. Then *Fox* shot down the first of four planes which went for her. She got two more but the fourth crashed her between the two forward gun mounts, putting both out of commission and killing seven men. Another kamikaze parted a lifeline before splashing close aboard, spattering gasoline over the fantail. Fires were under control by 1945 and *Fox* went to Kerama under her own power, with 35 wounded on board.[5]

The seventh major *kikusui* attack opened on the evening of 23 May and lasted into the 25th. Picket station No. 15 was under attack intermittently for seven hours from 2030 May 23. Several planes were shot down but the damage was slight, from a bomb which near-missed *LCS(L)-121*. There was also considerable activity the following night but the enemy inflicted no damage. At 0904 May 25 the weather was thick over this station, but bogeys were known to be in the vicinity. *Stormes* (Commander W. N. Wylie) sighted a plane in the overcast as it emerged from a cloud at about 2000 yards and took it under fire when apparently heading for *Ammen*, next ahead of her. Suddenly the plane flipped completely over and dove into *Stormes's* after torpedo mount. The bomb exploded in No. 3 magazine and heavy fires broke out. By 1055 all fires were out and the destroyer, with a hole in her hull between the propeller shafts, 21 killed and six wounded, proceeded to Hagushi at 20 knots.

Bogeys were also active on the morning of the 25th over picket station No. 5. *Braine* and *Anthony* shot down four attackers, including a Betty with its *baka* bomb.

During the eighth *kikusui* attack of 27–29 May, last to which the

---

[4] *Anthony* Action Report, and information from radarman B. C. Aldrich, 1947.
[5] *Douglas H. Fox* Action Report 24 May 1945. **Two men were missing.**

Japanese committed more than 100 planes, radar pickets again suffered. *Braine* (Commander W. W. Fitts) was in station No. 5 with *Anthony* (Commander C. J. Van Arsdall) and four LCS. The C.A.P. of eight Army Thunderbolts (P-47) requested and obtained permission from the fighter director in *Braine* to return to base, owing to foul weather. At 0744 three or four Vals were seen coming out of the clouds. Taken under fire by both ships, one was splashed; the second, set afire about 2000 yards from *Anthony*, passed over that destroyer, turned sharply to port and crashed *Braine* in her No. 2 handling room. The explosion demolished the wardroom country. Almost simultaneously the third Val which had been orbiting ahead of *Anthony* dived on her. Gunfire deflected it sufficiently to cause it to splash fifty feet on the starboard beam. The plane exploded, raising a huge geyser of water in the midst of which, like a tin ball on a park fountain jet, was the body of the Japanese pilot. As the geyser subsided his mangled corpse, dressed in a black-hooded funeral robe adorned with brightly colored dolls, dropped on board *Anthony*, along with various motor parts.

The troubles of station No. 5 were not finished. Simultaneously with the crash on *Anthony*, a Val which *Braine* had earlier taken under fire crashed the sickbay and its bomb exploded in No. 3 boiler uptake. The unfortunate ship was now divided by flames into three sections, unable to communicate with each other. She went dead in the water. While the two LCS on station picked up floating survivors, *Anthony* grappled and helped her bring the fires under control around noon and took her casualties on board. These were very heavy: — 66 killed or missing and 78 wounded; but the ship survived and *Anthony*, until relieved by tug *Ute*,[6] towed her into Kerama Retto.

On the 28th this eighth *kikusui* attack was directed mainly at station No. 15 where LCS(L)-52 suffered minor damage and eleven casualties from a near-miss. At 0650 *Lowry* and *Drexler* (Commander R. L. Wilson) reversed their patrol course, but having a contact on their radar screens turned column right to bring it abeam. This proved to be a well coördinated attack with excellent kamikaze pilots and fast planes. A Nick, first sighted on the starboard beam, was shot down by C.A.P. Another plane was seen coming in on the starboard bow. *Drexler* took it on, firing directly over *Lowry*. The plane, a Frances, missed *Lowry* and seemed about to splash but the pilot recovered sufficiently to hit *Drexler* obliquely on her topside. Steam lines were ruptured and gasoline fires sprang up, but these were put out in less than a minute. About half a minute later a second Frances was taken under fire when diving on *Lowry*, but gunfire deflected it into the water. At about 0703 a third came in from ahead, but Corsairs on its tail caused it to miss *Drexler* on the first pass. It appeared to be done for and to be about to splash astern; but its pilot had too much skill and energy to give up. He recovered, made another pass, and although repeatedly hit by fighters and gunfire, came in on *Drexler* from ahead, just missing the signal bridge, clipped the signal halyards and crashed the boat davits and superstructure. The explosion that followed was terrific, as this Frances carried two bombs. An oil fire shot several hundred feet up, parts of the ship were blown in all directions and she rolled over and sank in less than a minute. Her casualties were very heavy: 158 killed or missing and 51, including the captain, wounded.[7]

At 0013 May 29, under a full moon, *Shubrick* (Lieutenant Commander J. C. Jolly) was hit by a twin-engined plane. When proceeding to picket station No. 16 she sighted the plane at 2355 May 28 with running lights burning, flying low and about three miles away. Not sure that she had been seen, *Shubrick* slowed to ten knots. By 0008 there was no doubt that the plane had spotted her. It was taken under fire but crashed a gun director over the after engine room. The bomb blew a hole in the main deck about 30 feet in diameter, and the starboard side of the ship was blasted out. The after engine room and adjacent compartments were completely flooded and the usual fires raged. At 0113 *Van Valkenburgh*

---

[7] *Drexler* Action Report 26 June 1945. This action caused such concern that Cdr. Wilson was twice called to Washington to give more details of her loss.

came alongside and took off the wounded. By 0130 the fantail from No. 4 gun aft was awash and confidential publications and electronics gear were transferred. At 0135 all unnecessary men were ordered to leave the ship. The situation at that time looked hopeless, but with the aid of handy-billys from *Van Valkenburgh* the flooding was brought under control. Destroyer transport *Pavlic* arrived at 0200 with more handy-billys and at 0510 a tug took *Shubrick* in tow for Kerama Retto. She had 32 killed or missing and 28 wounded.

Thus, the eighth *kikusui* attack cost us another destroyer and 256 more sailors killed.

2. *The Fast Carrier Force* [8]

The heavy air attacks of 4 May left Task Force 58 relatively unmolested. Not for another week, in the course of the sixth *kikusui* assault, did it again suffer serious loss. During the preceding night the force had been snooped, but there was no warning or indication of anything but friendlies on the radar scope at 1005 May 11, when there suddenly appeared out of low broken clouds on the starboard quarter of Admiral Mitscher's flagship *Bunker Hill* a Zeke making a shallow dive. It crashed flight deck just abaft No. 3 elevator, skidded through parked planes, kindling huge fires en route, and fell over the side. Its bomb penetrated the flight deck, passed through topside at gallery deck level and exploded, riddling gun sponsons with fragments. Just as the Zeke hit the ship a Judy was spotted coming in from astern at a high angle. This plane, after an almost vertical dive, penetrated the flight deck at the base of the island, spreading flames through access passages and ladders of the superstructure. The bomb, released before the crash, exploded on the gallery deck; the motor was hurled into flag office, killing three officers and eleven men of the Admiral's staff.

Bunker Hill now became a mass of flames and smoke from well

[8] Same references as in Chap. XII Note 1 and Chap. XIII Note 1.

forward to the fantail and down through three decks. In a desperate maneuver Captain G. A. Seitz swung his ship 70 degrees, which threw the flaming mixture on the flight deck over the side, and enabled damage control parties to get the best of the fires in that quarter; but those below raged on, fed by parked planes, throwing out so much smoke and heat as to be difficult of access. Cruiser *Wilkes-Barre* and several destroyers closed to direct their pumps into the hangar deck fire, and some planes there were sent topside by the still intact No. 1 elevator to help fire-fighters to gain access. Not until 1530, when Captain Seitz felt that his crew could handle the situation, did the assisting ships cast off. One hour later Admiral Mitscher transferred his flag and the rest of his staff to *Enterprise* by a destroyer. *Bunker Hill* suffered unusually heavy casualties, mostly owing to smoke suffocation: 353 dead, 43 missing and 264 wounded and injured. The material damage was so extensive that she had to return to Bremerton for repairs. With the exception of *Franklin*, this was the most heavily damaged carrier to survive, although put out of action for the rest of the war.[9]

During the night of 12–13 May, Task Groups 58.1 and 58.3 steamed northward for two full days and nights in order to launch sweeps, strikes and heckling missions on airfields and air facilities on Kyushu and Shikoku. That these efforts had some value is suggested by the slacking off of air attacks on Okinawa; the Japanese could not lay on another *kikusui* attack until the 24th.

Returning from these diversionary strikes, TF 58 suffered another major casualty on 14 May. Shortly after daylight 26 Japanese planes attacked. Six were shot down by antiaircraft fire and 19 by C.A.P., but at 0656 the one survivor crashed *Enterprise* just abaft the forward elevator, blowing a hole and raising a big bulge in the flight deck. The bomb penetrated the flight deck and exploded deep in the ship, over 50 feet from where it broke through. The elevator was demolished and parts of it were blown 400 feet in the air. Fires broke out in the forward part of the hangar deck and in the elevator pit. These were quickly got under control and extinguished in half

[9] *Bunker Hill* Action Report; story in *Life* 9 July 1945.

an hour. Casualties were relatively light for the amount of damage inflicted — 13 killed and 68 wounded. *Enterprise* also had to be sent to a navy yard for major repairs.[10] This was the third time the "Big E" had been hit by a kamikaze, and the second time in four days that Admiral Mitscher had been on the receiving end. He transferred his flag to carrier *Randolph* next day.

An uneventful fortnight followed for Task Force 58.

The British Carrier Task Force sortied 1 May for another two to three weeks' go at the Sakishima Gunto. Early 4 May, after the carriers had topped off the destroyers with fuel, they launched strikes against Miyako and Ishigaki. Admiral Rawlings decided to bombard Miyako with the battleships and cruisers. He believed that air bombing would be more effective than naval gunfire, but felt that the battleship and cruiser gunners were spoiling for action and needed a morale booster. So, at 1000, in H.M.S. *King George V*, he led the bombardment group away from the carriers, and at noon they opened a 45-minute pounding of Nobara airfields and Sukuma airstrip.

The enemy took advantage of this weakening of the screen to attack the carriers. About 16 to 20 planes were involved, some acting as decoys. While C.A.P. took off after one group, another broke through. At 1131 a Zeke dove on H.M.S. *Formidable* through heavy antiaircraft barrage, crashing her flight deck near the island and kindling large fires among parked aircraft. Through a small hole that the impact made in the steel flight deck, splinters pierced the center boiler room, slowing the ship to 18 knots. Casualties were eight killed and 47 wounded with eleven aircraft destroyed. Flight deck gear was damaged but by 1254 *Formidable*, true to her name, had picked up speed to 24 knots.[11]

She was not the only carrier to suffer attack on 4 May. At 1134 a Zeke appeared on the starboard bow of H.M.S. *Indomitable*. After being taken under antiaircraft fire, it slipped into a cloud, but the kamikaze pilot soon took heart and dived. The task force was then

[10] *Enterprise* Action Report 22 May 1945.
[11] Vice Admiral Sir Philip Vian RN Action Report 14 May 1945.

maneuvering radically and Captain Eccles ordered *Indomitable's* rudder to be put hard over. The Zeke, set afire by automatic weapons, was splashed about ten yards on the carrier's starboard bow. C.A.P. accounted for two or three more enemy aircraft during the afternoon and prevented further attack on the carriers. The bombardment group rejoined at 1430.

The hole in *Formidable's* deck was so quickly patched up that she was able to recover aircraft at 1700. The armored flight decks of British aircraft carriers, which American ship planners disliked because the weight affected stability and reduced the number of planes that could be carried, proved their value in these actions. A kamikaze hitting a steel flight deck crumpled up like a scrambled egg and did comparatively little damage, whilst one crashing the wood flight deck of an American carrier usually penetrated to the hangar deck and raised hell below.[12]

Task Force 57 maintained a similar pattern of strikes, counterattacks and fueling periods through Operation ICEBERG. Sakishima Gunto fields were again plastered on 5 May, and there was then no counterattack. On the next two days the task force fueled, and on the 8th the weather was too foul for air operations. Next day TF 57 again struck Sakishima Gunto, and these strikes brought retaliation. At 1654 the flight deck of H.M.S. *Victorious* was crashed by a kamikaze, and two minutes later it happened again. That plane bounced over the side and a third was shot down at 1657. Casualties were three killed and 19 wounded, with no great damage to the ship. At 1705 a kamikaze dove into aircraft parked on the flight deck of H.M.S. *Formidable;* seven planes were destroyed, but all fires were extinguished in 15 minutes' time. Since *Formidable* now had only 15 planes serviceable, she retired for replenishment, together with H.M.S. *Victorious,* but returned to the fray three days later.

Sakishima Gunto was struck on 12–13 and 16–17 May, with no counterattacks and slight loss. A Corsair pilot who ditched three

[12] Compare in Appendix I the number of planes on each CV of TF 57 with those of TF 58. The ships were of about the same tonnage.

miles off Miyako was rescued by lifeguard submarine U.S.S. *Blue-fish*. Dense fog in the launching area on 20 May prevented air operations but caused a destroyer to collide with H.M.S. *Indomitable*, which then went to Sydney for repairs and refit. The final strikes on Sakishima Gunto were made on 24–25 May, by which time so few planes were operating from the cratered fields of these islands that they needed no further attention.

Shortly after, Admiral Rawlings received a congratulatory message from Admiral Spruance. The Pacific Fleet of the Royal Navy had demonstrated that it could take the grueling routine that the war with Japan required at this stage. And every unit of the Fifth Fleet operating off Okinawa was grateful for this southern shield against air attacks from the Sakishima Gunto.

The second fortnight of May was relatively uneventful for the United States Navy fast carriers. Two groups provided support off Okinawa while a third enjoyed rest and upkeep at Ulithi. On 27 May Admiral Halsey relieved Admiral Spruance off Okinawa and Fifth Fleet again became Third Fleet. Next day Admiral McCain took over from Admiral Mitscher and Task Force 58 again was designated Task Force 38.

3. *Operations on and near Okinawa*

On 1 May the Marines' III Amphibious Corps, having executed their mission of overrunning the Motobu Peninsula, were brought into the main action in the southern part of the island. At that time fire support ships were divided into two groups, one off the Hagushi beaches and one in Nakagusuku Wan. Spotting planes were supplied and extensive use was made of the float planes belonging to battleships and cruisers. This went on day after day, the last fire support ship mission assigned being on 20 June when the remaining Japanese on Okinawa were cornered in a small pocket in the extreme southern part of the island.

On 4 May General Ushijima launched an all-out offensive, hoping to deal a major defeat to Tenth Army. According to plan he was to be supported by *kikusui* mass attack No. 5, with the Japanese Navy alone contributing 280 planes; and although only 75 Navy and 40 Army planes were actually committed, they did plenty of damage. As we have seen, the radar pickets bore the brunt of the attack, two destroyers and two LSMs were sunk and several others badly damaged. But enough "floating chrysanthemums" broke through picket line to damage several ships. The oft-battered *Birmingham* (Captain H. D. Power), now flying the flag of Rear Admiral Deyo, having completed her forty-first gunfire support mission, anchored off Hagushi during the morning watch 4 May, hoping for a little peace and quiet. The forenoon watch had been on duty only five minutes when 14 planes were reported closing, 60 miles distant. They were intercepted by C.A.P., but apparently with slight success as ten or twelve broke through and made for the cruiser. While these were absorbing the gunners' attention, an Oscar, which had approached from over Okinawa, undetected by radar, was sighted by the lookouts about a mile distant and almost directly overhead. It dove through a barrage of 20-mm fire, at 0841 crashed *Birmingham* just to starboard of No. 2 six-inch turret, broke through main deck, passed through the communications officers' cabin, killing Lieutenant Henry Page who had just gone below, and exploded in the sickbay where sick-call was just being held, killing or severely wounding everyone there, including all but five corpsmen of the medical staff. And the bomb, too, exploded on first platform deck. Fires were under control by 0914, and the less badly wounded were transferred to hospital ship *Mercy*, which left some of her medical department on board to treat the severely wounded. Casualties were 51 killed, missing or died of wounds, 81 wounded. *Birmingham* now had to be sent to Guam for repairs.[13]

---

[13] *Birmingham* Action Report 5 July 1945; Deyo "Kamikaze." Vice Admiral Oldendorf, having recovered from his accident at Ulithi, had returned to *Tennessee* as Combatron 1 on 1 May. Rear Adm. Rodgers shifted his flag from *Birmingham* to *Crescent City*. *Birmingham* on 3 May relieved *Tennessee* and when she in turn left Okinawa, Rear Adm. Allan E. Smith became CTF 54, and Deyo went to *California* to fly his flag once more in *Santa Fe*.

Survey ship *Pathfinder* off the Motobu Peninsula, and seaplane tender *St. George* at Kerama Retto, were crashed by kamikazes on 6 May. *Pathfinder* had one man killed; *St. George* lost three killed and 30 wounded.

The heartening news of Germany's unconditional surrender reached the forces at Okinawa early on 8 May. This, reported Admiral Turner, was "the most quiet day yet experienced by our forces in this area. Many ships conducted Divine Services in Thanksgiving for Victory in Europe. At exactly 1200 one round from every gun ashore accompanied a full gun salvo from every possible fire support ship directed at the enemy, as a complimentary and congratulatory gesture to our Armed Forces in Europe."

This lull did not last long. On 9 May destroyer escort *Oberrender* (Lieutenant Commander Samuel Spencer USNR) was in the outer antisubmarine screen west of Okinawa. At 1840, hearing of planes being in the vicinity, she went to general quarters; and twelve minutes later, just before sunset, sighted a plane at 9000 yards. Repeatedly hit by gunfire in a gliding dive, one of its wings began flapping and fell off about 250 yards away. But this did not deflect the plane sufficiently to cause it to miss. It crashed *Oberrender* at 20-mm gun No. 5. The bomb exploded in the forward fire room and caused heavy damage, killing eight men and wounding 53. Towed to Kerama Retto, she was judged to be beyond profitable repair, and this gallant little ship was stricken from the Navy list.

During this same attack the veteran destroyer escort *England*, which in 1944 had performed the phenomenal feat of sinking six Japanese submarines in twelve days,[14] also got crashed. She was now under command of Lieutenant Commander J. A. Williamson USNR. The kamikazes apparently had her number, for she had been jolted though not damaged by one that near-missed her on 25 April. On 9 May *England* was in the outer antisubmarine screen northwest of Kerama Retto. At about 1853 she picked up three bogeys being chased by C.A.P., with a Val in the lead and diving for her. It was taken under fire by the main battery and automatic weapons while

[14] See Vol. VIII 224–231.

the ship maneuvered to evade. The Val, although hit, crashed the superstructure and the resulting bomb explosion not only demolished wardroom country, ship's office, radio room and adjacent compartments, but started heavy fires in them. The bridge was enveloped in flames but the skipper managed to make his way aft and there resume the conn. With the help of other vessels the fires were brought under control in about 45 minutes. *England* was towed into Kerama roadstead for patching up and then sent to the rear for major repairs. She lost 35 men killed or missing and 27 wounded.

One of the most unusual, persistent and daring feats of shooting down an enemy plane was performed by a Corsair piloted by 1st Lieutenant Robert R. Klingman USMCR of Marine Air Group 33, based on Kadena field. He was one of a four-plane C.A.P. during the forenoon of 10 May when a high-flying Nick passed over Okinawa. In a chase that lasted for one and three-quarters hours and extended over 185 miles, Klingman caught up with it at 38,000 feet only to find that his guns were frozen. Undaunted, he made three passes at the tail of the Nick, cut off rudder, stabilizer and finally the whole tail with his propeller, and saw his target splash. By that time the altitude of the action was well over a Corsair's service ceiling of 41,600 feet. He lost oxygen at 18,000, the engine cut out at 10,000, he had holes in his own wings and engine and both propeller and engine cowling were damaged, but he made a belly landing safely at Kadena field.[15]

New Mexico had just returned to Hagushi anchorage from replenishment at Kerama after sunset 12 May when, as the largest ship in the roadstead, she was attacked by two kamikazes which had tailed a returning C.A.P. The first attacker was thrown off by a 5-inch shell burst directly under, which lifted it clear of the mastheads. Its bomb exploded, making the stack look like a giant blowtorch. The second, although several times hit, crashed the gun deck and tore into the stack. Casualties were heavy: 54 killed or missing

[15] Marine Air Group 33 War Diary May 1945; Robert Sherrod *Marine Aviation* p. 392; my notes on Cincpac conference.

and 119 wounded; but efficient work by damage control had all fires quenched in 21 minutes. With the help of the crew of repair ship *Oceanus* the battleship was able to carry on until 28 May, when she was ordered to Guam for repairs.[16]

Matters were relatively quiet for several days in the transport, support and logistics areas. And wet days they were. Rains set in on the 16th, and from that day to the end of the month there was a precipitation of almost 21 inches. The resulting mixture of rain water and Okinawa soil produced such mud as none of the Americans present had seen or imagined. Tanks were almost completely immobilized.

On 17 May there was an important change of command. Vice Admiral Harry W. Hill, who earlier had relieved Admiral Turner as Commander Fifth Amphibious Force, now took over his second hat, CTF 51.

On 20 May several enemy planes penetrated the transport area and Kerama roadstead. Several ships were damaged, *Thatcher* most seriously. She was crashed by a kamikaze which caused extensive damage on the starboard side and a six-by-nine-foot hole between keel and bilge. She made her own way into Kerama Retto but had 14 killed or missing and 53 wounded.

During the unusually clear night of 24–25 May, under a full moon, the Japanese made an airborne attack on Kadena and Yontan airfields, in support of their counteroffensive on Okinawa. A Sally made a belly landing on the principal runway at Yontan. While it was still screeching along the concrete, ten members of the *giretsu* (a special airborne attack unit) tumbled out, head over heels, found their feet quickly and sprinted for the parked planes, tossing out hand grenades and phosphorus bombs. Blinding flashes and flames from burning planes illuminated the field. In the wild confusion that ensued two Americans were killed and 18 wounded before the attackers were hunted down and exterminated. They

[16] *New Mexico* Action Report 28 May 1945; "The Queen's Daily News" (the ship's paper) for 27 Oct. 1945.

succeeded in destroying seven planes, damaging 26 others, and blowing up two fuel dumps containing 70,000 gallons of gasoline. Four more *giretsu*-manned Sallys roared in but were shot down, and their crews, to the number of 56, were killed.[17]

On the same night enemy planes dropped 50 to 70 bombs on Ie Shima where a Seabee unit was making a temporary base for Marine Air Group 22. Nobody was killed, but many of the bombs were of the delayed-action kind, giving the bomb disposal officers plenty of nerve-wracking but necessary work.[18]

These exploits were part of the seventh major *kikusui* attack consisting of 165 planes, most of which managed to circumvent the radar pickets and penetrate the fire support area. Destroyer transport *Barry* (Lieutenant Commander C. F. Hand USNR) was in the screen when at 0034 May 25 she sighted two planes coming in low at about 2200 yards. They were taken under fire by the 40-mm quads. The lead plane began strafing and a few seconds later crashed the ship's starboard side at frame 42. Four compartments were penetrated and fires broke out around the radar transmitter room, radio shack and half deck. Internal communication was disrupted. Nobody was killed but 30 men were wounded. As fires prevented the flooding of magazines, the ship was abandoned temporarily for fear of an explosion. With the help of *Sims* the fires were brought partly under control by 0355 when a tug came alongside to tow *Barry* to Kerama. She was so badly damaged as to be decommissioned, and it was decided to use her hulk as a decoy for kamikazes.

Many other planes penetrated the transport area where heavy attacks lasted from about 0800 to 1300 May 25. Minesweeper *Spectacle* was crashed by a kamikaze, burned fiercely and had to be abandoned but was later towed to Kerama; she had 29 killed or missing. *LSM–135*, carrying *Spectacle* survivors, was hit at 0835, set on fire and abandoned after beaching on a reef near Ie Shima.

---

[17] C. W. Ruble et al. *The Earthmover: Chronicle of the 87th Seabee Battalion* (Baton Rouge 1946); *Okinawa: The Last Battle* pp. 361–62.

[18] R. G. Barwise of CBMU–509, paper written for this History, 1948.

At 0906 *Stormes*, at radar picket station No. 15, was crashed by a vertical diver which demolished the after torpedo mount, caused a bad fire in a 5-inch handling room, and flooded the ship aft. At 1120 APD *Bates* was hit by two kamikazes and had to be abandoned owing to fires that got out of control; she lost 21 killed or missing and 35 wounded. She was later towed to Hagushi anchorage but capsized and sank the same evening. On 26 May there was again heavy enemy air activity and some damage to ships off Okinawa.

The eighth *kikusui* assault of 27–29 May — the one that sank *Braine* and *Drexler* — spilled over into the transport area where the attack was favored by a 50 per cent overcast and full moon. Merchant ship *Josiah Snelling* off Ie Shima, merchant ships *Brown Victory* and *Mary Livermore* and transport *Sandoval*, off Nakagusuku Wan, were hit by kamikazes on 28 May but none were seriously damaged.

This attack coincided with the relief of Admiral Spruance by Admiral Halsey on 27 May, when Fifth Fleet again became Third Fleet, and TF 58, TF 38. Since 17 March Fifth Fleet had been at sea dishing it out, and taking the rap, exposed to the threat of deadly air attack day and night. With a count so far of 90 ships sunk or damaged badly enough to be out of action for more than a month, this Okinawa operation had proved to be the most costly naval campaign of the war, seldom exceeded in any war. Throughout the ordeal Admiral Spruance clung tenaciously to the objective that Okinawa must be secured. He never flinched, no more than did the officers and men of his command. A less serene and courageous man might, before reaching this point, have asked "Is this island worth the cost? Is there no better way to defeat Japan?" But no such doubts or questions ever even occurred to Raymond A. Spruance.

CHAPTER XVII

Okinawa Secured

June–September 1945

1. *The Last Month of Battle, 3 June–2 July*

WHEN the battle for Okinawa was almost over, some of the correspondents and armchair strategists in Washington began nasty criticisms of the way the campaign had been handled.[1] Homer Bigart, a *New York Herald Tribune* correspondent, seems to have started this ball a-rolling by criticizing General Buckner's tactics, alleging that instead of committing the Marines on the same front as XXIV Corps he should have landed them on the enemy's flank and made them the second arm of a pair of pincers. David Lawrence then went so far as to call the campaign a fiasco, and "a worse example of military incompetence than Pearl Harbor." Secretary Forrestal, Admirals Turner and Mitscher, issued statements defending the Army's tactics. Since that did not silence the "kibitzers," as Kelly Turner called them, Admiral Nimitz took the unprecedented step of discussing the campaign with 76 press correspondents at Guam. He praised the Army for a "magnificent performance," deprecated interservice criticism, and pointed out that, in view of the nature of the terrain and the Japanese tactics, a flank amphibious landing by the Marines would have been a waste of effort.

In June there were few air alerts, compared with the almost continuous "Condition Red" of earlier months, but enemy planes occasionally got through. During the evening of 6 June, light minelayer

[1] David Lawrence in Washington *Evening Star* 30 May and 4 June and *Sunday Star* 17 June; Secnav's statement in *N.Y. Times* 6 June, Nimitz's in *Washington Post* 17 June, and articles by George Fielding Eliot about the same time in *N.Y. Herald Tribune.*

J. William Ditter was screening with *Harry F. Bauer* southeast of Nakagusuku Wan when a raid was detected coming in from the sea, and at 1713 both ships were attacked by about eight aircraft. *Ditter* (Commander R. R. Sampson) claimed shooting down five, but one struck her No. 2 stack with its wing, and nine minutes later another hit her on the port side just below the main deck level, punching a hole 7 by 50 feet, killing ten men, wounding 27. The after fire room and forward engine room flooded and all power was temporarily lost, but she was towed into Kerama Retto.

The next to the last *kikusui* attack, a small one which spread over five days, 3–7 June, and comprised only 50 "floating chrysanthemums," was a complete failure. Station No. 1 had most of the excitement on 7 June. A Tony had been shot down by C.A.P. directly over destroyer *Anthony*. Her crew observed with amazement that the Japanese pilot, breaking all rules, bailed out; but his parachute failed to open in time, so his end was the same. C.A.P. splashed three that afternoon. Toward dusk two approached this station out of a low haze. One exploded as the result of innumerable 40-mm hits by *Anthony*, showering the destroyer's bridge, forecastle and director with burning gasoline. Fortunately the water from the plane's splash extinguished the flames with little help needed from Damage Control. Five men blown overboard used the plane's wreckage as a life raft and were recovered by an LCS; *Anthony* herself sustained slight damage.

A single Val on 10 June had the satisfaction of sinking a destroyer, *William D. Porter*, on picket station No. 15. She was not buttoned up aft when, at 0825, the kamikaze dove on her out of a 1500-foot overcast. Although the Val missed and splashed, its bomb exploded under water so close aboard as to create a mining effect. Sixty men were wounded, mostly with broken or badly sprained ankles, the seams opened aft and the after engine room flooded rapidly. Four LCS came alongside to help but the water gained, *Porter* settled by the stern and sank at 1119. None of her crew were killed.[2]

[2] Navy Dept. Interview with Cdr. C. M. Keyes 18 July 1945.

Next day, 11 June at 1900, LCS(L)–*122* splashed the first of three Vals which dove on her out of the clouds at station No. 15, but the second crashed the base of her conning tower. The bomb passed through her hull and exploded in the water on the port side, showering her with fragments. A heavy fire was brought under control and she made Hagushi anchorage under her own power with eleven killed, and a wounded skipper, Lieutenant R. M. McCool.

Four peaceful days followed for the radar pickets. At 2030 June 16, *Twiggs*, in the western fire support area, was hit on the port side by a torpedo dropped from a low-flying plane, which exploded her No. 2 magazine. The explosion was easily visible from other ships, especially to Captain Glenn R. Hartwig, the squadron commander in *Putnam*. He closed promptly and, through calling each of his ships by radio, by elimination identified the victim. *Twiggs*'s bow was bent upward at right angles to the keel, and the ship was enveloped in flames. Exploding antiaircraft ammunition kept would-be rescuers at a distance until *Twiggs* sank one hour after the hit. Some 188 survivors were picked up, but 126 were killed or missing, including her skipper, Commander George Philip.

After two months of bitter fighting on the big island, Tenth Army occupied the capital, Naha, on 27 May. Two days later the Japanese Thirty-second Army began withdrawing from the ruins of Shuri. At 1015 May 29 Company A 1st Battalion 5th Marines captured the shell of Shuri Castle, where Commodore Matthew C. Perry had been received in great state by the "King of Loochoo" almost exactly 92 years before.[3] As the Marines stormed in they saw Japanese soldiers trying to escape by swimming the medieval moat. Tenth Army kept up pressure and the Japanese were compressed into smaller and smaller pockets until their remnants were driven to the extreme southern point of the island.

Early in June the 2nd Marine Division returned to Okinawa from the Marianas, and its 8th Regiment (Colonel Clarence E. Wal-

[3] Arthur Walworth *Black Ships off Japan* pp. 50–51; Nichols & Shaw *Okinawa* p. 206.

lace USMC), attached to the 1st Marine Division, took part in the final push which jumped off on 18 June. At noon that day Lieutenant General Simon Bolivar Buckner was at Colonel Wallace's observation post when it was hit by five Japanese artillery shells. The explosion hurled a large block of coral at the general. Mortally wounded, he died within a few minutes, a scant two miles and four days short of his goal, the capture of Okinawa.

Major General Roy S. Geiger USMC assumed temporary command of Tenth Army. He was relieved five days later by Lieutenant General Joseph A. Stilwell USA.

On 19 June Lieutenant General Ushijima sent farewell messages to Japan and ordered what was left of his army to "fight to the last and die." Not all obeyed. Loud-speakers mounted on Army tanks and in LCIs that cruised along the coast invited both troops and civilians to surrender, and many did — 106 Japanese soldiers, 238 Okinawan auxiliaries and over 3000 civilians on 19 June alone. Two days later when, shortly after noon, Tenth Army drove through to Ara Saki, the southernmost point of Okinawa, General Geiger announced that organized resistance had ceased.[4] At 0300 June 22 General Ushijima and his chief of staff took their own lives. The Okinawa campaign was officially declared to be over on 2 July, but mopping up was still going on when the Japanese commander of the hitherto uninvaded islands of the Ryukyus formally surrendered the group to General Stilwell on 7 September 1945.[5]

2. *The Air and Naval Base* [6]

Base development began soon after the assault troops landed on Okinawa. Specialized Seabee battalions landed on L-day and the

[4] Officially confirmed at a formal ceremony at 1000 June 22.

[5] On 11 Nov. 1945 a large cave, sheltering several cold, half-starved and frightened stragglers, was captured; and in early 1946 a Japanese officer who had collected a few escaped P.O.W.s sent word to the base commander that he was ready for an honorable surrender, which was granted. Barwise Report.

[6] The Army and Marine Corps monographs earlier cited; Bureau of Yards and Docks *Building the Navy's Bases in World War II* Vol. II; Robert Sherrod *History of Marine Corps Aviation in World War II*.

build-up from the start was rapid. First object was to condition existing airfields. In addition, the Seabees directly supported the amphibious forces by handling pontoon causeways, and the troops by building and maintaining roads.

Practically none of the Japanese facilities on Okinawa were suitable for the United States Army. Roads were not only few in number but narrow and poorly surfaced. Hence, much of the early engineering effort had to be put into making existing roads wider, surfacing them for heavy military traffic, building new roads and repairing demolished bridges.

Engineers, both Army and Seabee, were under Commander Construction Troops who, in turn, was under the Island Commander, Major General Fred C. Wallace USMC. Within a week of the initial landings, General Wallace became responsible for directing unloading on the beaches, and the scope of his activities increased commensurate with the captured area of Okinawa, until it included a vast complex of concurrent projects. The military government of Okinawa, taking care of the tens of thousands of civilians who had to be fed and sheltered, was another responsibility. By the end of June he controlled 153,000 men, of whom 95,000 were construction troops and Seabees.

Airfield construction and supply roads had priority; other base developments could wait until the island was secured. When the heavy rains in late May bogged down Tenth Army, General Buckner ordered work on airfields to be suspended and put all available engineers on the supply roads. With the return of fair weather in June, base development went into high gear. Nakagusuku Wan (renamed Buckner Bay after the death of the General) and Kimmu Wan were transformed by Seabees into seaports, with docks and other cargo handling facilities. New airfields and a seaplane base were built on the eastern side of Okinawa, and airfields on Ie Shima. The face of the island was changed more than it had been for thousands of years by multi-lane roads, traffic circles, water points, quonset villages, tank farms, storage dumps and hospitals. And by the end of the war in mid-August base development had progressed to the point where Okinawa could well have performed its original purpose of serving as an advance base for the invasion of Japan proper. After the surrender, and until the future status of the island was settled, no new projects were started, but construction troops continued those already under way. By that time Okinawa as an advanced naval base was surpassed only by Guam, Leyte and Manus. Naval facilities on the island covered 20,000 acres by the end of 1945.

As new airfields became available there was a corresponding build-up of Tenth Army's Tactical Air Force under Major General F. P. Mulcahy USMC. Initially the planes were Marine fighters, but A.A.F. fighter planes were soon added to the command. Up to 1 May, 3521 C.A.P. sorties had been flown from Okinawan airfields. The fields were naturally the targets of Japanese bombers, but aviation engineers kept them operating and ground crews kept the planes serviced. As the build-up increased, so did the variety of air missions. On 17 May long-range Army P–47s from Ie Shima hit Kyushu in the first of many similar attacks. As the enemy-occupied part of Okinawa contracted, so did the need for close air support of troops, and the emphasis of air operations shifted to the aërial attack on Japan itself.

On 11 June General Mulcahy, in poor health, was relieved by Major General Louis E. Woods USMC, and by the end of June the tactical air force under his command had increased to more than 750 aircraft. It included a Marine aircraft wing, an Army fighter wing, and an Army Air Force bomber command with one light, one medium and two heavy bomber groups. Tactical was dissolved on 14 July since by that time Okinawa-based aircraft were devoted almost entirely to the bomber offensive. A.A.F. units passed to the operational control of General Kenney's Far Eastern Air Forces.

If the Japanese ashore knew that Okinawa was secured, their airborne fellows did not. The tenth and last *kikusui* attack, to which only 45 kamikazes were committed, began 21 June and lasted into the 22nd.

At 1830 June 21, five hours after Major General Geiger had declared Okinawa secured, a small group of kamikazes penetrated Kerama Retto. Seaplane tender *Kenneth Whiting* knocked down an Oscar, but part of it hit her, causing minor damage and wounding five men. Twenty seconds earlier her type sister *Curtiss* was hit by a Frank on the starboard side forward at third deck level. It took 15 hours to bring the resulting fires under control, and by that time the forward magazines had been flooded and only half the ship was livable. She lost 41 killed or missing and 28 wounded. On the same day *LSM-59* was towing the hulk of decommissioned *Barry* out to sea to act as a kamikaze decoy, when both were crashed. *LSM-59* sank in four minutes but lost only two killed and eight wounded; the former *Barry* floated a little longer but she too went down, prematurely fulfilling her mission. This raid continued into the early hours of 22 June when *LSM-213* was hit by a suicider in Kimmu Wan. Hull damage was severe, and she had three killed or missing and ten wounded. At 0920 *LST-534*, which was unloading on the beach in Nakagusuku Wan, was hit by a kamikaze and her bow doors and tank deck were damaged. She lost three killed and 35 wounded. *Ellyson* was near-missed, losing one killed and four wounded.

On 22 June between 0749 and 0925, radar picket station No. 15 was under attack. Owing largely to the superb work of two C.A.P. groups, controlled by fighter directors in *Massey* and *Dyson*, 29 out of an estimated 40 enemy planes were splashed and the rest driven away, without the ships present expending a single round of ammunition.

This was the last exploit of the "floating chrysanthemums." But, until the end of the war, radar pickets continued to be favorite targets of individual kamikazes.

On 3 July, because there were fewer ships operating in Okinawan waters and less frequent air attacks, the number of picket stations was reduced to two. Life there was uneventful until late July when *Callaghan* (Commander C. M. Bertholf, with squadron commander Captain A. E. Jarrell on board) chalked up her 13th enemy plane at a heavy price. She was in picket station No. 9A with *Cassin Young*, *Prichett* and three LCS. All were veterans of the Pacific war and *Callaghan* had been at Okinawa since Palm Sunday.

At 0028 July 29, early in the midwatch under a bright third-quarter moon, bogeys were reported. *Callaghan* opened fire with her main battery at a slow, low-flying plane which closed to about 2000 yards, started a kamikaze run, and hit the ship at 0041 in No. 3 upper handling room, which exploded four minutes later. The bomb itself exploded in the after engine room, which went completely out of action. Immediately after the handling room explosion the destroyer began to settle by the stern, automatic ammunition began going off when the fires swept aft, and only two minutes after the hit, the fantail was under water. Commander Bertholf ordered all but a few key men to abandon ship and at 0153 he and Captain Jarrell boarded an LCS which had closed to help. Gallant *Callaghan* went down by the stern at 0235. She had 47 missing and 73 wounded. It was an extra and bitter pill that the attacking aircraft was one of those ancient twin-float biplanes made of fabric and wood, against which proximity fuzes were not effective. The following night, at 0326 July 30, another antique crashed *Cassin Young*, which had survived a kamikaze attack on 12 April. It caused extensive damage, killing 22 and wounding 45 men.[7]

This was the last time that kamikazes seriously molested naval forces in the vicinity of Okinawa. The Japanese were now feverishly training pilots and building or repairing planes to operate against United States ships in the expected invasion of Japan.

Although the Navy had met the kamikaze by radar warning, C.A.P., and the proximity fuze for antiaircraft shells, and although average effectiveness of the suicide planes diminished, the prospect of thousands of them being used against our invasion forces in the autumn was disquieting. The Navy, far from satisfied with the

---

[7] It is a strange coincidence that both destroyers were named after officers killed on board cruiser *San Francisco* in the great Naval Battle of Guadalcanal, 12–15 Nov. 1942, Rear Adm. Daniel J. Callaghan and Capt. Cassin Young. See Vol. V 247.

situation,[8] detached from TF 58 Vice Admiral Willis A. Lee, one of the best brains in the service, to set up a research and experiment unit for devising a remedy for the kamikaze disease, at Casco Bay in Maine. Admiral Lee died before the end of the war in August, and his unit was then dissolved.

Captain Frederick Moosbrugger, over-all commander of the radar picket destroyers, paid a tribute to them in his action report of 20 July that might well be recorded in bronze: —

"The performance of . . . screening and radar picket ships . . . was superb throughout the Okinawa campaign. Acts of heroism and unselfishness, fighting spirit, coolness under fire, unswerving determination, endurance, and qualities of leadership and loyalty exceeded all previous conceptions . . . set for the United States Navy. . . . Never in the annals of our glorious naval history have naval forces done so much with so little against such odds for so long a period. Radar picket duty in this operation might well be a symbol of supreme achievement in our naval traditions." [9]

Although your historian himself has been under kamikaze attack, and witnessed the hideous forms of death and torture inflicted by that weapon, words fail him to do justice to the sailors on the radar picket stations. We need a poet to do it, as John Masefield did in his *Dauber* for old-time sailors in their freezing grind of rounding Cape Horn. Men on radar picket station, to survive, not only had to strike down the flaming terror of the kamikaze, roaring out of the blue like the thunderbolts that Zeus hurled at bad actors in days of old; they were under constant strain and unusual discomfort. In order to supply 650-lb. steam pressure to build up full speed rapidly in a destroyer, its superheaters, built only for intermittent use, had to be lighted for three and four days' running. For days and even nights on end, the crew had to stand general quarters, and the ship kept "buttoned up." Men had to keep in condition for the instant reaction and split-second timing necessary to riddle a plane bent

[8] It also issued, in June 1945, an information bulletin in the *Battle Experience* series, *Radar Pickets and Methods of Combating Suicide Attacks off Okinawa*.
[9] CTG 51.5 (Capt. Moosbrugger) Action Report 20 July 1945 p. 14.

on a crashing death. Sleep became the rarest commodity and
choicest luxury, like water to a shipwrecked mariner.

Thus, as the war against Japan drew to its close, Okinawa became a giant air and naval base which was destined to play a major
rôle in the cold war that followed the war with Japan. For it we
paid a heavy price. Thirty-two naval ships and craft had been sunk,
mostly by kamikaze attack, and 368 ships and craft had been damaged. The Fleet lost 763 aircraft. Over 4900 sailors were killed or
went missing in action, and an additional 4824 were wounded. This
was by far the heaviest loss incurred in any naval campaign in the
war. Tenth Army also suffered heavy casualties: 7613 killed or
missing in action, 31,807 wounded and more than 26,000 non-battle
casualties. Sobering thought as it is to record such losses, the sacrifice of these brave men is brightened by the knowledge that the
capture of Okinawa helped to bring Japanese leaders face to face
with the inevitable, and that their surrender in August saved many
thousand more Americans from suffering flaming death in an assault on the main islands of Japan.

However that may be, there is no reason to alter the verdict of
Winston Churchill, who in a message to President Truman on 22
June 1945 said: —

"The strength of willpower, devotion and technical resources
applied by the United States to this task, joined with the death
struggle of the enemy, . . . places this battle among the most intense and famous of military history. . . . We make our salute to
all your troops and their commanders engaged." [10]

[10] N.Y. Times 23 June 1945.

PART III

Miscellaneous Operations

CHAPTER XVIII

Pacific Fleet Submarines[1]

December 1944–August 1945

1. Offensive Operations

B Y DECEMBER 1944 United States submarines in the Yellow and East China Seas and off the coast of Japan were seldom encountering good targets. *Sea Devil* (Commander R. E. Styles), patrolling west of Kyushu on 2 December, ran into an eleven-ship convoy, and in spite of heavy weather managed to cut out of it a 6800-ton tanker and a 9467-ton freighter. Four days later *Trepang* (Commander R. M. Davenport), in a three-submarine pack, made contact on a seven-ship convoy with three escorts which imprudently tried to thread Luzon Strait. At 2045 she delivered the first of a series of attacks. Supported by the other members of her pack, *Segundo* (Commander J. D. Fulp) and *Razorback* (Commander C. D. Brown), *Trepang* worked over this convoy until midnight, sinking four cargo ships for a total of 20,000 tons and heavily damaging a fifth.

On 8 December at 2015 *Redfish* (Commander L. D. McGregor), west of Kyushu, began tracking a fast, zig-zagging target which, by 0110 on the 9th, she identified as a battleship, an aircraft carrier and three destroyers. At 0134, after the group had made a fortunate zig in her direction, *Redfish* got two hits on 24,000-ton carrier *Junyo*. That was the carrier whose planes had bombed Dutch Har-

---

[1] Patrol Reports of named submarines; *Imp. Jap. Navy World War II;* Monthly War Diary of Comsubpac; Theodore Roscoe *Submarine* (1949); Charles A. Lockwood *Sink 'em All* (1951). For the contemporary patrols of Southwest Pacific submarines, see Vol. XIII Chap. XIII.

bor in 1942, damaged battleship *South Dakota* in the Battle of the Santa Cruz Islands and which had survived the Battle of the Philippine Sea.[2] She was so badly damaged as to be out of the war. *Sea Devil*, which was operating in the same vicinity as *Redfish*, shares the credit; she also got a fish into *Junyo*.

Redfish was really in the money; on 19 December she had a crack at another carrier. Heading for the China coast just south of Shanghai she sighted a Japanese patrol plane which exploded a depth charge close aboard. Assuming that this plane was covering a convoy to seaward, Commander McGregor shaped an easterly course, sighted the masts of a southbound ship at 1624, and five minutes later identified it as a carrier. This was the new 17,500-ton *Unryu*, escorted by three destroyers. The group conveniently zigged towards *Redfish*, which at 1635 fired a spread of four torpedoes. One hit the carrier aft, stopping her dead, giving her a 20-degree list and causing her to burst into flame. While destroyers milled about dropping depth charges indiscriminately, *Redfish* reloaded her tubes and at 1650 fired an electric torpedo which hit just abaft the carrier's island. Explosions and heavy smoke followed. By 1659 a good periscope sweep failed to pick her up; *Unryu* had gone down. Her escorts almost avenged her loss by giving *Redfish* some heavy jolts from a cluster of depth charges, but she escaped by lying on the bottom until dark.

On the 22nd *Tilefish* (Commander R. M. Keithly) sank torpedo boat *Chidori* off the coast of Honshu. In Luzon Strait on 30 December *Razorback* sighted a convoy of four merchant ships with two escorts. She fired torpedoes and claimed having sunk at least one ship, but postwar checkups do not confirm this. Shortly after, however, she accounted for one of the escorts, destroyer *Kuretake*, by knocking its bow clean off.

January of 1945 proved to be a lean month for want of targets. *Kingfish* (Commander T. E. Harper), patrolling near Ogasawara

---

[2] *Redfish* Report of Second War Patrol; see Vol. IV 175, V 218, VIII 294. The carrier was erroneously named *Hayataka* in this and earlier reports, owing to misreading the Japanese characters.

Gunto in heavy weather, picked up a convoy of four ships and two escorts on the 3rd. First torpedo salvo missed but she trailed the convoy until dark, and around 2110 fired nine torpedoes. These accounted for two small *Marus*. Next day, *Puffer* (Lieutenant Commander Carl Dwyer), patrolling off the Ryukyus, observed a ship anchored off Yoron Jima. She closed through heavy seas to attack. Two torpedoes broached but a third at 1726 was observed to hit the vessel, which promptly disintegrated.[3] On 10 January *Puffer* had a curious experience when catching up with a ten-ship convoy, which had been reported by another submarine nearby. In a good position at 0250 January 10 she fired her first torpedoes, observed two hits, an explosion and a bright flash of light. "It looked like a C. B. De Mille movie," reported the skipper. Other attacks followed and at 0528 *Puffer* surfaced and fired torpedoes at two destroyer escorts. One took two hits and the other, one; but the second retaliated with radar-directed gunfire, using tracers. "There were straddles in range, deflection and morale," reported Commander Dwyer, but he was feeling pretty cocky and did not even submerge. His estimate was five ships sunk and two destroyers damaged; postwar assessment gives him destroyer escort *CD–42* sunk, *CD–30* badly damaged, but no merchant ships.

The story of "Loughlin's Loopers" — *Queenfish, Barb* and *Picuda* — in Formosa Strait has already been told for the most part.[4] One need only add that on 29 January *Picuda* picked up a two-ship convoy, claimed hits on both, and was later given credit for a 5500-ton *Maru*.

Spot (Commander W. S. Post), patrolling the Shanghai-Tsing-tao-Chefoo shipping lane in the Yellow Sea, enjoyed plenty of action. Shortly after midnight 19 January 1945 she picked up a target which turned out to be a passenger-freighter with portholes conveniently lit up; one torpedo disposed of her. Next day a small freighter was sighted and attacked by torpedoes without success.

[3] Neither JANAC nor *Imp. Jap. Navy W.W. II* show any ship hit here, but the detail and description in the patrol report is too vivid to throw it out entirely.
[4] See Vol. XIII 297–298. For earlier exploits of this pack, see Vol. XII 399, 409.

Spot having stopped the vessel with 40-mm gunfire, Commander Post decided to board and destroy her with demolition charges, and nosed his submarine's bow alongside. A boarding party scrambled aboard what turned out to be 1200-ton *Tokiwa Maru;* but before *Spot's* men managed to set their charges, the ship took a sudden list, the boarding party beat a hasty retreat and the *Maru* rolled over and sank.

An unfortunate mishap occurred near the Marianas. *Guardfish* (Commander D. T. Hammond) was returning to Guam from patrolling a "joint zone," one designated to be used both by submarines and surface vessels. In these zones no attack could be made without positive identification of the target as enemy. During the evening of 23 January *Guardfish* made radar contact on a westbound ship. As there were no indications of her character, and no sighting, the submarine sent off a report asking for information and continued tracking the target. Comsubpac answered promptly that no friendly submarines were known to be in the zone, but any surface contact should be presumed to be friendly. *Guardfish* was then ordered by her task group commander to continue tracking. Ten minutes before sunrise 24 January the target was wrongly identified through the periscope as an I-class Japanese submarine. Four torpedoes were fired and two hit; but as the unfortunate victim was plunging by the bow, it was seen to be no submarine, and when *Guardfish* surfaced she rescued 73 floating survivors of U.S.S. *Extractor*, an 800-ton salvage vessel. Six of the crew were lost. The presence of this ship in the joint zone was not reported to *Guardfish* because the day before she had been ordered to reverse course and return to port; but the order was received by *Extractor* in so garbled a form that her people could not decipher it and she continued on her course.

One Pacific Fleet submarine was lost during this month. *Swordfish* (Commander K. E. Montross) was last heard from on 3 January when she acknowledged receipt of an order to keep clear of the Nansei Shoto during carrier air strikes and to patrol off Yaku Island, south of Kyushu. On 12 January, when *Swordfish* was due to be in waters off Okinawa, submarine *Kete* heard a heavy depth charging there but was unable to ascertain what was going on. This may have marked the end of *Swordfish*, or she may have struck a mine.

February provided the underwater fleet with meager pickings around Japan and Formosa. The shallow Yellow Sea, where wintry weather limited operations, proved to be more fruitful. There on 4 February, *Spadefish* (Commander G. W. Underwood) sank a 4273-ton passenger-cargo steamer and recovered one survivor. Also in the Yellow Sea, veteran *Gato* (Commander R. M. Farrell), on her 11th war patrol, got destroyer escort *CD-9* on 14 February and a small *Maru* on the 21st. Three days later *Lagarto* (Commander F. D. Latta), on her first war patrol, bagged a small freighter and topped off the day by sinking submarine *I-371* east of the Bonins. *Sennet* (Commander G. E. Porter) sank a minelayer south of Kyushu on 16 February. Other submarines disposed of a variety of luggers and small craft during February, but important targets were conspicuously absent.

The same conditions prevailed the following month, which proved fatal for two United States submarines.

During the night of 9–10 March *Kete* (Lieutenant Commander Edward Ackerman), patrolling East China Sea southwest of Kyushu, sank three ships out of a convoy for a total of 6881 tons. Being low on torpedoes she was ordered to return to Pearl Harbor on the 20th, but the last heard from her was the transmission of a weather report on that date. What became of her is still a mystery.[5] On the same day *Devilfish* (Lieutenant Commander S. S. Mann), en route to her patrol station west of Iwo Jima, was crashed by a kamikaze. The radar antennas were damaged and a hole was punched in her after periscope shears, rendering both radar and periscope inoperable. *Trigger* (Commander D. R. Connole), operating in waters near Okinawa, reported 20 March that she had

[5] According to Comsubpac *U. S. Submarine Losses World War II* p. 153, three Japanese submarines were sunk in March in the waters through which *Kete* would have had to pass, and it is probable that one of these sank her before itself being sunk.

been held under by depth-charge attacks two days earlier after
sinking a small freighter out of a convoy, and had been unable to
regain contact. She sent a weather report on 26 March but failed
to acknowledge an order to join a wolf-pack the same day. On the
28th several submarines in her general vicinity reported hearing a
severe depth-charge attack, and postwar investigation has revealed
that the enemy made a combined air and surface attack on a submarine at that time in the waters where *Trigger* was operating. She
was lost with all hands.

Balao (Commander R. K. R. Worthington), operating in the
Yellow Sea on 17 March, sank a small lugger by gunfire and recovered two prisoners. Two days later, by way of compensation
for so small a prize, she bagged 10,413-ton transport *Hakozaki
Maru*, which, with one exception, was the biggest merchant ship to
be sunk by a United States submarine during this year.

Spot (Commander Post) celebrated St. Patrick's Day in Formosa
Strait near the China coast by sinking a 3000-ton cargo-passenger
vessel. Later she engaged in a fight with a Japanese minelayer escorting another convoy. Little or no damage was done on either
side. During the evening of 31 March, after she had been ordered
into waters off Iwo Jima, *Spot* had a radar contact which proved
to be the U.S.S. *Case* on aircraft lifeguard duty. Both ships claimed
to have sent out recognition signals but the destroyer, which either
failed to receive them or did not understand them, opened fire at a
range under 4000 yards. After the first salvo *Spot* shot off a red
flare and dove. Sonar recognition signals were then successfully ex-
changed and no damage, other than to tempers, resulted.

A far more unfortunate incident occurred in Formosa Strait on
1 April when *Queenfish* sank 11,259-ton passenger ship *Awa Maru*
at night in a dense fog, and only one survivor was recovered. This
ship was returning from Malaya and the Netherlands East Indies
after delivering Red Cross supplies to Allied prisoner of war camps.
For this mission the Allied governments had accorded her safe conduct for both outward and return passages, provided she burned
navigational lights and displayed illuminated white crosses. Mes-

sages about this ship, her schedule and routing had been broadcast to all submarines and received on board *Queenfish*, but those relating to schedule and routing were not shown to her skipper, Commander C. E. Loughlin. He was court-martialed and found guilty of negligence.[6]

The only overseas route which the enemy tried to keep open after 1 April, outside the Sea of Japan, was to South China. Most of the sightings and sinkings that took place after that were in the Yellow Sea and waters west of Kyushu. On 2 April *Sea Devil* sank three freighters from one convoy in the Yellow Sea for a total of 10,027 tons.

For this stage of the war *Tirante* (Lieutenant Commander A. L. Street) had an unusually successful first war patrol. In the waning days of March she bagged a converted subchaser and a freighter off Nagasaki. On 9 April, in the Yellow Sea, she got a 5057-ton transport. Prowling around Quelpart Island (Cheju do) on 14 April she made a night run into an anchorage behind a smaller island and caught three ships at anchor. This bold run inside the ten-fathom curve yielded her a 4000-ton freighter and two DEs, *Nomi* and *CD-31*. When returning to base two days later, she picked up two crewmen of a capsized Japanese plane east of Okinawa and destroyed the plane by rifle fire.

In waters off Honshu, *Parche* sank a minesweeper on 9 April. *Sunfish*, in the same waters, sank destroyer escort *CD-73* and a small freighter on the 16th. Three days later she accounted for two small freighters in convoy. *Sea Owl* (Commander C. L. Bennett) sank submarine *RO-46* near Wake Island on 18 April.

From May until the end of the war in August, Pacific Fleet submarines continued to sink vessels, most of them of 2000 tons or less. Army aircraft and mines that they laid in the Inland Sea and off the Korean coast did more damage to Japanese shipping at this time than did the underwater craft.

One of the most successful and carefully planned submarine op-

[6] Richard G. Voge "Too Much Accuracy," U.S. Naval Institute *Proceedings* LXXXVI (Mar. 1950) 257-263.

erations of the war was Operation BARNEY, the invasion of the Sea of Japan, the only remaining body of water in the Pacific where Japanese shipping still moved freely. This project of Admiral Lockwood's was calculated to complete the ring around Japan and shut her off from the Asian mainland. Enthusiasm did not close his mind to the dangers, and he took every precaution.[7] One guarantee of success was the fact that scientists had perfected a sonar device which enabled submarines to detect mines in the water.

Admiral Lockwood selected for the first penetration of the Sea of Japan a wolf-pack under Commander E. T. Hydeman in *Sea Dog*, known as "Hydeman's Hellcats." Sailing from Guam on 27 May, these nine submarines headed for the Strait of Tsushima. En route *Tinosa* picked up ten survivors from a B–29 which had splashed south of Kyushu, but when the rescued aviators learned of *Tinosa's* mission they expressed a unanimous desire to return to their rubber raft and wait for a different rescue! Their dilemma was solved by transferring them to nearby *Scabbardfish* before *Tinosa* made the dangerous passage through Tsushima Strait. She and her eight sister boats passed through the Strait successfully on 5 and 6 June. To permit all nine boats to reach their assigned patrol stations in the Sea of Japan it was ordered that no attacks be made until the 9th. Several skippers were sorely tempted to break this rule when sighting unescorted ships with running lights burning, but they obeyed orders with good results.

Between 9 and 20 June eight of Commander Hydeman's nine "Hellcats" sank 27 merchantmen, together with submarine *I–122* sunk by *Skate*, for a total of about 57,000 tons. But one of their number was lost. *Bonefish* received permission to run into Toyama Wan, a deep bay near the middle of Honshu, on 18 June. A ship was sunk there on 19 June, presumably by *Bonefish;* but she was never heard from again. She was the last United States submarine lost in the war.

[7] Lockwood *Sink 'em All* chap. xviii. Participating were *Sea Dog, Crevalle* Cdr. E. H. Steinmetz, *Spadefish* Cdr. W. J. Germershausen, *Tunny* Cdr. G. E. Pierce, *Skate* Cdr. R. B. Lynch, *Bonefish* Cdr. L. L. Edge, *Flying Fish* Cdr. R. D. Risser, *Bowfin* Cdr. A. K. Tyree, *Tinosa* Cdr. R. C. Latham.

The plan for this foray called for the submarines to leave the Sea of Japan by the Soya or La Pérouse Strait, between Hokkaido and Sakhalin Islands, on or about 24 June. All but *Bonefish* turned up at the rendezvous on the evening of 23 June and made a surface run through the Strait that night. They continued their passage into the broad Pacific through Kita Uruppu channel in the central Kuriles and returned safely to Pearl Harbor on 4 July.

The success of "Hydeman's Hellcats" prompted Admiral Lockwood to send other submarines into the Sea of Japan, and six of them [8] operated there until V-J Day.

Tirante's second war patrol was fruitless until 11 June when Lieutenant Commander Street spotted a ship moored to a dock on Ha Shima, a small island about seven miles southwest of Nagasaki. To reach this target he had to thread shoals and rocks at periscope depth, and when reaching firing position he observed that the ship mounted a 4.7-inch gun aft and that her gun crew was standing by. A ranging shot with a torpedo, fired to test current correction, hit the target forward and cascaded a stream of coal into the water. Street had planned to retire on the surface; but when he saw the Japanese gun crew elevating their piece and scanning the sky for aircraft, he turned around and fired a second torpedo. This failed to reach the target. The enemy gun crew now spotted his radar antenna and opened fire. *Tirante* then fired a third torpedo which hit amidships and finished off 2220-ton *Hakuju Maru*. The submarine, only 1800 yards from the target, surfaced and ran full speed for the open sea. To clear a shoal spot she had to run the gantlet of a headland from which several automatic weapons sprayed the water about her, but she reached deep water safely. Later in June, in the Yellow Sea, *Tirante* destroyed several cargo-carrying junks by the classic method of boarding, and on 8 July she bagged a small freighter off Kwantung Peninsula.

Veteran *Barb*, whose exploits we have described in earlier vol-

[8] *Jallao* Cdr. J. B. Icenhower, *Stickleback* Cdr. H. K. Nauman, *Torsk* Cdr. B. E. Lewellen, *Pargo* Lt. Cdr. D. B. Bell, *Piper* Lt. Cdr. E. L. Beach, *Pogy* Lt. Cdr. J. M. Bowers.

umes,[9] made her twelfth and final war patrol, still under Commander E. B. Fluckey. Leaving Pearl Harbor 8 June she entered the Sea of Okhotsk on the 20th. For the next month she sailed up and down the coasts of Hokkaido, and Karafuto in the Sakhalin Islands, but found few worthwhile targets. She had a launcher and a load of rockets on board and on several occasions dumped a rocket barrage on coastal towns, as well as bombarding other targets and sinking a number of small craft by gunfire. On 5 July she sank a small freighter off the harbor of Otomari on the south coast of Karafuto and on 18 July disposed of a destroyer escort in the same region. Her most bizarre exploit occurred during the short night of 23–24 July when she landed a party on the east coast of Karafuto to place demolition charges on a railroad, after which she lay-to offshore to watch a train explode. Before closing her patrol on 26 July she bombarded and set on fire a lumber mill and sampan building yard on Kunashiri Island.

By mid-July United States submarines had to be content with small stuff. The last important merchant vessel that they sank was 5800-ton cargo-passenger steamer *Teihoku Maru*, sunk by *Jallao* in the Sea of Japan on 11 August. Finally, in the closing hours of the war on 14 August, *Spikefish* sank 1926-ton submarine *I–373* in the South China Sea, south of Shanghai.

In the meantime *I–58* had more than revenged the heavy losses of the Japanese submarine service by sinking cruiser *Indianapolis* on 29 July.

2. *Lifeguard Service*

During the waning months of the war the aircraft lifeguard service by submarines was an even greater contribution to victory than the destruction of enemy shipping. This system, originally set up during the Gilbert Islands operation in November 1943 in order to rescue downed aviators from carrier strikes, had picked up no fewer than 224 airmen by the end of 1944. By the close of that year, when

[9] XII 399 and XIII 297–298.

U.S.S. *Laffey*, after Hits on 16 April

U.S.S. *Aaron Ward*, after Hits on 3 May

Kamikaze Victims off Okinawa

U.S.S. *Hazelwood*, after Hits on 29 April

Hazelwood Restored, with Helicopter Deck, 1959

A Kamikaze Victim Survives

the air effort had become one of the principal offensive elements against Japan, and B–29s were striking the Japanese home islands, it was necessary to step up the lifeguard service.

Before their first strike, representatives of XX Bomber Command conferred with Admiral Lockwood and staff to make plans, and Comsubpac issued a standard operating procedure for lifeguard work which contained detailed procedures for submarines and the air and surface forces involved. For each B–29 mission against Japan at least three submarines, and usually more, were stationed along the flight route and near the targets to pick up aviators who were forced to ditch. It was soon found that handling lifeguard assignments from Pearl Harbor was too slow and Admiral Lockwood delegated the details to his task group commander stationed at Saipan.

The land-based airmen were slow to appreciate this service; many a pilot preferred to try to work a damaged plane back to base rather than allow himself and crew to be rescued by a strange craft, which he regarded with some suspicion as operating under water, a medium with which he was unfamiliar. *Spearfish* (Lieutenant Commander C. C. Cole) picked up seven men of the crew of a B–29 near the Bonins on 19 December, almost a month after the Superforts began striking Japan.

Admiral Lockwood now re-assumed control of the lifeguards. When Fairwing 1 moved to Kerama Retto early in the Okinawa campaign, he sent an ex-lifeguard submarine skipper as liaison officer to the staff of Rear Admiral J. D. Price, to coördinate lifeguard work; and when land-based planes began to operate from Okinawa the liaison officer moved to that island. With two sets of lifeguard submarines operating from the Marianas and Okinawa, those working with the Ryukyu planes became the "Texas League" and those based in the Marianas the "National League." When P–51 Mustangs began to operate from Iwo Jima a submarine liaison officer was sent there to coördinate communications, fighter cover and relations with Air-Sea Rescue "Dumbos," which also operated from Iwo.

Lifeguard submarines were called upon to perform other services, such as photographing Iwo Jima and Okinawa for the planners of those operations.

In November 1944, when Admiral Halsey was planning a carrier strike on the Japanese home islands, the problem arose of dealing with the string of picket boats stationed offshore to give the enemy early warning of approaching air attacks. Destroyers could easily have disposed of the pickets, but in that event some Japanese craft would surely get off an alarm before being sunk, thus giving warning of the approach of carrier planes. Operation HOTFOOT – submarines sweeping along the proposed line of approach to Honshu waters – was the solution. Seven submarines were assembled at Saipan for this purpose. After several postponements of the proposed carrier strikes, Admiral Nimitz approved Admiral Lockwood's suggestion that these submarines make a trial sweep. They ran into the Japanese picket line in rough weather, succeeded in sinking four of them, but attracted a swarm of enemy aircraft and more picket boats. As an experiment this trial sweep could hardly be considered a success, but valuable lessons were learned to apply later.

Profiting by these lessons, wolf-pack "Mac's Mops" under Commander B. F. McMahon in *Piper*, with *Sterlet*, *Pomfret*, *Trepang* and *Bowfin*, departed Saipan 8 February 1945 to make an anti-picket sweep along the track which Task Force 58 intended to use in its first strikes against Tokyo; thereafter to act as lifeguards. The sweep was conducted without incident. *Pomfret* picked up two Japanese pilots and two United States carrier pilots on 16–17 February. On the 17th *Bowfin* (Commander A. K. Tyree) sank a destroyer escort off Mikura Jima. During the same period a diversionary sweep was made by a smaller pack ("Latta's Lancers") under Commander F. D. Latta in *Lagarto*, with *Sennet* and *Haddock*. This sweep started midway between Iwo Jima and Tokyo Bay and moved westerly toward Kyushu. The principal incident of it was the sinking of two small picket boats on 13 February.

During the eight months that the Pacific war lasted in 1945, 86 different submarines rescued a total of 380 aviators.[10] But submarines were not the only means of air-sea rescue. As the B-29 strikes on Japan intensified, more and more attention was paid to this problem, and towards the end of the war there was no point on their route that could not be reached by a rescue plane in half an hour, or by a destroyer or submarine in three hours. When the last B-29 strike on Japan was made on 14 August, the air-sea rescue team on station consisted of 14 submarines, 21 Navy seaplanes, nine "superdumbos" and five ships.[11]

[10] Roscoe p. 474.
[11] Craven & Cate V 605-606. "Superdumbos" were B-29s modified for search and rescue work.

CHAPTER XIX

Third Fleet in Japanese Waters

June–July 1945

1. *June Typhoon* [1]

W HEN Admiral Halsey relieved Admiral Spruance on 27 May he also assumed responsibility for supporting our forces in and around Okinawa until it was secured. Task Force 38 continued to furnish C.A.P. and strike aircraft, as had been the pattern for the past two weeks. On 2 and 3 June, while "Jocko" Clark's TG 38.1 took care of Okinawa, Radford's TG 38.4 launched fighter sweeps over the Kyushu airfields.

Again it was Third Fleet's fate to have a joust with a typhoon, under circumstances remarkably similar to those which had been so costly on 18 December 1944. Indications of trouble were first known on 1 June when Weather Central at Guam reported a storm forming north of the Palaus, at lat. 12° N, long. 135° E. In the early morning of the 3rd a search plane from Samar reported a storm 360 miles east of Manila, moving north. That was the last definite report of it until the evening of 4 June. In the meantime every interested command was making its own estimate of the storm's track.

During the evening of 3 June, Clark's task group proceeded to a rendezvous with the oilers at around lat. 24° N, long. 129° E, and

---

1 "Record of Proceedings of a Court of Inquiry . . . to inquire into the circumstances . . . of the . . . typhoon or storm on or about 4 June 1945 off Okinawa," 15 June 1945. Action Reports of Com Third Fleet (Admiral Halsey) 21 July; CTF 38 (Vice Adm. McCain) 7 July; CTG 38.1 (Rear Adm. Clark) 14 June; CTG 38.3 (Rear Adms. Sherman and Bogan) 18 June; CTG 38.4 (Rear Adm. Radford) 2 July 1945, and of all ships and lesser commands mentioned.

commenced fueling at 0550 June 4. At 0936 Admiral Halsey directed Rear Admiral Clark to break off and, with the fueling group, to prepare for heavy weather and to steam eastward (course 110°) at best speed to gain sea room and await developments. Admiral Halsey was closely following the estimated position and course of the storm center; but as the weather remained good during the day (4 June), he ordered fueling to be resumed, and it was completed around 2000. Already at 1732 he had ordered Radford's group to belay air operations and join Clark's group and the oilers. Junction was made at 2014. At about 2200 Admiral McCain resumed tactical command of TF 38. His flagship *Shangri-La* was attached to Radford's TG 38.4, which also included Halsey's flagship, battleship *Missouri*.

The force continued on course 110° for a little over two hours, when Halsey suggested that 150° might be better; but McCain preferred the more easterly one.

The first definite location of the storm in more than twenty-four hours came after 2200 June 4. Amphibious command ship *Ancon*, en route Leyte to Okinawa, had a radar bearing of the center, locating it at 1930 at lat. 21° 30' N, long. 130° E. This report reached Admiral Halsey at about 0100 June 5. "The estimated position of the storm area made by Weather Central Guam at 0900 June 4," observed the Court of Inquiry, "when considered with *Ancon's* estimate, would have given a track of about 26° with an advance of about 26 knots." But this "was not considered credible by Commander Third Fleet and his advisers."

At 0130, after a fresh consideration of the probable course and velocity of the typhoon, Halsey ordered the disposition to change course to 300° and to hold that course until the weather moderated. His intention was to cross the storm track to the northwestward, into the safe semicircle.

By 0230 wind and sea began definitely to make up from the southeast. Admiral Beary, commanding the fueling group then steaming about 30 miles south of Radford's, signaled at 0246 to CTF 38, "Believe this course [300°] is running us back into the storm." This prompted Vice Admiral McCain to change course of the disposition to 360° at 0300. Rear Admiral Beary, after steaming about twenty minutes due north, signaled "My CVEs riding very heavily on this course, am coming to previous course [300°]," and did so. His task group proceeded independently at slow speed on courses between 240° and 300°, which took it right into the center of the typhoon — as Admiral Beary predicted it would in a message to CTF 38. Radford's TG 38.4, by maintaining the due north course, escaped the worst of it and by 0600 was in moderate weather.

This typhoon, like the fatal one of 18 December 1944, was so small and tight that groups only a few miles apart experienced totally different weather. Clark's TG 38.1, which was steaming only fifteen miles south of Radford's, experienced increasingly heavy typhoon conditions on the same due north course. At 0240 his flagship *Hornet* obtained definite storm indications on her radar, 63 miles away, bearing 233°, and 60 miles away, bearing 259°. At 0336 destroyer *John Rodgers* of this group reported loss of steering control and one engine stopped. Clark then slowed his group to 12 knots in order to stay with *Rodgers*, but resumed standard speed of 16 knots at 0419.

At 0420 June 5 occurred the following exchange of messages between Rear Admiral Clark and Vice Admiral McCain, CTF 38: —

CLARK TO McCAIN: "I can get clear of the center of the storm quickly by steering 120°. Please advise."

McCAIN TO CLARK: "We have nothing on our scope to indicate storm center."

CLARK TO McCAIN: "We very definitely have. We have had one for one and a half hours."

Fifteen minutes later, McCain asked Clark for this information and was told that the storm center now bore 240°, distant 30 miles. Nevertheless, McCain decided to hold to course north, but (as he signaled at 0440) gave Clark permission to use his own judgment. Radford, about the same time (0443), reported to CTF 38 that his

Ticonderoga found the storm center by radar to bear 220°, distant 23 miles, and he advised course NW.

Referring to our chart of the storm track and of *Hornet*, it is clear that Clark was right; course 120° at 0420 would have got him clear. McCain made a mistake in not releasing him immediately from the task force disposition; and when he did, it was too late. By 0500 Clark's group was very close to the storm center. Barometer fell to 28.98 with gusts of wind up to 90 knots. In order to avoid excessive rolling by his light carriers, Clark tried a succession of courses, first changing to 330° at 0507, eight minutes later to 270°, and at 0519 he informed McCain "We are maneuvering to find best course, should be out soon. The wind is now 80 knots." In a few minutes *Maddox* on the new westerly course reported that she was rolling 60 degrees. At that, Clark slowed to 10 knots and ordered *Maddox* and *Mansfield*, on picket station, to maneuver independently. *Hornet* and *Bennington*, however, lost steerage way at that speed. By 0600 TG 38.1 had come all around the compass to 160°, the first course that the carriers were able to hold for half an hour. The rain was moderate with occasional heavy showers; visibility varied from zero to one mile and the ceiling was under 1000 feet. Barometer was now down to 28.30. Direction of the wind at 0545 was E by N, force 70 knots with gusts up to 100.

At 0640, after *Pittsburgh* had lost her bow, Admiral Clark signaled to his group to stop engines "and lay-to at discretion," an intelligent suggestion. For the net result of all this maneuvering to find a comfortable course was to score a bull's-eye on the typhoon center. Shortly after 0700, TG 38.1 entered the edge of the typhoon's eye, which proved to be about 12 miles in diameter. The seas there were extremely heavy, 50 to 60 feet from crest to trough in long curving swells radiating from the center. Within the eye itself the waves were pyramidal and confused. When the task group emerged on the other side of the eye it found less violent wind and sea; the wind velocity was only 55 to 60 knots and by 1500 it had steadied in the west at 15 knots.

Nearly every ship in TG 38.1 suffered some damage as a result of

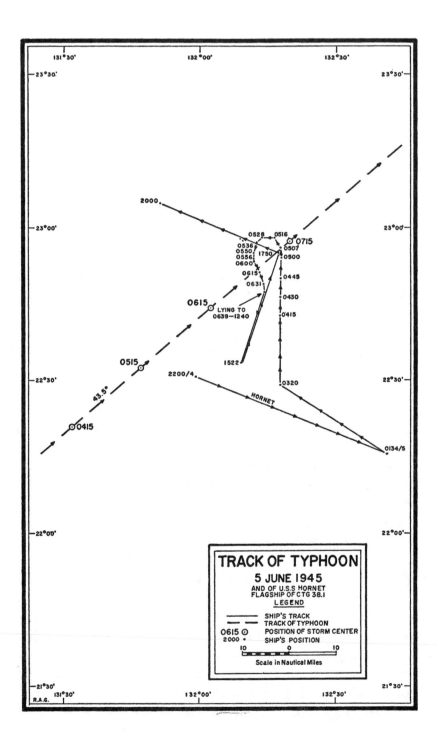

TRACK OF TYPHOON
5 JUNE 1945
AND OF U.S.S HORNET
FLAGSHIP OF CTG 38.1
LEGEND

SHIP'S TRACK
TRACK OF TYPHOON
0615 ⊙   POSITION OF STORM CENTER
2000 •   SHIP'S POSITION

Scale in Nautical Miles

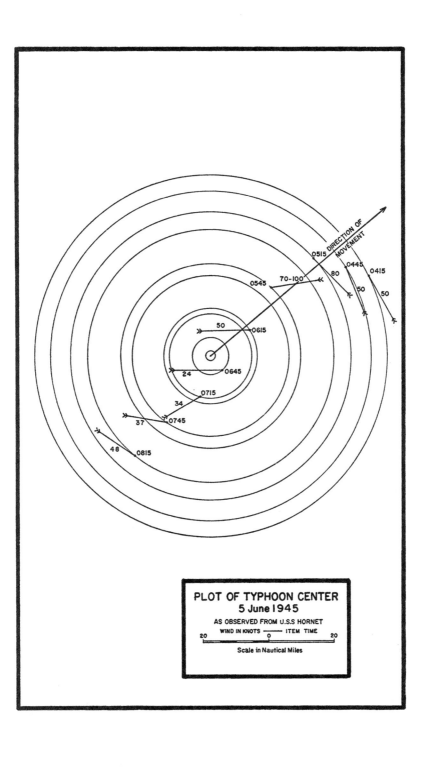

PLOT OF TYPHOON CENTER
5 June 1945

AS OBSERVED FROM U.S.S HORNET
WIND IN KNOTS ——— ITEM TIME

20   0   20

Scale in Nautical Miles

passing through the typhoon's eye. The most serious damage occurred to heavy cruiser *Pittsburgh*. During the afternoon watch of
4 June, she secured for heavy weather. At 0440 June 5 she plotted
the typhoon center at 240°, distant 30 miles, moving 030° at about
25 knots. At 0540 the wind increased to 60 knots, with gusts higher,
and *Pittsburgh* reduced speed to 3 knots. At 0555, when she was
steering 160° with the wind about due S, a plane was blown clean
off the port catapult, landing belly-up on deck. A fire broke out
in the anchor windlass room and was promptly quenched. At 0612
Captain Gingrich ordered Condition One damage control set,
which meant that the ship was completely "buttoned up" with all
watertight bulkheads dogged; and at 0615 he set Condition Z, battle stations, which pulled all men out of the berth compartments in
the forward part of the ship. That proved to be just in time to save
them. At 0630 the ship encountered two tremendous seas. The first
threw her off her course, and as the second sea passed under the
ship, the deck plates buckled and broke, and 104 feet of the
bow section ripped off at frame 26, floated clear and sailed merrily
off before the wind. Fortunately the watertight bulkheads at
frame 33 held where damage control shored them up, as the chief
carpenter's mate had obtained double his allowance of 4 by 4 inch
shoring.

At the moment of parting, the seas were about 15 degrees on the
starboard bow. Captain Gingrich first, to clear the floating bow,
backed full speed directly down wind, then let his ship pay off until
she presented her starboard quarter to both wind and sea, steadying
her on course 10° where she rode well and rolled not more than
20 degrees. *Pittsburgh* did not pass through the eye; and as the wind
veered westward with the passing of the typhoon, her head was
worked around to keep stern to wind.[2] By 1538 the wind had sub-

[2] *Pittsburgh* Deck Log and War Diary June 1945; Capt. Gingrich's testimony
in "Record" pp. 10–11. He told me in Dec. 1945 and confirmed it 14 years later
that the bow would not have broken off but for weak construction. The keel had
been riveted from the stern up to the bow section which was welded on with a
bad weld in which rust and verdigris had developed. Naval Constructor F. B.
Schultz who had examined her in drydock so testified at the Court (p. 111).

sided sufficiently to permit shaping course 130° for Guam. The decapitated cruiser, escorted by destroyer escorts, managed to make 8.5 knots, and arrived Guam 10 June.

In the late afternoon of 5 June, fleet tug *Munsee* and destroyer *Stockham* were ordered to round up the bow section, which had drifted beyond sight of the parent ship. *Munsee* after picking it up sent the following message: "Have sighted the suburb of *Pittsburgh* and taken it in tow." [3] *Munsee* (Lieutenant Commander J. F. Pingley) had a deal of trouble and showed much ingenuity in towing such a misshapen hunk of hardware. After one parting, at 0610 June 6, a tow wire was connected to the bow's starboard anchor by a 60-foot wire pendant wound around the shank and crown. Thirteen hours later the bow capsized, exposing twenty feet of keel. The towline was then connected to the bow chocks. Heavy seas slowed the speed of the tow to 1.3 knots. On the 10th, fleet tug *Pakana* joined, ran her tow wire, too, through the bow chocks, and the two ships towed parallel, increasing speed to 2.8 knots. They reached Guam 11 June, only a day later than *Pittsburgh*, and backed the bow into Agate Bay.

Pittsburgh's sister ship *Baltimore* got badly twisted and had to go into drydock, but she stayed together. Light cruiser *Duluth* (Captain D. R. Osborn) between 0400 and 0600 June took five or six mountainous seas, which buckled her bow upward at frame 21. Flooding occurred between frames 18 and 23 and the shell plating and longitudinal members were distorted and cracked.

All four carriers in TG 38.1 were damaged. In *Hornet* and *Bennington* the forward 25 feet of their flight decks collapsed, and the next 25 feet became too weak to support aircraft, owing to pounding by heavy seas shortly before entering the eye of the storm. Each lost a catapult, and *Bennington* had to jettison six damaged airplanes. *Belleau Wood* lowered elevators to improve her

---

[3] Story of the typhoon in *Phila. Eve. Bulletin* 13 July 1945 p. 2, interview with Capt. Gingrich, who specially commended Lt.(jg) F. I. Calfee, Cdr. J. J. Kircher and Chief Carpenter J. R. Webb for damage control. Their crews worked for 5 hours in partially flooded compartments, among floating debris, to get the bulkheads shored.

stability, but a heavy sea carried away the starboard forward cat-walk and swept a sailor overboard. While maneuvering to recover him the ship lay in the trough of the sea and rolled 35 to 40 degrees. A tractor which broke loose on the hangar deck damaged a number of planes before it could be secured. Captain W. G. Tomlinson, after passing through the western semicircle of the typhoon, maneuvered *Belleau Wood* so that she took the seas 20 to 30 degrees on her port bow, with wind broad on the starboard bow and with bare steerageway. The ship then "rode like a little lady." *San Jacinto* found this typhoon more intense though not so prolonged as that of 18 December 1944, in which she had suffered extensive damage. She measured a gust of wind making 97 knots for a full minute and her barometer hit 28.18 inches at 0622 when she was in the eye. Her hull was damaged, though not seriously, by buckling and flooding.

The destroyers rode out this typhoon very well; *Samuel N. Moore* was the only one to suffer serious damage. A big wave stove in a ten-foot section of her superstructure.

Admiral Radford's TG 38.4, ahead of and to the northward of Clark's group, continued on its northerly course, crossing the typhoon track ahead of the center, with comparatively moderate wind, about 43 knots with gusts up to 57. Between 0500 and 0700 it steered various courses, gradually working around to 290° and running directly away from the center. The lowest barometer record was 29.00. This group had only insignificant damage and by 1050 was able to launch C.A.P.

Admiral Beary's fueling group gave up trying to follow CTF 38 at about 0300 June 5 and maneuvered in the vain hope of evading the typhoon; at about 0330 it began to receive the full force of the wind and two hours later entered into the eye, where it spent a most uncomfortable half hour. Captain G. T. Mundorff, C.O. of *Windham Bay*, reported that at 0355 June 5 the seas were about 75 feet from trough to crest. He estimated the wind to be blowing 127 knots, "the ship was pitching violently, and the bow would alternately plunge deeply with screws clear of the water, racing madly, and then rise to extraordinary heights before plunging again." By 1000 the typhoon had passed and Beary reformed his group with all 48 ships present; only four had suffered serious damage. *Windham Bay's* forward elevator was inoperative, twenty feet of her flight deck demolished, and the catapult track ruptured. *Salamaua* was in about the same condition, and had lost one man killed and four seriously injured. Tanker *Millicoma* reported a badly cracked foremast with all booms on the port side destroyed. Destroyer escort *Conklin* had one boiler, one main engine and all radios and radars inoperative.

Aircraft losses in Task Force 38, including fueling group, amounted to 33 overboard, 36 jettisoned, seven damaged beyond economical repair and 16 requiring major overhaul. One officer and five men were killed or lost overboard, and four men were seriously injured.

On 6 June both task groups replenished from the oilers and again provided C.A.P. and direct support at Okinawa. During the night TG 38.4 made a high speed run to a launching point for attacking airfields in southern Kyushu. For this attack on 8 June, variable time fuzes on 260-lb. bombs were used for the first time for destroying revetted aircraft on the Kanoya airfield. Many observers felt that strafing was more effective.

While the rest of TF 38 refueled, Rear Admiral F. S. Low's Crudiv 16, large cruisers *Guam* and *Alaska* and five destroyers, bombarded Okino Daito for 90 minutes on 9 June with limited results. Next day *Massachusetts*, *Alabama* and *Indiana*, with five destroyers, laid on a bombardment of Minami Daito, experimenting with incendiary shell on these tiny islands. Course was then set for Leyte Gulf. Both groups arrived at Leyte 13 June after almost three months of continuous operation in support of the Okinawa campaign.

A court of inquiry on the typhoon, presided over by Vice Admiral John H. Hoover, met at Guam 15 June and sat for eight days. The opinion was pretty severe on Com Third Fleet and CTF 38. It pointed out that Fleet Admiral Nimitz's advice, in his letter

of 13 February on lessons of the earlier typhoon,[4] had not been followed; that there was a "remarkable similarity between the situations, actions and results" of the two encounters; that the change
of course from 100° to 300° at 0134 June 5 was "extremely ill-
advised" in view of storm information already in hand; that the
weather reporting organization under Cincpac "did not function
efficiently or effectively," that radio communications within Third
Fleet were so bad as to require "corrective action"; that "our new
cruisers are weak structurally"; and that the "primary responsibility" for the damage and loss rested on Admiral Halsey, secondary
responsibility on Vice Admiral McCain and Rear Admirals Clark
and Beary. The court even went so far as to recommend "that serious consideration" be given to assigning Admirals Halsey and
McCain "to other duty."

Secretary of the Navy Forrestal wished to retire Admiral Halsey
but was dissuaded on the ground that he was a popular hero, and
that any such action would boost enemy morale. Fleet Admiral
King, in an endorsement on the record of the earlier court of inquiry, asked Admiral Halsey if he had anything to say in view of
the second typhoon; and Halsey had plenty to say. His letter of 29
September 1945 to Secnav via Cincpac and Cominch includes the
following paragraphs: —

I have repeatedly made detailed recommendations for a typhoon warning service which would enable a task fleet commander at sea to conduct his forces to areas of comparative safety. This weather service did
not exist in December 1944, nor was adequate and timely information
available to me to completely avoid damage from a typhoon 4–5 June
1945; in the latter instance positive information as to the location and
direction of movement of the typhoon was not available to me from
any source until a matter of hours before the typhoon arrived among
the fleet forces. And it must be remembered that task fleets cover great
areas.

Subsequent to the 4–5 June typhoon, the typhoon warning service

---

[4] See Vol. XIII 85–86. Admiral Hoover presided over the earlier Court of Inquiry, and Vice Adm. G. D. Murray was a member of both courts. Capt. I. H.
Nunn was judge advocate of the June court.

was greatly improved and approximated the system recommended by me; planes actually located and tracked their centers and good information enabled me to avoid damage on several occasions.

I wish to point out that the "law of storms" can enable a single ship or very small unit to make a last-minute evasion and so escape the full devastating force of the center, but with fleets and large forces it may be, and has been, impossible to completely extricate all scattered groups. I also wish to emphasize that typhoon movements are erratic and frequently could not be predicted owing to lack of weather information concerning Empire areas. Forces under my command avoided no less than eleven typhoons without damage during extended operations in the typhoon belt.

I have no wish to avoid my proper responsibility in these instances; however, I also wish to state unequivocally that in both the December 1944 and June 1945 typhoons the weather warning service did not provide the accurate and timely information necessary to enable me to take timely evasive action. For that inadequacy I can not accept responsibility.

In conclusion: Admiral Halsey was certainly right about the inadequate weather warnings; Vice Admiral McCain made a mistake in not releasing TG 38.1 when Rear Admiral Clark had the right idea — course 120° — for evading the typhoon's eye; and Clark himself, after being released from following McCain, jockeyed about too long in search of a comfortable course before ordering his ships to lay-to at discretion. Rear Admiral Radford showed the best judgment of any task group commander in this encounter with the elements; and he also had the best luck.

2. *Honshu and Hokkaido Bombed and Bombarded* [5]

Vice Admiral Hill's TF 31, directly supporting troop operations on Okinawa, was steadily reduced during the last ten days of June

[5] Action Reports of Com Third Fleet (Adm. Halsey) 17 Sept. 1945; CTF 38 (Vice Adm. McCain) 31 Aug. 1945; CTG 38.1 (Rear Adm. T. L. Sprague) 27 Aug. 1945; CTG 38.3 (Rear Adm. Bogan) no date; CTG 38.4 (Rear Adm. Radford) 8 Sept. 1945; CTU 34.8.1 (Rear Adm. Shafroth) 18 Aug. 1945; CTG 35.3 (Rear

by assigning ships to other activities, and on 1 July was dissolved. At the same time a new striking force was set up under over-all command of Vice Admiral Oldendorf, who had established his headquarters at Buckner Bay, Okinawa. It was composed of large cruisers *Guam* and *Alaska*, four light cruisers and a number of destroyers. With Rear Admiral F. S. Low in *Guam* as O.T.C. this force dashed into the East China and Yellow Seas between 16 and 23 July to sink shipping. Direct results were few; but the fact that a surface sweep of Japan's home waters could be made with impunity demonstrated how low the enemy's air and naval power had sunk.

In Admiral Nimitz's Operation Plan 4-45, of 15 May 1945, to be placed in effect by signal, Admiral Halsey's Third Fleet was given the mission to "attack Japanese naval and air forces, shipping, shipyards and coastal objectives," as well as to "cover and support Ryukyus forces." Now that organized resistance on Okinawa had ceased, Halsey was free for what he had been chafing to do since the fall of 1944 — to strike at the heart of Japan from within its home waters.

After a two weeks' upkeep at Leyte, Task Force 38 sortied from Leyte Gulf 1 July with "blood in the eye," to operate close to Japan; and there it stayed until Japan surrendered.

At the time of this sortie Task Force 38 consisted of three task groups: TG 38.1, now under Rear Admiral T. L. Sprague; Admiral Bogan's TG 38.3 and Admiral Radford's TG 38.4. Each group had three *Essex*-class carriers and two CVLs, together with a powerful battleship, cruiser and destroyer screen. Course was set for a fueling rendezvous east of Iwo Jima on 8 July and the first strikes against Tokyo were planned for the 10th.

The Tokyo strike took the Japanese by surprise. One of the pilots of *Yorktown's* VF 88, in combat for the first time, described it as follows: —

Adm. J. C. Jones) 27 July 1945; CTF 37 (Vice Adm. Rawlings RN) 1 Oct. 1945; CTF 95 (Vice Adm. Oldendorf) Op Plan 3-45; USSBS *Reports of Naval Bombardment Survey Parties* after the war, which assess the damage at each target.

U.S.S. *Enterprise* Crashed off Kyushu, 14 May

Deck Crew Preparing to Catapult Planes, CVE *Mission Bay*

Aircraft Carriers

The Angry Sea — from U.S.S. *Pittsburgh* during the Typhoon

U.S.S. *Pittsburgh* minus her Bow

June Typhoon

We struck at Katori and Konoike airfields on the coast of Honshu. The great Tokyo plain was so thickly studded with airfields that ten or a dozen were visible from almost any point at 5000 feet altitude. No aërial opposition was encountered although several of our planes were damaged by antiaircraft. Our pilots discovered that the Japs were playing it very cagey with their air force. Planes were cunningly camouflaged and hidden in dispersal areas and covered revetments sometimes as far as two miles from the field itself. Hunting out and destroying such planes was a primary mission of the squadron and a tough one, in the face of the enemy's concentration of antiaircraft fire. However, at Konoike alone in two attacks, our pilots destroyed or damaged 20 planes plus an undeterminable number knocked out by 13½ tons of fragmentation bombs. The pilots disliked these fragmentation bombs because they couldn't determine the amount of damage done; but as inspection after the war disclosed, they were very destructive. The pilots were quite disappointed over the lack of Jap planes in the air, and neither antiaircraft fire nor other occupational hazards seemed to bother even the greenest of them.[6]

Following that strike, TF 38 retired to a fueling rendezvous in preparation for the next series of strikes on northern Honshu and Hokkaido. Elaborate preparations were made to cover targets in these strikes. Photographic reconnaissance of northern Honshu and southern Hokkaido was made by XX Army Air Force. Submarines searched for possible mine fields menacing ships that closed the shore. The first strikes on this relatively untouched part of Japan were scheduled for 13 July but heavy and thick weather prevented them being carried out. Next day the weather slightly improved and the fast carriers launched the grand total of 1391 sorties against targets in northern Honshu and Hokkaido, parts of Japan that so far had escaped hostile action as beyond B–29 range. Although the carriers launched their planes from only 80 miles off shore there was no air opposition; one lone Betty snooper was shot down and another damaged by C.A.P. Only 25 aircraft were claimed destroyed but the pilots had a field day on shipping, espe-

---

[6] Lt.(jg) Henry J. O'Meara, Report on Operations of VF 88 written for this History. Air Group 88 had reported on board *Yorktown* 16 June, relieving Air Group 9.

cially in the harbors of Muroran and Hakodate. Of naval vessels, destroyer *Tachibana*, two DEs and eight naval auxiliaries were sunk; destroyer *Yanagi*, three escort craft and four auxiliaries damaged. Twenty merchant ships, including seven car ferries that operated on the Aomori-Hakodate run, were sunk, and 21 damaged.

An unfortunate loss on this strike was that of Lieutenant Commander Richard G. Crommelin, one of five brothers in the Navy. When leading a flight through a weather front his plane collided with another and was knocked down.

On 15 July the fast carriers repeated their strikes of the previous day. The most important result of this two-day effort was the complete disruption of the Aomori-Hakodate car ferry system. About 30 per cent of the coal trade between Hokkaido and Honshu was carried in railway cars over this ferry route of 65 miles. Eight of the twelve-car ferries were sunk, two beached in shallow water and the other two, then under repair, were damaged. In addition 70 out of 272 auxiliary sailing colliers used for this service were sunk and eleven severely damaged; ten steel freighters were sunk and seven damaged. These losses, irreplaceable at that stage of the war, reduced the coal-carrying capacity by a good 50 per cent.

Simultaneously with the air strikes, and for the first time, a naval gunfire force bombarded a major installation within the home islands of Japan. This target was the iron works at Kamaishi, one of the seven plants of the big Japan Iron Company. The factory and the city of 40,000 people lay in the narrow valley of the Otatari River with steep hills on each side. Rear Admiral Shafroth [7] com-

[7] John F. Shafroth, b. 1887 Denver; Naval Academy '08. Served in *Virginia* and three destroyers before World War I in which he was C.O. of *Terry* and of an SC squadron based on Queenstown. C.O. of three destroyers in succession, duty in BuEng, aide to Rear Adm. W. C. Cole Com Special Service Squadron in *Birmingham*, and to Cincus, Admiral R. E. Coontz. Senior course Naval War College; instructor in Army War College to 1928. Navigator of *Arkansas* to 1930, duty in BuNav, exec. *West Virginia* 1933–1935, C.O. *Indianapolis* 1938–1940. Duty in BuNav, to outbreak of W.W. II, when as Rear Admiral became Comcrudiv 3 and Com Southeast Pacific Force in *Trenton*, Deputy Comsopac June 1943; Inspector General Pacific Fleet 7 Mar. 1944 to 12 Dec. 1944, when assumed duty as Combatdiv 8, and Combatron 2 when Vice Adm. W. A. Lee was detached. Com Seven and Gulf S. F. 1 Dec. 1945; Com Fifteen and Panama S. F. July 1946, General Board 1948; retired 1949; President Naval Historical Foundation 1956.

manded the bombardment unit, which comprised battleships *South Dakota, Indiana* and *Massachusetts,* heavy cruisers *Quincy* and *Chicago,* and nine destroyers. "Big Jack" Shafroth approached undetected, and, opening fire at 1210 from a range of 29,000 yards, made six passes across the harbor mouth. The bombardment, lasting for over two hours, was conducted without a hitch and evoked no enemy reaction. Heavy smoke from fires kindled by the explosions blanked out air spot, but the detailed targets had been so well mapped that this hardly mattered. Most of the shells fired (802 16-inch, 728 8-inch and 825 5-inch) fell within the limits of the ironworks, and fires sprang up in the city. These, however, were not started as a result of direct hits, but from concussion which spread cooking fires in the people's houses to paper partitions and straw matting.

Shortages of raw materials, particularly coking coal, had reduced the output of the Kamaishi plant to less than half its capacity. Damage from this bombardment on 14 July was very extensive and production ground to a halt. After the war it was estimated that this bombardment caused a loss of the equivalent of two and one half months of coke production and one month of pig iron production. On 9 August Rear Admiral Shafroth's bombardment unit, with two more heavy cruisers (*Boston* and *St. Paul*) and ten destroyers, delivered a second two-hour bombardment on Kamaishi. Four runs were made past the town and the battleships and cruisers fired 803 16-inch and 1383 8-inch shells into the iron works and docks. A Royal Navy bombardment unit, consisting of light cruisers H.M.S. *Newfoundland* and H.M.N.Z.S. *Gambia,* with three destroyers, under Rear Admiral E. J. P. Brind RN, added 733 rounds of 6-inch shell to the general destruction. This bombardment was delivered on the same day that the second atomic bomb was dropped.

During the night of 14–15 July Rear Admiral J. Cary Jones's Crudiv 17, consisting of *Pasadena, Springfield, Wilkes-Barre* and *Astoria,* with six destroyers, made an anti-shipping sweep along the east coast of northern Honshu, without a single contact. Next day a task unit under Rear Admiral Oscar C. Badger, comprising battleships *Iowa, Missouri,* and *Wisconsin,* light cruisers *Dayton* and *Atlanta* and eight destroyers, bombarded the Nihon Steel Company and the Wanishi Ironworks, second largest producer of coke and pig iron in Japan, at Muroran, Hokkaido. A one-hour bombardment, expending 860 rounds of 16-inch shell, was delivered at ranges between 32,000 and 28,000 yards. There was no enemy opposition. One hundred and seventy shells struck within the plant areas and the damage caused an estimated loss of two and one half months' coke production and slightly less pig iron production. Considerable damage was also done to the city of Muroran.

While these bombings and bombardments were going on, the expert hunter-killer group built around escort carrier *Anzio*[8] was prowling off the east coast of Honshu in search of Japanese submarines. At 0747 July 16 a search plane from the carrier sighted one on the surface and damaged it with rockets. The boat submerged, trailing oil. Destroyer escorts *Lawrence C. Taylor* and *Robert F. Keller* were sent to get it. At 1000, before they arrived at the spot, another plane, which had been tracking the submarine by its oil slick, made an attack which apparently inflicted further damage. *Taylor,* guided to the target by the second plane, made a hedgehog attack at 1140. Several explosions, including two heavy ones, were heard, and miscellaneous debris floated to the surface. These were the remains of *I-13* (Captain T. Ariizumi) flagship of Subdiv 1.[9]

Upon completion of its 14–15 July strikes, TF 38 retired for fueling. The British carrier force (TF 37) under Vice Admiral Rawlings RN rejoined TF 38 after a period of upkeep at Sydney. The combined fleet planned to strike Tokyo again on 17–18 July, but very heavy weather on the 17th resulted in only the first two strikes reaching their targets.

During the following night Admiral Badger's task unit, augmented by *North Carolina* and *Alabama,* bombarded six major industrial plants (copper, steel, arms, electric appliances) at Hitachi, about eighty miles northeast of Tokyo. This was conducted at long

[8] See Vol. XII 79.
[9] *Anzio* War Diary July 1945; letter from Capt. T. Ohmae 17 July 1959.

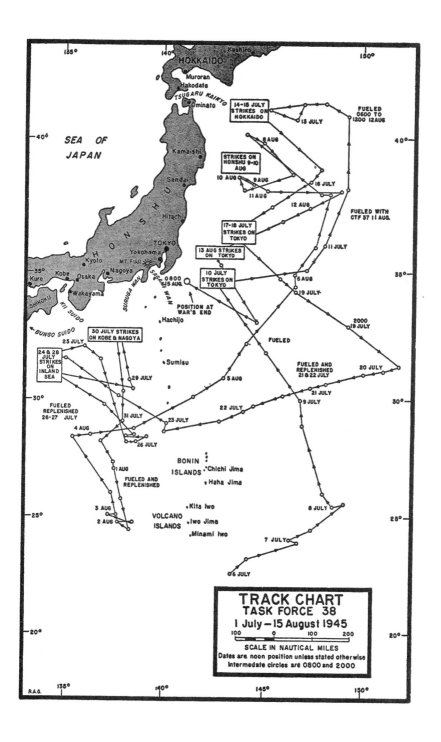

SEA OF
JAPAN

HOKKAIDO

Kushiro
Muroran
Hakodate
Ominato

TSUGARU KAIKYO

Kamaishi

Sendai

Hitachi

TOKYO
Yokohama
Kyoto
MT. FUJI
Kobe Nagoya
Osaka
Kure
Wakayama

SHIKOKU

KII SUIDO

BUNGO SUIDO

SURUGA WAN

SAGAMI WAN

14-15 JULY STRIKES ON HOKKAIDO

STRIKES ON HONSHU 9-10 AUG

17-18 JULY STRIKES ON TOKYO

13 AUG STRIKES ON TOKYO

10 JULY STRIKES ON TOKYO

POSITION AT WAR'S END

0800 15 AUG.

Hachijo

30 JULY STRIKES ON KOBE & NAGOYA

24 & 28 JULY STRIKES ON INLAND SEA

Sumisu

FUELED REPLENISHED 26-27 JULY

FUELED AND REPLENISHED 21 & 22 JULY

FUELED

FUELED 0600 TO 1200 12 AUG

FUELED WITH CTF 37 11 AUG.

8 AUG

13 JULY

16 JULY

10 AUG   9 AUG
11 AUG

12 AUG

11 JULY

6 AUG
19 JULY

2000 19 JULY

20 JULY

21 JULY
9 JULY

22 JULY

5 AUG

25 JULY

29 JULY

31 JULY   23 JULY

4 AUG

26 JULY

1 AUG

FUELED AND REPLENISHED

3 AUG
2 AUG

BONIN ISLANDS
Chichi Jima
Haha Jima

Kita Iwo
VOLCANO ISLANDS   Iwo Jima
Minami Iwo

7 JULY

8 JULY

6 JULY

TRACK CHART
TASK FORCE 38
1 July – 15 August 1945

100   0   100   200

SCALE IN NAUTICAL MILES
Dates are noon position unless stated otherwise
Intermedate circles are 0800 and 2000

R.A.G.

135°   140°   150°

40°

35°

30°

25°

20°

135°   140°   145°   150°

range (35,000 to 23,000 yards) around midnight in a heavy overcast and rain which precluded plane spot or illumination. A total of 1238 16-inch shells were expended on Hitachi, and the two light cruisers shot off 292 rounds of 6-inch at radar and electronic installations a few miles south of the city. Astern of Admiral Badger's unit steamed H.M.S. *King George V* and two British destroyers, to bombard a plant about eight miles north of the city. The damage resulting from this bombardment cannot be isolated from what was inflicted by B–29s in June and again on 19 July; but the cumulative effect was to cut production almost to zero, and to interrupt rail service, electricity and water supply. Individual Japanese, however, considered the naval bombardment more terrifying than either aërial attack.

On 18 July the weather improved slightly and the carriers launched heavy strikes on the shores of Tokyo Bay, concentrating on the naval shipyard at Yokosuka. The principal target was battleship *Nagato*, moored close to the shore, heavily camouflaged and well protected against the only practicable air approach by antiaircraft batteries. These were first neutralized by a well-coördinated bombing attack, after which *Yorktown's* VF 88, armed with bombs, went for the battlewagon.[10] (Fortunately she was not too badly damaged to be used in the postwar atomic tests at Bikini atoll.) Submarine *I–372*, destroyer *Yaezakura*, two escort vessels and a PT boat were sunk and five small vessels damaged at Yokosuka. The task force then retired for replenishment.

Although night anti-shipping sweeps had not been productive, Admiral Halsey believed that they kept a certain pressure on Japan and should be continued. So, on the night of 18–19 July Rear Admiral Cary Jones's Crudiv 17 returned to the fray, sweeping around Cape Nojima, at the end of the peninsula southeast of Tokyo. The cruisers again encountered no ships, but threw 240 rounds of 6-inch shell at the Cape Nojima station. Apparently no hits were obtained.

Admiral Halsey now shifted his field of operations to the southwestern part of Kyushu and the Inland Sea.

[10] Lt.(jg) H. J. O'Meara USNR Report.

CHAPTER XX

Parthian Shots and Final Passes

24 July–15 August 1945

1. The Kaitens Score

BY THE END of July the Japanese surface and air navies were knocked out or impotent; but, just as German U-boats swarmed into the Western Atlantic up to the very end of the war, so Japanese submarines continued active in the Western Pacific.

The final Japanese naval offensive of the war was the last war patrol of Subdiv 15, Captain K. Ageta. It comprised six I-boats, each carrying six *kaiten* one-man midget submarines, better known as the human torpedoes. The initial *kaiten* attack delivered in Ulithi lagoon on 20 November, 1944, resulted in the sinking of a fleet tanker; but three of the four *kaiten* carriers committed in the Iwo Jima campaign, and two out of six sent to waters around Okinawa, were sunk,[1] and not one accomplished anything. *I–47* claimed a highly successful patrol southeast of Okino Daito; but the only trace of her on our side is a brief fight on 27 April in which nobody was damaged. Destroyer transport *Ringness*, escorting a convoy of beaching craft from Saipan to Okinawa, saw what appeared to be a midget submarine explode; this was probably a *kaiten* from *I–47*.

After Okinawa was secured, *I–53* and *I–58* sortied in company, and the former scored a notable success. DE *Underhill* (Lieutenant Commander R. M. Newcomb USNR), with five PC and three SC, was escorting a convoy of several LST and a reefer from Okinawa to Leyte. At 0909 July 24 they picked up a bogey at a range of ten

[1] See Vol. XII 51–52 and this volume end of Chapter I.

miles. This plane made no effort to close but horsed around for about half an hour, either watching for a chance to attack, or, more likely, homing in *I–53*. Nothing happened until 1415, when *Underhill* sighted a mine, which she attempted to sink by gunfire. Shortly after, a submarine sound contact was reported, and *Underhill* called in *PC–804* to investigate. The PC made a sound contact at 1451 and two minutes later *Underhill* attacked with depth charges. Lieutenant Commander Newcomb believed that he had sunk a human torpedo, and had just informed his crew to that effect when *PC–804* sighted a periscope and the shape of a submarine very near the surface. In rapid succession Newcomb reported that he was chasing another human torpedo, that he sighted torpedoes, and that he was about to ram. Whether he actually did ram, or was hit by a *kaiten*, nobody knows; for at 1507 *Underhill* blew up. The explosion tossed flames and debris 1000 feet into the air, and the entire bow of the ship down to the forward fireroom bulkhead blew off, sinking immediately with all hands who were in it, including the Captain, nine other officers and 102 men. The after section remained afloat for four hours, during which more *kaitens* were sighted and fired on by *PC–803* as she was bringing over a surgeon from an LST. After the PCs had rescued 116 of the crew who were in the after section, it was sunk by gunfire.[2]

The loss of *Underhill*, about 250 miles east of Cape Engaño, proved that Japanese submarines were still active in the Philippine Sea. Yet we are unable to find that the battle created any special stir in the commands which should have been concerned, or that a submarine alert was sent out. The general sentiment seems to have been that the hunter-killer groups could handle enemy submarines. Indeed they could, if they were around; but the *Anzio* and *Kasaan Bay* groups were then operating east of the Marianas, *Tulagi* was in dry dock, and none was anywhere near the Philippine Sea. Air

---

[2] Interview with Lt. E. M. Rich USNR 29 Aug. 1945 (Division of Naval History); *PC–803* Action Report; Com LST Grp. 46 Action Report; *LST–647* Action Report. The position of *Underhill's* sinking was lat. 19° 20.5′ N, long. 126° 42′ E.

searches covered that Sea, as well as all waters within several hundred miles of Saipan, daily; that was routine.

Routine is the key word to the sad events that we are about to relate.

2. *The Loss of* Indianapolis [3]

Sad indeed that the war with Japan should have begun with a disaster caused by the observance of peacetime routine after a war warning, and that during the final fortnight there occurred another preventable tragedy, owing to an unimaginative observance of wartime routine.

Heavy cruiser *Indianapolis* was a happy ship, lovingly remembered by her former commanding officers. But she was not what one would call a "safe" vessel, even for a warship. As in the case of many destroyers and cruisers built before the age of radar, she had had so much new equipment added topside as to make her very tender. Admiral Spruance, after going on board before the Iwo Jima campaign, ascertained that her metacentric height was less than one foot, and remarked to his staff that if she ever took a clean torpedo hit she would capsize and sink in short order.[4]

In the Okinawa campaign, as we have seen, *Indianapolis* was crashed by a kamikaze and had to be sent to Mare Island for extensive repairs; but these did not improve her stability. Her C.O. since November 1944 had been Captain Charles Butler McVay III, third generation of that name in the Navy. His father, a veteran of the Spanish American War and World War I, had finished a distinguished naval career as Admiral and C. in C. Asiatic Fleet.[5] Young

---

[3] Navy Department release "Narrative of the Circumstances of the Loss of *Indianapolis*," 23 Feb. 1946; Richard F. Newcomb *Abandon Ship!* (1958), a detailed account including interviews with survivors ten years later; Mochitsura Hashimoto *Sunk* (1954), by the submariner who did it; war diaries of ships engaged in the rescue of survivors and of VPB-152; other records in the Navy Department.

[4] Admiral Spruance letter to writer 25 Dec. 1959.

[5] His grandfather, strictly speaking, was not Navy; but he did so much for the Naval Academy that he was made an honorary member of the Class of 1890.

McVay, who graduated with the Naval Academy Class of 1920, was an amiable, popular and competent officer.

The first mission of the newly repaired *Indianapolis* was a high speed run from San Francisco to Tinian with key elements for the atomic bombs to be dropped on Japan. She delivered this lethal cargo on 26 July 1945 and was then ordered to Guam en route to Leyte, where she was to undergo two weeks' training before reporting to Vice Admiral Oldendorf's Task Force 95 off Okinawa. At Guam, Captain McVay and the navigating officer received from the port director their routing, and a briefing on the general enemy and submarine situation. They were informed of two recent submarine contacts within 100 miles of the ship's projected route, but not, apparently, of the sinking of *Underhill*.

Indianapolis departed Guam at 0900 July 28 on her assigned direct route for Leyte, with an economical speed of advance — 15.7 knots, slightly short of the routine speed, 16 knots. Her ETA (estimated time of arrival) at Leyte Gulf was 1100 July 31. Port Director, Guam, sent this information in a message addressed to Commander Philippines Sea Frontier (Vice Admiral Kauffman), into whose jurisdiction she was headed, to Port Director, Tacloban, and to Rear Admiral Lynde D. McCormick, who commanded a training unit in Leyte Gulf and to whom *Indianapolis* was to report upon arrival. All this was normal, routine procedure; but in one vital respect routine was not followed. The message was received on board Admiral McCormick's flagship *Idaho* in such garbled form that it could not be deciphered; and her communications officer failed to ask for a repeat. Thus the most important addressee, who should have expected the cruiser to arrive on a certain date, was not even looking for her.

Indianapolis made her last and fatal passage unescorted, as she had sailed from San Francisco to Tinian. Captain McVay, when receiving his routing order at Guam, inquired about an escort. Although it does not appear that he specifically asked for one, he would not have got it if he had. The routing officer, a reserve lieutenant, made a routine request to Naval headquarters to ask if one was available, and was informed that no escort was needed. Again, this was routine. In rear areas, such as the Philippine Sea was then assumed to be, warships were supposed to take care of themselves; all escorts available in the Marianas were being used to convoy reinforcement and supply echelons, or to patrol "up the ladder of the Bonins" to pick up B–29 crews who ditched.

Without an escort possessing sound gear, the cruiser was dependent on radar and eyesight to detect a submarine. And she was not zigzagging when she encountered the underwater enemy. It was an overcast night and standing fleet instructions required ships to zigzag only in good visibility. Captain McVay's routing instructions directed him to zigzag "at discretion," which he did by day, but not at night. He did not appear to be disturbed that in his briefing there was a report of a submarine near his estimated position at 0800 next day, and of another 105 miles from his ship's track on 25 July. Nor was the ship "buttoned up" above the second deck. Since these old heavy cruisers had no air conditioning, the Captain, to make sleep possible for his men in tropical waters, allowed all ventilation ducts and most of the bulkheads to remain open. The entire main deck was open, as well as all doors on the second deck, and all hatches to living spaces below.

All went well until Sunday evening 29 July, second day out. The weather had been foul during the afternoon but began to clear about moonrise, 2200. An 11 to 16 knot breeze was blowing from the SW. Sea was choppy to rough; horizon visible to the lookouts.

Directly in the track of *Indianapolis* was *kaiten* submarine *I–58*, Lieutenant Commander Mochitsura Hashimoto. He had served in one of the mother subs to the crude and unsuccessful midgets off Pearl Harbor in December 1941, and had been chosen to fit out and command *I–58* in 1944. So far his patrols had been fruitless and he was feeling frustrated on 16 July when, in company with *I–53*, he departed Kure on another. Eight days later, when the moon began to wane, the skipper was still feeling depressed and, according to his own narrative, "went to pray at the ship's shrine." By the 28th he was feeling better, having launched two *kaitens* against a tanker and hearing them explode — although, in our books, they failed to connect with anything. Hashimoto then had the good judgment to proceed to a point where the direct courses from Guam to Leyte and from Peleliu to Okinawa cross. There he would be almost sure to encounter a worthwhile target.

During daylight on 29 July, *I-58* submerged owing to poor visibility, but at about 2305 rose to periscope depth. The skipper, observing that the moon was up and the overcast thin, decided to surface. Scarcely had the conning tower been opened when he sighted a ship on the eastern horizon at 90 degrees true, distant 10,000 meters (about five and a half miles), silhouetted by a moonbeam shining through a rift in the clouds. By good luck *I-58* had a submariner's dream of a setup. She dived at once, and did not even have to maneuver for attack, as the ship was fast approaching. Neither lookouts nor radar on board *Indianapolis* picked up the submarine during the few minutes it spent on the surface. The cruiser steamed steadily on to her doom.

It was not even necessary for Hashimoto to expend his *kaitens*.[6] Taking about ten minutes to find a firing solution, he came up again to periscope depth. The cruiser was about to cross his bows to the southward, distant only 1500 meters. Only a fool could have missed at this short range. At 2332 July 29 *I-58* fired six torpedoes. Set for a speed of 48 knots, it took them only a minute and a quarter to reach their target. Two hit *Indianapolis* on the starboard side forward — one under No. 1 turret, the other under the wardroom. Two violent explosions followed, ripping away sections of the cruiser's bottom and topsides as if they had been made of cotton cloth. All internal communications were knocked out, all fire mains ruptured; but the engines kept turning over, and, as the officer of the deck could not get word to the engine room to secure, the ship scooped up countless tons of water while they ran full speed for an estimated 45 seconds. Almost immediately she began to list badly to starboard. Captain McVay by messenger ordered a distress

[6] Cdr. Edward L. Beach, the well-known submariner, in his introduction to Hashimoto's *Sunk* pp. 17–18, questions this; argues that *I-58* must have used *kaitens*.

signal to be sent out. A surviving chief radioman reported that he keyed a code message meaning "We have been hit by two torpedoes, need immediate assistance," with the ship's position, and that several SOS's were also keyed. But no one could be sure that the transmitter was working, so sudden and complete had been the

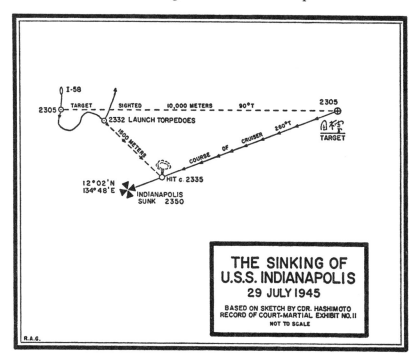

THE SINKING OF
U.S.S. INDIANAPOLIS
29 JULY 1945

BASED ON SKETCH BY CDR. HASHIMOTO
RECORD OF COURT-MARTIAL EXHIBIT NO. 11
NOT TO SCALE

loss of power, and there is no record that any such message was received by any ship or shore station.[7]

The list rapidly increased and Captain McVay ordered Abandon

[7] The Court of Inquiry found that *no* SOS from the cruiser was picked up by *any* station. The following story, however, appeared in the *Los Angeles Times* 30 July and *Saturday Evening Post* 6 Aug. 1955. The SOS was received at radio station Tolosa, Leyte, around 0030 July 30, 1945. A yeoman carried it personally to his senior officer, Commo. H. H. Jacobson, who read it and remarked, "No reply . . . if any further messages are received, notify me immediately," or words to that effect. By the time this story came out Commo. Jacobson was dead and the radio log at Tolosa had been destroyed, so the story could not be checked; but Adm. Kauffman, who had gone over all the records personally on 16–17 Aug. 1945, believes the story to be completely false, as do I. Obviously, if the SOS had reached Tolosa it would have reached several other stations.

Ship. It had to be passed by word of mouth, but the crew seemed to sense what was coming and at the suggestion of junior officers began going over the side. A few minutes before midnight, less than a quarter of an hour after the torpedoes hit, the "great shroud of the sea" enveloped *Indianapolis*. She rolled over on her side and went down bow first into a 1200-fathom deep.[8]

Only about a dozen life rafts and six floater nets were released in time. Most of the survivors had life jackets; the lucky ones, those made of kapok; the unlucky, inflatable rubber life belts which leaked and were of little use. It was later estimated by senior survivors that 350 to 400 out of 1199 men on board were killed in the explosion or went down with the ship, and that approximately 800 to 850 got into the water alive.

At daylight, Captain McVay and other officers began rounding up the men in groups to await rescue. During the night an estimated 50 to 100 sailors who had been badly burned or otherwise injured, or who had no life jackets, died in the water. For the rest a terrible ordeal was just beginning.

The sun rose Monday morning 30 July, and passed the zenith, but no ship or aircraft approached. A high-flying plane passed over at 1300 but kept on without sighting anything. Another was seen on the southern horizon at 1500; a third, with running lights on, at 2200. Captain McVay fired flares but the plane saw them not. At about 0200 Tuesday July 31, according to the Captain's watch, a fourth plane was seen and heard overhead, and at that the men in the rafts fired off about everything they had.

Strangely enough, this pathetic effort was witnessed from the air, inaccurately estimated, promptly reported, and dismissed as unimportant. Captain Richard G. LeFrancis USA was piloting a C–54 between Manila and Guam, when from a point about 430 miles east of Manila, at 0400 July 31, he sighted what he took to be star shell, tracers and heavy gunfire coming from the surface of the sea. It looked to him like a naval action — two ships engaging a third!

---

[8] Position, according to U.S.N., lat. 12°02′ N, long. 134°48′ E; according to Hashimoto, 12°31′ N, 134°16′ E. This was about 300 miles from nearest land.

Upon arrival at Guam, he reported this remarkable spectacle and "was dismissed with the statement that if it was a Naval action the Navy knew about it." [9]

Routine again; naval battles were no concern of the Army Air Force.

During the second daylight period, on Tuesday 31 July, no planes were seen. By this time the survivors were suffering severely from thirst, exposure and the effect of their burns. Many became delirious and gave up the struggle. The reader who wants heart-rending details will find plenty in Mr. Newcomb's *Abandon Ship*. I will give only one incident, the death of Lieutenant J. L. Freese, exactly as it was told by radioman Elwin L. Sturtevant.

He was aboard another raft, but we brought him aboard the raft I was on when they signaled that his hand was burned badly. He was somewhat hysterical from the burns he had received and his hands were burned very badly. His face was also burned and he had lost one of his front teeth. We did not know that he was an officer until he told us where he was sleeping, and that was in room JJ. At one time he asked for a petty officer from the 4th division but there were none on our raft. He then asked for some water, but we had none and we could not find any. In the morning he crawled out of the raft into another raft where they had some water, and he drank a lot all day Monday. Tuesday evening he went to sleep, and when they tried to awaken him, he was dead. Because there were sharks following the raft, we decided to keep him aboard till Wednesday morning. On Wednesday morning, just before dawn we buried him without services because half the men were still asleep and we thought it better to get it over with.

During the third day, Wednesday 1 August, several planes approached and the weakened men tried to attract their attention with flares and signals, again to no avail. They were doomed to two more full days, and, some of them, part of another, in the water.

At about 1000 Thursday August 2, Lieutenant (jg) Wilbur C. Gwinn USNR, flying a routine search out of Peleliu in a land-based

---

[9] Letter of Col. Benjamin B. Cain at HQ IV A.A.F. to O.N.I. Western Sea Frontier 21 Aug. 1945, forwarded to Cincpac 23 Aug. The time given by Capt. LeFrancis was 1900 Z 30 July. This would be 0400 I 31 July, near enough to Capt. McVay's probably not too accurate watch.

Ventura, moved aft to fix his radio antenna, which was not hanging out far enough. He looked down, saw an oil slick on the water, followed it, and lost altitude to 900 feet to investigate. The oil slick appeared to be spotted with men's heads. He sent off an urgent message, "Sighted 30 men in water, position 11°30′ N, 133°30′ E," both to his C.O. at Peleliu and to Commander Marianas. By the time his radioman was through transmitting, some 150 heads had been counted. Gwinn dropped all the life rafts he had; but, being land based, was unable to come down to rescue survivors.

Now at last, 84 hours after the sinking, events moved quickly. A Catalina from Peleliu, commanded by Lieutenant R. Adrian Marks, arrived on the scene at 1550 August 2. After dropping life rafts and life-saving gear to those survivors who appeared to be in greatest need of help, Lieutenant Marks at 1630 landed his plane in a 12-foot swell to pick up swimmers, and sent out messages for more help. An Army PBY (Lieutenant R. C. Alcorn USA) followed suit, but made only one rescue; Marks gathered in no fewer than 56 men.

Destroyer escort *Cecil J. Doyle* (Lieutenant Commander W. G. Claytor USNR), then east of Babelthuap, and two destroyers at Ulithi, were ordered to the spot indicated by Lieutenant Gwinn. Philippine Sea Frontier ordered destroyer transport *Bassett* and destroyer escort *Dufilho*, then at sea east of Leyte, to the rescue. *Doyle*, by bending on top speed (24 knots), was the first ship to arrive, about midnight 2–3 August. She recovered her first survivors at 0030 August 3. Destroyers *Madison* (Commander D. W. Todd) and *Ralph Talbot* (Commander W. S. Brown USNR) arrived from Ulithi at 0430, or shortly after. By that time five ships were on the scene and more were coming. Commander Todd became O.T.C. of the search, which continued for five days. First efforts were made to rescue the living; the last group, which included Captain McVay, was picked up by *Ringness* around noon August 3. Ships and aircraft continued to comb the area until the afternoon of 8 August, when they were satisfied that there were no more survivors. *Doyle* took on board the men rescued by Marks's PBY; she and *French* were the last to depart from the scene, at 2000 August 8.

Deducting the men who died of burns and exposure after being rescued, there were only 316 survivors from *Indianapolis* as against 883 who lost their lives. If the estimate that 800 men abandoned ship is correct, this means that no fewer than 484 died in the water.

How could it be that the survivors of a great ship could drift about for three and a half days before anyone ashore or aloft even guessed that something was wrong? Why did nobody miss the cruiser when overdue at Leyte? Even after Lieutenant Gwinn's report of survivors came in, nobody ashore figured out what ship they belonged to. Lieutenant Commander Claytor's dispatch from *Cecil J. Doyle* in the early hours of 3 August was the first to inform any shore command that *Indianapolis* had gone down.

Admiral Nimitz promptly ordered a court of inquiry to go into the matter. This court, presided over by Vice Admiral Charles A. Lockwood,[10] met at Guam 13 August and completed hearings on the 20th. The results were not made public. The Navy Department's first release of news of the sinking was made on 15 August, adding a sour note to the glad news of Japan's consent to surrender. This delay brought the Navy plenty of criticism and aroused public interest in the case. As a result of the inquiry, the court reprimanded Captain McVay for failing to zigzag or to get out a distress message; but, not deeming this as sufficient, recommended that he be brought to trial by general court-martial for (1) culpable inefficiency in the performance of his duty and (2) negligently endangering the lives of others. Never, at least for a century, had the United States Navy subjected a commanding officer to court-martial for losing his ship to enemy action; but Secretary Forrestal, against the advice and wishes of high-ranking officers, decided to go ahead with the trial, partly to silence the clamor of indignant relatives of the men lost, partly to satisfy the press. In a mild way the case of Captain McVay recalls the famous trial and execution of Admiral John Byng RN in 1757 for failing to defeat the French off Minorca — the subject of Voltaire's famous quip that in England "it

---

[10] Other members were Vice Admiral G. D. Murray, Rear Admiral F. E. M. Whiting, and Captain W. E. Hilbert as judge advocate.

is found good, from time to time, to kill one admiral to encourage the others." [11]

The court-martial of seven officers, presided over by Rear Admiral Wilder D. Baker, sat in early December 1945. Commander Hashimoto was flown to Washington to testify. This provoked angry editorials in the press and was denounced by a concurrent resolution of Congress; but the Japanese testimony tended to exonerate Captain McVay.

Charges against the Captain were (1) hazarding his ship's safety through failure to zigzag, and (2) failing to issue timely orders to abandon ship. He was acquitted of the second charge but found guilty of the first. Probably *Indianapolis* would not have escaped if she had been zigzagging; Hashimoto testified that it would have made no difference to him: [12] *I-58* sighted the cruiser fast approaching an optimum position for torpedo attack. Nevertheless, it was thought that Captain McVay should have zigzagged, considering that there was enough moonlight to make his ship visible to an enemy submarine five and a half miles away. On 23 February 1946 the Navy Department announced that the Captain had been sentenced to lose 100 numbers in grade. Upon recommendation of the court the sentence was remitted and he was restored to duty.

Nobody was court-martialed for the delay in organizing rescue, but letters of reprimand were sent to Commodore Norman C. ("Shorty") Gillette, acting commander Philippine Sea Frontier in the absence of Vice Admiral Kauffman, to his operations officer, and to the acting port director at Leyte and his operations officer. This procedure also was unprecedented because none of these officers had been made "interested parties" to the court of inquiry and so had had no opportunity to defend themselves.

[11] *Candide* ch. xxiii.
[12] His chart, which we have reproduced, indicates that if *Indianapolis* had zigzagged after the sighting, Hashimoto, in view of *I-58's* slow speed (7 knots submerged, 15 on surface) and his inaccurate estimate of the cruiser's speed (12 instead of 15.7 knots), might have had difficulty reaching a good launching position for conventional torpedoes. In that event, however, he would have used his *kaitens*, which had a human pilot and sufficient speed to overtake *Indianapolis* on any probable course. As it was, 4 of the 6 torpedoes missed.

Responsibility for the long delay in locating survivors was due primarily to a faulty system, and to flaws in routine procedures then being followed at shore stations. As Commodore Gillette vigorously pointed out, identical fleet letters of Pacific and Seventh Fleets had ordered port directors *not* to report arrivals of combatant ships. This they reasonably interpreted to mean that movements of combatant ships were of no concern to port directors and sea frontiers. These orders, the court of inquiry found, created an attitude of "complacency" over the cruiser's nonarrival.[13] After these facts had been pointed out by Commodore Gillette, the letters of reprimand were withdrawn. Instructions had already been issued requiring port directors to report all naval vessels sailing independently which failed to arrive within eight hours of their estimated time.

Since *Indianapolis* had been ordered to report to Admiral McCormick, who was at sea off Leyte engaged in training exercises, there was no assurance that the ship would even have entered the Gulf on arrival; and her routine message, as we have seen, was received on board flagship *Idaho* in so garbled a form that it was never decoded. Admiral McCormick was ordered to reprimand his communications personnel for their failure to ask for a repeat. It would seem, however, that some slight blame might be imputed to the Admiral himself; since, even though he failed to receive the routine message, he had earlier been told to expect *Indianapolis* at about that time. He later admitted that he assumed the cruiser had either been delayed at Guam or had been diverted to another command. That word "assumed" is the key to almost as much naval disaster as "routine."

One more case of routine seems, in retrospect, to have been the most reprehensible. Within two hours of having torpedoed *Indi-*

---

[13] The cruiser's course was plotted at Philippine Sea Frontier HQ, and entered as "arrived" at her ETA. Admiral Kauffman adds, in a letter of 11 Jan. 1960, "I do not agree that the P.S.F., at least, was complacent. . . . Every morning and night the ships on the Operation Board were checked, and the Sub-Board to the right of the Big Board, which held the ships and planes in my own command, were constantly checked. The Information Board to the left of the Big Board was given the most careful attention by me, although we had no responsibility to check on ETA's, or to send messages inquiring why an ETA was not met."

anapolis, Lieutenant Commander Hashimoto sent off his radio report to Tokyo declaring that he had sunk a "battleship of *Idaho* class," giving the latitude and longitude. This was intercepted and decoded at Pearl Harbor or at Washington; but, since Japanese claims of sinkings were usually wildly exaggerated, it received very little attention. Cincpac headquarters at Guam had it 16 hours after the sinking, and Seventh Fleet also received a copy.[14] If the combat intelligence evaluators at Guam had observed that the position of the sinking given by *I-58* was on the direct route to Leyte, and very near a point through which *Indianapolis* should have passed, they would have had the area checked by air search; and if that had been done, rescue operations might have started on 30 July instead of 2 August.

While *Indianapolis* survivors were struggling for life in the water, Hashimoto and his merry men were celebrating the sinking with a dinner of beans, corned beef, boiled eel, and sake. On 2 August the skipper heard that the Japanese communications unit at home had picked up the heavy radio traffic attendant on the search for survivors. He was still hunting for more victims when news was received of the two atomic bombs; but that meant nothing to Hashimoto. He launched *kaitens* at American ships on 10 and 12 August without result, and entered the Inland Sea by the Bungo Suido on the 16th, expecting to receive an ovation. Instead, he was handed a dispatch containing the Imperial order to cease fire, which he read to his people with eyes full of tears. One wonders whether he reflected on the futility of a war in which he had witnessed both the opening and the concluding events.

3. Last Swipes at Japan [15]

To return to Task Force 38 operations in Japanese home waters: its three-day refueling and replenishment on 21–22 July was probably the largest logistics operation ever performed on the high

[14] Navy Department Release of 23 Feb. 1946 p. 5.
[15] Same references as in note to Chap XIX sec. 2.

seas. Admiral Beary's TG 30.8 provided 6369 tons of ammunition, 379,157 barrels of fuel oil, 1635 tons of stores and provisions, 99 replacement aircraft and 412 replacements of officers and men.[16]

Replenishment completed 23 July, TF 38 proceeded to launching points for strikes on the Inland Sea. These strikes, delivered on 24 and 28 July, were among the heaviest of the war (1747 sorties on the 24th alone) and the most destructive of shipping. At Kure and Kobe most of the heavy ships still left to the Imperial Navy were moored in coves and difficult of access to bombers, which nevertheless scored heavily on warships that had been slugging it out with the United States Navy since early 1942. The lucky battleships *Haruna*, *Ise* and *Hyuga*, which had escaped from numerous fights, were now so heavily damaged that they filled with water, settled on the bottom and were abandoned. The same fate was met by two battle-scarred heavy cruisers, *Tone* and *Aoba*, and two obsolete cruisers.[17] Cruiser *Kitagami*, five destroyers and many smaller vessels were damaged in varying degrees. Strikes on the new aircraft carrier *Amagi* were assisted by 11 B-24s and followed by a second attack of 30 carrier planes. Her sister carrier *Katsuragi*, and *Ryuho*, were put out of business. Night hecklers, "zippers" and "intruders" attacked during the night; bad weather finally stopped these round-the-clock strikes at 1305 July 25. No aërial opposition met these massive attacks, since the Japanese were conserving aircraft to meet the expected invasion.

During the night of 24-25 July, Admiral Cary Jones's cruisers swept across the Kii Suido and conducted a brief bombardment of a naval seaplane base on Shionomisaki, the southernmost point of Honshu. Damage was not extensive. On 29-30 July, when most of the Tokyo plain was shielded by bad weather, the carrier planes struck Maizuru, a naval base on the Japan Sea, and the north coast of Honshu. One destroyer escort, two smaller naval vessels, and 12 merchantmen were sunk in these attacks and many others damaged.

---

[16] Com Third Fleet War Diary 22 July; CTF 38 Action Report 31 Aug. 1945.
[17] *Campaigns of the Pacific War* pp. 340-349.

During the night of 30–31 July Desron 25 (Captain J. W. Lude-wig in *John Rodgers*) swept Suruga Wan, the bay adjoining Sagami Wan, in search of shipping, and found none. It then sailed to within three miles of the innermost reaches of the bay, to fire 1100 rounds of 5-inch shell at main-line railroad yards and an aluminum plant at Shimizu. This did not accomplish much, because production in Shimizu industrial plants had already fallen almost to zero owing to lack of raw materials; and the railroad yards were not hit.

On the last day of July, an approaching typhoon caused a radical change of plan; Admiral Halsey did not care to risk another en-counter with foul weather. Fast carrier forces retired to the vicinity of lat. 25° N, long. 137° E, to keep clear of the typhoon's path. There all ships were replenished from the logistic support group during the first three days of August. Adverse weather conditions prevented action during the first week of August.

There then came an order from Admiral Nimitz to TF 38 to re-turn to waters off northern Honshu and wipe out a reported con-centration of enemy aircraft. It was well that they did so, because the Japanese Navy had assembled about 200 bombers, planning to crash-land them, with 2000 suicide troops, on the major B–29 bases in the Marianas.[18]

Devastating strikes were launched against northern Honshu on 9 August. Careful pilot briefing and attacks at tree-top level were successful in rooting out camouflaged aircraft dispersed in revet-ments. No fewer than 251 aircraft were claimed destroyed, and 141 damaged, and the planned crash mission to Saipan was completely broken up. No kamikazes approached the carriers, but one almost "did for" destroyer *Borie* (Commander Noah Adair). She was part of a four-ship picket station about 50 miles southwest of Task Force 38. At 1456 a Val came near enough to be taken under fire by the four destroyers. It headed for *Borie's* stern. Before she could maneu-ver to unmask batteries the plane crashed her between mast and 5-inch gun director at bridge level. Large fires broke out imme-diately, and the bridge became untenable, but damage control got

[18] USSBS *Japanese Air Power* (1946) p. 73.

the best of things within two hours and *Borie* survived. She lost 48 killed or missing and had 66 wounded.

On this same day, 9 August, the second atomic bomb was dropped, on Nagasaki.

What effect had these conventional bombings and bombardments during the three concluding weeks of the war? A group of the Strategic Bombing Survey which considered this question immediately after the surrender concluded that these attacks, "in combination with other pressures being applied, had considerable influence in lowering the will to continue the war of the local populations which were subjected to gunfire from heavy ships." [19] This estimate may be correct, but the Japanese popular will had little if anything to do with ending the war.

On 10 August heavy air strikes were again sent against northern Honshu, plastering two previously undetected airfields where planes were being assembled for the big crash on Saipan. That evening word reached the Fleet that Japan had accepted, in principle, the Potsdam Declaration, but was still haggling over terms. Admiral Halsey properly decided to continue pressure until the Japanese government definitely decided to surrender. He planned to strike the Tokyo region after refueling on the 11th.

On that day Admiral Halsey invited Admiral Rawlings to a conference and suggested that the British flagship fuel from the same tanker as his. While H.M.S. *King George V* and U.S.S. *Missouri* were fueling from *Sabine*, the two admirals and their staffs conferred. Later in the day, Admiral Rawlings received word from Admiral Fraser, C. in C. British Pacific Force, that Admiral Nimitz had agreed to incorporate a number of his ships in Task Force 38, for the naval occupation of Japan. Accordingly H.M.S. *King George V, Indefatigable, Gambia* and *Newfoundland*, with ten destroyers, under Admiral Rawlings, became TG 38.5 on 12 August and passed under the command of Vice Admiral McCain, CTF 38. The rest of the British force, excepting Admiral Fraser's flagship *Duke of York*, then headed for Manus.

[19] USSBS *Ships' Bombardment of Japan*, General Summary.

Threat of a typhoon forced a postponement of the Tokyo strikes from 12 to 13 August, when complete deckloads were launched. TF 38 claimed 254 planes destroyed on the ground and 149 damaged, C.A.P. accounting for 18 more in the air. Admiral McCain refueled his ships on 14 August and next day at 0415 began to launch what proved to be the final air strike against Tokyo.

Two hours later these planes were over Tokyo, and a second strike was approaching the coast, when Admiral Halsey received an urgent message from Cincpac ordering air operations suspended, since word had come through of the Emperor's promise to surrender. Admiral McCain promptly canceled all subsequent strikes and recalled planes already in the air. The second strike jettisoned its bombs in the open sea and returned, but the first was not so fortunate. Six Hellcats of *Yorktown's* VF–88 got the word when over Tokurozama airfield. The strike leader had barely got off his "Roger" when the formation was jumped by 15 to 20 Japanese planes. A wild fight — last important air battle of the war — ensued; and although the outnumbered Hellcats shot down nine of the enemy, they lost four of their own.[20]

In mid-forenoon watch of the same day, 15 August, Admiral Halsey received orders from Cincpac ordering the Navy to "cease all offensive operations against Japan." Commander Third Fleet then broke his four-starred admiral's flag and celebrated the end of the fighting by having flagship *Missouri* blow her whistle and sound her siren for a full minute, at 1100.[21] Yet, even while this informal paean of victory was sounding and starry flags were blossoming on

[20] *Yorktown* Action Report 6 Sept. 1945.
[21] Other task force and group commanders declared the war to be over on their own responsibility. Rear Admiral Deyo in *Santa Fe*, then en route Pearl Harbor to Leyte with *Birmingham*, *Antietam* and seven destroyers, picked up President Truman's broadcast from the White House during the evening of 14 Aug. and signaled to his TG 12.3:
"The war has been won. Your Navy has borne the brunt of this War in the Pacific. You may well be proud of your Navy. Tomorrow all exercises and drills will be suspended. It is suggested that ceremonies be held at 1100 in which the Captains will speak to their crews and that a prayer of thanksgiving be offered to God for His great blessings to our country. . . . Full war readiness will be maintained. . . ."

every flag officer's ship, a number of enemy planes, whose pilots had not been ordered to cease fire, approached to attack TF 38. All were shot down or driven off by combat air patrol.

It was ironic that the last major ship to receive damage in action was the old *Pennsylvania*, flagship of the United States Fleet before the war. On 12 August she was anchored in Buckner Bay, Okinawa, having just returned from extensive modernization at the Bremerton Navy Yard; and Vice Admiral Oldendorf, who had recovered from his accident in Ulithi, had just transferred his flag to her from *Tennessee*. At 2045 a single Japanese plane made a surprise attack on *Pennsylvania*. Its torpedo exploded near the starboard outboard propeller, killing 20 men and wounding many, including the Admiral, who again went on the binnacle list for several months.

The fighting ended so abruptly that peace was difficult to accept, and the Allied Navies in Japanese waters took no chance of the surrender being a ruse. Air search, antisubmarine patrol and C.A.P. continued on wartime basis, and every ship maintained a high measure of defensive alert until 2 September, when the formal surrender was signed on board battleship *Missouri*.

CHAPTER XXI

Victory and Peace[1]

1. The Approach to Peace, January–August 1945

IN VOLUME III of this series, *The Rising Sun in the Pacific*, we
traced the process by which the Japanese Army obtained control of the government, dictated foreign policy, and maneuvered
the country into war against the advice of wiser minds, including
high-ranking officers of the Imperial Navy. Once that irrevocable
step was taken, national pride refused to admit any other end to
the war than victory. The Japanese people were never told that
their country was losing the war; even our capture of such key
points as Saipan, Manila and Okinawa was explained as a strategic
retirement. Hence, anyone high in the government or armed forces
who recognized the symptoms of defeat found himself in a cruel
dilemma. Love of country impelled him to seek a way out of the
war, but admission of defeat exposed him to disgrace or assassina-
tion. Even the Emperor, who had always wished to preserve the
peace, found himself caught in the same trap. When General Mac-
Arthur after the war asked Hirohito why he did not earlier take a
stand against it, he made a symbolic gesture of his throat being cut.

[1] MacArthur *Historical Report* II chap. xx, Toshikazu Kase *Journey to the
Missouri* (1950), Mamoru Shigemitsu *Japan and Her Destiny* (1958), and Shigenori
Togo *The Cause of Japan* (1956), are the best accounts in English by important
Japanese. The best work by an American is Robert J. C. Butow *Japan's Decision
to Surrender* (1954). The most important accounts by American participants in
the final decisions are Henry L. Stimson and McGeorge Bundy *On Active Service*
(1948), Fleet Admiral William D. Leahy *I Was There* (1950), Joseph C. Grew *The
Turbulent Era* II (1952), Harry S. Truman *Years of Decisions* I (1955), Karl T.
Compton "If the Atomic Bomb Had Not Been Used" *Atlantic Monthly* Dec. 1946
pp. 54–56. Also Craven & Cate *Army Air Forces in World War II*. Dr. Elting E.
Morison has kindly allowed me to use the ms. of chap. xxxii of his forthcoming
biography of Stimson.

Thus, any Japanese peace move had to be made with the utmost circumspection.

As early as September 1943, certain conservative leaders felt that peace should be sought through negotiation. This move centered in the *jushin* or "important subjects," former Premiers and the Presidents of the Privy Council. These men, like the extinct *genro* or "elder statemen," had no constitutional standing as a group but enjoyed great prestige as individual counselors to the Emperor. When, in July 1944, the loss of Saipan caused General Tojo to resign as Premier and chief of staff, the Emperor replaced him by a diumvirate, with General Kuniaki Koiso as Premier and Admiral Mitsumasa Yonai, one of the *jushin*, as Deputy Premier. Yonai, however, was unable to move Koiso, who made pronouncements fully as bellicose as Tojo's. He would contemplate attempting to split Chiang Kai-shek from his Allies with offers of a separate peace, then to obtain the aid of a powerful country such as Russia to mediate a favorable peace with the Allies. But he insisted that an important military victory was necessary before any such move. And the goddess of victory smiled no longer on Japan.

Early in 1945, following the Allied invasion of Luzon, the Emperor himself began to play an active part in the peace movement. His intervention had to be done cautiously and discreetly so as not to disturb the established tradition and machinery of government. In late January and early February he conferred with seven of the *jushin* individually and found their feeling to be like his, that an early peace was necessary. Prince Konoye, the former Premier, stated bluntly that Japan faced certain defeat and urged his cousin the Emperor to take positive action to end the war.

Fear of the powerful military clique was so pervasive that nothing could be done until the invasion of Okinawa, and Russia's denunciation of the Soviet-Japanese neutrality pact, a few days later, precipitated a new crisis. When General Koiso resigned the premiership on 5 April 1945, the *jushin* provided his relief. These men now had the confidence of the Lord Keeper, Marquis Kido, closest adviser and personal friend of the Emperor, who gave his approval to a political deal. The new Premier, who took office on 7 April, was the octogenarian Baron Kantaro Suzuki, who as a junior naval officer, forty years earlier, had participated in the Battle of Tsushima Straits. Now a retired admiral and President of the Privy Council, it was ironic that, on the very day he took office, battleship *Yamato* was sunk. Shigenori Togo, also an advocate of peace, was appointed Foreign Minister.

The Army chiefs insisted, as their price for allowing Suzuki to form a cabinet, that he prosecute the war to a victorious finish. Consequently the new Premier had to pretend to be doing just that. He knew that he was expected by the Emperor to bring the war to an end; but as he held office at the Army's sufferance, he had to continue making die-hard public pronouncements.

Although it takes but one antagonist to start a war, at least two are required to conclude peace; so it is natural to inquire what if anything the United States and the other Allies were doing about it. The answer is, almost nothing except to press the war more and more vigorously. It is possible that if President Roosevelt had lived six weeks longer he would have taken the advice of Joseph C. Grew, to give public assurance that if Japan surrendered "unconditionally," she could keep her Emperor. The Department of State had envisaged just that, even at the beginning of the war. Following this line, government agencies in propaganda for home consumption had consistently ignored Hirohito, and directed popular rage and hatred against Tojo and his military clique.[2] The Imperial palace had been conspicuously spared in the successive bombings of Tokyo; and owing to the Secretary of War's insistence, the Army Air Force had not bombed the two principal religious and artistic centers in Japan, Nikko and Kyoto.

Mr. Grew, an old schoolmate and personal friend of President Roosevelt, had been American Ambassador to Japan for several years before Pearl Harbor. Knowing Japanese personalities and

[2] This attitude was due in part to knowledge by the insiders that Hirohito had never wanted war; partly to experience of World War I, in which the Kaiser was played up as principal culprit, and his removal led to a weak government which was overthrown by Hitler.

politics as did no other American, he detected through the double talk of the Suzuki government a genuine desire to end the war. He knew that the one essential gesture to help the peace party in Japan was to promise that the Emperor would not be deposed as a condition of peace. From 20 December 1944 Mr. Grew was Under Secretary of State. He found that many top people in the Department did not share his views. A popular demand, "Hirohito must go," was being whipped up by a section of the American press, and by certain columnists and radio commentators. Admiral Leahy observed that some of the civilians who had access to the President wanted Hirohito to be tried as a war criminal, and the nationalist press in China demanded that he be hanged. The Soviet government, of course, aimed to break up the Imperial system so that communism could profit from the ensuing anarchy.

After hearing reports of the destructive bombing raids on Tokyo of 23 and 25 May 1945, Mr. Grew called on the President and begged him to make an explicit statement, in an address that he was planning to deliver on the 31st, that Hirohito could retain his throne if Japan surrendered. Harry Truman, who had been in the presidential office only six weeks, was sympathetic but felt unqualified to make so vital a policy pronouncement without military advice. At his request Mr. Grew consulted General Marshall and Secretaries Forrestal and Stimson. They too were sympathetic but advised against making any such assurance at that time, because the Okinawa campaign had almost bogged down, and the Japanese government would interpret any such statement as evidence of war weariness on our part. So this opportunity to proffer a friendly hand to Japanese advocates of peace was missed. It is very unlikely that it would have been accepted; since, as we shall see, the Japanese military and naval chiefs were against concluding peace even after two atomic bombs had been dropped, and explicit assurances about the Emperor had been given.

On 1 June the President's Interim Committee, composed of high officials and top atomic scientists, recommended that the new bomb be used against Japan as soon as possible, without warning, and against a target that would reveal its "devastating strength." A well-considered alternative, to drop one bomb on a relatively uninhabited part of Japan, after due warning, in order to demonstrate the uselessness of further struggle, was rejected. It was feared that Japan would move in Allied P.O.W.s as "guinea pigs"; and nobody could predict whether or not the bomb would work. If, after a warning, it proved a dud, the United States would be placed in a ridiculous position. And anyone who has followed our account of the senseless destruction and suffering inflicted by the kamikazes around Okinawa will appreciate the fact that compassion for Japan formed no factor in this decision.

Again on 18 June, when Okinawa was almost secured, Mr. Grew urged the President to issue a proclamation on the subject of the Emperor. Again the service chiefs asked for more time and the President decided to refer the whole matter to Potsdam, where his conference with Churchill, Stalin and the Combined Chiefs of Staff was scheduled to open on 16 July.

On that very day the experimental atomic bomb was exploded in New Mexico. Churchill was told about it at Potsdam. "This is the Second Coming, in wrath," said he.

In Japan, in the meantime, responsible statesmen were groping and fiddling and getting exactly nowhere. After the news of Germany's surrender came through on 9 May, the more realistic Army chiefs realized that if Russia entered the war against them, a successful defense of the home islands would be impossible. The Suzuki cabinet agreed that every effort should be made to keep Stalin neutral and to seek his good offices to negotiate a favorable peace. Some half-hearted, unofficial feelers were put out to the Soviet ambassador in Tokyo, but nothing came of them, and on 8 June the Supreme Council for the Direction of the War, (S.C.D.W.), consisting mainly of the Premier, the War, Navy and Foreign Ministers and the Army and Navy chiefs of staff,[3] approved a basic war

[3] These were the "big six" of the S.C.D.W., which had been organized in August 1944. When the S.C.D.W. met with the Emperor it became an Imperial Conference. The Council had other members, but the "big six" handled the important matters.

policy that committed Japan to fight to the bitter end. Then, ten days later, they voted to propose peace through neutral powers, especially the Soviet Union.

Marquis Kido, who got wind of their first decision, prepared a plan, which the Emperor approved, to circumvent the S.C.D.W. He opened a series of personal and private negotiations with responsible government members. These dragged along for several days without result.[4] The Emperor then summoned the S.C.D.W. to the palace (22 June) and supported Foreign Minister Togo in his determination to send a special envoy to Moscow, hoping to work out some means of ending the war through diplomatic negotiation.

By that time the Japanese government knew that Okinawa was lost; that the B-29s were capable of wiping out one Japanese city after another; that, in a word, the war was lost. But nothing was done to prepare the people for the inevitable. On the contrary, Premier Suzuki issued a statement that the loss of Okinawa "improved Japan's strategic position," and dealt America a "severe spiritual blow." "Peace agitators" were threatened in official broadcasts, efforts were made to increase war production, a program of building solid houses with underground shelters was announced to protect the people from air bombing, and of stockpiling food to render them self-sufficient. This talk, as Mr. Kase wrote, "was not only nonsense but extremely harmful" at that juncture.

In the meantime the Japanese ambassador in Moscow was being brushed off by Stalin, and the Soviet ambassador in Tokyo also refused to negotiate. The Emperor, concerned by the delay, summoned Suzuki and proposed that a special envoy be sent to Moscow with a personal message from himself to Stalin. Togo jumped at the idea, and Prince Konoye consented to be the envoy. Permission had to be asked of the Soviet foreign office, and not until 18 July did the Soviet government send an evasive and discouraging reply. For Stalin had already decided to declare war on Japan.

[4] On 13 June Kido called on Yonai, now Navy Minister, and asked if he had given any thought to ending the war. "What can I do?" he said. "Suzuki is very set in his views." He posed the same query to Suzuki, who replied "What can I do? Yonai is very stubborn!" Shigemitsu *Japan and Her Destiny* p. 356.

Then out of a clear sky, on a summer day of sweltering heat, came the Potsdam Declaration of 26 July by President Truman, Prime Minister Churchill and Chiang Kai-shek, stating the conditions under which Japan would be called upon to surrender "unconditionally." The principal terms of the Potsdam Declaration were: — [5]

1. The authority and influence of the Japanese militarists "must be eliminated for all time."

2. Until a "new order of peace, security and justice" is established in Japan, Allied forces will occupy Japanese key points "to secure the achievement" of this basic objective.

3. Terms of the Cairo Declaration [6] will be carried out and Japanese sovereignty will be limited to Hokkaido, Honshu, Kyushu, Shikoku and adjacent smaller islands.

4. Japanese military forces, "after being completely disarmed, shall be permitted to return to their homes with the opportunity to lead peaceful and productive lives."

5. "We do not intend that the Japanese shall be enslaved as a race or destroyed as a nation, but stern justice shall be meted out to all war criminals. . . . Freedom of speech, of religion, and of thought, as well as respect for the fundamental human rights, shall be established."

6. Japan may retain such industries as will sustain her economy, but not re-arm; and she may look forward to "participation in world trade relations."

7. Occupation forces "shall be withdrawn from Japan as soon as these objectives have been accomplished and there has been established a peacefully inclined and responsible government."

8. The Japanese government is called upon "to proclaim now the unconditional surrender of all Japanese armed forces." The alternative is "prompt and utter destruction."

---

[5] Text in Truman *Years of Decision* I 390–392.

[6] The Cairo Declaration of the SEXTANT Conference stated that Japan would be deprived of all conquests gained by aggression since the opening of Japan by Commodore Perry in 1853. Manchuria, Formosa and the Pescadores would accordingly be restored to China, Korea would recover her independence, and the southern half of Sakhalin be returned to Russia.

A broadcast of this declaration, received in Tokyo 27 July, caused a flurry of discussion in high governmental circles as to how it should be handled. Foreign Minister Togo wished to play a waiting game and avoid any official statement, because (a typically Japanese condition) if any official declaration were made it would have to be a flat rejection, to please the military men in the cabinet. Unfortunately Premier Suzuki "upset the applecart" when, at a press conference on 28 July, he indicated that the cabinet considered the Potsdam Declaration to be a mere rehash of the earlier and unacceptable Cairo Declaration, and as such unworthy of official notice.[7] And, he added, the increase of aircraft production gave renewed hope of a Japanese victory.

No explicit assurance about the Emperor had issued from Potsdam; but (so Shigemitsu assured me in 1950) [8] the reference in paragraph 7 to withdrawing occupation forces after a "peacefully inclined and responsible government" had been set up indicated to the Japanese that they would be permitted to determine their own future government.

If the Suzuki government could have made up its mind promptly to accept the Potsdam Declaration as a basis for peace, there would have been no explosion of an atomic bomb over Japan. Suzuki's bumbling statement to the press triggered it off.

Secretary of State Byrnes found the Premier's statement "disheartening." Both he and President Truman hoped that before the Potsdam Conference broke up, the Japanese government would change its mind.[9] The President had already decided to use the bomb if Japan did not accept the Declaration, and on 25 July had issued the necessary order to XX Army Air Force to "deliver its first special bomb as soon as weather will permit visual bombing

[7] See Butow pp. 145–148 for discussion of just how Suzuki's words should be translated. The sensational story by W. J. Coughlin, "The Great *Mokusatsu* Mistake" in *Harper's* March 1953, to the effect that Suzuki's real intentions were completely reversed by the translation, does not meet the test of facts. Suzuki succeeded in doing just what Togo was trying to avoid – closing the door.

[8] Mamoru Shigemitsu, a strong advocate of peace, had been Foreign Minister in the Koiso cabinet, and was in close touch with what was going on.

[9] Byrnes *Speaking Frankly* p. 263.

after about 3 August." But this could have been revoked, just as the Japanese strike on Pearl Harbor could have been recalled before 6 December 1941. Not until after the Conference had broken up with no further word from Tokyo, and when President Truman was at sea on board U.S.S. *Augusta*, did he give the final order to drop the bombs on two Japanese cities.[10]

That was on 2 August, west longitude date. All parts and materials for assembling the bombs had arrived at Tinian — some of them in the doomed *Indianapolis* — before the first of the month. Weather on 3 and 4 August (east longitude dates) was unfavorable; but on the 4th, with a good forecast for the next two days, General LeMay decided to load the first bomb on 5 August and drop it on the 6th.

The B–29 nicknamed "Enola Gay," commanded by Colonel Paul W. Tibbets USA, was chosen to carry the first atomic bomb. Captain William S. Parsons, a Navy ordnance specialist who had had charge of the ordnance aspects of the bomb and of its safety features, came along to assemble it and make the final adjustments en route.

At 0245 August 6 "Enola Gay" took off from North Field, Tinian, followed by two observation planes. Over Iwo Jima she began a slow climb to 30,000 feet. At 0730 Captain Parsons and his assistant made the final adjustments to the bomb. Weather reconnaissance planes reported all clear over Hiroshima. The B–29 was over the city at 0911 when controls were passed to the bombardier, Major Thomas W. Ferebee, USA, who at 0915 "toggled the bomb out" at an altitude of 31,600 feet and speed of 328 m.p.h. No enemy planes attacked "Enola Gay." She landed on Tinian at 1458.

Results were catastrophic. The bomb exploded right over the parade ground where the Japanese Second Army was doing calisthenics. The soldiers were wiped out almost to a man. Everything in the city within an area of over four square miles was razed or fuzed. An estimated 71,379 people, including the military, were

---

[10] Craven & Cate V 714–715; Leahy *I Was There* p. 431. The Presidential plane "Sacred Cow" landed at Plymouth, where Mr. Truman transferred to *Augusta* on 2 August. See note by Herbert Feis in *Amer. Hist. Rev.*, LXVIII, 309–10 (Oct. 1963).

killed; 19,691 were seriously injured, and about 171,000 rendered homeless.[11]

President Truman got the word at noon 6 August (west longitude date) on board cruiser *Augusta* while crossing the Atlantic. He told the officers and men about it, saying "This is the greatest thing in history."

Before sunrise 9 August the Russian declaration of war on Japan was known in Tokyo. At 1000 Marquis Kido conveyed to Premier Suzuki the Emperor's belief that it was urgent to accept the Potsdam Declaration immediately. The S.C.D.W., promptly summoned to the Imperial Palace, was already in session when the second atomic bomb exploded over Nagasaki, at 1101. All agreed to insist that the prerogatives of the Imperial family be preserved, but beyond that there was no agreement. War minister General Anami, Army chief of staff General Umezu, and Admiral Toyoda, the Navy chief of staff, insisted on three conditions: (1) the Japanese would disarm their own troops overseas, (2) war criminals would be prosecuted by Japanese courts, and (3) only a limited military occupation of Japan would be permitted. Togo pointed out that the Allies were certain to refuse such conditions, that all hope of Japanese victory had vanished, and that Japan must no longer delay seeking peace. But as Anami, Umezu and Toyoda held out, nothing could be decided.

Nor could agreement be reached at a cabinet meeting which opened at 1430, even after sitting for over seven hours and hearing more bad news from Hiroshima and Nagasaki. When that meeting broke up at 2230 August 9, Suzuki and Togo called on the Emperor, and told him that, as neither cabinet nor S.C.D.W. could reach a decision, he must summon the Council to meet with him. Hirohito agreed. The S.C.D.W. met as Imperial Conference with the Emperor in an underground air-raid shelter at the Palace, at 2350 August 9.

[11] Craven & Cate V 717, 722–725. This seems, however, to have been an overestimate. A Japanese official notice of 31 July 1959 stated that the total number of deaths attributed to the bombing of Hiroshima, including all that had occurred in the nearly 14 years since it happened, was 60,175.

This was what Togo, Shigemitsu and Kido had been working toward for months. At the Imperial Conference Suzuki took the floor and presented his arguments for immediate acceptance of the Potsdam Declaration. Togo and Navy Minister Yonai supported him. Generals Anami and Umezu and Admiral Toyoda argued for a resolute prosecution of the war, unless the Allies accepted the three above-mentioned conditions. There was a long discussion of possibilities, ably led by Baron Hiranuma. Suzuki requested an "Imperial Decision" to break the deadlock, an unprecedented step.[12] The Emperor rose, said that ending the war was the only way to relieve Japan from unbearable distress, and left the room. Suzuki then declared, "His Majesty's decision should be made the decision of this conference as well," and the S.C.D.W. adjourned at 0230 August 10.

Since an Imperial Conference had no formal power to decide anything, a cabinet meeting was called at about 0300 August 10. There, the "Imperial Decision" was unanimously approved.

At 0700 August 10, a message was sent to the governments of the United States, Great Britain, the Soviet Union and China, stating that Japan was ready to accept the terms of the Potsdam Declaration with the understanding that the prerogatives of the Emperor as a sovereign ruler were not prejudiced.

During that day the cabinet debated whether to announce this to the public. It was decided to make no announcement until after the publication of an Imperial rescript accepting the Potsdam terms, because of the fear of a militarist *coup d'état*. That possibility was real indeed. On the morning of 10 August, War Minister Anami summoned all officers in Tokyo of the rank of lieutenant colonel and above, told them what had happened and appealed to them to keep the Army quiet. Increasing restiveness at the war ministry during the day caused him to issue a warning against any overt effort to obstruct the government's decision. And Admiral Yonai issued a comparable warning to the Japanese Navy.

---

[12] In Japanese constitutional practice the Emperor was supposed only to ratify decisions already reached by cabinet or S.C.D.W.

But the wireless waves and cables between Tokyo and Washington were working, via Switzerland. The message of 0700 August 10 accepting the Potsdam Declaration was received at about the same hour next day — 10 August, west longitude date. At Washington this created a flurry only less agitated than the one at Tokyo. Was it or was it not an acceptance of the Potsdam terms? At a conference in the White House between President Truman, Secretaries Byrnes, Stimson and Forrestal, Admiral Leahy and a few others, the question was threshed out. "Terrible political repercussions" were anticipated if a promise to keep the Emperor on his throne should backfire by encouraging the Japanese government to continue the war. The President decided, nevertheless, to take the risk, and Secretary Byrnes drafted a note in reply to the Japanese offer, which, after obtaining telegraphed approval from London, Moscow and Chungking, was sent to Tokyo via Switzerland on 11 August (west longitude date) and immediately broadcast. The foreign office at Tokyo intercepted it at about noon the same day, which was 12 August in Japan.

The Byrnes note of 11 August comprised five pertinent provisions: —

1. "From the moment of surrender the authority of the Emperor and Japanese government . . . shall be subject to the Supreme Commander of the Allied Powers who will take such steps as he deems proper to effectuate the surrender terms."
2. The Emperor will authorize his government and Imperial General Headquarters to sign the surrender and shall command all his armed forces to lay down their arms.
3. Immediately upon the surrender the Japanese government shall transport prisoners of war and interned civilians to places of safety where they can be embarked in Allied transports.
4. The ultimate form of the government of Japan shall be established by the free will of the Japanese people.
5. Allied occupation forces will remain in Japan "until the purposes set forth in the Potsdam Declaration are achieved."

The Byrnes note created new tensions and a fresh crisis in high circles at Tokyo. It left no doubt in anyone's mind that the Japanese would be permitted to retain the Emperor, and most of the cabinet were for accepting; but Anami, Umezu and Toyoda were adamant, holding out for self-disarmament and a limited occupation or none. A fanatical *coup d'état*, with the purpose of continuing the war, was narrowly averted. Soon after receipt of the Allied reply, a group of young Army officers in the War Ministry approached Anami with a direct suggestion that the Army intervene to stop all peace moves. He succeeded in putting them off, but this powder-keg atmosphere persisted while the cabinet for two days longer remained deadlocked. Togo received support on 13 August in the form of a cablegram from the Japanese minister in Stockholm, reporting that the United States had resisted strong pressure from the Soviet Union and China to remove the Emperor.

On the 11th, when the Byrnes note was dispatched, President Truman ordered all "strategic" air operations (B–29 flights by XX A.A.F.) to be suspended; but on the 14th, apparently with a view to helping the Japanese make up their minds, the bombers were ordered to resume. That order in turn was canceled after over 1000 B–29s were in the air, but most of them were recalled before doing any further damage.[13]

During the night of 13–14 August, seven B–29s dropped on Tokyo over five million leaflets, containing the text of the Japanese note accepting the Potsdam Declaration and a Japanese translation of Secretary Byrne's reply.[14] This was the first intimation the people had of what was going on. At 0830 August 14, Marquis Kido brought one of these leaflets to the Emperor and urgently advised him to take prompt action, predicting that the leaflets would have a profound effect. Unless the Emperor declared immediately for peace he might lose control of armed forces in the field. Shortly after, Premier Suzuki arrived at the palace. He and Marquis Kido, who had vainly endeavored to convert General Anami to reason, urged the Emperor to convoke an Imperial Conference (the

[13] Craven & Cate V 699, 733.
[14] Cincpac "Report of Surrender and Occupation of Japan" 11 Feb. 1946.

S.C.D.W. in the "presence") on his own initiative.[15] The Emperor, before taking so drastic a step, requested several senior Army and Navy officers to take measures to secure the obedience of all armed forces to his orders to cease fire. He then summoned the S.C.D.W. to the palace.

The meeting opened at 1100 August 14 in the air-raid shelter. Suzuki reported that most of those present favored an immediate acceptance of the Byrnes note but suggested that the Emperor hear the objectors before making his decision. In a highly emotional atmosphere, Anami, Umezu and Toyoda repeated their earlier arguments for continuing to fight. The Emperor then spoke the thoughts that he had long firmly held. Continuing the war, he said, will merely result in additional destruction. The whole nation will be reduced to ashes. The Allied reply is a virtually complete acknowledgment of the position of his note of 0700 August 10, and evidence "of the peaceful and friendly intentions of the enemy." It is the Imperial desire that his ministers of state accept it. They will at once prepare an Imperial rescript broadcasting this decision directly to the people.

The deed was done. At 1449 August 14 Radio Tokyo flashed the Emperor's decision around the world. The cabinet was already making a final draft of the rescript, which had been in preparation since 10 August. At 2100 it was completed and taken to the Emperor, who signed it at 2250 August 14. Ten minutes later it was officially proclaimed that Japan would accept the Allied terms; and a note to that effect was sent to the Allied governments through a neutral country. This important news reached President Truman at 1550 August 14, west longitude date. He announced it from the White House at 1900 the same day, and declared a two-day holiday of jubilation.[16]

[15] This was unprecedented. By Japanese constitutional procedure, an Imperial Conference could be convoked only after the Premier and chiefs of staff had agreed on the agenda.

[16] Leahy p. 508; *Washington Evening Star* Extra 14 Aug. 1945.

Despite every care to prevent "incidents," the situation in Tokyo almost got out of hand. Hotheads in the War Ministry and on the General Staff were still planning a military *coup*. During the night of 14–15 August (east longitude date) they called on Lieutenant General Takeshi Mori, commanding the Imperial Guards Division, to demand that he order his men to disobey the surrender order. Mori refused and was then assassinated. With the connivance of two officers of his staff, orders were prepared, over his forged seal, to isolate the palace and the Emperor, and impound the disc-recording of the surrender message that was to be broadcast at noon next day. When General Tanaka of the Eastern District Area Army heard of this plot, he proceeded to the palace, took personal command of the Imperial Guards, countermanded the forged orders and by 0800 August 15 had suppressed the nascent insurrection.

In the course of the day attempts were made to assassinate Premier Suzuki, Marquis Kido and Baron Hiranuma. General Anami, who knew what was going on but either dared not or cared not do anything about it, felt that the only honorable way out was to commit hara-kiri, and did so. His example was followed by four of the principal conspirators and by General Tanaka, whose prompt action had defeated their plans, and (most appropriately) by Vice Admiral Takijiro Onishi, father of the Kamikaze Corps.

Throughout the morning of 15 August Japanese radios announced that a most important broadcast would be made at noon. When listeners were told that the next voice would be that of the Emperor, which they had never before been permitted to hear, they anticipated something tremendous, and generally assumed that it would be a plea for resistance to the bitter end. On the contrary — Hirohito reviewed the course of the war, announced that he had accepted the terms of the Allies, appealed to the people to rebuild the country, and ended: "We charge you, Our loyal subjects, to carry out faithfully Our will." The word "surrender" was carefully omitted from the text, but almost every listener realized that his ruler was announcing the end of the war on Allied terms. The people were stupefied by this revelation, and still appeared stunned when the first occupation troops arrived two weeks later.

The Japanese note of 2300 August 14 (east longitude date) was promptly acknowledged by Secretary Byrnes, together with an order that the Japanese cease hostilities at once, as our forces had already been ordered to do. This was received in Tokyo early 16 August (east longitude date) and the Emperor's definite order to cease fire went out at 1600 that day. As we have seen in the previous chapter, the United States Navy had stopped all offensive operations 35 hours earlier, at 0615 August 15. The Emperor's order to his armed forces to surrender was not issued until after the signing of the surrender document on board *Missouri*, 2 September.

It was the Emperor who cut governmental red tape and made the great decision. This required courage. The Army chiefs and Admiral Toyoda were not greatly moved by the atomic explosions. They argued that the two bombs were probably all that the United States had; and if more were made we would not dare use them when invading Japan; that there was a fair chance of defeating the invasion by massed kamikaze attacks, and that in any event national honor demanded a last battle on Japanese soil. All the fighting hitherto had been little more than peripheral skirmishes; the way to victory was to "lure" the Americans ashore and "annihilate" them, as had been done by the original kamikaze "divine wind" to the hordes of Kublai Khan in A.D. 1281. Such had been the propaganda line given to the Japanese people to explain the series of defeats; they had no idea that Japan was really beaten.[17] Nothing less than an assertion of the Imperial will could have overcome these arguments and objections.

[17] Shigemitsu *Japan and Her Destiny* 334. An intelligent and patriotic French banker, M. Jacques Bardac, who was interned at Peiping through the entire war and cut off from all news and propaganda except Japanese, told me that it was so well done as to convince him up to the very last that Japan was winning. The older Japanese on Oahu, who could not understand English, believed even after the end of the war that Japan had won, and scores of them assembled one day on Aiea Heights to see the victorious Imperial Fleet enter Pearl Harbor. War Research Lab. Univ. of Hawaii Report No. 8 of 1 Mar. 1946; Y. Kimura "Rumor among the Japanese" *Social Process in Hawaii* XI (1947) 84–92.

On the Allied side it has been argued that the maritime blockade, virtually complete by mid-August, would have strangled Japanese economy and that the B–29s and naval gunfire ships would have destroyed her principal cities and forced a surrender before long, without the aid of the atomic bombs, or of invasion. Fleet Admirals King and Leahy lent their distinguished advocacy to this view. Whether or not they were correct, not even time can tell. But of some facts one can be certain. The stepped-up B–29 bombings and naval bombardments, had they been continued after 15 August, would have cost the Japanese loss and suffering far, far greater than those inflicted by the two atomic bombs. And the probable effects of the projected invasions of Kyushu and Honshu in the fall and winter of 1945–1946, and of a desperate place-to-place defense of Japan, stagger the imagination. It is simply not true that Japan had no military capability left in mid-August. Although 2550 kamikaze planes had been expended, there were 5350 of them still left, together with as many more ready for orthodox use, and some 7000 under repair or in storage; and 5000 young men were training for the Kamikaze Corps. The plan was to disperse all aircraft on small grass strips in Kyushu, Shikoku and western Honshu, and in underground hangars and caves, and conserve them for kamikaze crashes on the Allied amphibious forces invading the home islands.[18] Considering the number of planes, pilots and of potential targets, all within a short distance of principal airfields, it requires little imagination to depict the horrible losses that would have been inflicted on the invading forces, even before they got ashore. After accepting these losses there would have been protracted battles on Japanese soil, which would have cost each side very many more lives, and created a bitterness which even time could hardly have healed. Japan had plenty of ammunition left; the U. S. Army after the war found thousands of tons holed up in Hokkaido alone.[19] And, as Russia would have been a full partner in this final campaign, there is a fair chance that Japan would have been divided like Germany

[18] USSBS *Japanese Air Power* (1946) pp. 70–73.
[19] CTF 56 (Rear Adm. Deyo) Action Report 23 Nov. 1945 p. 3.

and Korea, if not delivered completely to the mercy of the Communists.

We must also point out that even after two atomic bombs had been dropped, the Potsdam Declaration clarified, the guards' insurrection defeated and the Emperor's will made known, it was touch and go whether the Japanese actually would surrender. Hirohito had to send members of the Imperial family to the principal Army commands to ensure compliance. His younger brother Prince Takamatsu was just in time to make the Atsugi airfield available for the first occupation forces on 26 August, and to keep the kamikaze boys grounded. They were boasting that they would crash the *Missouri* when she entered Tokyo Bay.[20] If these elements had had their way, the war would have been resumed with the Allies feeling that the Japanese were hopelessly treacherous, and with a savagery on both sides that is painful to contemplate.

When these facts and events of the Japanese surrender are known and weighed, it will become evident that the atomic bomb was the keystone of a very fragile arch.

2. *Allied Plans for the Occupation* [21]

The surrender of Japan before her home islands were invaded had been foreseen months before the event.

Admiral Nimitz by 25 July had a plan ready for the initial occupation of Tokyo Bay and other strategic points by Third Fleet and the Marine Corps, pending the arrival of normal occupation forces under General MacArthur's command. General MacArthur's staff produced another plan which envisaged initial landings in Japan by all three arms, and in great force. After the Pentagon had pointed

[20] Kase p. 264.
[21] Cincpac-Cincpoa "Report of Surrender and Occupation of Japan" 11 Feb. 1946; Com Third Fleet (Admiral Halsey) "Report on Operations of Third Fleet 16 Aug.–19 Sept." 6 Oct. 1945; Com Fifth Fleet (Admiral Spruance) Action Report 15 Aug.–8 Nov. 1945; CTF 31 (Rear Adm. Badger) Action Report 19 Aug.–8 Sept. 1945; CTG 30.6 (Commo. Simpson) Action Report 29 Aug.–19 Sept. 1945. J.C.S. ms. History "Evolution of Global Strategy" chaps. 96, 97.

out that at least two weeks would elapse after the surrender before a landing in force could be made, the J.C.S., at Potsdam, accepted the Nimitz concept. They further proposed that the formal surrender would be "received jointly by General MacArthur and Admiral Nimitz"; informed all commanders in the Far East that the order of mainland surrenders would be Shanghai, Pusan, Chefoo and Chinwangtao; and that preliminary landings at these points would be effected by United States Marines.

Owing to the gradual breakup of the Potsdam Conference between 26 July and 1 August, members returning home by different routes and President Truman's traveling by sea, there was a hiatus of eleven or twelve days in top command, during which nothing could be done about Japan. In the meantime General MacArthur sent in his views on the occupation to the J.C.S. He objected to the idea of a prior occupation by the Navy, both because sailors alone might be unable to cope with opposition from Japanese ground elements and because "it would be psychologically offensive to ground and air forces of the Pacific Theater to be relegated from their proper missions at the hour of victory." [22]

Japan, of course, was not the only country to be occupied. The Imperial government estimated that over 3,000,000 of its subjects were under arms overseas. These, and the tense situation in China between Nationalists and Communists, with Soviet Russia promising to burst in, made occupation priorities a matter of vital importance for the future. The best prophet was General A. C. Wedemeyer USA, commanding the China Theater. In dispatches of 12 and 14 August to the J.C.S. he urgently demanded priority for occupation of Manchuria and the Chinese seaports, in order to prevent the Chinese Reds from taking over. Japan, a country under orderly government, could wait; but Asia was then "an enormous pot, seething and boiling, the fumes of which may readily snuff out the advancements gained by Allied sacrifices the past several years. . . ." Which is just about what happened.

Admiral Nimitz did not agree, believing that the occupation of

[22] General MacArthur to J.C.S. 27 July, J.C.S. ms. History chap. 96 pp. 45–46.

Japan and Korea should have priority over Chinese ports and the Yangtze Valley. He felt that the primary consideration in planning the occupation of China should be "to avoid participation in fighting between the Chinese." General MacArthur replied even more strongly to Wedemeyer's proposal, insisting the "the prompt occupation of Japan proper" was "paramount," and should be given highest priority in the allotment of forces and logistics. He added that two Marine divisions should occupy Shanghai as soon as shipping became available, but that any further occupation of the Chinese coast should "be placed in a contingent category." [23]

In accordance with President Truman's instructions, the J.C.S. had directed General MacArthur and Admiral Nimitz to occupy Seoul and Dairen before the Russians got there. They wished "that every effort be made to expedite the movement of U.S. forces into key ports on the China coast."

Representatives of Admiral Nimitz and General Wedemeyer met Commander Seventh Fleet (Admiral Kinkaid) and members of SCAP staff at General MacArthur's Manila headquarters on 18–19 August. At this conference it became clear that no shipping would be available to lift Marines into China before 30 September. The following priority list of Seventh Fleet participation in the occupation of China was then drawn up: —

1. North China Naval Force to be set up, immediately, to control Yellow Sea and Gulf of Chihli and support occupation of Korea.
2. Yangtze Patrol to be set up as soon as minesweeping permits.
3. South China Patrol to be set up as soon as Chinese Nationalist forces had a seaport in their possession.

It was also agreed that 72 LCI be allotted to help move Chiang Kai-shek's troops down rivers and along the coastline.

Correspondence followed between General MacArthur and the J.C.S. about the joint Soviet-U.S. occupation of Korea. The General was urged by the J.C.S. on 24 August to make haste lest Russian troops push south of lat. 38° N — a line of grim significance for the postwar history of Korea. The Royal Navy occupied Hong

[23] MacArthur to J.C.S. 14 and 15 Aug., J.C.S. ms. History chap. 97 pp. 18–25.

Kong 30 August and restored the British colonial administration there. It was assumed that the same procedure would be followed by the French in Indochina. Allied intentions respecting the Dutch administration were similar; but, as we have seen, the delay in oc-cupying Java gave the rebels an edge that could not be blunted.[24] Admiral Lord Mountbatten, the Southeast Asia commander, re-quested permission to accept the surrender of Japanese troops in Burma, Thailand, etc., ahead of schedule, because his occupation troops were already at sea in small craft, but General MacArthur did not consent.

Trouble with Russia began immediately. The Russian Army in Manchuria ignored the Japanese cease-fire of 16 August, pressing on to Mukden and into Jehol Province, ordering all Japanese forces in Manchuria to surrender to Marshal Vassilevski on 20 August, two weeks before the general surrender. A Stalin-Chiang treaty of al-liance and friendship, signed 14 August at Moscow, was broken by Russia before the ink was dry. Fortunately no Russian troops occu-pied Japan proper. They could not, however, be kept out of south-ern Sakhalin, which had been Russian territory before 1904.

As early as 11 August, the Joint Chiefs had sent to Admiral Nimitz and to General MacArthur, designated Supreme Com-mander for the Allied Powers, drafts of the actual instrument of surrender, a proclamation to be made by the Emperor, and military and naval general orders to be issued upon the capitulation of Japan.

The occupation plan finally agreed upon between General Mac-Arthur and Admiral Nimitz was based on those for Operation OLYMPIC, the invasion of Kyushu planned for the fall of 1945, and for Operation CORONET, the invasion of the Tokyo plain tentatively scheduled for March 1946. If the war had not ended earlier, General Krueger's Sixth Army, lifted and supported by Admiral Spruance's Fifth Fleet and V Amphibious Force, would have landed on Kyushu 1 November 1945. The invasion of the Tokyo plain would have been effected by Lieutenant General Eichelberger's Eighth Army

[24] See Vol. XIII 276–277.

lifted and supported by Admiral Halsey's Third Fleet. No formal directive for CORONET had been issued by the J.C.S. but General Eichelberger and staff had been working on it while Eighth Army was mopping up in the Philippines. They were able to use some of this for key occupational functions, saving much additional paper work.

For the actual occupation Eighth Army, lifted and supported by Admiral Halsey's Third Fleet, was assigned Honshu east of the 135th meridian; Sixth Army and Fifth Fleet took key points on western Honshu, Kyushu and Shikoku; XXIV Corps and Admiral Kinkaid's Seventh Fleet occupied Korea south of latitude 38° N. Hokkaido was assigned to Vice Admiral Frank J. Fletcher's North Pacific Force, using elements of Eighth Army. Three phases of the occupation, geared to the day Japan accepted the surrender terms, were planned. These decisions were made on 27–28 July.

Admiral Halsey and Third Fleet, already actively engaged in offensive operations against the home islands, were given an important rôle in the occupation, to seize the Yokosuka naval base on Tokyo Bay, operate Japanese naval facilities ashore and assist in the occupation of the Tokyo region. Third Fleet was scheduled to return to Ulithi and Leyte in August, but indications that Japan might collapse in a matter of days caused Halsey to issue orders to keep the logistics pipeline full in case it became necessary to prolong operations in Empire waters indefinitely. By 10 August planning was well in hand for the contingency of surrender; lists of ships, facilities and equipment were ready for submission to Admiral Nimitz.

Since a landing force would be required for Yokosuka, all available Marines in Third Fleet were organized into a provisional regiment and strengthened by another Marine regiment from Guam. In addition, three Naval landing battalions of about 400 men each were organized within Task Force 38 [25] and one Royal Navy landing battalion was contributed by Task Force 37. Rear Admiral Oscar C. Badger headed this expeditionary force. Plans included

[25] This was the first time in World War II that a landing force of American bluejackets, a familiar feature of earlier wars, had been organized.

not only the occupation of Yokosuka naval base and air station, but the manning of enemy ships, demilitarizing installations, supply drops to P.O.W. camps, and rescue of the prisoners themselves. For this last object, which had highest priority, a task group was organized under Commodore R. W. Simpson. From the time of the cease-fire order on 15 August, the fast carriers maintained daily observation patrols over Japan, locating many P.O.W. camps with the help of signal panels laid out by the prisoners themselves.

President Truman, upon receipt of the Emperor's acceptance of surrender terms at 1550 August 14, proclaimed the fact to the world, and at the same time announced that General of the Army Douglas MacArthur would be Supreme Commander of the Allied Powers (SCAP) for the surrender and occupation of Japan. MacArthur was so informed by General Marshall at 2305 the same day. Thus, there were set in motion the wheels of an occupation which rolled smoothly but not quite so fast as that of Germany, because the Imperial government was intact and the greater part of the Japanese Army, still undefeated, was in a position to resist any premature attempt of the Allies to take over. General MacArthur, who understood the situation perfectly, was responsible for the sequence of events which gave time for the Emperor's commands to reach all his armed forces, as well as time for his own command to prepare the first landings of occupation troops. He set 17 August as the date for Japanese representatives to meet him at Manila, to arrange for the formal surrender.

3. Japan Surrenders, 15 August–2 September [26]

On 15 August General MacArthur directed the Japanese government by radio to order "immediate cessation of hostilities" and to

[26] Com Third Fleet (Admiral Halsey) Action Report and War Diary; *Missouri* Action Report 8 Sept. 1945; *Admiral Halsey's Story* (1947) chap. xvi; Eichelberger *Our Jungle Road to Tokyo;* National Archives booklet *The End of the War in the Pacific, Surrender Documents in Facsimile* (1945); *N.Y. Sunday Times* and *Herald Tribune* 2 Sept.; *Time* 10 Sept.; *Life* Magazine 17 Sept. 1945, with good pictorial coverage.

send "a competent representative" by air to Manila to receive instructions for the formal surrender and the reception of occupation forces. No action on this was taken at Tokyo until Secretary Byrnes's note of acceptance of the Japanese surrender offer was officially received during the morning of 16 August. An Imperial order then went out at 1600 "to the entire Armed Forces to cease fire immediately."

By that time the Emperor had a new cabinet. The Suzuki government offered to resign three hours after the Imperial broadcast of noon 15 August, but the Emperor ordered it to function until a new cabinet could be formed. The choice fell upon General Prince Naruhiko Higashikuni, uncle-in-law of the Emperor. Mamoru Shigemitsu, who had been working for peace all along, became the new Foreign Minister.

The delegation to General MacArthur at Manila was delayed two days, 17–19 August, owing in part to the Higashikuni government's not having been completely formed, partly to a Japanese request for clarification as to the purpose of the mission,[27] and partly because hotheads of the Japanese Army Air Force threatened to shoot down any surrender mission that took off. This delay caused a brief but unfounded suspicion in America that the Japanese government was stalling.

Lieutenant General Kawabe, deputy chief of the Army general staff, headed the delegation, which took off in darkness and secrecy from Kizarazu in two planes painted white with green crosses, early on 19 August. At Ie Shima they transferred to an A.A.F. transport plane, which landed them at Manila in the late afternoon. Members of General MacArthur's staff, with Rear Admiral Forrest Sherman as Admiral Nimitz's representative, there presented them with a copy of the instrument of surrender and instructions for the reception of occupying forces. When told that the first troops would arrive in Japan on 23 August the Japanese asked for more time, stating the problem of controlling their own armed forces and pleading that delay would enable them to prevent regrettable incidents.

[27] J.C.S. ms. History chap. 97 pp. 34–35.

The date for the first airborne soldiers to arrive at Atsugi airport, near Yokohama, was then set for 26 August and the first major landings for the 28th. The Japanese delegation was impressed by the firmness but fairness of the American officers. As one member expressed it, their attitude was "stern, but they were not arrogant nor did they mock the vanquished." [28] Shortly after noon 20 August the delegation returned to Tokyo.

Some of the outlying Japanese garrisons obeyed their Emperor's order even before the formal surrender. On 22 August, at Mili in the Marshall Islands, 2395 ragged and half-starved soldiers, sailors and construction workers surrendered to Captain H. B. Grow USNR in destroyer escort *Levy*, representing Rear Admiral W. K. Harrill, commanding the Gilberts-Marshalls area. The American flag was raised over Mili 28 August, and next day all but twelve officers were embarked on a Japanese merchant ship for repatriation. The twelve exceptions were sent to Majuro for the investigation of an outrage which occurred in January 1944, when five American airmen who bailed out on Mili were tortured and then decapitated. The then Japanese island commander committed suicide, leaving a note in which he assumed responsibility but disclaimed issuing the order.

The tiny garrisons which had been holding out in the Kerama Retto began to surrender to Tenth Army on 29 August. On the same day Major General H. H. Johnson USA, of the 93rd Division on Morotai, took the surrender of all Japanese in the Halmahera group, 36,700 servicemen and 5000 civilians. About 2500 emaciated troops on Marcus Island surrendered to Rear Admiral F. E. M. Whiting, in *Bagley*, on the last day of August.

General MacArthur planned that an advance party fly into Atsugi airfield 26 August to prepare for the arrival of the 11th Airborne Division two days later, and that on the same day Admiral Halsey's landing force would go ashore at Yokosuka. Owing to foul weather the General postponed these moves two days. It was not too foul for a "brash young pilot" from *Yorktown*, who made an unauthorized solo "occupation of Atsugi" on the 27th. At his

[28] MacArthur *Historical Report II* 294 *n.46*.

orders, the Japanese ground crews painted and posted a large sign, "Welcome to the U.S. Army from Third Fleet," which greeted the Army paratroops when they arrived next day.

Admiral Halsey decided to anchor major units of Third Fleet in Sagami Wan, under the shadow of Mount Fuji. Emissaries from the Japanese Navy in destroyer *Hatsuzakura*, carrying a number of local pilots, made rendezvous with flagship *Missouri* at the entrance of the Bay on 27 August. On board the battleship, Admiral Halsey's chief of staff, Rear Admiral Robert B. Carney, gave them detailed instructions to prepare for occupation of Yokosuka and the naval control zone, and received hydrographic information and a chart of mine fields. *Missouri*, H.M.S. *Duke of York* wearing the flag of Admiral Sir Bruce Fraser RN, and other ships of Third Fleet, then entered Sagami Wan and proceeded to selected berths, piloted by the Japanese. From the anchorage, the sun appeared to set that evening directly into the crater of Mount Fuji. It seemed symbolic – a dismal setting of that sun which had risen triumphant over Oahu on 7 December 1941.

Aircraft carriers remained outside Sagami Wan to maintain surveillance over Tokyo and eastern Honshu. Minesweepers, preceding advance elements of Third Fleet, began sweeping the entrance to Tokyo Bay at once and on 28 August entered it, together with a few of the lighter ships. By 1400 August 29, when Admiral Nimitz arrived by air to join his flagship *South Dakota*, three battleships, two light cruisers and numerous destroyers were anchored off Yokosuka. The older battleships remained in Sagami Wan to render fire support at Atsugi in case it were needed. The same day, Commodore Simpson's TG 30.6 began to rescue prisoners of war from camps around Tokyo Bay.

At 0600 August 30, landings began at the Japanese forts guarding the entrance to Tokyo Bay to insure their neutralization, and at 1000 Admiral Badger landed his bluejackets and Marines at Yokosuka naval base and airfield without incident. On the waterfront, Vice Admiral Tozuka transferred custody and control of base and airfield to Rear Admiral Carney. On Atsugi airfield the 11th Airborne's band greeted General MacArthur, who appeared at the door of his plane with shirt open at the neck and smoking the familiar corncob pipe. To General Eichelberger, on hand to greet him, he said, "Bob, this is the payoff!" With Eichelberger in company, MacArthur set off for Yokohama, twenty miles away, in an ancient American car. Owing to repeated breakdowns the trip required two hours. Both sides of the road were lined with Japanese soldiers.

General MacArthur established temporary headquarters in the Yokohama customhouse and various Japanese agencies located themselves nearby. Here the final arrangements were made for the formal signing of the instrument of surrender, now set for 0900 September 2. It was intended that it be done in a frame of impressive dignity, accompanied by an appropriate display of Allied air and sea power. General MacArthur, having obtained the prior occupation of Japan proper, gracefully yielded to Admiral Nimitz the choice of place. Battleship *Missouri* (Captain S. S. Murray), which was named for President Truman's native state and sponsored by his daughter Margaret, and which had been Admiral Halsey's flagship during the last weeks of the war, became the scene of the ceremony. She anchored in Tokyo Bay, about four and a half miles NE ½ E from Commodore Perry's second anchorage.[29] On a bulkhead overlooking the surrender ceremony was displayed the 31-starred flag that Perry carried into Tokyo Bay in 1853. In contrast to the tiny fleet that had opened Japan 92 years earlier, there were now anchored in Tokyo Bay 258 warships of all types from battleship to the smallest beaching craft, representing the Allied nations which had been at war with Japan. Most of the aircraft carriers remained outside the bay in order to launch planes at the appropriate moment of this "V-J Day."

Sunday, 2 September, dawned with scattered clouds that dissipated during the morning. *Missouri* was especially rigged for the occasion. On the admiral's veranda deck on the starboard side was

---

[29] The anchorage of "Mighty Mo" was around lat. 35°22' N, long. 139°45'35" E.

set up an ordinary mess table covered with a green baize cloth. There the surrender documents, in English and Japanese, were laid out ready for signature. At Morning Colors the flag that had flown over the Capitol in Washington on 7 December 1941 was raised on the battleship's flagstaff. It had also been displayed at Casablanca, Rome, and Berlin, and would rise again over the American Embassy in Tokyo when General MacArthur moved in, a few days later.

Visitors began to arrive on board shortly after seven. Destroyer *Buchanan* closed the starboard side at 0803 to deliver high-ranking officers and Allied representatives. When Fleet Admiral Nimitz came on board at 0805, his five-starred flag was broken at the main, Admiral Halsey in the meantime having shifted his four-starred flag to *Iowa*. General of the Army Douglas MacArthur came up *Missouri's* starboard gangway from destroyer *Buchanan* at 0843, to be received by Admirals Nimitz and Halsey and a full set of sideboys. His personal flag was promptly broken alongside that of Admiral Nimitz. The General and the two Admirals went directly to flag cabin.

At 0856 the Japanese delegation, lifted from Yokohama in destroyer *Lansdowne*, mounted the starboard gangway. They were headed by the Foreign Minister, Mamoru Shigemitsu, who, having lost a leg to an assassin's bomb many years before, negotiated the ladder with difficulty. He was followed by General Yoshijiro Umezu, chief of the Army general staff, to sign on behalf of Imperial General Headquarters. It was reported that the General, who had consistently opposed surrender, turned white with rage when he learned that he was being considered for this part and threatened to commit hara-kiri; but after personal intervention by the Emperor he consented to carry it out. The rest of the party consisted of three representatives each from the Foreign Office, the Army and the Navy.[30] The civilians were in formal morning dress with top hats, in contrast to the ill-fitting uniforms of the military mem-

[30] The Navy representatives were Rear Adm. S. Tomioka, chief Navy planner for Imperial General Headquarters, Rear Adm. I. Yokoyama and Capt. K. Shiba of Navy section Imperial General Headquarters.

bers and to the khaki uniforms with open-necked shirts worn by the United States Navy and Army officers. Sideboys were stationed and the Japanese delegation were piped on board. As they arrived on deck, their faces expressing no emotion, complete silence fell over the assembled multitude.

Immediately abaft the table on which the documents lay stood representatives of the Allied Nations to sign the surrender for their respective governments, and observers from their armed services. On their right and under *Missouri*'s No. 2 turret were a score of flag and general officers of the United States who had taken a leading part in the war against Japan. Cameramen were everywhere and bluejackets manned every vantage point from which to view the proceedings.

The Japanese were not asked to present their formal credentials. As translated into English, these began:

HIROHITO, by the Grace of Heaven, Emperor of Japan, seated on the Throne occupied by the same Dynasty changeless through ages eternal, To all to whom these Presents shall come, Greeting!

And the Instrument of Surrender, drafted in Washington and slightly amended by General MacArthur, contained these pregnant paragraphs: —

We hereby proclaim the unconditional surrender to the Allied Powers of the Japanese Imperial General Headquarters and of all Japanese armed forces and all armed forces under Japanese control wherever situated.

We hereby command all Japanese forces wherever situated and the Japanese people to cease hostilities forthwith, to preserve and save from damage all ships, aircraft, and military and civil property and to comply with all requirements which may be imposed by the Supreme Commander for the Allied Powers or by agencies of the Japanese Government at his direction. . . .

We hereby command all civil, military and naval officials to obey and enforce all proclamations, orders and directives [issued] by the Supreme Commander for the Allied Powers . . . and we direct all such officials to remain at their posts and to continue to perform their noncombatant duties unless specifically relieved by him or under his authority. . . .

The authority of the Emperor and the Japanese Government to rule the state shall be subject to the Supreme Commander for the Allied Powers, who will take such steps as he deems proper to effectuate these terms of surrender.

The atmosphere was frigid. The Japanese, performing an act unprecedented in their country's history, preserved their dignity. Toshikazu Kase, a member of the Foreign Office who noted the significance of the miniature rising sun flags painted on the wing of *Missouri's* bridge, felt that the delegation was "subjected to the torture of the pillory. A million eyes seemed to beat on us with the million shafts of a rattling storm of arrows barbed with fire." [31] As they stood immobile, facing the table, in position indicated by an aide, the ship's chaplain spoke an invocation over the loud-speaker system, and was followed by "The Star-Spangled Banner" played from a disc. A Russian photographer tried to secure a position close to the table and was firmly removed to his proper place.

After three or four minutes had elapsed, General MacArthur appeared with Admirals Nimitz and Halsey. The General took his place before the microphones to open the ceremony. At his side were Lieutenant General Jonathan M. Wainwright USA, who had surrendered the Philippines in 1942, and Lieutenant General Sir Arthur E. Percival, who had surrendered Singapore the same year. Both had been flown from prison camps in Manchuria. General MacArthur made a short speech stating the purpose of the occasion, concluding with a ringing expression of hope for the future: —

It is my earnest hope — indeed the hope of all mankind — that from this solemn occasion a better world shall emerge out of the blood and carnage of the past, a world founded upon faith and understanding, a world dedicated to the dignity of man and the fulfillment of his most cherished wish for freedom, tolerance and justice.

Mr. Kase, at least, was profoundly moved by the General's speech. It transformed the battleship's quarterdeck, he recorded, "into an altar of peace."

[31] *Journey to the Missouri* (1950) p. 7.

The General now pointed to a chair at the other side of the table, and motioned to the Japanese delegates to come forward and sign. Mr. Shigemitsu fumbled with his hat, gloves and cane and seemed puzzled as to which paper he was supposed to sign. It was a tense moment; some of the onlookers suspected the Foreign Minister of stalling, but what really bothered him was pain from his ill-fitting artificial leg. MacArthur's voice punctuated the dead silence with a crisp order to his chief of staff, "Sutherland, show him where to sign." Sutherland did, and Shigemitsu signed the instrument of surrender at 0904, thus officially ending the war, which had lasted exactly 1364 days, 5 hours and 44 minutes. He was immediately followed as signatory by General Umezu.

General of the Army Douglas MacArthur then signed the acceptance of the surrender for all Allied powers. Next, Fleet Admiral Nimitz, with Admiral Halsey and Rear Admiral Forrest Sherman as supporters, signed for the United States. Then, in order, came General Hsu Yung-chang for China, Admiral Sir Bruce Fraser RN for the United Kingdom, Lieutenant General Derevyanko for the Soviet Union, General Sir Thomas Blamey for Australia, Colonel Moore-Gosgrove for Canada, General Jacques LeClerc for France, Admiral Helfrich for the Netherlands, and Air Vice Marshal Isitt for New Zealand.

After all had signed, General MacArthur spoke a final word: —

"Let us pray that peace be now restored to the world and that God will preserve it always. These proceedings are now closed."

In this firm and stern setting, Japan acknowledged her defeat in a war forced upon her by an ambitious and reckless military clique. The ceremony was conducted in an atmosphere of cold formality; no pageantry, no roll of drums, no handing over of swords or colors, not even a handshake; nothing to recall historic surrenders such as those of Saratoga, Yorktown and Appomattox. Nevertheless, the atmosphere was charged with emotion. Vice Admiral John S. McCain, who had only four more days to live, thought that the mask behind which the Japanese delegation hid their feelings

Congratulations: Fleet Admiral King, Mr. Secretary Forrestal,
Admiral Halsey, Fleet Admiral Nimitz

Ships of Third Fleet in Sagami Wan, 27 August — Mount Fuji in the
Background

Victory

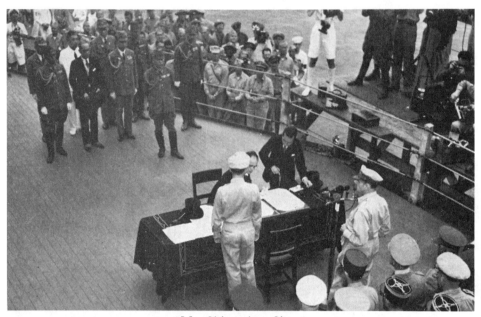

Mr. Shigemitsu Signs

Mr. Kase is standing by. General Sutherland has back to camera; General MacArthur is at right, General Umezu at head of Japanese delegation

General MacArthur Signs

Behind him, standing, left to right: General Wainwright, General Sir Arthur Percival, General Sutherland, Rear Admiral John F. Shafroth. Commodore Perry's flag is behind them

The Surrender on board U.S.S. Missouri, 2 September 1945

The Japanese Delegation Departs

Wings over U.S.S. *Iowa*

Immediately after the Surrender

U.S. Submarine *Sand Lance* Flying Presidential Unit Citation Flag
below her Battle Ensign

Homeward Bound

concealed a spirit of non-compliance or revenge; he could not have been more wrong. Admiral Halsey's feeling was one of undisguised elation. "If ever a day demanded champagne, this was it," he recorded; but when, after the ceremony, the Allied representatives flocked into flag cabin he had nothing to offer but coffee and doughnuts. General MacArthur and Admiral Nimitz entertained a feeling of compassion toward the fallen foe; Nimitz revoked an order from Halsey to the C.O. of destroyer *Lansdowne* not to offer coffee, cigarettes or other courtesies to the Japanese delegation. The Japanese delegates received customary honors as they approached the gangway in order to symbolize the fact that they were no longer enemies.

As the formalities came to a close at 0925, the sun broke through, and a flight of 450 carrier aircraft, together with several hundred of the Army Air Force, swept over *Missouri* and her sister ships.

Immediately after, Admiral Nimitz released a statement that was broadcast throughout the Pacific and the United States: —

On board all naval vessels at sea and in port, and at our many island bases in the Pacific, there is rejoicing and thanksgiving. The long and bitter struggle . . . is at an end. . . .

Today all freedom-loving peoples of the world rejoice in the victory and feel pride in the accomplishments of our combined forces. We also pay tribute to those who defended our freedom at the cost of their lives.

On Guam is a military cemetery in a green valley not far from my headquarters. The ordered rows of white crosses stand as reminders of the heavy cost we have paid for victory. On these crosses are the names of American soldiers, sailors and marines — Culpepper, Tomaino, Sweeney, Bromberg, Depew, Melloy, Ponziani — names that are a cross-section of democracy. They fought together as brothers in arms; they died together and now they sleep side by side. To them we have a solemn obligation — the obligation to insure that their sacrifice will help to make this a better and safer world in which to live.

Now we turn to the great tasks of reconstruction and restoration. I am confident that we will be able to apply the same skill, resourcefulness and keen thinking to these problems as were applied to the problems of winning the victory.

General MacArthur, with his usual felicity, assumed the prophet's mantle in a broadcast addressed to the people of the United States: —

Today the guns are silent. A great tragedy has ended. A great victory has been won. The skies no longer rain death — the seas bear only commerce — men everywhere walk upright in the sunlight. The entire world is quietly at peace. The holy mission has been completed . . . I speak for the thousands of silent lips, forever stilled among the jungles and the beaches and in the deep waters of the Pacific. . . .

A new era is upon us. Even the lesson of victory itself brings with it profound concern, both for our future security, and the survival of civilization. . . .

Men since the beginning of time have sought peace. Various methods through the ages have been attempted to devise an international process to prevent or settle disputes between nations. . . . Military alliances, balances of power, leagues of nations, all in turn failed, leaving the only path to be by way of the crucible of war. . . .

The utter destructiveness of war now blots out this alternative. We have had our last chance. If we do not devise some greater and more equitable system, Armageddon will be at our door. The problem basically is theological and involves a spiritual recrudescence and improvement of human character. . . .

To the Pacific basin has come the vista of a new emancipated world. Today, freedom is on the offensive, democracy is on the march. Today, in Asia as well as in Europe, unshackled peoples are tasting the full sweetness of liberty. . . .

And so, my fellow countrymen, today I report to you that your sons and daughters have served you well and faithfully.[32]

One famous flag officer of the Pacific Fleet, Vice Admiral Theodore S. Wilkinson, was too busy to attend the surrender, since as Commander III Amphibious Force he was responsible for landing the 1st Cavalry Division while the ceremony was going on. Owing to this circumstance we have a good description of what happened in Tokyo Bay outside the *Missouri* in a letter from the Admiral to

[32] Maj. Gen. Courtney Whitney *MacArthur* (1956) pp. 222–224; Maj. Gen. C. A. Willoughby & John Chamberlain *MacArthur* (1954) p. 297 supplies a sentence left out in the Whitney version.

his wife, written that evening on board his flagship *Mount Olympus*.[33]

We stood in after an all night approach through several islands, in a rainy night, in a long column of thirty-odd transports. We reached the lower entrance . . . just after dawn and filed slowly up the harbor, to avoid fouling four destroyers reported to be bringing out visitors (including the Japs) to the surrender party. As we approached last night I got a general message from Bill Halsey that all flag officers not engaged in operations were invited to the ceremony at 9, to be aboard by 8:15. I couldn't leave my flock, but I lowered a fast boat and sent Dick Byrd[34] on ahead at 6. Our column, however, passed during the ceremony, and should have made an impressive 10-mile long backdrop. . . .

We anchored our large squadron off Yokohama and sent our boats scurrying in, filled with men. By shortly after noon all our "assault" troops were landed, though fortunately without the usual accompaniment of an assault, and the reserve troops went ashore, followed by the usual tedious and lengthy unloading of supplies, which we hope to complete in two days.

In the afternoon I went down the harbor to see Bill Halsey and the old Third Fleet crowd; they were most cordial. He promptly took me over to a very impressive sunset ceremony Admiral Fraser was having in the *Duke of York*. Massed bands of all the British ships played splendid martial music and a hymn. The flags of all the signatory Allies were flying from the signal yards, and all were slowly lowered in unison during the sunset hymn.

The hymn was John Ellerton's "The Day Thou Gavest, Lord, Is Ended."

> The day thou gavest, Lord, is ended,
> The darkness falls at thy behest;
> To thee our morning hymns ascended,
> Thy praise shall sanctify our rest.
>
> So be it, Lord; thy throne shall never,
> Like earth's proud empires, pass away:
> Thy kingdom stands, and grows for ever,
> Till all thy creatures own thy sway.

[33] 2 Sept. 1945, by kind permission of the recipient, now Lady Moore, wife of Admiral Sir Harry Moore RN.

[34] Rear Admiral Richard E. Byrd, the noted explorer, who had come up from Manila with Admiral Wilkinson.

Nothing could have been more appropriate to the occasion than this Sunday evening hymn to the "Author of peace and lover of concord." The familiar words and music, which floated over the now calm waters of the Bay to American bluejackets, touched the mystic chords of memory and sentiment, reminding all hands of the faith that had sustained them through travail and sacrifice. It brought sailors back to base and made them feel that their Navy had achieved something more than a military victory.

They were right. If victory over Japan meant anything beyond a change in the balance of power, it meant that eternal values and immutable principles, which had come down to us from ancient Hellas, had been reaffirmed and reëstablished. Often these principles are broken, often these values are lost to sight when people are struggling for survival; but to them man must return, and does return, in order to enjoy his Creator's greatest gifts — life, liberty and the pursuit of happiness.

Task Organization for the Capture of Okinawa[1]

14 March–30 June 1945

AS THIS is the longest and most complicated task organization that we have published, an explanation may help the reader to find his way around. We attempt to list groups in the order of their arrival off Okinawa, and to include all ships committed to that operation before the island was secured. The campaign lasted so long that many commanders were relieved before it was over, which accounts for frequent mentions of two C.O.'s for the same ship.

We begin with the Gunfire and Covering Force, TF 54, which remained fairly constant.

Admiral Blandy's Amphibious Support Force including Escort Carriers, which arrived early and stayed late, begins on page 373.

The Western Islands Group, which took the Kerama Retto, starts on p. 375.

The Minecraft, also early arrivals, begin on p. 376.

Northern Attack Force for Okinawa itself begins on p. 378; Southern Attack Force on p. 379.

Admiral Wright's Demonstration Group for the simulated landing, and the Seaplane Air Groups and Tenders, are on p. 381.

---

[1] Compiled from the op plans, action reports and war diaries of participating ships and commands. Air groups, squadrons and their C.O.s have been verified from action reports, war diaries and histories; numbers and types of planes also from the "Weekly Location of U.S. Naval Aircraft."

The first ship in a group is the flagship unless otherwise stated, and ships are listed only once, but they were constantly joining and being detached from the various groups,

TF 58, the Fast Carrier Force, begins on p. 382.
Admiral Beary's Logistics Support Group begins on p. 386;
Commodore Carter's Servron 10 will be found on p. 387.
A simplified task organization of TF 57, the British Carrier Force,
p. 388, concludes this long appendix.

COMMANDER–IN–CHIEF PACIFIC FLEET AND PACIFIC OCEAN AREAS

Fleet Admiral Chester W. Nimitz

Chief of Staff, Vice Admiral C. H. McMorris

FIFTH FLEET

Admiral Raymond A. Spruance in INDIANAPOLIS

Captain C. B. McVay III

Chief of Staff, Rear Admiral A. C. Davis

TF 51 JOINT EXPEDITIONARY FORCE

Vice Admiral Richmond K. Turner in ELDORADO

Capts. J. R. Wallace & M. J. Tichenor
Chief of Staff, Commodore P. S. Theiss
* Lieutenant General Simon B. Buckner USA, Commanding
General Expeditionary Troops (TF 56), embarked

TF 54 GUNFIRE & COVERING FORCE Rear Admiral M. L. Deyo
in TENNESSEE Capt. John B. Heffernan

Chief of Staff, Captain Richard W. Bates

Unit One, Rear Admiral P. K. Fischler: Battleships TEXAS Capt. C. A. Baker, MARYLAND Capt. J. D. Wilson; heavy cruiser TUSCALOOSA Capt. J. G. Atkins; destroyers LAWS (with Comdesdiv 110, Cdr. W. H. Price, embarked) Cdr. L. O. Wood, LONGSHAW Cdr. T. R. Vogeley & * Lt. Cdr. C. W. Becker, MORRISON Cdr. J. R. Hansen, PRICHETT Cdr. C. M. Bowley.

Unit Two, Rear Admiral C. Turner Joy: Heavy cruisers SAN FRANCISCO Capt. J. E. Whelchel, MINNEAPOLIS Capts. H. B. Slocum & R. C. Hudson; battleships ARKANSAS Capt. G. M. O'Rear, COLORADO Capt. W. S. Macaulay; destroyers HALL (with Comdesron 51 Capt. H. J. Martin embarked) Cdr. L. C. Baldauf & Lt. Cdr. J. D. P. Hodapp, * HALLIGAN * Lt. Cdr. E. T. Grace, PAUL HAMILTON Cdr. Dan Carlson, LAFFEY Cdr. F. J. Becton, * TWIGGS * Cdr. George Philip.

Unit Three, Rear Admiral B. J. Rodgers: Light cruisers BIRMINGHAM Capt. H. D. Power, ST. LOUIS Capt. J. B. Griggs; battleships TENNESSEE Capt. Heffernan, NEVADA Capt. P. M. Rhea; heavy cruiser WICHITA (with Rear Admiral F. G. Fahrion em-

Lost in this operation.

barked) Capts. D. A. Spencer & C. J. Rend; destroyers * MANNERT L. ABELE (with Comdesron 60 Capts. W. L. Freseman & B. R. Harrison embarked) Cdr. A. E. Parker, ZELLARS Cdr. L. S. Kintberger, BRYANT Cdr. G. C. Seay, BARTON Cdr. E. B. Dexter, O'BRIEN Cdr. W. W. Outerbridge.

Unit Four, Rear Admiral Lynde D. McCormick: Battleships IDAHO Capt. H. J. Grassie, WEST VIRGINIA (with Rear Admiral I. C. Sowell embarked) Capts. H. V. Wiley & R. W. Holsinger; heavy cruisers PENSACOLA Capt. A. P. Mullinnix, PORTLAND Capt. T. G. W. Settle; light cruiser BILOXI Capt. P. R. Heineman; destroyers PORTERFIELD (with Comdesron 55 Capt. A. E. Jarrell embarked) Cdr. D. W. Wulzen, * CALLAGHAN Cdr. C. M. Bertholf, IRWIN Cdrs. D. B. Miller & R. B. Kelley, CASSIN YOUNG Cdr. J. W. Ailes, PRESTON Cdr. G. S. Patrick.

Unit Five, Rear Admiral Allan E. Smith: Heavy cruisers SALT LAKE CITY Capt. E. A. Mitchell, INDIANAPOLIS Capt. McVay; battleships NEW MEXICO Capt. J. M. Haines, NEW YORK Capt. K. C. Christian; destroyers NEWCOMB (with Comdesron 56, Capt. R. N. Smoot embarked) Cdr. I. E. McMillian, HEYWOOD L. EDWARDS Cdr. A. L. Shepherd, LEUTZE Lt. Leon Grabowsky, RICHARD P. LEARY Cdr. D. P. Dixon, BENNION Cdr. R. H. Holmes.

Unit Six, Commander W. B. Hinds USNR: Destroyer escorts SAMUEL S. MILES Lt. Cdr. H. G. Brousseau USNR, WESSON Lt. Henry Sears USNR, FOREMAN (with Comcortdiv 40 Cdr. F. W. Hawes embarked) Lt. Cdr. W. J. Carey USNR, WHITEHURST Lt. J. C. Horton USNR, ENGLAND Lt. Cdr. J. A. Williamson USNR, WITTER Lt. George Herrmann USNR, BOWERS Lt. Cdr. C. F. Highfield USNR & Lt. T. B. Hinkle USNR, WILLMARTH Lt. Cdr. J. G. Thorburn USNR. The following reported to TF 54 after L-day: Heavy cruiser NEW ORLEANS Capt. J. E. Hurff; light cruiser MOBILE Capt. C. C. Miller; destroyer DALY Cdr. R. R. Bradley; fast minesweeper FORREST Lt. Cdr. S. E. Woodward.

TF 52 AMPHIBIOUS SUPPORT FORCE

Rear Admiral W. H. P. Blandy in ESTES Capt. B. O. Mathews

Chief of Staff, Captain N. A. Chapin

TG 52.1 SUPPORT CARRIER GROUP, Rear Admiral C. T. Durgin

Unit One, Rear Admiral C. A. F. Sprague: 2 Escort carriers MAKIN ISLAND Capts. W. B. Whaley & I. E. Hobbs with VC-84: 16 FM-2 (Wildcat), 11 TBM-3 (Avenger), Lt. D. K. English USNR. FANSHAW BAY Capt. M. E. Arnold with VOC-2: 24 FM-2, 6 TBM-3, Lt. Cdr. R. M. Allison. LUNGA POINT Capt. G. A. T. Washburn with VC-85: 18 FM-2, 11 TBM-3, 1 TBM-3P, Lt. Cdr. F. C. Herriman. SANGAMON Capts. M. E. Browder & A. I. Malstrom with Air Group 33 (Cdr. F. B. Gilkeson) 24 F6F (Hellcat) Lt. Cdr. P. C. Rooney, 6 TBM-3E Cdr. Gilkeson. NATOMA BAY Capts. A. K. Morehouse & B. B. Nichol with VC-81: 20 FM-2, 11 TBM-1C, 1 TBM-1CP, Lt. Cdr. W. B. Morton USNR. SAVO ISLAND Capt. W. D. Anderson with VC-91: 20 FM-2, 11 TBM-1C, 4 TBM-3, Lt. F. M. Blanchard USNR. ANZIO Capt. G. C. Montgomery with VC-13: 12 FM-2, 12 TBM-1C, Lt. Cdr. R. P. Williams USNR.

Screen, Commander J. C. Zahm (Comdesdiv 120)

Destroyers INGRAHAM Cdr. J. F. Harper, PATTERSON Lt. Cdrs. W. A. Hering & A. H. Angelo, BAGLEY Cdr. W. H. Shea, HART Cdr. W. D. Coleman, BOYD (with Comdesdiv 92 Cdr. J. B. Maher embarked) Cdr. A. E. Teall, BRADFORD Cdr. W. W.

* Lost in this operation.

2 Relieved by Rear Adm. E. W. Litch 7 April, Rear Adm. G. R. Henderson 9 May, Rear Adm. Litch 17 May, and Rear Adm. H. M. Martin 24 May.

Armstrong; destroyer escorts LAWRENCE C. TAYLOR (with Comcortdiv 72 Cdr. Alex Jackson USNR embarked) Lt. Cdr. J. R. Grey, MELVIN R. NAWMAN Lt. Cdr. F. W. Kinsley, OLIVER MITCHELL Lt. Cdr. K. J. Barclay USNR, ROBERT F. KELLER Cdr. R. J. Toner USNR & Lt. Cdr. G. Q. Thorndike USNR, TABBERER Lt. Cdrs. H. L. Plage USNR & D. A. DeCoudras USNR, RICHARD M. ROWELL (with Comcortdiv 63 Cdr. J. V. Bewick embarked) Lt. Cdr. N. D. Bullard USNR, RICHARD S. BULL Lt. Cdr. F. S. Moseley USNR, DENNIS Cdr. Sigurd Hansen USNR, SEDERSTROM (with Comcortdiv 31 Cdr. C. A. Kunz embarked) Lt. Cdr. J. P. Farley USNR, FLEMING Lt. Cdr. K. F. Burgess USNR, O'FLAHERTY Lt. Cdr. P. L. Callan USNR.

Unit Two, Rear Admiral F. B. Stump: Escort carriers SAGINAW BAY Capts. F. C. Sutton & Robert Goldwaite with VC–88: 20 FM–2, 12 TBM, Lt. E. L. Kemp USNR; SARGENT BAY Capt. R. M. Oliver with VC–83: 16 FM–2, 12 TBM–1C, * Lt. Cdr. B. V. Gates & Lt. M. S. Worley USNR; RUDYERD BAY, Capts. C. S. Smiley & J. G. Foster with VC–96: [3] 20 FM–2, 11 TBM–1C, Lt. Cdr. W. S. Woollen USNR; MARCUS ISLAND Capt. H. V. Hopkins with VC–87: 20 FM–2, 12 TBM–3, Lt. H. N. Heisel. PETROF BAY Capt. R. S. Clarke with VC–93: 16 FM–2, 12 TBM–3, Lt. Cdr. C. P. Smith; TULAGI Capts. J. C. Cronin & W. V. Davis with VC–92: 19 FM–2, 12 TBM–3, Lt. Cdr. J. B. Wallace; WAKE ISLAND Capt. A. V. Magly with VOC–1: 26 FM–2, 6 TBM–3, Lt. Cdr. W. F. Bringle.

Screen, Captain G. P. Hunter (Comdesdiv 91)

Destroyers CAPPS Cdr. J. M. Wood, LOWRY Cdr. E. S. Miller, EVANS Cdrs. B. N. Wev & R. J. Archer, JOHN D. HENLEY Cdr. C. H. Smith; destroyer escorts WILLIAM SEIVERLING (with Comcortdiv 70 Cdr. Ralph Cullinan embarked) Lt. Cdr. F. W. Larson USNR, ULVERT M. MOORE Lt. Cdr. F. D. Roosevelt Jr. USNR, KENDALL C. CAMPBELL Lt. Cdr. R. W. Johnson USNR, GOSS Cdr. C. S. Kirkpatrick USNR, TISDALE Lt. Cdr. J. S. Hatfield USNR, EISELE Lt. Cdr. S. C. Ranta USNR.

Unit Three, Rear Admiral W. D. Sample: Escort carriers: SUWANNEE Capt. D. S. Cornwell with Air Group 40 (* Lt. Cdr. R. D. Sampson & Lt. Cdr. J. C. Longino): 17 F6F, 10 TBM. CHENANGO Capts. George Van Deurs & H. D. Felt with Air Group 25 (* Lt. Cdr. R. W. Robinson, Lt. B. Phillips & Lt. Cdr. P. M. Paul): 17 F6F–5, 1 F6F–5P, 12 TBM; SANTEE Capt. J. V. Peterson with Air Group 24 (* Lt. Cdr. R. J. Ostrom & Lt. P. N. Charbonnet): 18 F6F, 12 TBM; STEAMER BAY Capt. J. B. Paschal with VC–90: 19 FM–2, 12 TBM–3, Lt. Cdr. R. A. O'Neill.

Screen, Captain A. D. Chandler (Comdesron 58)

Destroyers METCALF Cdr. D. L. Martineau, DREXLER Cdr. R. L. Wilson, FULLAM Lt. Cdr. G. M. Boyd, GUEST Cdrs. M. G. Kennedy & J. B. Weiler, HELM Lt. Cdr. A. F. Hollingsworth; destroyer escorts EDMONDS Lt. Cdr. J. S. Burrows USNR, JOHN C. BUTLER Lt. Cdrs. J. E. Pace & C. M. Jenkins USNR.

Special Escort Carrier Group, Captain C. L. Lee

These CVEs brought up Marine Air Groups 31 (Col. J. C. Munn USMC) and 33 (Col. W. E. Dickey USMC), with 192 F4U (Corsair) and 30 F6F, to operate from Okinawa airfields, arriving 4 April: HOLLANDIA Capt. Lee, WHITE PLAINS Capts. D. J. Sullivan & Frederick Funke, SITKOH BAY Capts. R. G. Lockhart & J. P. Walker, BRETON Capt. Frank Obeirne.

Screen, Commander R. A. Wilhelm USNR

Destroyer transports KILTY Lt. L. G. Benson USNR, MANLEY Lt. Cdr. L. M. Shepard USNR, GEORGE E. BADGER Lt. Cdrs. E. M. Higgins USNR & E. C. Stokes USNR, GREENE Lt. Cdr. G. O. Scarfe USNR.

* Lost in this operation.

[3] VC–96 operated from *Shamrock Bay* between 23 May and 30 June.

TG 51.1 WESTERN ISLANDS ATTACK GROUP Rear Admiral
I. N. Kiland in MOUNT MCKINLEY Capt. W. N Gamet

Embarking Western Islands Landing Force (77th Infantry Division and one
Marine BLT) Major General A. D. Bruce USA, and Air Support Control Unit
Capt. A. E. Buckley.

Transport Group "Fox," Commodore T. B. Brittain, with Beach Parties under
Lieutenant Commanders A. W. Lunt, C. J. Nath, Ebenezar Learned USNR and
J. Jeffries USNR.

Transdiv 49, Commo. Brittain: Attack transports CHILTON Capt. H. W. Turney,
LAGRANGE Capt. H. D. McIntosh, TAZEWELL Cdr. H. S. Olsen USNR, ST. MARY's Capt.
E. R. Glosten USNR; attack cargos OBERON Capt. J. C. Goodnough, TORRANCE Lt.
Cdr. G. A. Euerle USNR.

Transdiv 50, * Capts. Elmer Kiehl & R. W. Abbott: Attack transports HENRICO
* Capt. W. C. France & Lt. W. D. Craig USNR & Capt. J. H. Willis, PITT Capt.
W. S. Mayer, NATRONA Capt. E. E. Winquist USNR, DREW Capt. D. H. Swinson
USNR; attack cargo TATE Lt. Cdr. R. E. Lyon USNR; evacuation transport RIXEY
Capt. P. H. Jenkins & Lt. Cdr. M. S. Pratt USNR.

Transdiv 51, Capts. J. H. Willis & J. L. Allen: Attack transports GOODHUE Capt.
L. D. Sharp, EASTLAND Cdr. G. L. Harriss, TELFAIR Cdr. L. O. Armel USNR, MOUNT-
RAIL Cdr. R. R. Stevens USNR, MONTROSE Cdr. H. J. Davis; attack cargos WYANDOT
Lt. Cdr. R. B. Alderman, SUFFOLK Cdr. E. C. Clusman USNR.

Reconnaissance Section, Lt. Cdr. G. M. Street USNR: Destroyer transports
SCRIBNER Lt. Cdr. Street, KINZER Lt. R. C. Young USNR.

Western Islands Tractor Flotilla, Capt. R. C. Webb in LCI–783: 18 LST.
Western Islands Reserve Tractor Group,⁴ Cdr. E. A. Anderson USCG: 10 LST.
Western Islands LSM Group, Cdr. H. Doe in LCI–656: 11 LSM.
Western Islands Control Unit, Lt. C. S. Baker USCG in PCE–873: 3 PC, 4 SC.
Western Islands Support Craft Flotilla, Capt. T. W. Rimer: Mortar support
Divisions 6, 7, 8; RCM and Rocket Div. 3, and Gunboat Support Divs. 1, 3, 4, 5,
Cdr. A. R. Montgomery, from TGs 52.20, 52.22, 52.15; and LSM (R) Group,
Cdr. D. L. Francis, from gunboat support (p. 378).
Western Islands Hydrographic Survey Group, Lt. F. A. Woodke: 4 PCS.
Western Island Service & Salvage Unit, Capt. L. H. Curtis USNR: Salvage vessel
CLAMP, landing craft repair ship EGERIA; fleet tugs YUMA, TEKESTA; 2 LCI(L), 1 LCT.

WESTERN ISLANDS ATTACK GROUP Screen,⁵ Captain
Frederick Moosbrugger in BISCAYNE Lt. Cdr. R. H. Bates USNR

Comdesron 49, Capt. B. F. Brown: Destroyers PICKING Cdr. B. J. Semmes,
SPROSTON Cdr. R. J. Esslinger, WICKES Lt. Cdr. J. B. Cresap, * WILLIAM D. PORTER
Cdr. C. M. Keyes, ISHERWOOD (with Comdesdiv 98 Capt. M. H. Hubbard embarked) Cdr. L. E. Schmidt, KIMBERLY Cdr. J. D. Whitfield, LUCE Cdr. J. W. Waterhouse, CHARLES J. BADGER Cdr. J. H. Cotten.

Comcortdiv 69, Cdrs. T. C. Phifer & G. R. Keating USNR: Destroyer escorts
RICHARD W. SUESENS Lt. Cdr. R. W. Graham USNR, ABERCROMBIE Lt. Cdr. B. H.
Katschinski USNR & Lt. J. R. Hicks USNR, OBERRENDER Lt. Cdr. Samuel Spencer
USNR, RIDDLE (with Comcortdiv 44 Cdr. W. B. Hinds USNR embarked) Lt. Cdr.
F. P. Steel USNR, SWEARER Lt. J. M. Trent USNR, STERN Lt. Cdrs. J. R. Hinton USNR

* Lost in this operation.

⁴ These groups, with Sweep Unit 19, were organized as "Western Islands Tractor
Group HOW" for Tsugen Jima expedition, under Cdr. E. D. McEathron in *Buoyant*.
⁵ This organization effective until L-day only.

& C. F. Wilson; destroyer transports HUMPHREYS Lt. Cdr. O. B. Murphy USNR, HERBERT Lt. G. S. Hewitt USNR, * DICKERSON * Lt. Cdr. R. E. Lounsbury USNR; PCE(R)-853.

Western Islands Pontoon Barge & Causeway Unit, Lt. W. C. Zeigler USNR: 7 Pontoon Causeways, 8 Warping Tugs and 4 Pontoon Barges, in 10 LSTs. Also 18 LST carrying LCT.

TG 52.2 MINE FLOTILLA

Rear Admiral Alexander Sharp [6] in TERROR Cdr. H. W. Blakeslee

Chief of Staff, Captain R. P. Whitemarsh

TG 52.3 DESTROYER MINESWEEPER GROUP, Capt. R. A. Larkin in ELLYSON

Unit 2, Cdr. F. P. Mitchell: FORREST Lt. Cdr. S. E. Woodard, HOBSON Cdr. J. I. Manning & Lt. R. M. Vogel USNR, MACOMB Lt. Cdr. A. L. C. Waldron, DORSEY Lts. J. M. Hayes USNR & G. G. Powell USNR, HOPKINS Lt. P. D. Payne USNR; light minelayer, GWIN Cdr. F. S. Steinke.

Unit 3, Capt. Larkin & Cdr. W. R. Loud: ELLYSON Lt. Cdr. R. W. Mountrey USNR, HAMBLETON Cdr. G. A. O'Connell, RODMAN Cdr. W. H. Kirvan & Lt. Cdr. D. M. Granstrom USNR, * EMMONS Lt. Cdr. E. N. Foss USNR; light minelayer, LINDSEY Cdr. T. E. Chambers.

Unit 4, Cdr. M. D. Matthews: BUTLER Cdr. R. M. Hinckley, GHERARDI Lt. Cdr. W. W. Gentry, JEFFERS Cdr. H. Q. Murray & Lt. Cdr. R. D. Elder USNR, HARDING Lt. Cdr. D. B. Ramage; light minelayer, AARON WARD Cdr. W. H. Sanders.

TG 52.4 MINESWEEPER GROUP ONE, Captain T. F. Donohue

Unit 5, Cdr. J. H. Howard USNR & Lt. Cdr. A. D. Curtis USNR: CHAMPION Cdr. Howard USNR & Lt. Cdr. M. A. Rusteen USNR, HEED Lt. J. J. Lind USNR, DEFENSE Lt. Cdr. Gordon Abbott USNR, DEVASTATOR Lt. W. F. Remington USNR, ARDENT Lt. Cdr. A. D. Curtis USNR; light minelayer, ADAMS (with Comindiv 8, Capt. J. H. Sides, embarked), Cdr. H. J. Armstrong; PC-584.

Unit 6, Lt. Cdrs. H. R. Peirce USNR & J. L. Jackson USNR: REQUISITE Lt. Cdr. Peirce & Lt. J. D. Swartout USNR, REVENGE Lt. Cdr. Jackson, PURSUIT Lt. A. A. Mattera USNR, SAGE Lt. Cdr. F. K. Zinn USNR & Lt. D. L. Brantley USNR; light minelayer TOLMAN Cdr. C. A. Johnson; PC-1128.

Unit 7, Lt. Cdrs. G. M. Estep USNR & Richard Bassett USNR: SHELDRAKE Lt. B. E. Taylor USNR, * SKYLARK Lt. Cdr. Estep, STARLING Lt. Cdr. M. D. Duffield USNR, * SWALLOW Lt. Cdr. W. F. Kimball USNR; light minelayer HENRY A. WILEY Cdr. P. H. Bjarnason; PC-1179.

Unit 8, Lt. Cdr. R. W. Costello USNR: GLADIATOR Lt. Cdr. Costello, IMPECCABLE Lt. Cdr. B. H. Smith USNR, SPEAR Lt. Cdr. A. M. Savage USNR, TRIUMPH Lt. Cdr. C. R. Cunningham USNR & Lt. W. T. Bell USNR, VIGILANCE Lt. Cdr. W. C. Hayes USNR & Lt. J. L. Morton USNR; light minelayer SHEA Cdr. C. C. Kirkpatrick; PC-1598.

TG. 52.5 MINESWEEPER GROUP TWO, Captain L. F. Freiburghouse

Unit 9, Lt. Cdr. J. C. Kettenring USNR: SKIRMISH Lt. B. M. Hyatt USNR, STAUNCH Lt. Cdr. Kettenring, SIGNET Lt. Cdr. C. L. Grabenhorst USNR & Lt. E. H. Gentry

---

* Lost in this operation.

6 Relieved by Capt. R. P. Whitemarsh 5 April; returned to duty 16 April; TERROR relieved 23 Apr. by BIBB Cdr. H. T. Diehl USCG.

USNR, SCURRY Lt. C. E. Dunston USNR, SPECTACLE Lt. G. B. Williams USNR, SPECTOR Lt. Jacques Chevalier USNR; light minelayer TRACY Lt. Cdr. R. E. Carpenter USNR; PGM-9.
Unit 10, Lt. N. R. Hanson USNR: SUPERIOR Lt. Hanson, SERENE Lt. J. E. Calloway USNR, SHELTER Lt. S. D. Letourneau USNR, STRATEGY Lt. V. A. Brown USNR, STRENGTH Lt. W. D. White USNR, SUCCESS Lt. R. N. Hall USNR; light minelayer J. WILLIAM DITTER Cdr. R. R. Sampson; PGM-10.
Unit 11, Lt. Cdr. W. N. McMillen USNR: RANSOM Lt. Cdr. McMillen, DIPLOMA Lt. A. B. Baxter USNR, DENSITY Lt. Cdr. R. R. Forrester USNR, FACILITY Lt. C. R. Jennette USNR, REBEL Lt. F. S. Wooster USNR, RECRUIT Lts. C. L. Henley USNR & W. O. Hankinson USNR; PGM-11.

TG 52.6 MOTOR MINESWEEPER GROUP, Lt. Cdr. C. A. Bowes USNR

Four units, each consisting of one light minelayer: ROBERT H. SMITH Cdrs. Henry Farrow & W. H. Cheney, SHANNON Cdr. E. L. Foster & Lt. Cdr. W. T. Ingram, THOMAS E. FRASER Cdrs. R. J. Woodaman & N. B. Atkins, HARRY F. BAUER Cdr. R. C. Williams.
6 YMS, plus PGM-17 and * PGM-18.
Investigation & Disposal Unit, Cdr. D. N. Clay: light minelayer BREESE Lt. G. W. Knight USNR; 1 YMS; PGM-20.

TG 52.7 RESERVE SWEEP GROUP, Cdrs. E. D. McEathron & J. W. Wyckoff

Unit 19, Cdr. McEathron: BUOYANT Lt. Cdr. W. L. Savell USNR, GAYETY Lts. R. B. Harrell USNR & R. H. Crowe USNR, DESIGN Lt. L. A. Young USNR, DEVICE Lt. Russell Remage USNR, HAZARD Lt. C. B. Tibbals USNR, EXECUTE Lt. R. E. Brenkman USNR.
The following minecraft reported in May: CHIEF Lt. Cdr. A. Winslow USNR, COMPETENT Lt. A. S. Furtwangler USNR, TOKEN Lt. W. T. Hunt USNR; ZEAL Lt. Cdrs. E. W. Woodhouse USNR & S. A. Brand USNR, STRIVE Lt. Cdr. E. B. Knowlton USNR, ORACLE Lt. Cdr. D. W. Deits USNR, VELOCITY Lt. G. J. Buyse USNR, FIXITY Lt. Cdr. A. P. Krieger USNR, PREVAIL Lt. W. M. Mark USNR, DOUR Lt. W. V. Byrd USNR.
Unit 17, Lt. R. N. Compton USNR: 7 YMS (including * YMS-104); Unit 18, Lt. R. E. Crowley USNR: 7 YMS; Unit 20: LCP(R) equipped with sweep gear— embarked in destroyer transports REEVES Lt. Cdrs. J. J. Durney USNR & P. A. Dallis USNR, DANIEL T. GRIFFIN Lt. Cdr. J. A. Eastwood USNR & Lt. E. R. Ferguson USNR, WATERS Lt. Cdr. Sam Halfon USNR, SIMS Lt. F. M. Donahue USNR; Support Unit Cdr. K. F. Horne, minelayers WEEHAWKEN Cdr. W. P. Wrenn USNR, MONADNOCK Lt. Cdr. J. E. Cole USNR; repair ship MONA ISLAND Cdr. Horne.

TG 52.8 NET & BUOY GROUP, Cdr. G. C. King USNR in minelayer SALEM

Three units under Lt. Cdr. J. F. Eddy USNR and Cdrs. R. P. Lewis USNR and L. B. Hillsinger USNR, comprising net tenders SNOWBELL, TEREBINTH, CORKWOOD, SPICEWOOD, CLIFFROSE, STAGBUSH, ABELE, MAHOGANY, ALOE, CHINQUAPIN, WINTERBERRY, PINON; net cargo ships KEOKUK, SAGITTARIUS, TUSCANA.

TG 52.11 UNDERWATER DEMOLITION FLOTILLA
Captain B. Hall Hanlon in GILMER Lieutenant W. C. Quant USNR
Chief of Staff, Cdr. D. L. Kauffman USNR

Group ABLE, Cdr. J. S. Horner: Destroyer transports BATES Lt. Cdrs. H. A. Wilmerding USNR & H. G. Powell USNR, BARR Lt. Cdr. P. T. Dickie, BULL Lt. J. B. McLaughlin & Lt. Cdr. M. Berner USNR, KNUDSON Lt. D. C. Sharp USNR & Lt. Cdr. T. K. Dunstan USNR, with *UDT-12* Lt. Cdr. E. S. Hochuli USNR, *UDT-13* Lt. Cdr.

V. J. Moranz USNR, *UDT–14* Lt. A. B. Onderdonk USNR, *UDT–19* Lt. G. T. Marion USNR.
Group BAKER, Capt. R. D. Williams: Destroyer transports LOY Lt. Cdr. R. W. Pond USNR, HOPPING Lt. W. J. McNulty USNR, KLINE Lt. B. F. Uran USNR, RAYMON W. HERNDON Cdr. S. C. Hale USNR, CROSLEY Lt. Cdr. A. W. P. Trench USNR, BUNCH Lt. B. D. Hyde USNR, with *UDT–4* Lt. Cdr. W. G. Carberry USNR, *UDT–7* Lt. Cdr. R. F. Burke USNR, *UDT–11* Lt. L. A. States USNR, *UDT–16* Lt. E. A. Mitchell USNR, *UDT–17* Lt. A. M. Downes USNR, *UDT–21* Lt. E. P. Clayton.

TG GUNBOAT SUPPORT FLOTILLA, Captain T. C. Aylward in LCI–988
Group One, Cdr. M. J. Malanaphy in LCI–627: 36 LCI (G).
Group Two, Capt. Aylward: 42 LCS(L).
Radio Countermeasures & Rocket Group, Commander C. E. Coffin in LCI–370: 34 LCI(R).
LCM(R) Group Cdr. D. L. Francis: 12 LCM(R).

MORTAR SUPPORT FLOTILLA, Captain T. W. Rimer in LCI–657
Group One, Cdr. L. M. Bailliere USNR in LCI–679: 25 LCI(M); Group Two, Capt. Rimer: 21 LCI(M).

TF 53 NORTHERN ATTACK FORCE

Rear Admiral L. F. Reifsnider in PANAMINT Capt. E. E. Woods
Chief of Staff, Captain E. G. Fullinwider
Major General Roy S. Geiger USMC commanding Northern Landing Force (III Amphibious Corps) embarked

TG 53.1 Transport Group "ABLE," Commodore H. B. Knowles, embarking 6th Marine Division, Major General L. C. Shepherd USMC

Comtransdiv 34, Commo. Knowles: Attack transports CAMBRIA Capt. C. W. Dean USCG, MARVIN H. MCINTYRE Capt. J. J. Hourihan, ADAIR Capts. S. P. Comly & C. V. Lee, GAGE Cdr. L. J. Alexanderson USNR, NOBLE Cdr. S. S. Isquith, GILLIAM, Cdr. H. B. Olsen USNR; attack cargos SHELIAK, Cdr. S. J. Lowery USCG, HYDRUS Lt. Cdr. R. J. Wissinger USNR.
Comtransdiv 35, Capts. S. P. Jenkins & R. C. Bartman: Attack transports CLAY Capt. N. B. Van Bergen, LEON Capt. H. B. Southworth, GEORGE CLYMER Capt. W. H. Benson, ARTHUR MIDDLETON Capt. S. A. Olsen USCG, CATRON Lt. Cdr. D. MacInness USNR; attack cargos CASWELL Lt. Cdr. F. M. Diffley USNR, DEVOSA Lt. Cdr. R. C. Wilkinson USNR.
Comtransdiv 36, Capts. G. W. Johnson & C. L. Tyler: Attack transports MONROVIA Capts. J. D. Kelsey & Olin Scoggins, WAYNE Capt. T. V. Cooper, SUMTER Cdr. J. T. O'Pry USNR, MENIFEE Capt. P. P. Spaulding USNR, FULLER Capt. N. M. Pigman & Cdr. C. B. Hamblett USNR; attack cargos AQUARIUS Cdrs. I. E. Eskridge USCG & E. C. Whitfield USCG, CIRCE Lt. Cdr. V. J. Barnhart USNR; LSD CASA GRANDE Lt. Cdr. F. E. Strumm USNR; landing ship vehicle CATSKILL Capt. R. W. Chambers USNR.

TG 53.2 Transport Group "BAKER," Commodore J. G. Moyer
Embarking 1st Marine Division, Major General Pedro A. del Valle USMC
Comtransdiv 52, Commo. Moyer: Attack transports BURLEIGH Cdr. D. G. Greenlee & Capt. P. G. Wrenn, MCCRACKEN Cdr. B. N. Bock, THOMAS JEFFERSON Capts. J. R. Barbaro & J. F. Madden, CHARLES CARROLL Capt. E. B. Strauss, BARNETT Capts. S. S. Reynolds & W. P. McCarty; attack cargos ANDROMEDA Lt. Cdr. D. W. Ward

USNR, CEPHEUS Cdrs. R. C. Sarratt USCG & D. E. McKay USCG; LSD OAK HILL Cdr. C. A. Peterson USNR; landing ship vehicle MONITOR Cdr. K. J. Olsen USNR. Comtransdiv 53, Capt. W. N. Thornton: Attack transports MARATHON Cdr. John W. McElroy USNR, RAWLINS Cdr. C. S. Beightler USNR, RENVILLE Capt. W. W. Ball USNR, NEW KENT Capt. Frank Monroe & Cdr. J. E. Baker USNR, BURLESON Lt. Cdr. Barnard Hartley USNR; attack cargos CENTAURUS Cdr. J. P. Gray USCGR, ARCTURUS Cdr. C. H. K. Miller.

Comtransdiv 54, Capt. J. R. Lannom: Attack transports DADE Cdr. M. P. DuVal, MAGOFFIN Capt. M. W. Graybill, NAVARRO Cdr. F. E. Angrick USNR, EFFINGHAM Cdr. C. H. McLoughlin, JOSEPH T. DICKMAN Capt. F. A. Leamy USCG; attack cargos BETELGEUSE Lt. Cdr. W. E. Webb USNR, PROCYON Cdr. C. H. Minckler; LSD WHITE MARSH Cdr. G. H. Eppelman USNR & Lt. Cdr. J. V. Hewitt USNR.

TG 53.3 Northern Tractor Flotilla, Capt. J. S. Laidlaw in LC(FF)–1080 [7]

Tractor Group "ABLE" Cdr. A. A. Ageton in LC(FF)–1081: 16 LST carrying 6 LCT, 22 pontoon barges and 6 pontoon causeways; 7 LSM.
Tractor Group "BAKER" Capt. Laidlaw: 16 LST carrying 10 LCT, 16 pontoon barges and 6 pontoon causeways.
Tractor Group "CHARLIE" Capt. Ethelbert Watts in LC(FF)–786: 14 LST carrying 20 pontoon barges; 8 LSM.
Northern Control Group, Capt B. M. Coleman in PCE–872: 4 PC, 5 PCS, 9 SC; Northern Beach Party, Lt. Cdr. R. R. Nelson in SC–630.

TG 53.6 Northern Attack Force Screen,[8] Captain J. H. Wellings: Destroyers MORRIS Cdr. R. V. Wheeler, MUSTIN Lt. Cdr. J. G. Hughes, LANG (with Comdesdiv 4 Cdr. W. T. McGarry embarked) Lt. Cdr. J. T. Bland, STACK Lt. Cdr. S. J. Caldwell, STERETT Lt. Cdr. G. B. Williams, * PRINGLE Lt. Cdr. J. L. Kelley, HUTCHINS (with Comdesdiv 90 Capt. J. W. Schmidt embarked) Lt. Cdr. A. R. Olsen, MASSEY Cdr. C. W. Aldrich, RUSSELL Lt. Cdr. J. E. Wicks, WILSON Cdr. C. J. McKenzie & Lt. Cdr. W. L. Roberts USNR, STANLY Cdr. R. S. Harlan, HOWORTH Cdr. E. S. Burns, HUGH W. HADLEY Cdrs. B. J. Mullaney & R. J. Newton; destroyer escorts GENDREAU (with Comcortdiv 73 Cdr. R. H. Groff USNR embarked) Lt. Martin Victor USNR, FIEBERLING Cdr. E. E. Lull USNR & Lt. Cdr. A. M. Gendreau USNR, WILLIAM C. COLE Lt. Cdr. C. Harrold USNR, PAUL G. BAKER Lt. Cdr. W. G. Cornell USNR, BEBAS Lt. Cdrs. J. R. Schweizer USNR & M. M. Dichter USNR; destroyer transports CHARLES LAWRENCE Lt. Cdr. G. R. Seidlitz USNR, ROPER Lt. Cdr. U. B. Carter USNR & Lt. W. B. Sanderson USNR; 2 PCE(R); 1 SC.

TG 53.7 Northern Defense Group, Capt. W. W. Weeden in LC(FF)–790, embarking Marine Corps support units and high priority cargo: 21 LST carrying LCT & pontoon causeways; oil storage ships ELK, CAMEL; destroyer escort FAIR Lt. Cdr. W. E. Biggerstaff USNR; 2 SC; 7 YMS.

TF 55 SOUTHERN ATTACK FORCE

Rear Admiral John L. Hall in TETON, Capt. D. R. Tallman

Chief of Staff, Captain M. N. Little

Major General John R. Hodge USA Commanding Southern Landing Force (XXIV Army Corps), and Air Support Control Unit, Capt. M. F. Leslie, embarked

TG 55.1 Transport Group "DOG," Commodore M. O. Carlson, embarking 7th Infantry Division, Maj. Gen. A. V. Arnold USA.

* Lost in this operation.

[7] An LC(FF) is an LCI equipped as flagship for a control group.
[8] To 1 April when screening destroyers received new assignments.

Transdiv 37, Commo. Carlson: Attack transports HARRIS Capts. M. E. Murphy & G. L. Burns USNR, LAMAR Capts. B. K. Culver & J. P. Rockwell, SHERIDAN Capt. P. H. Wiedorn, PIERCE Capt. F. M. Adams & Cdr. C. C. Ray, TYRRELL Lt. Cdr. J. L. McLean USNR; attack cargo ALGORAB Cdr. T. C. Green.

Transdiv 38, Capt. P. P. Welch: Attack transports BARNSTABLE Capt. H. T. Walsh, ELMORE Capt. J. L. Reynolds, ALPINE Cdr. G. K. G. Reilly; attack cargos LYCOMING Cdr. D. B. Coleman, ALSHAIN Lt. Cdr. B. W. Strickland USNR; LSD EPPING FOREST Capt. Lester Martin USNR & Lt. Cdr. R. J. Kaltenbacher USNR.

Transdiv 39, Capts. D. L. Ryan & G. E. Maynard: Attack transports CUSTER Capts. W. E. Terry & W. A. McDowell, FREESTONE Capt. C. L. Carpenter, KITTSON Capts. G. B. Helmick & W. A. P. Martin, BAXTER Capt. V. R. Sinclair; attack cargos ALGOL Lt. Cdr. A. T. Jones USNR, ARNEB Cdr. E. T. Collins USNR.

Transdiv 13, Capt. F. P. Williams: Landing ship vehicle OZARK Capt. Williams; attack transports APPLING Cdr. A. L. Stuart USNR & Lt. Cdr. E. T. Conlon USNR, BUTTE Lt. Cdr. J. A. Gillis USNR, AUDRAIN Cdr. G. O. Forrest USNR, LAURENS Capt. Donald McGregor; attack cargos AURELIA Cdr. E. G. MacMurdy USNR, CORVUS Cdr. C. M. Gregson USNR.

Tractor Group "DOG," Capt. W. H. Brereton in LCI-994: 16 LST, 12 LSM, 2 LCI.

Tractor Group "FOX," Capt. E. A. Seay in LCI-425: 14 LST carrying LCT and pontoon barges; 10 LSM.

TG 55.2 Transport Group "EASY," Commo. C. G. Richardson, embarking 96th Infantry Division, Maj. Gen. J. L. Bradley USA.

Transdiv 40, Commos. Richardson & D. L. Ryan: Attack transports MENDOCINO Capts. W. R. Read & Frank Monroe, SARASOTA Cdr. J. I. MacPherson USNR, HASKELL Cdr. A. L. Mare, OCONTO Cdr. Paul Jackson USNR; attack cargos CAPRICORNUS Lt. Cdr. B. F. McGuckin USNR & Cdr. C. A. Joans USNR, CHARA Cdr. J. P. Clark USNR; LSD LINDENWALD Capt. R. W. Cutler USNR & Lt. Cdr. D. F. Owen USNR.

Transdiv 41, Capt. H. J. Wright: Attack transports OLMSTEAD Capt. C. E. A. Spigel USNR, LA PORTE Cdr. M. C. Thompson, FOND DU LAC Capt. E. P. Creehan, BANNER Lt. Cdr. J. R. Pace USNR; attack cargos DIPHDA Lt. Cdr. R. C. Willson USNR, UVALDE Lt. Cdr. W. M. McCloy USNR.

Transdiv 42, Capts. E. T. Short & A. R. Mack: Attack transports NESHOBA Capt. M. J. Drury, OXFORD Capts. P. S. Crandall & J. C. Goodnough, LATIMER Capts. J. P. Dix & J. J. O'Donnell, EDGECOMBE Cdr. F. W. Wauchope USNR; attack cargo VIRGO Lt. Cdr. H. E. Randall USNR; LSD GUNSTON HALL Lt. W. F. Bentley USNR & Lt. Cdr. M. A. Powell USNR.

Transdiv 14, Capt. J. J. Twomey: Attack transports ALLENDALE Capt. Twomey, MERIWETHER Capt. A. M. Cohan, MENARD Cdr. J. B. Bliss, KENTON Capt. V. B. Tate & Cdr. G. B. Ogle; attack cargo ACHERNAR Lt. Cdr. J. R. Lange USNR.

Tractor Group "EASY," Capt. C. H. Peterson USCG in LCI-398: 23 LST, 5 LSM.

Beach Party Unit "EASY," Lt. Cdr. T. H. Ochiltree USNR.

LCS Support Division 5, Lt. B. A. Thirkfield USNR: 6 LCS(L).

Southern Control Group, Capt. B. B. Adell in PCE-877: 4 PCS, 4 PC, 7 SC;

Southern Beach Party, Cdr. L. C. Leever USNR in SC-1272.

Southern Support Gunboats, Cdr. L. M. Bailliere USNR in LC(FF)-679: 11 LCS(L); 6 LSM(R) including * LSM(R)-190.

* Lost in this operation.

TG 55.6 Southern Attack Force Screen,[9] Capt. E. W. Young: Destroyers ANTHONY Cdr. C. J. Van Arsdall, BACHE Lt. Cdr. A. R. McFarland, * BUSH (with Comdesdiv 48 * Cdr. J. S. Willis embarked) Cdr. R. E. Westholm, MULLANY Cdr. A. O. Momm & Lt. Cdr. A. R. Drea, BENNETT (with Comdesron 45 Capt. J. C. Daniel embarked) Cdr. J. N. McDonald, HUDSON Cdr. R. R. Pratt, HYMAN Cdr. R. N. Norgaard, PURDY Cdr. F. L. Johnson, BEALE Cdr. D. M. Coffee & Lt. Cdr. A. B. Register, WADSWORTH Cdr. R. D. Fusselman, AMMEN Cdr. J. H. Brown & Lt. Cdr. G. V. Rogers, PUTNAM (with Comdesron 66 Capt. G. R. Hartwig embarked) Cdr. F. V. H. Hilles, ROOKS Cdr. J. A. McGoldrick; destroyer transport SIMS Lt. F. M. Donahue USNR; destroyer escorts CROUTER Lt. Cdr. C. F. Braught USNR, CARL-SON Lt. Cdr. M. S. Loewith USNR, DAMON M. CUMMINGS Lt. Cdr. C. R. Millett USNR, VAMMEN Cdr. L. M. King USNR & Lt. G. Washburn USNR, O'NEILL Lt. Cdr. D. S. Bill & Lt. N. A. Townsend USNR, WALTER C. WANN Lt. Cdr. J. W. Stedman USNR; 1 PCE(R), 2 SC. Comdesdiv 126, Capt. C. A. Buchanan, was in HYMAN, later PURDY.

TG 55.7 Southern Defense Group Cdr. B. T. Zelenka: Destroyer escort MAN-LOVE Lt. Cdr. E. P. Foster & Lt. J. R. McKee USNR; destroyer transport STRINGHAM Lt. J. B. Schlel USNR; 34 LST (including * LST-447), 14 LSM, 6 YMS, 2 LCI; oil storage ship GRUMIUM Lt. Cdr. B. J. Parylak USNR.

TG 55.9 Southern LCT & Pontoon Barge Group, Cdr. A. J. Benline USNR. LCT Flotillas 16 & 21, Lt. Cdrs. C. P. Lewis USNR & W. B. Gillette USNR: 60 LCT.

TG 51.3 Floating Reserve, Commo. J. B. McGovern (Comtransron 16), with Major General G. W. Griner USA commanding 27th Infantry Division: 21 trans-ports, 10 LCM, 6 destroyer escorts. Mounted at Espiritu Santo, arrived Ulithi 2 April, and landed troops Okinawa 9 April.

TG 50.5 SEARCH & RECONNAISSANCE GROUP
Commodore Dixwell Ketcham

Seaplane tenders HAMLIN Capt. G. A. McLean supporting VPB-208: 12 PBM-5 (Mariner) Lt. Cdr. A. J. Sintic USNR; ST. GEORGE Capt. R. G. Armstrong supporting VPB-18: 12 PBM-5 Lt. Cdr. R. R. Boettcher; CHANDELEUR Cdr. J. S. Tracy sup-porting VPB-21: 12 PBM-3 Lt. Cdrs. J. E. Dougherty & J. D. Wright.

Small seaplane tenders YAKUTAT Cdr. G. K. Fraser, ONSLOW Cdr. A. D. Schwarz, SHELIKOF Cdr. R. E. Stanley, supporting VPB-27: 12 PBM-5 Lt. Cdr. E. N. Chase; BERING STRAIT Cdr. W. D. Innis supporting VH-3: 6 PBM-3R Lt. Cdr. W. D. Bon-villian.

Destroyer seaplane tenders * THORNTON Lt. L. F. Beibel USNR, GILLIS Lt. J. C. Sul-livan USNR; destroyer WILLIAMSON Lt. W. H. Ayer.

TG 51.2 DEMONSTRATION GROUP "CHARLIE"

Rear Admiral Jerauld Wright in ANCON Capts. M. S. Pearson & W. E. Lankeneau Embarking Demonstration Landing Force (2nd Marine Division) Major General T. E. Watson USMC.

Transron 15, Commo. H. C. Flanagan: Attack transports BAYFIELD Capt. W. R. Richards USCG, MELLETTE Cdr. F. H. Spring USNR, HENDRY Capt. R. C. Welles, SIBLEY Cdr. E. I. McQuiston, BERRIEN Lt. Cdr. J. M. Gallagher USNR; attack cargos SHOSHONE Lt. Cdr. S. E. Melville USNR & Cdr. J. A. Flenniken, THEENIM Cdr. G. A. Littlefield USCG, SOUTHAMPTON Lt. Cdr. L. V. Cooke USNR; evacuation transport PINKNEY Cdr. A. A. Downing USNR.

---

[9] To 1 April when screening destroyers were given new assignments.

TF 58 FAST CARRIER FORCE PACIFIC FLEET
Vice Admiral Marc A. Mitscher in BUNKER HILL

Chief of Staff, Commodore Arleigh A. Burke

TG 58.1 TASK GROUP ONE Rear Admiral J. J. Clark

Carrier		HORNET	Capt. A. K. Doyle

Air Group 17: Commander E. G. Konrad

VF-17	61	F6F-5, 6 F6F-5P, 4 F6F-5N	Lt. Cdrs. M. U. Beebe & H. W. Nicholson USNR
VB-17	9	SB2C-3 2 SB2C-4, 4 SBW (Helldivers)	Lt. Cdr. R. M. Ware
VT-17	15	TBM-3	Lt. Cdr. W. M. Romberger USNR

Carrier		WASP	Capts. O. A. Weller & W. G. Switzer

Air Group 86: Commander G. R. Luker

VBF-86	36	F4U-1D (Corsair)	Lt. Cdr. H. E. Tennes USNR
VF-86	28	F6F-5, 2 F6F-5E, 2 F6F-5P, 2 F6F-5N	Lt. Cdr. C. J. Dobson USNR
VB-86	15	SB2C-4	Lt. Cdr. P. R. Nopby USNR
VT-86	15	TBM-3	Lt. Cdr. L. F. Steffenhagen USNR

Carrier		BENNINGTON	Capts. J. B. Sykes & B. L. Braun

Air Group 82: Commander G. L. Heap

VF-82	29	F6F-5, 2 F6F-5E, 2 F6F-5P, 4 F6F-5N	Lt. Cdr. E. W. Hessel
VB-82	15	SB2C-4E	Lt. Cdr. Hugh Wood
VT-82	15	TBM-3	Lt. Cdr. E. E. DeGarmo
VMF-112	18	F4U-1D	Maj. Herman Hansen USMC
VMF-123	17	F4U-1D	Maj. T. E. Mobley USMCR

Light Carrier		BELLEAU WOOD	Capts. John Perry & W. G. Tomlinson

Air Group 30: Lieutenant Commander D. A. Clark

VF-30	24	F6F-5, 1 F6F-5P	Lt. Cdr. Clark
VT-30	8	TBM-3, 1 TBM-3P	Lts. F. C. Tothill USNR & R. F. Regan USNR

Light Carrier		SAN JACINTO	Capt. M. H. Kernodle

Air Group 45: Commander G. E. Schecter

VF-45	24	F6F-5, 1 F6F-5P	Cdr. Schecter
VT-45	9	TBM-3	Lt. J. G. Pregari USNR

Batdiv 8, Rear Admiral J. F. Shafroth: MASSACHUSETTS Capts. W. W. Warlick & J. R. Redman, INDIANA Capts. T. J. Keliher & F. P. Old.

Crudiv 10, Rear Admiral L. J. Wiltse: Heavy cruisers BALTIMORE Capt. C. K. Fink, PITTSBURGH Capt. J. E. Gingrich.

Crudiv 14, Rear Admiral F. E. M. Whiting: Light cruisers VINCENNES Capt. W. G. Lalor, MIAMI Capt. T. H. Binford, VICKSBURG Capt. W. C. Vose, SAN JUAN Capts. J. F. Donovan & G. H. Bahm.

Desron 61 & Desdiv 121, Capts. J. H. Carter & T. H. Hederman: DEHAVEN Cdrs. J. B. Dimmick & W. H. Groverman, MANSFIELD Cdr. L. W. Smythe, LYMAN K. SWENSON Cdrs. F. T. Williamson & W. B. Braun, COLLETT Cdr. J. D. Collett, MADDOX Cdr. S. K. Santmyers. Desdiv 122, Cdr. C. K. Bergin & Capt. R. J. Archer:

Appendix I 383

BLUE Cdrs. Lot Ensey & L. A. Bryan, BRUSH Cdrs. J. E. Edwards & J. V. Smith, TAUSSIG Cdrs. J. A. Robbins & W. H. McClain, SAMUEL N. MOORE Cdr. H. A. Lincoln. Desdiv 106, Capts. J. H. Hogg & G. K. Carmichael: WEDDERBURN Cdr. C. H. Kendell & Lt. Cdr. R. W. Clark, TWINING Cdr. F. V. List, STOCKHAM Cdrs. M. G. Johnson & D. L. Moody. Desron 25 & Desdiv 49, Capt. J. W. Ludewig: JOHN RODGERS Cdr. J. G. Franklin, STEVENS Cdr. G. W. Pressey & Lt. Cdr. R. A. Schelling, HARRISON Cdr. W. V. Combs, MCKEE Cdr. R. B. Allen, MURRAY Cdr. P. L. de Vos. Desdiv 50, Capts. H. O. Parish & W. C. Winn: SIGSBEE Cdrs. G. P. Chung-Hoon & H. A. Barnard, RINGGOLD Cdr. W. B. Christie, SCHROEDER Cdr. R. W. McElrath, DASHIELL Cdr. D. L. L. Cordiner.

TG 58.2 TASK GROUP TWO, Rear Admirals R. E. Davison & G. F. Bogan

	Carrier	ENTERPRISE	Captain G. B. H. Hall
	Night Air Group 90: Commander W. I. Martin		
VFN-90	11 F6F-5E, 2 F6F-5P, 19 F6F-5N		Lt. Cdr. R. J. McCullough USNR & Lt. C. B. Collins USNR
VTN-90	21 TBM-3D		Lt. R. F. Kippen USNR
	Carrier	FRANKLIN	Captain L. E. Gehres
	Air Group 5: Commander E. B. Parker		
VF-5	2 F6F-5P, 4 F6F-5N, 2 FG-1D (Corsair), 30 F4U-1D		Lt. Cdr. M. Kilpatrick
VB-5	15 SB2C-4E		Lt. Cdr. J. G. Sheridan
VT-5	15 TBM-3		Lt. Cdr. A. C. Edmands
	Carrier	RANDOLPH	Captain F. L. Baker
	Air Group 12: Commanders * C. L. Crommelin, E. J. Pawka USNR		
VF-12	25 F6F-5, 2 F6F-5E, 2 F6F-5P, 4 F6F-5N		Cdr. N. A. M. Gayler
VBF-12	24 F6F-5		Lt. Cdr. J. C. Lawrence
VB-12	15 SB2C-4E		Cdr. R. A. Embree
VT-12	15 TBM-3		Lt. Cdr. T. B. Ellison

Light cruiser SANTA FE Captain H. C. Fitz

Desron 52 & Desdiv 103, Capts. J. P. Womble & H. C. Daniel: OWEN Cdr. C. B. Jones, MILLER Lt. Cdr. D. L. Johnson, STEPHEN POTTER Lt. Cdr. G. R. Muse, TINGEY Cdr. K. S. Shook & Lt. Cdr. W. K. Rogers. Desdiv 104, Cdr. P. L. High: HICKOX Cdrs. J. H. Wesson & G. L. Christie, HUNT Cdr. H. A. Knoertzer & Lt. Cdr. F. E. McEntire, LEWIS HANCOCK Cdrs. W. M. Searles & R. E. Babb, MARSHALL Cdr. J. D. McKinney & Lt. Cdr. C. Holovak.

TG 58.3 TASK GROUP THREE, Rear Admiral F. C. Sherman

Carrier		ESSEX	Captain C. W. Wieber
	Air Group 83; Cdr. H. T. Utter		
VF-83	28 F6F-5, 2 F6F-5E, 2 F6F-5P, 4 F6F-5N		Cdr. J. J. Southerland
VBF-83	36 F4U-1D		Lt. Cdr. F. A. Patriarca
VB-83	15 SB2C-4		Lt. Cdr. D. R. Berry
VT-83	15 TBM-3		Lt. Cdr. H. A. Stewart

* Lost in this operation.

Carrier	BUNKER HILL	Captain G. A. Seitz

Air Group 84: Commander G. M. Ottinger

VF–84	6 F6F–5P, 4 F6F–5N, 27 F4U–1D	Lt. Cdr. R. R. Hedrick
VB–84	2 SB2C–4, 13 SB2C–4E	Lt. Cdr. J. P. Conn USNR
VT–84	15 TBM–3	Lt. Cdr. C. W. Swanson
VMF–221	18 F4U–1D	Maj. E. S. Roberts USMCR
VMF–451	18 F4U–1D	Maj. H. A. Ellis USMC

Carrier	HANCOCK	Captain R. F. Hickey

Air Group 6: Commander H. L. Miller

VF–6	28 F6F–5, 2 F6F–5E, 2 F6F–5P, 4 F6F–5N	Lt. Cdr. R. L. Copeland USNR
VBF–6	36 F6F–5	Lt. Cdr. R. W. Schumann
VB–6	5 SB2C–3 & –3E, 3 SB2C–4, 4 SBW–3 & –4E	Lt. Cdr. G. P. Chase
VT–6	10 TBM–3	Lt. Cdr. W. G. Privette USNR

Light carrier	CABOT	Captain Walton W. Smith

Air Group 29: Lieutenant Commander W. E. Eder

VF–29	25 F6F–5	Lt. Cdr. Eder
VT–29	9 TBM–3	Lt. Cdr. I. H. McPherson USNR

Light carrier	BATAAN	Captain J. B. Heath

Air Group 47: Cdr. Walker Etheridge & Lt. Cdr. A. H. Clancy

VF–47	23 F6F–5, 1 F6F–5P	Cdr. Etheridge & Lt. Cdr. Clancy
VT–47	12 TBM–3	Lt. Cdr. H. R. Mazza USNR

Batdiv 6, Rear Admiral T. R. Cooley: WASHINGTON Capts. R. F. Good and F. X. McInerney, NORTH CAROLINA Capts. O. S. Colclough & B. H. Hanlon, SOUTH DAKOTA (Combatpac Vice Adm. W. A. Lee embarked) [10] Capts. C. F. Stillman & C. B. Momsen.

Heavy cruiser INDIANAPOLIS (flagship of Admiral Spruance), Capt. C. B. McVay. Crudiv 17, Rear Admiral J. Cary Jones: Light cruisers PASADENA Capts. R. B. Tuggle & J. H. Doyle, SPRINGFIELD Capts. F. L. Johnson & T. J. Kelley, ASTORIA Capts. G. C. Dyer & W. V. Hamilton, WILKES-BARRE Capt. R. L. Porter.

Desron 62 & Desdiv 123, Capts. J. M. Higgins & W. D. Brown: AULT Cdrs. J. C. Wylie & D. S. Edwards, ENGLISH Cdrs. J. T. Smith & W. H. Baumberger, CHARLES S. SPERRY Cdrs. H. H. McIlhenny & J. B. Morland, WALDRON Cdr. G. E. Peckham, HAYNSWORTH Cdr. S. N. Tackney. Desdiv 124, Capt. Richard W. Smith: WALLACE L. LIND Cdr. George Demetropolis, JOHN W. WEEKS Cdrs. R. A. Theobald & W. L. Harmon, HANK Cdr. G. M. Chambers, BORIE Cdr. Noah Adair. Desron 48 & Desdiv 95, Capts. W. J. Marshall & H. H. Henderson; ERBEN Cdr. Morgan Slayton & Lt. Cdr. W. H. Snyder, WALKER Cdr. P. D. Quirk, HALE Cdr. D. W. Wilson, STEMBEL Cdr. M. S. Schmidling. Desdiv 96, Cdr. L. C. Chamberlin: BLACK Cdr. E. R. King, BULLARD Cdr. B. W. Freund & Lt. Cdr. E. T. Steen, KIDD Cdr. H. G. Moore [11] CHAUNCEY Cdr. L. C. Conwell & Lt. Cdr. P. B. Haines.

---

[10] Until 27 May, when detached to set up anti-kamikaze research unit at Casco Bay, Maine, where he died 25 Aug. 1945.

[11] Wounded 11 Apr., Lts. B. H. Brittin USNR and R. L. Kenney USNR assuming command; Lt. Cdr. F. M. Bush became C.O. 30 Apr.

TG 58.4 TASK GROUP FOUR, Rear Admiral A. W. Radford

Carrier YORKTOWN Captains T. S. Combs & W. F. Boone

Air Group 9: [12] Commander P. H. Torrey & Lieutenant Commander
H. N. Houck USNR

VF-9	40 F6F-5, -5E, -5P & -5N	Lt. Cdr. Houck USNR &
		Lt. J. S. Kitchen USNR
VBF-9	33 F6F-5	Cdr. F. L. Lawlor USNR
VB-9	15 SB2C-4	Lt. Cdr. T. F. Schneider
VT-9	6 TBM-3, 1 TBM-3P	Lt. Cdr. B. E. Cooke &
		Lt. T. H. Stetson

Carrier INTREPID Captain G. E. Short

Air Group 10: Commander J. J. Hyland

VF-10	2 F6F-5P, 4 F6F-5N, 1 FG-1, 29 F4U-1D	Lt. Cdr. W. E. Clarke
VBF-10	36 F4U-1D	Lt. Cdr. W. E. Rawie
VB-10	15 SB2C-4E	Lt. Cdr. R. B. Buchan
VT-10	15 TBM-3	Lt. Cdr. J. C. Lawrence

Light carrier LANGLEY Captain J. F. Wegforth

Air Group 23: * Lt. Cdr. Merlin Paddock USNR & Cdr. J. J. Southerland

VF-23	3 F6F-3, 21 F6F-5, 1 F6F-5P	* Lt. Cdr. Paddock & Cdr.
		Southerland
VT-23	9 TBM-1C	Lt. D. A. Pattie USNR

Light carrier INDEPENDENCE Captain N. M. Kindell

Air Group 46: Commander C. W. Rooney

| VF-46 | 24 F6F-5, 1F6F-5P | Cdr. Rooney |
| VT-46 | 8 TBM-3 | Lt. J. P. Barron |

Batdiv 9, Rear Admirals E. W. Hanson & L. E. Denfeld: WISCONSIN Capts. E. E. Stone & J. W. Roper, MISSOURI Capts. W. M. Callaghan & S. S. Murray, NEW JERSEY Capt. E. T. Wooldridge.

Crudiv 16, Rear Admiral F. S. Low: Large cruisers ALASKA Capt. K. H. Noble, GUAM Capt. L. P. Lovette; light cruisers ST. LOUIS Capt. J. B. Griggs, FLINT Capt. C. R. Will, OAKLAND Capt. K. S. Reed, SAN DIEGO Capt. W. E. A. Mullan.

Desron 54 & Desdiv 107, Capt. P. V. Mercer: REMEY Cdr. R. P. Fiala & Lt. Cdr. J. B. Balch, NORMAN SCOTT Cdr. W. B. Porter, MERTZ Cdr. W. S. Maddox, MONSSEN Lt. Cdr. E. G. Sanderson. Desdiv 108, Cdrs. R. H. Phillips & W. A. Cockell: McGOWAN Cdr. W. R. Cox & Lt. Cdr. T. H. W. Connor, McNAIR Cdrs. M. L. McCullough & B. P. Ross, MELVIN Cdr. B. K. Atkins. Desron 47, and Desdiv 93, Capts. I. H. Nunn & J. H. Sides: McCORD Cdr. F. D. Michael, TRATHEN Cdr. J. R. Millet, HAZELWOOD * Cdr. V. P. Douw, Lt. D. N. Mobey USNR, & Lt. Cdr. J. C. Mathews, HEERMANN Cdr. A. T. Hathaway. Desdiv 94, Capt. L. K. Reynolds & Cdr. W. M. Searles: HAGGARD Lt. Cdr. V. J. Soballe, FRANKS * Cdr. D. R. Stephan, Lt.

* Lost in this operation.

[12] Replaced 27 June by AG 88, Commander S. S. Searcy: —
VF-88: 30 F6F-5, 3 F6F-5P, 6 F6F-5N, * Lt. Cdr. R. G. Crommelin & Lt M. W. Cagle.
VBF-88 37 FG-1D (Corsair), Lt. Cdr. J. E. Hart USNR.
VB-88 9 SB2C-4, 6 SB2C-4E, Lt. Cdr. J. S. Elkins.
VT-88 14 TBM-3, 1 TBM-3E, Lt. Cdr. J. C. Huddleston USNR.

G. F. Case, & Lt. Cdr. E. B. Henry, HAILEY Lt. Cdr. J. N. Payne. Desron 53 & Desdiv 105, Capts. H. B. Jarrett & W. G. Beecher: CUSHING Cdr. L. F. Volk & Lt. Cdr. W. D. Adams, COLAHAN Cdr. M. A. Shellabarger, UHLMANN Cdrs. S. G. Hooper & S. E. Small, BENHAM Cdr. F. S. Keeler & Lt. Cdr. W. L. Poindexter.

As Reorganized 7 April, TG 58.1, Rear Admiral Clark, comprised HORNET, BENNINGTON, BELLEAU WOOD, SAN JACINTO, MASSACHUSETTS, INDIANA, VINCENNES, MIAMI, VICKSBURG, SAN JUAN, Desrons 25, 61.

TG 58.2, Rear Admiral Bogan, comprised RANDOLPH, ENTERPRISE, INDEPENDENCE, WASHINGTON, NORTH CAROLINA, BALTIMORE, PITTSBURGH, FLINT, OAKLAND, Desrons 52, 53, Desdiv 106.

TG 58.3, Rear Admiral Sherman, comprised ESSEX, BUNKER HILL, SHANGRI-LA,[13] BATAAN, NEW JERSEY, SOUTH DAKOTA, PASADENA, SPRINGFIELD, ASTORIA, WILKES-BARRE, Desrons 45, 62, 84.

TG 58.4, Rear Admiral Radford, comprised YORKTOWN, INTREPID, ENTERPRISE,[14] LANGLEY, WISCONSIN, MISSOURI, ALASKA, GUAM, SAN DIEGO, Desrons 47, 54.

TG 50.8 LOGISTICS SUPPORT GROUP FIFTH FLEET, Rear Admiral D. B. Beary in DETROIT Captain Duncan Curry

Support escort carriers SHAMROCK BAY, Captains F. T. Ward & J. E. Leeper with VC-94: 18 FM-2, 12 TBM-3 * Lt. Cdr. J. F. Patterson USNR & Lt. L. E. Terry; MAKASSAR STRAIT Captain H. D. Riley with VC-97: 14 FM-2, 12 TBM-3 Lt. Cdr. M. T. Whittier USNR.

TU 50.8.4 CVE Plane Transport Unit

Escort carriers ATTU Capt. H. F. MacComsey, ADMIRALTY ISLANDS Capt. M. E. A. Gouin, BOUGAINVILLE Capt. C. A. Bond, WINDHAM BAY Capt. G. T. Mundorff.

Ammunition ships: AKUTAN Lt. Cdr. W. B. Murphey & Cdr. R. C. Brown, FIREDRAKE Cdr. Aloysius Elb USNR, LASSEN Cdr. J. E. Wade USNR, MAUNA LOA Capt. G. D. Martin, SHASTA Lt. Cdr. W. H. St. George USNR, VESUVIUS Lt. Cdr. F. J. George USNR, WRANGELL Cdr. H. C. Todd, * CANADA VICTORY Master William MacDonald, BEDFORD v. Lt. Cdr. D. A. Durrant USNR, BUCYRUS v. Lt. Cdr. F. A. Geissert, MANDERSON v. Lt. Cdr. John Larsen, LAS VEGAS v. Lt. Cdr. W. F. Lally USNR, * LOGAN v., GREENBURG v., PIERRE v., * HOBBS v.

Reefers (store ships): ADRIA Lt. Cdrs. L. W. Borst USNR & C. R. Paul USNR, ATHANASIA Lt. J. J. Borden USNR, BRIDGE Cdr. T. N. Saul USNR, LATONA Lt. Cdr. N. W. Landis USNR, LIOBA Lt. S. T. Boisdore USNR, MERAPI Lt. Cdr. W. W. Wood USNR.

Survey ships: ARMISTEAD RUST Lt. J. G. Carlson USNR, BOWDITCH Cdr. H. C. Behner.

Hospital ships: BOUNTIFUL Lt. Cdr. P. W. Mallard USNR, COMFORT Lt. Cdr. Adin Tooker USNR, HOPE Cdr. A. E. Richards USNR, MERCY Capt. T. A. Esling USNR, RELIEF Lt. Cdr. J. C. Sever USNR, SAMARITAN Cdr. W. A. McCreery USNR, SOLACE Cdr. E. B. Peterson; transport WHARTON Capt. W. D. Ryan USNR.

Cargo ships: ADHARA Lt. Cdr. A. W. Callaway USNR, ALKAID Cdr. E. G. Gummer USNR, ALKES Lt. Cdr. C. L. Wickman, ALLEGAN Lt. Cdr. J. S. Hulings USNR, APPANOOSE Cdr. V. H. S. Holm USNR, FOMALHAUT Capt. R. V. Mullany, MATAR Lt.

* Lost in this operation.

13 Joined toward end of April.
14 Detached from TG 58.2 on 10 April.

H. A. Weston USNR, MINTAKA Lt. Cdr. M. J. Johnson USNR, ROTANIN Lt. Cdr. C. H. Lehlleitner USNR.

Stores-Issue ships: ANTARES Lt. Cdr. J. E. Kendall USNR, CASTOR Capt. F. C. Huntoon USNR, KOCHAB Lt. Cdr. R. E. King USNR.

Oilers: CUYAMA Lt. Cdr. C. R. West USNR, BRAZOS Lt. Cdr. G. A. Haussler USNR, CIMARRON Lt. Cdr. H. G. Schnaars USNR, PLATTE Capt. F. S. Gibson USNR & Cdr. L. M. Fabian USNR, SABINE Lt. Cdr. H. C. VonWeien USNR, KASKASKIA Lt. Cdrs. W. F. Patten USNR & T. D. Arthur USNR, GUADALUPE Lt. Cdr. C. A. Boddy USNR & Cdr. R. N. Gardner USNR, CHICOPEE Lt. Cdr. C. O. Peak USNR, HOUSATONIC Lt. Cdr. J. Ducat USNR, MERRIMACK Capt. V. Bailey, KANKAKEE Lt. Cdr. W. G. Frundt USNR, LACKAWANNA Cdr. A. J. Homann, MONONGAHELA Cdr. F. J. Ilsemann, TAPPAHANNOCK Cdr. H. Corman, PATUXENT Lt. Cdr. F. P. Ferrell USNR & Lt. Cdr. K. R. Hall USNR, NECHES Cdr. H. G. Hansen USNR, SUAMICO Cdr. A. S. Johnson & Lt. Cdr. N. C. Bishop USNR, TALLULAH Lt. Cdr. W. F. Huckaby USNR, ASHTABULA Lt. Cdr. M. K. Reece USNR, CACAPON Cdr. G. D. Arntz USNR, CALIENTE Lt. Cdr. F. N. Lang USNR & Cdr. G. L. Eastman USNR, CHIKASKIA Lt. Cdr. G. G. Boyd USNR, AUCILLA Lt. Cdr. C. L. Cover USNR, MARIAS Cdr. J. G. Olsen USNR, MANATEE Lt. Cdr. J. B. Smyth USNR, NANTAHALA Cdr. A. C. Larsen USNR, SEVERN Lt. Cdr. Owen Rees, TALUGA Cdr. H. M. Mikkelsen USNR, CHIPOLA Cdr. E. G. Genthner USNR, TOLOVANA Lt. Cdr. C. G. Long USNR, PECOS Lt. Cdr. G. W. Renegar USNR, ATASCOSA Cdr. H. L. de Rivera, CACHE Lt. Cdr. C. R. Cosgrove USNR, ENOREE Lt. Cdr. E. L. Jurewicz USNR, ESCALANTE Capt. W. I. Stevens USNR, NESHANIC Capt. A. C. Allen USNR, NIOBRARA Cdr. R. C. Spalding USNR, MILLICOMA Cdr. G. E. Ely USNR & Lt. Cdr. J. W. Home USNR, SARANAC Lt. Cdr. C. G. Strom USNR, COSSATOT Lt. Cdr. C. H. Glenwright USNR, COWANESQUE Capt. L. S. McKenzie USNR, ESCAMBIA Lt. Cdr. R. Goorigian USNR, CAHABA Lt. Cdr. J. Burnbaum USNR, MASCOMA Lt. Cdr. H. P. Timmers USNR, OCKLAWAHA Lt. Cdr. R. C. Foyt USNR, PONAGANSET Capt. J. R. Sanford USNR, SEBEC Cdr. H. M. Elder USNR, TOMAHAWK Lt. Cdr. W. L. Eagleton USNR, ANACOSTIA Lt. Cdr. T. H. Hoffman USNR.

Gasoline tankers: WABASH, GENESEE, KISHWAUKEE, NEMASKET, ESCATAWPA, HIWASSEE, ONTONAGON, YAHARA, PONCHATOULA, SACANDAGA.

Station tankers: ARMADILLO, GIRAFFE, MARMORA, MOOSE, WHIPPET, LCI(L)-993.

Repair ships: VESTAL, ARISTAEUS, NESTOR, OCEANUS, ANCHOR, CLAMP, CURRENT, DELIVER, GEAR, SHACKLE.

Floating drydocks: ARD-13, -22, -27, -28; AFD-14; AFDL-32.

Fleet tugs: ARIKARA, CHICKASAW, CREE, LIPAN, MATACO, MENOMINEE, MUNSEE, PAKANA, TAWAKONI, TEKESTA, TENINO, UTE.

4 ocean tugs; 3 ocean tugs, rescue.

LOGISTICS SUPPORT GROUP SCREEN

From a pool of 11 destroyers and 24 destroyer escorts, escorts were assigned to TG 50.8 units as required. The squadron and division commanders were Capts. W. M. Cole, H. F. Stout & J. R. Pahl; Cdrs. B. N. Wev, C. K. Hutchison, W. S. Howard, J. W. Golinkin USNR, D. C. Brown USNR.

TG 50.9 SERVICE SQUADRON 10, Commodore W. R. Carter at Ulithi

Destroyer tenders DIXIE Capt. G. H. Lyttle, PRAIRIE Capts. O. A. Kneeland & F. S. Gibson USNR, CASCADE Capt. H. K. Gates, PIEDMONT Capt. F. L. Robbins, SIERRA Capt. P. B. Koonce, MARKAB Capts. L. B. Farrell & A. L. Prosser, WHITNEY Capt. C. D. Swain, YOSEMITE Capt. G. C. Towner, HAMUL Capt. C. C. Hoffner.

14 Floating drydocks (8 mobile); 9 Miscellaneous auxiliaries.

Repair ships PROMETHEUS Cdr. H. E. Barden USNR, AJAX Cdr. G. C. Weldin, HECTOR Cdr. J. W. Long, BRIAREUS Cdr. C. T. Corbin, MEDUSA Capt. P. E. Kuter,

PHAON Lt. C. L. Husted USNR, ZEUS Lt. Cdr. C. W. Groves, NESTOR Lt. Cdr. S. N. Davis USNR, LUZON Cdr. E. R. Runquist, MINDANAO Cdrs. G. B. Evans & J. A. Ivaldi USNR, OAHU Cdr. A. M. Loker, CEBU Capt. G. W. Stott, JASON Cdr. E. F. Beck. Salvage vessels GRAPPLE, CURRENT.

Fleet ocean tugs ARAPAHO, ZUNI, HITCHITI, JICARILLA, MOCTOBI, PAWNEE, CHOWANOC, POTAWATOMI, SERRANO, YUMA; ocean tugs ONTARIO, TERN, TURKEY, ATA–122, ATA–124, 8 ATR.

Destroyer minesweeper ZANE Lt. Cdr. R. H. Thomas USNR; 6 Liberty tankers, 12 oil storage ships, 218 miscellaneous small craft.

TF 57 BRITISH CARRIER FORCE
Vice Admiral Sir H. B. Rawlings RN

TG 57.1 FIRST BATTLE SQUADRON, Vice Admiral Rawlings: H.M.S. KING GEORGE V Capt. T. E. Halsey RN, HOWE Capt. H. W. U. McCall RN

TG 57.2 FIRST AIRCRAFT CARRIER SQUADRON
Rear Admiral Sir Philip L. Vian RN

H.M.S. INDOMITABLE, Capt. J. A. S. Eccles RN: 15 Avengers, 29 Hellcats
H.M.S. VICTORIOUS, Capt. M. M. Denny RN: 14 Avengers, 37 Corsairs, 2 Walruses
H.M.S. ILLUSTRIOUS,[15] Capt. C. E. Lambe RN: 16 Avengers, 36 Corsairs
H.M.S. INDEFATIGABLE, Capt. Q. D. Graham RN: 20 Avengers, 40 Seafires, 9 Fireflies
H.M.S. FORMIDABLE,[16] Capt. P. Ruck-Keene RN: 15 Avengers, 28 Corsairs

TG 57.4 FOURTH CRUISER SQUADRON, Rear Admiral E. J. P. Brind RN

Light cruisers H.M.S. SWIFTSURE Capt. P. V. McLaughlin RN, H.M.S. BLACK PRINCE Capt. G. V. Gladstone RN, H.M.S. EURYALUS Capt. R. Oliver-Bellasis RN, H.M.S. ARGONAUT [15] Capt. W. P. McCarthy RN, H.M.C.S. UGANDA [17] Capt. E. R. Mainguy RCN, H.M.N.Z.S. GAMBIA Capts. N. J. W. William-Powlett & R.A.B. Edwards RN, H.M.N.Z.S. ACHILLES [18] Capt. F. J. Butler RN.

TG 57.8 Screen, Rear Admiral J. H. Edelsten RN in EURYALUS

24th Destroyer Flotilla Capt. F. G. Burghard RN, 27th D.F. Captain E. G. McGregor RN, 4th D.F. Capt. R. G. Onslow RN, and 25th D.F. Capt. H. P Henderson RN.

TF 112 BRITISH FLEET TRAIN
Rear Admiral D. B. Fisher RN in H.M.S. TYNE

Two repair ships, 2 aircraft repair ships, 2 armament stores ships (chartered), 7 other stores ships, 1 distilling ship, 1 water tanker, 3 hospital ships, 3 accommodation & base ships, 1 fleet tug, 1 collier, 13 R.A.N. minesweepers.

TG 112.2 Logistic Support Group: 5 escort and replenishment carriers, 4 destroyers, 4 sloops, 3 frigates, 5 oilers, 4 chartered merchantmen.

TG 112.3 Fleet Train at Manus: 1 netlayer, 2 oilers, 1 accommodation & base ship, 1 destroyer depot ship, 1 deperming ship, 1 fleet tug, 4 armament stores ships, 2 other stores ships.

15 Detached 1 May.
16 Joined 14 April.
17 Joined 10 April.
18 Joined 23 May.

United States Ships Sunk or Badly Damaged by Enemy Action in the Iwo Jima and Okinawa Operations[1]

17 February–30 July 1945

* Asterisked ships were sunk or scuttled. † Daggered ships were scrapped or decommissioned as result of damage. †† Double-daggered ships' repairs were not completed until after the war was over.

Air = air attack, usually kamikaze; M = mine explosion; CB = coastal battery; SB = suicide boat.

IWO JIMA

Date	Name	Cause	Casualties [2]	
			Killed	Wounded
17 Feb	LCI(G)–438	CB	0	4
	LCI(G)–441	"	7	21
	LCI(G)–449	"	21	18
	LCI(G)–450	"	0	6
	LCI(G)–457	"	1	20
	LCI(G)–466	"	5	19
	LCI(G)–469	"	0	7
†† LCI(G)–473	"	0	31	
* LCI(G)–474	"	3	18	
18 Feb	BLESSMAN	Air	42	29
	† GAMBLE	"	5	9
20 Feb	† LSM–216	"	0	0
21 Feb	* BISMARCK SEA	Air	119	99
	SARATOGA	"	123	192
	NAPA	"	0	0
25 Feb	LCI(M)–760	CB	0	2
28 Feb	TERRY	CB	11	19
	WHITLEY	Air	0	5

[1] Comprising all ships out of action for over 30 days.
[2] Casualties taken from individual action reports. *Killed* include *missing*.

OKINAWA

Date	Name	Cause	Casualties Killed	Wounded
19 Mar	†† FRANKLIN	Air	724	265 [3]
	WASP	"	101	269
20 Mar	HALSEY POWELL	"	12	29
26 Mar	* HALLIGAN	M	153	39
	KIMBERLY	Air	4	57
27 Mar	MURRAY	"	1	16
	O'BRIEN	"	50	76
28 Mar	* SKYLARK	M	5	25
	†† LSM(R)–188	Air	15	32
29 Mar	WYANDOT	M	0	1
31 Mar	INDIANAPOLIS	Air	9	20
1 Apr	ADAMS	"	0	0
	ALPINE	"	16	27
	†† HINSDALE	"	16	39
	† LST–884	"	24	21
2 Apr	* DICKERSON	"	54	23
	GOODHUE	"	24	119
	†† HENRICO	"	49	125
	ACHERNAR	"	5	41
3 Apr	WAKE ISLAND	"	0	0
	PRICHETT	"	0	0
	FOREMAN	"	0	3
	†† LST–599	"	0	21
	† LCT–876	"	0	2
4 Apr	* LCI(G)–82	SB	8	11
5 Apr	NEVADA	CB	2	16
6 Apr	* BUSH	Air	94	32
	* COLHOUN	"	35	21
	HOWORTH	"	9	14
	HYMAN	"	10	40
	† LEUTZE	"	7	34
	† MORRIS	"	13	45
	†† MULLANY	"	30	36
	† NEWCOMB	"	40	24
	HAYNSWORTH	"	7	25
	† WITTER	"	6	6
	FIEBERLING	"	0	0
	* EMMONS	"	64	71
	†† RODMAN	"	16	20
	†† DEFENSE	"	0	9
	* LST–447	"	5	17
	* HOBBS VICTORY	"	15	3
	* LOGAN VICTORY	"	16	11
7 Apr	HANCOCK	"	72	82
	†† MARYLAND	"	16	37
	†† BENNETT	"	3	18

[3] Figures furnished by BuPers 1959. The Navy Department on 19 May 1945 gave out 385 killed, 447 missing.

Date	Name	Cause	Killed	Wounded
7 Apr	WESSON	"	8	23
	* PGM–18	M	14	14
	* YMS–103	"	5	0
8 Apr	†† GREGORY	Air	0	2
	YMS–92	"	0	0
9 Apr	†† CHARLES J. BADGER	SB	0	0
	STERETT	Air	0	9
	HOPPING	CB	2	18
11 Apr	KIDD	Air	38	55
12 Apr	TENNESSEE	"	25	104
	* MANNERT L. ABELE	"	79	35
	PURDY	"	13	27
	CASSIN YOUNG	"	1	59
	†† ZELLARS	"	29	37
	RALL	"	21	38
	WHITEHURST	"	37	37
	†† LINDSEY	"	56	51
	†† LSM–189	"	0	4
	* LCS(L)–33	"	4	29
	LCS(L)–57	"	2	6
14 Apr	†† SIGSBEE	"	4	74
16 Apr	INTREPID	"	10	87
	†† BRYANT	"	34	33
	†† LAFFEY	"	31	72
	* PRINGLE	"	65	110
	†† BOWERS	"	48	56
	† HARDING	"	22	10
	†† HOBSON	"	4	8
	LCS(L)–116	"	12	12
18 Apr	LSM–28	"	0	0
22 Apr	†† ISHERWOOD	Air	42	41
	* SWALLOW	"	2	9
	* LCS(L)–15	"	15	11
27 Apr	† HUTCHINS	SB	0	0
	† RATHBURNE	Air	0	0
	* CANADA VICTORY	"	12	27
28 Apr	†† PINKNEY	"	35	12
	COMFORT	"	30	48
29 Apr	† HAGGARD	"	11	40
	HAZELWOOD	"	46	26
	† LCS(L)–37	SB	0	4
30 Apr	TERROR	Air	48	123
3 May	* LITTLE	"	30	79
	† AARON WARD	"	45	49
	MACOMB	"	7	14
	* LSM(R)–195	"	8	16
4 May	† SANGAMON	"	46	116
	BIRMINGHAM	"	51	81
	†† INGRAHAM	"	14	37
	* LUCE	"	149	94
	* MORRISON	"	159	102
	†† SHEA	"	27	91
	†† CARINA	SB	0	6

Date	Name	Cause	Killed	Wounded
4 May	* LSM (R)–190	Air	13	18
	* LSM (R)–194	"	13	23
9 May	† ENGLAND	"	35	27
	† OBERRENDER	"	8	53
11 May	†† BUNKER HILL	"	396	264
	† HUGH W. HADLEY	"	28	67
	† EVANS	"	30	29
	†† LCS (L)–88	"	7	9
13 May	†† ENTERPRISE	"	13	68
	†† BACHE	"	41	32
	†† BRIGHT	"	0	2
17 May	†† DOUGLAS H. FOX	"	9	35
18 May	* LONGSHAW	CB	86	97
	* LST–808	Air	11	11
20 May	† CHASE	"	0	35
	† THATCHER	"	14	53
	JOHN C. BUTLER	"	0	0
25 May	†† STORMES	"	21	6
	†† O'NEILL	"	0	16
	† BUTLER	"	0	15
	† SPECTACLE	"	29	6
	* BARRY	"	0	30
	* BATES	"	21	35
	† ROPER	"	1	10
	* LSM–135	"	11	10
	WILLIAM B. ALLISON	"	8	2
27 May	†† BRAINE	"	66	78
	† FORREST	"	5	13
	†† REDNOUR	"	3	13
	LOY	"	3	15
	†† LCS (L)–119	"	12	6
28 May	* DREXLER	"	158	51
	†† SANDOVAL	"	8	26
29 May	SHUBRICK	"	32	28
3 Jun	† LCI (L)–90	"	1	7
6 Jun	† J. WILLIAM DITTER	"	10	27
	HARRY F. BAUER	"	0	0
10 Jun	* WILLIAM D. PORTER	"	0	61
11 Jun	LCS (L)–122	"	11	29
16 Jun	* TWIGGS	"	126	34
21 Jun	HALLORAN	"	3	24
	†† CURTISS	"	41	28
	* LSM–59	"	2	8
22 Jun	†† LSM–213	"	3	10
	†† LST–534	"	3	35
29 July	* CALLAGHAN	"	47	73
30 July	†† CASSIN YOUNG	"	22	45

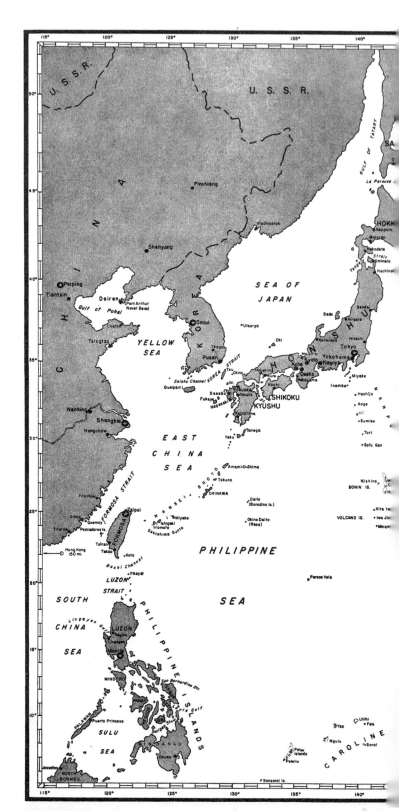

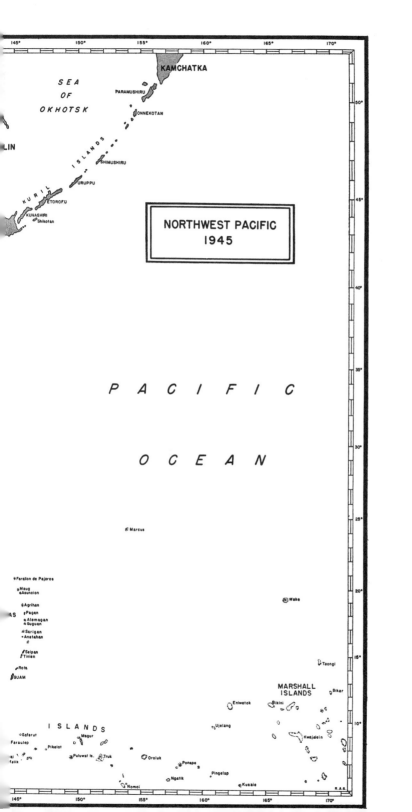

Index

Index

Names of Combatant Ships in SMALL CAPITALS
Names of Lettered Combatant Ships such as LSTs, and of
Merchant Ships, in *Italics*

Only main Task Force organizations are indexed (T.O.), and main headings of Appendices.

Schrier, 1st Lt. H. G., 61
SCRIBNER, 220
SEA DEVIL, 285, 291
SEA DOG, 292
SEA OWL, 291
Seabees, 70, 276–77
Seay, Cdr. G. C., 237
Sedgwick, Lt. Cdr. Ellery, 120
SEGUNDO, 285
Seitz, Capt. G. A., 263
SENNET, 289, 296
Seoul, 355
SERPENS, 9n
SEVERN, 161
Shafroth, Rear Adm. John F., 312–13;
    biog., 312n
Shanghai, 354–55
SHANGRI-LA, 299
SHANNON, 252
Sharp, Rear Adm. Alex, 26, 113
SHASTA, 8, 165–67
SHEA, 116, 248, 255
Sherman, Rear Adm. Forrest, 7, 256,
    359, 366
Sherman, Rear Adm. Frederick C., 21,
    34, 44, 52, 199
Sherrod, Robert, 47–48, 73–75
Sheya Retto, 258
Shiba, Capt. K., 363n
Shigemitsu, M., 343, 346, 359, 363, 366
Shimizu bomb't, 332
Shintani, Capt. K., 202
Shionomisaki bomb't, 331
Shipping control system, 162
Shore fire control party, 41, 48, 152
SHUBRICK, 261–62
Shuri, 171, 240–243, 275
SIGSBEE, 247
Sima, Cdr. F. F., 193
Simms, Lt. (jg) R. L., 204, 208
Simpson, Commo. R. W., 358, 361
SIMS, 271
SIOUX, 160, 169
SKATE, 292
SKYLARK, 134
Smart, Lt. (jg) C. A., 231n
Smith, Rear Adm. Allan E., 11–12, 129,
    267n
Smith, Lt. H. L., 223
Smith, Lt. Gen. H. M., 7, 48, 61, 64, 70,
    73
Smith, Vice Adm. W. W., 168
Smoot, Capt. R. N., 110, 185
Sneddon, Lt. (jg) J. B., 144

Soballe, Lt. Cdr. V. J., 112, 249
SOLACE, 110
SOUBARISSEN, 161
SOUTH DAKOTA, 21, 242, 313, 361
SPADEFISH, 289, 292n
SPEARFISH, 18, 295
SPECTACLE, 271
Spencer, Lt. Cdr. Samuel, 268
SPIKEFISH, 294
SPOT, 287–90
Sprague, Rear Adm. C. A. F., 132
Sprague, Rear Adm. T. L., 310
SPRINGFIELD, 313
Spruance, Admiral R. A., strategic
    plans, 4; relieves Halsey, 20; Iwo, 7,
    73; Japan strike of Feb. 1945, 21;
    Okinawa, 87–88, 101, 162, 198, 203,
    208, 217; shifts flag to *New Mexico*,
    138; Japan strike of Mar. 1945, 97;
    Royal Navy (TF 57), 103–106, 214,
    250, 266; relieved by Halsey, 272; *Indianapolis* sinking, 319; occupation of
    Japan, 356–57
ST. GEORGE, 268
ST. LOUIS, 132, 191, 226, 246
ST. PAUL, 313
Stalin, 340–341
STANLY, 225
STARR, 218
Steinmetz, Cdr. E. H., 292n
STERETT, 197, 221
STERLET, 296
STICKLEBACK, 293n
Stilwell, Lt. Gen. J. A., 276
Stimson, H. L., 339, 347
STOCKHAM, 58, 305
STOCKTON, 136, 243
STORMES, 259, 271
Strategy, 3–9, 17, 79–80, 92–93, 104
Street, Lt. Cdr. A. L., 291–93
Struckey, Boatswain E. F., 231n
Stump, Rear Adm. F. B., 132
Sturtevant, Radioman E. L., 325
Styles, Cdr. R. E., 285
Submarine operations, Japanese, 132,
    136, 243–44, 317–30; midgets, 136; U.S.,
    91, 285–97; in Sea of Japan, 292–93;
    Lifeguard, 294–97
Suicide boats, 124, 217, 243
SUMNER, 72
Sumner, Lt. (jg) W. C., 111n
SUNFISH, 291
Suribachi, Mt., 6, 15, 29, 30, 34, 37, 40–
    41, 44, 49–51, 61–62

Index

407